This book examines the analytical basis and practical experience of financial reforms in a number of countries, primarily developing countries. A key finding is that financial reforms have led to improved resource allocation – an a priori belief not hitherto tested. This finding is consistent with the argument that efforts in developing countries to maximize efficiency of resource utilization cannot be underestimated in their importance. Three key lessons suggest the importance of managing the reform process rather than adopting a laissez-faire approach: First, more successful reform must take account of information capital; second, initial conditions in finance – balance sheets, human and information capital, and incentive systems – are fundamental in determining how to go about reform; and third, different sequences of reforms can be tolerated and, with certain preconditions, do well.

Financial reform

Financial reform
Theory and experience

Edited by
GERARD CAPRIO, JR.
IZAK ATIYAS
and
JAMES A. HANSON
The World Bank

CAMBRIDGE
UNIVERSITY PRESS

Published by the Press Syndicate of the University of Cambridge
The Pitt Building, Trumpington Street, Cambridge CB2 1RP
40 West 20th Street, New York, NY 10011-4211, USA
10 Stamford Road, Oakleigh, Melbourne 3166, Australia

© Cambridge University Press 1994

First published 1994

Printed in the United States of America

Library of Congress Cataloging-in-Publication Data
Financial reform : theory and experience / edited by Gerard Caprio,
Jr., Izak Atiyas, James A. Hanson.

iographical references.
6562-1

– Developing countries – Case studies.   I. Caprio,
Atiyas, Izak.   III. Hanson, James A.
1994
– dc20   94-5692
                                                                                      CIP

A catalog record for this book is available from the British Library.

ISBN 0-521-46562-1 hardback

Contents

v

Figures and tables

Figures

ix

Tables

Foreword

The reform of financial systems is an area of economics that has led broader swings in economic thought. At times economists – going back to John Stuart Mill – and policymakers have viewed the financial sector as irrelevant, except in times of crises, and hence have tried to repress finance and use it for the convenience of government. More recently, the pendulum has swung back toward Schumpeter, who viewed finance as the key sector for its role in allocating credit efficiently. In the past 20 years the move has been toward financial sector deregulation, in part out of ideology and in part in response to technological change, which has made regulatory arbitrage a popular sport. Among developing countries, initial reform efforts in finance – the Southern Cone experience – had such well-publicized problems that the reform effort lost some momentum.

However, other countries did persevere in attempting to reform their financial systems, not always as dramatically as in the earlier experiments, and in some cases in a less far-reaching manner. But reform they did, making it appropriate to look at these cases and review their successes and failures. While economists always want a bigger cross section and a longer time series, authorities in many countries, including those with very low incomes and the formerly socialist economies, need to know what has worked and what has failed. Thus the present study is without doubt a timely one.

The most notable finding, that financial reforms have led to improved resource allocation, confirms beliefs that had been held but had not previously been as convincingly tested. This finding is consistent with the argument that efforts to maximize the efficiency with which developing countries utilize resources cannot be underestimated in their importance. The three key lessons, that more successful reform must take account of real sector links, that initial conditions in finance – balance sheets, human and information capital, and incentive systems – are crucial in determining how to go about reform, and that different sequences of reforms can be tolerated and may even do well, with certain preconditions, all suggest the importance of managing the process rather than adopting a laissez-faire approach. This message surely is crucial for countries emerging from a period of significant government intervention in resource allocation.

The study turns up some evidence that banks may need to be sheltered from competition at times of reform. What it does not address directly is whether or not this is more widely true. If governments are providing some type of deposit insurance, and if, judging from the experience of industrial countries, bank supervision alone is not sufficient to prevent large losses, then as I have argued elsewhere (with Jerry Caprio), it may make sense to increase the charter value of bank licenses so that bank management will have greater incentive to police itself.

This volume is part of the World Bank's ongoing effort to disseminate best practices in various aspects of financial sector reform, and it is hoped that it will be of value to policymakers and to those who study developing countries. Special thanks go to the Korea Development Institute, Bank Negara Malaysia, the Central Bank of Turkey, and the Reserve Bank of New Zealand, both for providing expert researchers and data. In keeping with usual practice, the views expressed should be regarded as personal ones: they do not necessarily reflect the views of any institution.

Lawrence H. Summers
Undersecretary for International Affairs, U.S. Treasury
Formerly, Vice President and Chief Economist,
The World Bank

Acknowledgments

The list of people who contributed directly and indirectly to this volume is long indeed. Any partial list must include Alan Gelb, who, through numerous conversations and comments on early outlines, provided invaluable assistance to the thinking through of the research plans underlying this study, while Patrick Honohan and Millard Long contributed at the outset insights and comments without which the resultant product surely would have been less useful. But none of the above have yet seen the final product, and so can only share in any "upside" to this volume. Many colleagues helped both in discussions and in reading and commenting on some or all of the chapters: Yoon Je Cho, Ross Levine, Diana McNaughton, Mary Shirley, and Dimitri Vittas provided much input, both directly and indirectly. Participants at the April 2–3, 1992, Conference on the Impact of Financial Reform and the May 25–28, 1992, seminar on Financial Sector Reforms in Asian and Latin American Countries served as a sounding board for some of the conclusions ventured in Chapter 7. Larry Summers's penetrating questions also had a notable influence on the tilt of that chapter. Andrew Sheng and I enjoyed/suffered a virtually simultaneous "birthing" process of our manuscripts, and in particular, he helped shelter me from other work demands so that this volume could get out. Notwithstanding his own book and many other demands, he managed to contribute many insights into the reform process. Along with Nancy Birdsall and my aforementioned colleagues, he helped make the intellectual climate in which this book was produced a stimulating one.

Over the course of two years, Bo Wang proved to be an immensely valuable research assistant without whom we would still be working away at the data. Wilai Pitayatonakarn helped type parts of and assemble the manuscript, kept the project as close to schedule as possible, and did that and much more in her usual efficient and unflappable way. All of the above offered views that were not always accepted, and they cannot be held responsible for any shortcomings or errors. However, two colleagues who cannot be divorced from all blame but must share any praise are my "coconspirators," Jim Hanson and Izak Atiyas, who helped with the conceptualization of the project, the drawing together of the summary material, and the editing of the papers. I learned a lot from both and hope that this intellectual trade was not too unbalanced. Last, but certainly not least, Jeanne, Peter, and Marisa contributed much love and support and put up with less attention than was their due, but I am making up for that now.

Gerard Caprio, Jr.

Contributors

Ismail Alowi
Bank Negara Malaysia

Izak Atiyas
The World Bank

John Chant
Boston University

Gerard Caprio, Jr.
The World Bank

Hasan Ersel
Central Bank of Turkey

Mark Gertler
New York University

James A. Hanson
The World Bank

John Harris
Boston University

Awang Adek Hussin
Bank Negara Malaysia

Dean Hyslop
Reserve Bank of New Zealand

Dimitri Margaritis
*University of Waikato, New Zealand
and Reserve Bank of New Zealand*

Sang-Woo Nam
Korea Development Institute

Mari Pangetsu
*Centre for Strategic and
International Studies,
Jakarta*

Salvador Valdés-Prieto
*Pontificia Universidad Católica
de Chile*

David Rae
Reserve Bank of New Zealand

Andrew Rose
*University of California,
Berkeley*

Fabio Schiantarelli
Boston University

Lim Chee Sing
Bank Negara Malaysia

Sukhadave Singh
Bank Negara Malaysia

Andrew Weiss
Simon Fraser University

Zainal Aznam Yusof
Bank Negara Malaysia

Financial reform

CHAPTER 1

Introduction

Gerard Caprio, Jr.

Money . . . is a machine for doing quickly and commodiously what would be done, though less quickly and commodiously, without it; and like many other kinds of machinery, it exerts a distinct and independent influence of its own only when it gets out of order.

John Stuart Mill

One can easily exaggerate the importance of finance, both when it is skillfully conducted and when it is not, but the suggestion that it usually falls into line and accommodates real forces – discoveries, inventions, population change, and the like – stretches belief.

Charles P. Kindleberger, *A Financial History of Western Europe*

Interest in reforming financial markets in developing economies has been rising, especially since the early 1980s, in part as a result of the reduction in international lending by commercial banks and the consequent need to increase domestic resources and maximize the efficiency with which they are invested. Reform programs also have often been the by-product of recognition of widespread financial distress. Developing countries' authorities that have embarked on reform recognized the inefficiencies associated with heavy intervention in the financial sector, especially with interest-rate controls and large directed-lending programs, and in many cases also were responding to difficulties in maintaining the efficacy of controls. Moreover, reforms have by no means been confined to developing nations: Rapid and sizable declines in computing and communication costs, product innovation, increased competition, and deregulation have changed the financial landscape in many industrialized countries in the last 20 years.[1]

Attempts to adopt more market-oriented policies plainly have not been limited to the financial sector. Many developing and formerly

1

socialist economies have begun in recent years to adjust their so-called real – that is, nonfinancial – sectors through deregulation of prices, realignment of overvalued currencies, reductions in the degree of protectionism, and decreases in inefficient government expenditures. In this environment, efforts to reform finance often reflect a general reconsideration of government's role in the economy. The near simultaneity of financial sector and real sector reforms complicates attempts to evaluate the separate contribution of either.

Moreover, the types of financial reforms undertaken in developing countries subsume a diversity of phenomena. Various expressions, such as deregulation, liberalization, innovation, privatization, and internationalization, have been employed to describe different parts of the process. A key aspect of most reforms has been a shift toward market-oriented allocation of credit through an easing or abandonment of portfolio requirements, directed-credit programs, and credit and interest-rate ceilings. In some cases, public sector entities have been privatized and entry, by domestic and foreign institutions, has been eased. Decreased segmentation between different branches of the finance industry has promoted greater competition among various types of intermediaries. New financial products and new combinations of existing instruments have appeared and, less frequently, barriers to international capital transactions have been reduced. Last, reform programs at times have included a reduction in the taxation of the financial sector. To be sure, these changes have been neither uniform nor universal, and have depended not only on the disposition of the authorities but, often more important, on the institutional structure preceding reforms. As will become clear in Parts II and III, the reform episodes reviewed here constitute a diverse set of experiences.

Financial reform has been recognized to have both benefits and costs. Borrowers and investors usually gain a wider choice of financial products (added breadth), including new and increasingly sophisticated tools for hedging various risks, and may enjoy lower transactions costs as well. Some observers expect savings to rise, though the more certain effect is that the portion of saving intermediated by the financial sector rises with increases in real interest rates and with added savings vehicles. The financial sector itself usually is expected to become more efficient following liberalization. Moreover, and most important, a more market-based allocation of capital is expected to enhance efficiency by allocating capital to its most productive uses. However, at least until now, there has only been some broad macroeconomic evidence pointing toward efficiency gains; Part II includes evidence, using firm-level data, which confirms the presence of these gains following the onset of financial reforms.

Some countries have clung to controls, perhaps out of concern for the destabilizing forces that could be released by reform. Financial reform entails a number of risks, associated with more variable asset prices and the consequences of trying to operate financial markets with institutions and a supervisory framework often unsuited to evaluating the risks inherent in a liberalized system. Most notably, bank behavior is susceptible to significant change following reform, especially if state intervention previously had been shielding bankers from market forces. Two dramatically opposite reactions – on the one hand, a retrenchment from all but the lowest-risk lending and, on the other, a reckless expansion of lending, even to insolvent clients – have been observed following reform.

Moreover, the manner in which monetary policy is implemented often must change following reforms. Officials long accustomed to direct methods of implementation often are reluctant to adopt less direct and seemingly less certain instruments.[2] Even more visibly, those countries that deregulated interest rates often saw them rise relative to actual inflation rates and, in some cases, remain at elevated levels in (ex post) real terms for extended periods of time. Dramatic fluctuations of real rates have also been noted. In certain countries interest rates increased generally, while in others spreads rose, reflecting changed tax or reserve policies, or perceptions of increased risk.

In fact, some experiences – most visibly, the episodes in South America (in the "Southern Cone"), during the late 1970s and early 1980s with sustained high real interest rates and financial crises – have been sufficiently turbulent to deter officials of developing countries from liberalizing. Indeed, many identify financial reform with these episodes. Chile, Argentina, and Uruguay suddenly reformed highly controlled financial markets in the 1970s and saw a dramatic expansion of intermediation centered around instruments with short maturities and high returns. In Chile, for example, the period was one of increasing domestic and external indebtedness, high real interest rates, and financial crisis (1982–3), ultimately requiring massive bailouts of a large portion of the domestic banking system. Many of these problems cannot be laid at the doorstep of the financial sector: A perverse macroeconomic environment (and policies) and a series of real shocks are widely recognized as having played an important role in the crisis. Still, the Southern Cone experience has been generalized to suggest that financial reforms should be delayed until after real sector adjustments have been made.

In addition to misleading relative prices, poor decisions by financial institutions were related at least in part to an underinvestment in risk assessment and monitoring skills during the long period of repression, as well as to portfolios dominated by nonperforming loans at the start of the reform process. Officials in liberalizing countries, when confronted by high real rates and collapsing financial institutions, have tended to slow or halt further liberalizing moves.[3] An emerging consensus, and one that is based overwhelmingly on the Southern Cone experience, appears to be that gradual financial liberalization – indeed, perhaps very little – is to be preferred. Cho and Khatkhate (1989), McKinnon (1988), and Villanueva and Mirakhor (1990) all urge caution in liberalization, emphasizing the achievement of macroeconomic stability and adequate bank supervision as preconditions for successful financial reform, while Calvo (1988) and Rodrik (1989a,b) use credibility arguments to support a narrow focus of adjustment programs, leaving the financial sector for last.

Dornbusch and Reynoso (1989) are even more doubtful about the benefits of liberalization in all but the most repressed economies, arguing that it instead exacerbates macroeconomic instability by robbing the government of tax revenue. Indeed, they go so far as to echo the sentiments of John Stuart Mill when they state that "financial factors are important only when financial instability becomes a dominant force in the economy."[4] This sentiment is an extreme, old-style Keynesian (but certainly not Keyneslike) view of the world, namely that money – worse still, the entire financial system – is just a veil. And the apparent consensus is supported by the notion that since asset prices adjust quickly and may be prone to overshooting, they should be restrained, perhaps permanently. One point made in this book is that while asset prices adjust quickly, financial institutions do not, hence the need to begin some financial reforms – those on the institution-building side – early in the broader reform effort. In terms of the epigraphs to this chapter, the view of Kindleberger seems more defensible than the view associated with Mill, especially given the efficiency gains that were uncovered in this study.

The intellectual heritage for the modern approach to financial sector reform dates back to the work of Gurley and Shaw (1955), and found its more recent expression for developing countries in the seminal works of McKinnon (1973) and Shaw (1973). Their argument, in brief, was that financial repression – a combination of heavy taxation, interest controls, and government intervention in the credit-allocation process – led to both a decrease in the depth of the financial system and a loss of the efficiency with which savings are intermediated. This argument has been extended to suggest that immediate and complete liberalization of finance is a preferred approach, but several papers, including the aforementioned work by McKinnon (1988), suggest at least a more gradual approach to reform. The seminal article by Stiglitz and Weiss (1981) emphasizes that even a free market system may be characterized by credit rationing, suggesting therefore that neither a rapid nor complete withdrawal of government from credit decisions is likely to be optimal.

With all of this controversy, it is timely both to reexamine the role of finance and financial reform, and, most important for policymakers charged with decision making about the financial sector, to look at a diverse group of cases to see how countries have reformed their financial sectors and how they have fared. This book is intended to do both.

Scope of the study

The present study, which took shape in the form of two research projects organized at the World Bank beginning in 1989, aims to examine financial reform analytically and empirically, focusing several key issues:

- The relationship between the financial and real sectors, and how these linkages affect reforms
- The behavior of banks around the time of reform, and how this behavior can affect the economy at large
- The process of reform and the sequencing of various elements, including in particular the timing of opening of the capital account
- The impact of financial reforms on the efficiency with which capital is allocated

The first part of the study focuses on theoretical and empirical overviews of some of these issues. Chapter 2, Finance, public policy, and growth, by Mark Gertler and Andrew Rose, applies insights from the recent literature to draw out the connection between finance and macroeconomic performance, emphasizing how the financial sector depends on real sector performance and how this dependence affects the reform process. Chapter 3, Banking on financial reform? A case of sensitive dependence on initial conditions (Caprio), complements this analysis by focusing on the behavior of banks and on how various aspects of their initial condition at the time of reform can affect subsequent performance. This chapter also touches on the links between structural (real sector) and financial sector reforms; here, in effect, the links go both ways, but the emphasis is on the dependence of the real sector on finance.

Chapter 4 examines the real effects of financial sector reforms in selected economies for which detailed firm-level data were obtained. Many have doubted the importance of finance, but in this chapter Schiantarelli, Atiyas, Caprio, Harris, and Weiss provide concrete evidence of real sector effects of financial reform. We also find cases in which small firms become less credit constrained following financial reform, in contrast to the branch of the literature that suggests that market-oriented financial systems tend to ration credit to small firms.

Part II, on the reform experiences, begins with an overview of the case studies it includes (by Atiyas, Caprio, and Hanson). It summarizes the macroeconomic background on the eve of reform in the countries covered, surveys the initial state of their financial systems, succinctly reviews the steps taken, and comments on the adjustment issues following the onset of reforms.

The case studies of domestic financial reform for Turkey, New Zealand, Korea, Indonesia, and Malaysia present the elements of the financial reform experiences and focus on the key issues in each episode. A variety of factors determined country coverage. Malaysia and Korea are known to have reformed at a very gradual pace, and are usually viewed as success stories, so it seemed logical to include them. New Zealand is at the opposite extreme, having reformed at least as abruptly as any of the Southern Cone countries but without some of the latter's macroeconomic constraints.[5] Turkey and Indonesia present interesting "in between" cases, with reform programs that are rapid in some areas and gradual in others, so they offer an intriguing middle ground.

Part III, on links between domestic and international financial reforms, commences with Chapter 11, by James Hanson, who focuses on the analytics of when to open the capital account. Domestic and international financial liberalization can be accomplished simultaneously or in different sequences, with the overwhelming body of the literature arguing that the domestic financial system should be liberalized first, and that international liberalization can be delayed. Hanson reviews the literature in this area and questions both the optimality and practicality of delaying capital account opening, and notes that it is a process that must be managed.

Chapter 12 follows with a study of the Chilean case. Much of the domestic financial reform story is well known for Chile, but the role in this process of its international financial reform effort has been of a "post hoc, ergo propter hoc" nature. An open capital account and large inflows were followed by, and perceived to have contributed to, a period of economic instability in Chile. However, Chapter 12 analyzes Chile's experience with capital account opening and argues that this popular conclusion is at best misleading, as a variety of other factors were dominant in their role in the crisis. Moreover, Salvador Valdés-Prieto maintains that the precise manner in which Chile opened its capital account, by not allowing banks to perform international financial intermediation until several years after nonbanks were performing this function, may have contributed to these problems. This chapter also shows clearly the consequences of allowing free entry into banking, which erodes the franchise value of bank licenses.

Chapter 13 ends with a review of some of the main lessons of the reform experiences studied here, and sketches the elements of a strategy for financial sector reform. The main lessons concern the importance of real and financial sector linkages in financial reform, and of the initial conditions in the banking sector. Not just analytically but in practice a number of sequences appear sustainable, including that of reforming the domestic financial system with an open capital account. However, where this unconventional sequence appears to have worked, special factors may well have helped to prevent the disasters feared in the literature. In particular, the domestic authorities achieved fiscal control and thus were able to avoid excessive reliance on taxation of financial intermediation.

The importance of institutional development – arguably the key initial condition in the financial sector – comes through in the experience of reforming economies and thus is emphasized both among the lessons and in the construction of a strategy in reforming a financial system following a period of marked government intervention. Countries that begin reform attempts with a heavily repressed financial sector will need to devote much time and effort in developing market-oriented institutions, staff, and incentives. Reforms can readily encounter severe problems, as in the Southern Cone in the 1970s and Turkey in its first reform attempt, when these fundamentals are ignored.

For those readers not inclined to wade through the entire volume, in addition to the summary chapters, those concerned with the issue of monetary control and financial reform will find Chapter 7 (New Zealand) of greatest interest, as well as Chapters 9 (Indonesia) and 10 (Malaysia). Chapters 8 and 10 will appeal not only to those who enjoy (still) happy endings, as Korea and Malaysia certainly stand out on various macro indicators, but also by those interested in comparing how significant nonperforming loan problems were handled, in particular the related difference between these two countries in the balance between banks and nonbanks as a result of reforms (or lack thereof). Readers interested in reform in more difficult macroeconomic circumstances will likely first jump to Chapters 6 and 7 (Turkey and New Zealand), to see how authorities there have either stayed or strayed from the reform course. And, as noted, Chapters 10 and 11 are for those most interested in reconsidering the conventional wisdom on sequencing of domestic and international reforms, while Chapters 2 and 3 offer a conceptual framework of finance and its reform.

Both the country coverage and the topics highlighted were chosen on the basis of their perceived relevance to policymakers, in addition to the availability of data. All of these liberalization experiments have attracted the interest of government authorities worldwide, but often there is a misunderstanding of the actions taken and the apparent results. Most important, misconceptions about reform attempts often induce authorities to resist changes for fear of repercussion, when in fact, as in the case of Chile, the disturbances experienced appear to have been the result of a number of perverse circumstances. It is hoped that the cases presented here provide a more balanced mix of successes and failures.

As is emphasized in several places, the reform effort in these economies is not over, and financial reform is most definitely not an event, but rather a process. The episodes reviewed in this book are relatively recent, and their evaluation will undoubtedly continue for many years to come, as is the case with ongoing reexaminations of finance in various industrialized economies. However, authorities in developing countries facing the need to utilize their domestic resources more efficiently cannot await "final" lessons, but rather must make decisions based on what is known at present. In view of the determination of authorities to continue the reform process, albeit at different paces, they certainly seem convinced of its benefits. And the very real efficiency gains turned up in Chapter 5 suggest that they are right. So to recall again Kindleberger, it is easy to exaggerate the role of finance, but the papers presented here suggest that it is a key sector in economies, and in many of them it is one in which the direction of change, in favor of less intervention, rather than more, remains clear.

NOTES

1 Australia, Denmark, France, Greece, Italy, Japan, New Zealand, Portugal, Spain, Sweden, the United Kingdom, and the United States are prominent among the industrialized countries in their liberalization efforts.

2 Perceived complications for monetary policy, which have been noted mainly in the industrial countries, include enhanced substitutability among financial assets and the loss of precision involved in the reliance on indirect means of achieving monetary targets. In part, however, these changes have resulted not just from changes in the way monetary policy is implemented but from competition and technology, both of which have combined to make more and better substitutes for money.

3 To take two examples, in the United States, despite the popularity of deregulation in the last 15 years, the combination of the savings and loan (S&L) crisis and the stock market crash of 1987 has put moves to dismantle the Glass–Steagall act on hold. The Zambian authorities reregulated interest rates even though ex post real rates remained negative throughout the 18-month period of freely determined interest rates, in part reflecting high and variable inflation.

4 Dornbusch and Reynoso (1992, p. 204).

5 While New Zealand's presence may be objected to in a volume otherwise focusing on developing countries, it is useful to note that with 35% of GDP in the agricultural sector, it is the least industrial of the economies of the member-countries of the Organization for Economic Cooperation and Development (OECD) and actually is more commodity oriented than some countries classified as developing. Also, the uniqueness of its reform effort and the relevance for transitional socialist economies were advantages that could not be resisted.

PART I

REFORMING FINANCE: APPROACHES
AND IMPORTANCE

CHAPTER 2

Finance, public policy, and growth

Mark Gertler and Andrew Rose

2.1   Introduction

Development economists have long argued that the evolution of financial markets is an important dimension of growth. A corollary view is that financial repression in many less developed countries (LDCs) is a serious obstacle to progress. But, unfortunately, many countries have had disappointing experiences with liberalization. Freeing up financial markets at times has appeared to produce chaos rather than growth, forcing many countries to retreat from deregulation. With economic stagnation seeming to persist in many developing and transitional economies, policymakers face a dilemma: Should they cling to repressed financial markets or, instead, should they try the road to reform – in some cases, once again?

In this paper we reconsider the relation between finance and growth, and the appropriate role of government policy. We update earlier treatments of the subject by applying insights from recent theoretical literature that draws out the connection between the efficiency of financial markets and macroeconomic performance.[1] We try to sketch informally a paradigm meant to be useful for thinking about the special problems that plague financial systems of developing countries. The overriding objective is to provide a basis for thinking about the process of financial reform. In addition, we present some macroeconomic evidence bearing on the relation between finance and growth.

Section 2.2 develops a benchmark for analysis by characterizing the role of financial markets in a setting of perfect markets. Section 2.3 provides a brief overview of the stylized facts on the relation between

This paper was prepared for a World Bank research project (The Impact of Financial Reform, RPO 676-13). The authors wish to thank Izak Atiyas, Jerry Caprio, Steven Kamin, and Salvador Valdés-Prieto for their comments.

13

finance and growth. Section 2.4 presents a nontechnical discussion of the relevant theory. The theory emphasizes not only how the efficiency of financial markets may contribute to growth, but also how the real sector feeds back to influence the performance of the financial system.

Section 2.5 extends the analysis to the special problems of developing countries, including financial repression and obstacles to financial reform. We draw several related kinds of policy conclusions. First, even though frictions exist which impede the performance of private financial markets, a decentralized capital market is vastly superior to a system of publicly managing credit flows. To flourish, a private capital market requires an efficient system of contract enforcement and a viable borrowing class. Public policy should be directed specifically toward these objectives, and away from directly tinkering in credit flows. Second, liberalization must be coordinated with policies that encourage both growth and stability of the real sector. Financial reform alone is insufficient to generate recovery, and some aspects of reform may even be counterproductive in the short term due to an initial adverse impact on borrowers' creditworthiness. Enhancing the creditworthiness of borrowers through prudent "real sector" policies is crucial to the success of any liberalization. Finally, to avoid potentially massive efficiency costs, any deregulation of financial markets must be coordinated with the design of the financial sector safety net. While some (or all) of these policy conclusions may not be new, we think that our way of deriving them may offer a fresh perspective.

Section 2.6 presents some formal econometric evidence on the relation between finance and growth, in order to confirm that the evolution of the financial sector is an important dimension of the growth process, and to give some feel for the rough magnitudes. We use a panel of developing countries, and differ from most existing studies, beginning with Goldsmith (1969), by formally exploiting both the time series and cross-sectional dimensions of the panel. Our results are consistent with the earlier studies. We find that, across developing countries, a 1 percentage point rise in per capita income is associated with a 1.5 percentage point increase in private domestic credit. While differences arise across continents (stronger for Asia, weaker for Africa), the relation is otherwise very robust. Concluding remarks are in Section 2.6.

To narrow the focus, we ignore specific issues related to sovereign borrowing – in particular, the issues posed by the inability to enforce contracts across national borders. Our analysis, however, will have something to say about the consequences of a large foreign debt over-hang for the economic performance of LDCs.

2.2   Financial systems under perfect markets

A financial system contributes to growth and development by mobiliz-ing saving and then efficiently allocating this saving across investment projects. Related to effectively engineering flows of funds is providing insurance to risk-averse savers and investors. An added task within an open economy is helping domestic lenders and borrowers compete effectively in international capital markets.

As a way to organize our thinking, we first consider how financial markets work in an idealized economy, one with the key features of the Arrow–Debreu paradigm. We begin with this paradigm because it often serves as the basis of policy recommendations. Suppose that perfect competition exists, that information is freely available, and that individuals can credibly commit to honoring all agreements. The financial system performs flawlessly in this environment. The absence of informational frictions and the ability of contracting parties to make credible promises implies that everyone is able to lend and borrow freely at risk-corrected rates of interest. Market forces consequently allocate income efficiently between consumption and saving, and then in turn allocate saving efficiently across investment projects. Each individual adjusts his saving to equalize the marginal utility of a unit of forgone consumption with the expected marginal benefit – the ex-pected product of the gross return on saving and the discounted mar-ginal utility of future consumption. The total funds furnished from saving flow to equalize risk-corrected marginal returns across invest-ment projects. Competitive forces ensure that lending and borrowing rates adjust to clear markets and that no one earns extra-normal profits. And the entire process is costless; the flow of funds from savers to borrowers does not absorb any resources.

An open economy differs in that there is no exact link between domestic saving and investment. In the pure Arrow–Debreu version of the international economy, country borders are essentially meaning-less. Domestic borrowers compete on an equal footing with foreign borrowers in the international capital market, much the same as corpo-rations located in New York and New Jersey compete for funds in the U.S. capital market. The analogous point is true for savers. These individuals are able to search over the entire world capital market for the best possible risk-corrected returns. Notably, the basic Arrow–Debreu framework – with constant returns to scale – predicts that funds will flow from low marginal product of capital-rich countries to high marginal product of capital-poor countries, just as the capital market works to equalize risk-corrected marginal products of capital within a country's border.[2]

An aspect of allocating saving and investment is providing insurance. Through a variety of mechanisms such as diversification, futures markets, debt–equity swaps, individuals are able to completely shed exposure to idiosyncratic risks and to share optimally the impact of systemic risks. Borrowers thus need only pay lenders a premium for the systemic risk associated with their particular investments, regardless of the amount of idiosyncratic risk. The key point is that, with perfect markets, the financial system washes a considerable quantity of risk out of the economy.[3] In equilibrium, only (optimally shared) systemic risks are left to influence saving and investment. And, given that the variation in GNP is a rough measure, this may not be much risk at all. Diminishing the impact of risk, therefore, is an important way in which the financial system increases the attractiveness of saving and investing, and ultimately contributes to growth.

Another dimension of allocating saving and investment is liquidity provision. Indeed, liquidity problems never arise in the Arrow–Debreu economy. Borrowers and lenders are able to make fully contingent arrangements to insure against unanticipated short-term needs for funds. Similarly, since information is perfect and markets for all financial claims are thick, "distress" sales of assets always yield the true market value. For this reason, and also because a full set of contingent claims markets exists, there is no need for precautionary holdings of safe assets.

Relatedly, there is no need for a public lender of last resort as safeguard against a liquidity crisis. Here, the government cannot outperform the private sector. Through private contracts, individuals are able to obtain the efficient amount of insurance. In general, any public intervention in financial markets is only counterproductive since the private market outcome is fully efficient.

Finally, the perfect markets paradigm is silent about the role of financial contracts and institutions. The theory only makes predictions about real allocations. Financial structure is both irrelevant and indeterminate, in keeping with the Miller–Modigliani theorem. Growth accordingly depends only on real factors – mainly, changes in technology and the supply of productive inputs. Because it is costless to obtain information and enforce contracts, individuals can enter financial relationships without the aid of institutions. That is, financial intermediaries are not essential. The theory accordingly offers no particular predictions about the evolution of financial relationships and institutions in the growth process.

2.3 Financial and real development: An overview

Even in the most advanced economies, financial markets perform less well than the Arrow–Debreu model predicts. Studies of U.S. microeconomic data, for example, consistently suggest that frictions are present in loan markets which raise the cost of borrowing, particularly for low-wealth consumers and small firms. Panel data studies of individual households, for example, indicate that consumption spending by low-wealth consumers is "excessively sensitive" to current income (Zeldes 1988). Similarly, panel data studies of firms show that investment is sensitive to current cash flow, even after controlling for expected future profits (Fazzari, Hubbard, and Peterson 1988; Gilchrist 1990). And the cash flow effect is stronger for firms likely to be constrained a priori (e.g., small firms). In addition, both households and firms hold sizable quantities of liquid assets. This suggests that the need for (at least some degree of) self-insurance arises even in industrialized economies.

Determinant financing patterns are also present in U.S. data, implying a clear violation of Miller–Modigliani. Small firms rely on internal funds and bank credit. Typically, only large, mature firms directly obtain funds from lenders. Issues of equity, commercial paper, and debt are concentrated among these firms. Evidence from other countries is broadly consistent with this pattern.

At the macroeconomic level, the collapse of financial markets in the Great Depression demonstrates that major disruptions in the flow of funds are possible, and that these episodes can severely impede real activity, even within industrialized countries (Bernanke 1983). Recent examples are the financial crises in several Southern Cone countries that followed in the wake of the liberalizations of the 1970s (Diaz-Alejandro 1983). The possibility of financial crises also raises the difficult question of public policy. Most policymakers and economists agree that some kind of safety net is essential. However, the provision of public insurance introduces some clear efficiency trade-offs. The current crisis in the U.S. banking and saving and loan industries provides a clear example. A similar message follows from the outcomes of the financial reforms in Latin America, as we will discuss.

A broader point is that international evidence suggests a determinate relation between the states of development in the real and the financial sectors.[4] The general patterns hold across countries, as well as across time within a country. In the poorest of the LDCs, individuals and firms rely heavily on internal resources and informal credit arrangements. As well, they hoard inventories of goods to self-insure, in effect siphoning saving from productive investments. Commercial banks are the predominant financial institutions. Formal markets for direct credit, particularly for long-term debt and equity, are virtually nonexistent. These countries also borrow relatively little from abroad. A sizable fraction of external funds, moreover, is obtained from public sources.

Financialization appears to accompany growth in the real sector.[5] As economies develop, nonbank intermediaries crop up, offering borrowers and lenders a greater range of options. Another outcome is that more capital tends to flow in from abroad, in contrast to the prediction of the simple neoclassical model. Across developing countries, the ratio of external borrowing to gross domestic product tends to rise with GDP.[6] Further, the composition shifts from public sources to private sources.

As development proceeds further, markets for direct debt and equity emerge.[7] The variety and magnitude of financial institutions and services continues to grow, improving the allocation of saving and investment. For example, insurance companies and pension funds become important sources of long-term credit. They also improve the allocation of saving by reducing the need for individuals to self-insure.[8] Because less saving is needed for safe assets like government debt and inventories of durable goods, more can flow to productive investments.

The observed link between financialization and growth is suggestive that financial factors may be important in development, but of course is not definitive about the exact nature and importance of the interaction, or about the proper role of public policy. To explore these issues further, it is useful to turn to a discussion of theories that may rationalize a meaningful interaction between the real and financial sectors.

2.4   Financial factors in growth and development: Theory

A major challenge for any theory of finance and growth is to explain the joint evolution of the financial and real sectors. It is insufficient, for example, simply to posit that financial markets work less well in poorer countries, and then proceed to explore the consequences. Financial systems are endogenous, after all. And they change over time. Required is an understanding of what determines the relative efficiency of a country's financial system, and how this efficiency may evolve.

A useful way to organize thinking is first to identify the primitive factors that might explain why the Miller–Modigliani theorem doesn't apply in practice. The most natural candidates are limited information and limited ability to enforce contracts.[9] Either factor is, to varying degrees, characteristic of real-world financial markets, particularly financial markets in developing countries. And incorporating either factor in a model is conceptually the most basic way to step outside the confines of the Miller–Modigliani.

In this section we first present a general description of how informational and enforcement problems introduce frictions in the relationship between individual borrowers and lenders. As we argue, these factors effectively force borrowers to pay an additional premium for uncollateralized loans and for insurance. We refer to this added cost generically as "the premium for external finance." We then illustrate the implications for financial structure, including the nature of both financial contracts and institutions. Next is a discussion of what we view as an important general prediction of these kinds of theories: an inverse relation between the borrower's net worth and the premium for external finance. We conclude by describing the general predictions of our story regarding the link between finance and growth. Along the way, we try to draw out the issues pertinent to public policy.

The premium for external finance

To sharpen the analysis, consider the example of farmer who is in need of funds to obtain seed for growing corn. The investment is risky because the quantity of corn harvested is random. It is a stochastic function of the amount of seed planted, the soil quality, and the effort the farmer puts into planting and maintaining a crop.

In the Arrow–Debreu setting, the farmer borrows funds from lenders and in the process enters a financial agreement that specifies all the relevant actions he is to take under every potential circumstance, as well as a set of state-contingent payoffs to each party. In particular, the parties agree in writing to the time and effort the farmer must place into harvesting and planting. They also agree to the payments each party should receive, depending on the realized harvest of corn. Soil quality figures into this calculation because it affects the probability distribution of the harvest outcome. If the crop risk is purely idiosyncratic, the expected payment to lenders must equal the riskless interest rate. To the extent there is systemic risk, perhaps due to weather conditions, lenders are compensated with an additional premium.

A key point is that with perfect information and perfect contract enforcement the farmer's real investment decision is both socially efficient and independent of the farmer's financial position. Regardless of the farm's balance sheet, it is always optimal for the farmer to invest so as to maximize the value of the farm – that is, to plant seed until the expected gain from the corn harvest equals the risk-corrected opportunity cost of funds. Further, the kind of financial claims the farmer issues is indeterminate. Though the total expected payments to lenders must properly reflect the systemic risk, the exact pattern of payoffs across risky output realizations may take numerous forms. Whether the firm issues equity or risky debt does not matter so long as lenders receive in expectation the risk-corrected opportunity cost of funds. Also immaterial is whether the farmer purchases seed with internal funds, by borrowing from financial institutions, or by obtaining credit directly from individual lenders.

As we have emphasized, the prediction of efficient allocations of saving and investment – independent of the nature of financial institutions – relies on the supposition that individuals may costlessly write and enforce richly detailed financial contracts. This "completeness" of financial markets, however, may not be a reasonable approximation of reality if either information or the ability to enforce contracts is significantly limited. In our example of the farmer, both these restrictions are quite plausible.

It is reasonable to hypothesize that real-world lenders may not be able to freely observe all the relevant aspects of the farmer's investment project. They may have less knowledge than the farmer about the soil quality. They may have difficulty monitoring how hard he works. They may find it costly to verify the size of the harvest. In each of these situations, the farmer can potentially gain by exploiting his advantage in information.

It is also plausible that enforcing particular aspects of the financial contract is costly, perhaps even prohibitively costly. Even if lenders can freely observe all the relevant economic variables, the same may not be true for third-party institutions such as courts, making it difficult to enforce contracts based on these contingencies. For example, even if lenders can freely determine that the farmer has misrepresented the size of his crop, it may still involve considerable expense to demonstrate this point in court. Costs of carrying out punishments –

for example, costs of collecting fines or imprisoning offenders – may also be factors, particularly for developing countries. In either case, enforcement costs permit circumstances to arise where the farmer gains on net by walking away from his debts, much as does a sovereign country.[10]

Rational lenders recognize the potential for conflicts of interest with the farmer, and try to structure the financial arrangements accordingly. The information and enforcement problems, however, limit the scope of the financial contract – the feasible set of contingencies and covenants – and, in doing so, limit the flexibility lenders have in regulating the farmer's behavior. Mitigating the possible incentive problems, therefore, may involve restrictions on the financial contract that introduce some kind of real costs. In this way, frictions enter the financial process.

Intuitively, a wedge emerges between the cost of (uncollateralized) external funds and internal funds.[11] That is, the farmer pays a premium for uncollateralized external funds. Roughly speaking, this premium compensates for the costs of resolving the conflict of interests with lenders. It may consist of both explicit and implicit components, depending on the nature of the incentive problem and the informational structure. If the soil quality of his farm is not publicly observable, for example, the farmer may have to pay an explicit "lemons" premium for external funds.[12] This is because lenders are forced to use the average soil quality in the region to calculate the expected harvest yield.[13] Lenders will also charge an explicit premium to compensate for any expected costs of evaluation or monitoring.[14]

The implicit component of the premium reflects loss in the value of the borrower's investment that stems from any constraints on the financial relationship. One example is the reduction in expected profits the farmer suffers if lenders restrict the size of the loan, perhaps in fear that he will misuse the funds or renege on his debts. Another one is the reduction in expected utility owing to restrictions on the amount of insurance lenders are willing to provide. If lenders are unable to observe how well the business is managed, they may restrict the extent to which they insure the farmer against bad harvests. They may instead require that the farmer bear a good portion of the risk, as a way to motivate him to properly plant and harvest his crop.[15] This limitation on insurance reduces the expected utility gain to the farmer, and thus reduces the value of his investment.

Figures 2.1 and 2.2 illustrate how the premium for external finance distorts the farmer's real investment decision. In each diagram, the dotted lines represent the demand and supply curves for investment

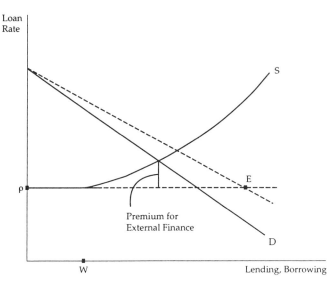

Figure 2.1 The premium for external finance

funds under perfect information, and the solid lines represent these curves when incentive problems are present. Under perfect information, the farmer faces a perfectly elastic supply curve of investment funds. The discount rate is ρ, equal to the sum of the riskless rate and a premium that reflects any systemic risk. The demand curve is downward sloping because the expected marginal increase in the harvest yield is diminishing. Point E, where the two dotted lines intersect, is the value-maximizing choice of investment. This outcome, however, may not be feasible if incentive problems are present.

Limits on either information or enforcement potentially affect the position of both the demand and the supply curves. Up to the point where the quantity of funds equals the farmer's collateralizable net worth – call this value W – the supply curve is unchanged. The opportunity cost of funds remains the same as under perfect information since the farmer is able to either self-finance his investment or provide perfect collateral for any funds borrowed. Beyond W, uncollateralized external finance is required. The supply curve rises, reflecting the premium on external funds that emanates from the incentive problems. The supply curve continues to rise as external finance increases, and may eventually bend backward. This might be the case, for example, if the quality mix of borrowers declines with increases in the loan rate.[16,17] After a point, further increases in the loan rate may actually reduce the expected return to lenders, given the impact on the quality mix. The farmer's demand for funds may decline as well, if solving the incentive problem requires restricting the quantity of insurance he can obtain against a bad crop yield. Presuming he is risk averse, this restriction reduces the farmer's expected gain in marginal utility at each level of investment, thereby pushing downward his demand curve for investment funds.

The combined impact on the demand and supply curves forces the farmer's desired investment level below the socially efficient value, as Figure 2.1 illustrates. Indeed, if the supply curve bends backward before it intersects the demand curve for funds, the farmer is "rationed" in the sense that his demand for investment funds exceeds the supply at the prevailing rate of interest. Figure 2.2 illustrates this possibility. Regardless of whether there is rationing, though, the costs imposed by incentive problems ultimately distort the farmer's investment decision. Investment in either case is below the level that would prevail under perfect information.

The premium attached to external funds equals the wedge between the perfect information demand and supply curves arising at the equilibrium level of investment. This value reflects the real cost that the incentive problem adds to the marginal dollar of external finance. Note that the sum of the premium and ρ divided by ρ equals the firm's marginal Q ratio.[18] As Figure 2.1 makes clear, the farmer's marginal Q

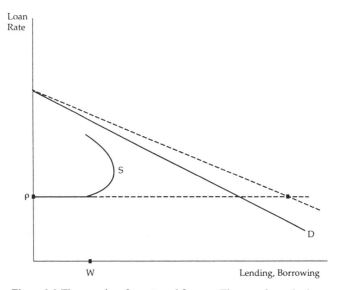

Figure 2.2 The premium for external finance: The case for rationing

value exceeds unity, and if it is larger, the more severe the impact of the incentive problems.

The relationship between Q values and exposure to credit problems is consistent with the evidence.[19] Fazzari, Hubbard, and Peterson (1988) show that, on average, Q values are higher for U.S. corporations firms that are likely to face credit-constraints. (See also Gilchrist 1990.) Cross-country evidence is supportive as well. Kong (1991) demonstrates that the average Q values for Korean corporations are considerably above the norm for U.S. firms, and cites credit market problems as a likely explanation.

Financial structure

The nature of the financial arrangement – the payoff structure, covenants, and so on – affects the incentives of borrowers. In this respect, financial structure influences real decisions when either limited information or limited enforcement are factors. One would expect that individuals design financial relationships to minimize any loss in the value of the investment owing to potential incentive problems. By pursuing this logic, we are able to pin down financial structure.

The exact financial structure that arises of course depends on the nature of the informational and enforcement problems. No general results are available. In many cases, particularly ones where moral hazard is a problem, standard debt emerges as the optimal contract. Debt mitigates the incentive problem by forcing the borrower to internalize the consequences of his actions.[20] It does so by making him the residual claimant for his investment.

Under a debt contract the borrower pays a fixed obligation contingent on not defaulting, and gets to keep the remainder of his net earnings; while he loses everything (including possibly his job) in the event of default.

This result is somewhat fragile though. In general, it is desirable to condition payoffs and covenants on all economically relevant variables that are publicly observable (and thus easily verified in court). Optimal contracts often look something like equity, or perhaps a combination of debt and equity. For example, if systemic risk – business cycle risk – affects the investment outcome, then the optimal arrangement is not likely to be simple debt, but rather a mixture of debt and equity, where equity acts as a kind of cushion against the business cycle: Incentive considerations dictate that the borrower should bear a considerable portion of the idiosyncratic risk, but that the outside lenders should absorb the lion's share of the systemic risk.[21] Intuitively, it is not optimal to punish the borrower if his investment is performing poorly because the economy is in recession, as this is clearly a circumstance beyond his control. Equity facilitates sharing aggregate risks, as dividends may be lowered in recessions and raised in booms.

Other devices to address the informational and enforcement problems include: evaluation and monitoring; credit ceilings; collateral or balance sheet requirements; and restrictions on the use of inputs (to the extent input use is observable). Adjusting the maturity structure is also a possibility. Lenders may exert greater control over borrowers by issuing short-term debt, which in effect forces borrowers to regularly account for their actions. This consideration is likely an important factor underlying the absence of markets for long-term credit in many developing countries.

Relatedly, lengthening the horizon of the borrower–lender relationship improves financial efficiency. An ongoing relationship increases the control lenders have over borrowers. Informational barriers lessen with time. A richer menu of incentive devices is available.[22] Lenders can restrict access to future credit in the wake of a poor earnings performance, for example. Long-term borrower–lender relationships, facilitated by financial intermediaries, are characteristic of credit markets throughout the world. Indeed, only in a few developed countries, such as the United States, are arm's-length credit transactions popular.

The general framework here also allows us to think about financial institutions. Financial intermediaries play two interrelated roles in this kind of environment. One is loan evaluation and monitoring. The other is liquidity provision. These features are central in traditional stories about intermediation. What is new in the last decade is capturing these features with endogenously motivated intermediary structures.

Evaluation and monitoring of borrowers is the most direct way to confront incentive problems. Economies of scale explain why lenders delegate the job to financial institutions. In this way, intermediaries reduce the premium on external finance. A theory of intermediary financial structure emerges once one recognizes the potential for conflict of interests between the intermediary and its depositors. In the process of evaluating and monitoring, the intermediary obtains information about borrowers that is not readily available to depositors. For the same general reasons as any borrower of funds, the intermediary may wish to exploit its informational advantage. Further, just as the intermediary might find it impossible or at least very costly to enforce certain kinds of agreements with borrowers, depositors may similarly have difficulty enforcing certain kinds of agreements with the intermediary.

Like any rational borrower, the intermediary picks a financial structure that minimizes the premium it must pay for external funds (depositor and short-term wholesale funds in the case of an intermediary). An additional device available to the intermediary is diversification. By diversifying its portfolio, the intermediary is able to reduce the impact of idiosyncratic risk and, in doing so, reduce the scope it has for cheating its depositors.[23] In the limiting case of perfect diversification the only risk to the bank's portfolio is systemic. Systemic shocks, however, are typically beyond the intermediaries' ability to disguise or control. Diversification accordingly reduces the "incentive" premium required to attract deposits.

Wrapped in the same package, thus, is an explanation for several basic features of intermediation: evaluation and monitoring, heavily diversified portfolios, and asset transformation (liabilities safer than assets). It is possible to extend the basic story to capture additional characteristics. For example, one hypothesis for why intermediaries issue demandable debt is that the short maturity provides depositors a way to discipline the intermediary, much the same way as shortening the maturity structure gives any lender greater leverage over a borrower.[24]

We can extend our thinking to interpret the role of intermediaries in providing liquidity.[25] Problems of limited information and enforcement preclude most individuals and firms from using the securities market to perfectly insure against sudden needs for funds. Intermediaries offer liquidity in two basic ways. One is by issuing liabilities that are safe and short-term, possibly demandable. The other is by entering arrangements to provide loans on short-term notice, either explicitly by offering a line of credit or implicitly as the outcome of an ongoing relationship with a borrower. By overcoming informational barriers that could slow the process, intermediaries are able to facilitate the delivery of loanable funds required on short-term notice.

Liquidity provision contributes to financial efficiency in two related ways. First, it reduces both the risk of saving and the risk of investing, and therefore lowers the premium on external finance. Second, it mitigates the need for inefficient forms of self-insurance. By diversifying independent risks, intermediaries can minimize the quantity of safe assets needed to provide liquidity insurance, and can therefore minimize the diversion of funds from productive investments. This latter point really applies to the role of intermediation in all forms of insurance.

Along with the benefits of having financial institutions provide liquidity come potential costs. The costs stem from the potential strain placed on intermediary balance sheets. The process of liquidity provision (often) appears to involve supplying liquid liabilities in conjunction with holding illiquid assets. This is particularly true for commercial banking. Asset illiquidity results from the information-intensive nature of most bank loans. As we have suggested, a bank is likely to possess considerably greater information about the quality of its loans (and so on) than substitute lenders. For "lemons" reasons, accordingly, liquid secondary markets for commercial bank loans typically do not exist. Even in the United States, markets for loan sales are in a relatively primitive form. Those kinds of markets that do succeed often involve assets with a recognizable collateral value, such as houses or automobiles. (Indeed, it is interesting to note that U.S. financial markets could not support an active secondary market for junk bonds.)

The particular combination of liquid deposits and illiquid loans makes banks subject to the risk of depositor panics. This basic feature of commercial banking is often cited as the reason for public intervention in banking in most countries.[26] Interventions take the form of either explicit deposit insurance, as in the United States, or concentration of banking with implicit government guarantees, as in Japan and most of Europe.

The issue of public intervention is subject to considerable debate, however. The cost of publicly safeguarding financial institutions is reducing the incentives of these institutions to safeguard themselves. Undertaking costly evaluation and monitoring of loans is less profitable, for example, if an intermediary can always rely on readily available, publicly insured deposits. In addition, it may be directly profitable for institutions to take advantage of the publicly provided insurance subsidy by investing in risky projects, even if they yield negative present value. The institution profits if its loan portfolio pays off, while the taxpayers pick up the tab in the opposite case. The U.S. savings and loan scandal, in which savings banks with negative net worth (in large part as a result of an interest rate mismatch between assets and liabilities) were deregulated and allowed to invest in high-risk (so-called junk) bonds, attests to this point. Having lost their capital already and with limited liability, S&L owners gambled unsuccessfully in risky investments. Aspects of the liberalization calamity in South America, which we discuss later, also bear some similarity to this case.[27]

Key to the debate over public intervention is whether intermediaries can design private financial arrangements to insulate themselves from distress.[28] One device, for example, is suspension of convertibility. As many have argued, though, this mechanism does not work well if systemic factors are responsible for depositor outflows. Other possibilities include indexing deposit contracts to systemic disturbances. The advantage of this approach is that it forces depositors to share the impact of systemic shocks, as opposed to having the payoff depend on their respective places in line at the bank.[29] It is this latter feature of bank liabilities, in conjunction with illiquid bank assets, that makes these institutions subject to depositor panics.

On the other hand, it is an open question as to whether in fact it is practical for depository institutions to offer suitably indexed deposits. Even if it is difficult to pin down the precise theoretical reasoning, historical experience suggests that purely private attempts to insure the financial system do not work well in the presence of systemic disturbances. The experience of the Great Depression in the United States is perhaps the best example of this point.

Borrower net worth and financial efficiency

The predictions about real activity and financial structure that evolve from these kinds of models are often closely tied to the details of the particular environment, including the exact nature of the incentive problem. Empirical relevance, however, requires general predictions. One broad implication of these theories is that the premium for external finance – and hence the magnitude of the distortion of real activity – depends inversely on borrower net worth, broadly defined.[30] As we will argue, the behavior of borrower net worth is at the core of the link between finance and aggregate economic activity. This includes being a factor that determines the extent of intermediation. Financial crises, further, can often be interpreted as involving severe disruptions of borrower net worth.

We define a borrower's net worth as the sum of his net liquid assets and the collateral value of his assets not in liquid form. The latter consists of not only tangible physical assets, but also any prospective future earnings that the borrower can credibly offer as collateral. In the example of the farmer, borrower net worth includes the farmer's financial assets and the unencumbered value of the farm's capital equipment (e.g., tractors) and land. Suppose further that the farmer is especially talented at managing that particular plot of land. Then any expected future rents earned from this skill that can be credibly posted as collateral for a current loan also enter the measure of the farmer's relevant net worth.[31]

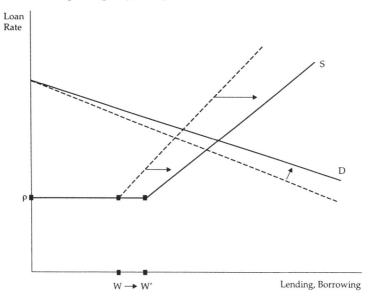

Figure 2.3 Impact of a rise in borrower net worth

Simply put, greater net worth implies either additional funds available for internal finance or additional collateral available to back external finance. More precisely, greater net worth increases a borrower's potential stake in his or her investment. This serves to align the borrower's incentives more closely with outside lenders' and thus lower the required premium on external funds. In the limiting case where the borrower's net worth is sufficient to effectively permit him a 100% stake in his investment, the borrower completely internalizes all the consequences of his actions.[32] The premium for external finance disappears. Conversely, if his net worth is sufficiently low – negative net worth is a possibility, if past debts are high – the required premium may be prohibitive. Lenders may refuse to supply funds despite the fact the investment may have a positive present value in setting of perfect markets.

Figure 2.3 illustrates the impact of a shift in borrower net worth on investment. An increase in net worth raises the threshold value of investment above which suppliers of external finance impose a premium. The supply curve shifts rightward as a consequence. The demand curve may also shift rightward, partly because greater net worth might permit the borrower to obtain more insurance, and partly because his willingness to bear risk may rise (if his relative risk aversion is declining in wealth). The combined effect of the shifts in the supply and demand curves is to lower the premium attached to external finance at each level of investment. The equilibrium level of investment rises accordingly.

It is important to emphasize the simultaneous nature of the interaction between financial and real factors. A kind of financial propagation mechanism emerges. The borrower's accumulated net worth depends both on past earnings and on anticipated future prospects.[33] Thus, previous economic shocks persist into the future by affecting the current premium for external finance. A streak of good harvests, for example, allows the farmer to build up his stock of financial assets, and consequently improve the terms under which he receives new loans. Conversely, beliefs about future economic fundamentals feed into the present, also by influencing the premium for external finance. News that corn prices are likely to be low for the next five years reduces the value of the farmer's land. Expected future quasi-rents owing to his particular farming talent decline as well. The combined effect of this pessimism about the future on his net worth raises the premium he must pay to borrow funds for the current planting season.

Overall, financial factors magnify swings in economic activity. This kind of prediction is true both at the cyclical and secular frequencies, implying that the analysis is relevant to growth as well as business fluctuations.[34]

The simple framework also provides some insight into how a collapse in borrower net worth could generate a financial crisis. There are several ways this might come about. One is a revaluation of unindexed debt due to a large unanticipated shift in the price level or the exchange rate. A classic example of the former is the sharp deflation of the Depression which, over a four-year period, raised the real value of outstanding debts nearly 30%.[35] As we will discuss later, sharp rises in exchange rates in the 1980s similarly raised the real value of foreign debts owed by borrowers in Latin American countries.[36] Another possibility is a sharp fall in the value of collateral owing to events in the real economy. The decline in real estate prices in the United States is a good example, as is the decline in export prices for Latin American countries or the decline in coffee prices for Sub-Saharan countries in the latter half of the 1980s. The sharp rise in world interest rates in the late seventies and early eighties had a qualitatively similar impact on discounted values of collateral assets. Finally, policy changes that have redistributive effects, such as structural adjustment programs, are capable also of producing the kind of sharp swing in borrower net worth that could lead to a financial crisis (see Caprio 1992).

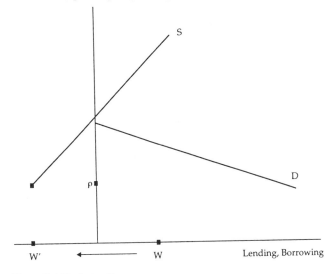

Figure 2.4 Market collapse

In each of these cases, the sudden large drop in the borrower's net worth yanks both the supply and demand curves for funds inward, sharply contracting investment. Indeed, if the borrower's net worth becomes sufficiently negative, investment is no longer feasible. In this case, the supply curve moves leftward to the point where it no longer intersects the demand curve at a positive value of investment (or, where it bends backward before it reaches a positive investment level). Figure 2.4 illustrates an "investment collapse," owing to insufficient borrower net worth.[37]

Net worth is also a relevant consideration for the efficiency and extent of financial intermediation.[38] By building up its capital base, an intermediary is able to reduce the premium it must pay for depositor funds, just as any borrower with greater net worth is able to reduce the premium required for external finance. A fluid system of financial intermediation is therefore more likely with a well-capitalized group of financial institutions. It also follows that a sharp decline in intermediary net worth is a potential source of disruption. As with individual borrowers, possible causes are sudden declines in the collateral value of assets or in expected future profits. A sharp rise in interest rates, for example, could reduce the value of an intermediary's long-term assets. It could also lower expected future profits by reducing both the quantity and quality of the intermediary's potential loan customers.

Summary implications for finance and growth

Our analysis suggests a symbiotic relation between finance and growth. Development of the real sector tends to reduce the premium attached to external finance, which in turn serves to stimulate further development. Several broad empirical regularities are associated with this process: evolution from self-finance to external finance; development of intermediation, and subsequent development of markets for direct credit; increased access to world capital markets; and, finally, narrowing of the spread between loan and deposit rates, along with a rise in the riskless rate. Underlying the general process are several interrelated factors.

First, as economies develop, the average net worth of its borrowers improves. An analogy may be drawn with the experience of a firm over its life cycle. When the firm starts up, it has low net worth for two basic reasons: Its financial resources and collateralizeable assets are limited, and its horizon is unsure. The cost of external finance is high, accordingly. The firm thus relies heavily on internal funds to finance investments. Over time it accumulates both financial and physical assets. Also, by establishing a track record and gaining experience, it possibly raises the market's assessment of its survival probability. The resulting rise in net worth makes obtaining external finance feasible. The likely first candidate is bank credit, since net worth is probably still insufficient to eliminate gains from evaluation and monitoring. As the firm grows further and establishes a more certain horizon, it may eventually reach the point where net worth is sufficient to obtain direct credit. Indeed, one may think of a developed country relative to a developing one as having the cross section of its borrowers consist of a greater fraction with characteristics resembling firms in the mature phase of its life cycle, as opposed to the early phase.

External effects are likely to be important as well. If increasing returns are important, the evolution of net worth is likely to depend on the development of the aggregate economy, as well as on individual factors. That is, there are likely to be external effects on expected profitability, and therefore external effects on borrower net worth.

In this regard, our story is quite compatible with recent growth theory (e.g., Romer 1986; Lucas 1988). This literature appeals to spillover effects on productivity stemming from increasing returns to explain why persistent growth rates between developed and less developed countries are possible – that is, why the law of diminishing returns doesn't take over – and relatedly why development traps are possible. To the extent the external effects impact on borrower net worth, financial factors – via the effect on the premium attached to external finance – amplify the impact of increasing returns on growth. Relatedly, they tighten the potential development trap. Net worth is likely to be lower than would be otherwise, for borrowers in a country that is not exploiting increasing returns – for example, due to low human capital development. Consequently the typical premium on external finance is higher, which in turn inhibits investment further, making it even more difficult to exploit the increasing returns (via human capital accumulation, etc.) Thus, financial considerations would seem to exaggerate the dispersion in output growth rates owing to increasing returns. Along with this prediction comes a theory of relative capital market development.

There is another respect in which increasing returns may be a factor in financial development. As the pool of quality borrowers increases, the potential for a thick secondary market for the securities of these borrowers rises. Thus stock markets are not active when there are only a few suppliers of equity. When there are many potential suppliers, the liquidity of the market correspondingly rises and the presence of the liquid market in turn lowers the cost of the issuing equity. The experience of the U.S. "junk bond" market is informative here. In the early and mid-1980s, the costs of issuing below-investment-grade (junk) bonds fell when it was perceived that a liquid market was possible. This perception emerged during the expansionary phase of the business cycle, when default rates were low. When the secondary market fell apart (in the wake of increasing defaults on these bonds), the cost of issuing junk rose precipitously, with spreads between junk bonds and treasuries rising back to historic norms.

Another important factor involves the evolution of the auditing and enforcement technologies that occurs as economies develop. To the extent there are increasing returns in developing legal systems, we would expect the ability to enforce contractual relationships to rise as economies develop. Development and adoption of monitoring and evaluation technologies should contribute to reduce the premium on external finance.

Growth also stimulates the development of financial intermediation, which in turn feeds back into growth.[39] Intermediaries of course benefit from improvements in monitoring and enforcement technologies. Competition ensures that these benefits are passed on to savers and investors. Improvements in the overall quality of borrowers increases the base of potential loan customers, facilitating accordingly the development of intermediation, especially to the extent increasing returns is important to the development of financial institutions. Also, fixed costs in developing an effective regulatory system suggests that richer countries may have an advantage in mitigating the bad incentive effects associated with providing a public safety net for the financial system.

Finally, the reduction in the premium for external finance that accompanies the development of intermediation (and the growth of borrower net worth) manifests itself in a reduced spread between the loan and deposit rates.[40] Further, the increased liquidity provision connected with an enhanced intermediary sector reduces the need for self-insurance. This tends to lower the value placed on riskless securities. The riskless rate rises for this reason, and also because the decline in the premium for external finance pushes up the competitive equilibrium return on saving.

In sum, a natural product of improved development of the real sector is a more efficient financial sector, and vice versa. The reduction in the premium for external funds increases investment and improves the allocation of existing investment funds. For an open economy, the improved efficiency of the domestic financial system enables more funds to flow in from abroad relative to the existing benchmark.

2.5   Problems of developing countries

We now turn our attention to two closely related issues that are particularly relevant to the experiences of developing countries. The first involves the consequences of financial repression and the second the consequences of financial liberalization. Mentioned as well in this discussion are the consequences of the debt crisis.

Financial repression

As we have been emphasizing, a well-functioning financial system features private contracts and private institutions designed to minimize the problems of limited information and enforcement. The most direct way a government can contribute to this process is by offering an efficient judicial/regulatory system, one that facilitates the enforcement of private contracts and punishes fraud effectively. There is also a role for some kind of public safety net to guard against a disruptive liquidity crisis, as we have discussed. But this objective must be balanced against the efficiency costs of providing public insurance.

Historically, public intervention in credit markets in developing countries seems to go well beyond the minimalist approach just described, despite virtually unanimous agreement that these interventions have been largely detrimental. As we see it, the traditional approaches fail by not attacking the basic sources of frictions in credit markets: the incentive problems owing to limited information and limited enforcement. Instead, governments have tried to directly manage credit flows through systems of subsidies, interest rate ceilings, and direct government intermediation. Not only do these policies inhibit the functioning of the price system; if anything, by inhibiting the formation of disciplining mechanisms in the private market, they tend to magnify the adverse consequences of the information and enforcement problems.

Conventional discussions of financial repression focus on the allocative consequences of interest-rate ceilings, targeted-credit programs, and regulatory costs imposed on intermediation such as reserve requirements. The analysis usually proceeds by taking a market that would otherwise function perfectly well, and then exploring the consequences of a government-induced distortion such as a loan or deposit rate ceiling. In our view, the relevant laissez-faire benchmark should allow for distortions in financial markets prior to government intervention, owing to the kinds of incentive problems we have been discussing. An additional consideration then, is how government policies affect the incentives of borrowers (including financial intermediaries) to exploit the environment of limited information and limited enforcement.

Government-managed and -controlled intermediaries are likely less efficient at confronting incentive problems. One example of this is a lax approach to collecting delinquent debts, cited by Veneroso as pervasive in many developing countries. Because the intermediaries in these countries are heavily subsidized (either explicitly or implicitly), they lack the internal incentives required to ensure that they properly screen and monitor loans. This allows the potential for abuse by borrowers, resulting in a poor overall performance of the loan portfolio. The reduced return on assets lowers the rate feasible for payment to depositors. In turn, the quantity of private funds the intermediary may attract falls.

The experience of many LDCs with state development banks is highly relevant to this discussion. These institutions were introduced to provide a conduit for long-term finance as a first step toward developing private markets for equity and long-term debt. As we have argued, however, there is a chicken-and-egg aspect to this problem. To thrive, private markets for long-term capital require large numbers of quality borrowers – that is, borrowers with high net worth. Unfortunately, because of the incentive problems inherent in the process, a system of publicly managed and subsidized funds is unlikely to create a core of borrowers who would be creditworthy in the absence of government help. Not surprisingly, state development banks have generally failed to produce well-functioning private markets for long-term finance.

A better approach to developing a thriving capital market, in our view, is to concentrate directly on promoting a viable borrowing class. We would recommend direct investment tax credits for borrowers, with borrowers then competing for private funds, as an alternative superior to publicly managed and subsidized credit. Tax credits not only increase the incentive to invest, they also reduce the premium for external finance by raising borrowers' net worth. The overall increase in borrowers' creditworthiness raises the likelihood of a well-functioning private capital market. We of course do not mean to suggest that tax credits alone would suffice. A strong system of contract enforcement and a stable policy environment are also crucial.

Financial liberalization

In the 1970s and 1980s, a number of developing countries liberalized their financial markets. In a number of Latin American countries the reforms initially produced chaos.[41] The much desired efficiency gains did not seem to materialize. The Asian countries that liberalized fared somewhat better. In a few countries, such as Korea and Malaysia, the experiment appears to have worked.

In our view, the liberalizations failed to meet expectations for three main reasons. First, accompanying the rise in loan rates – as an unfortunate side effect – was a rise in the required external finance premium for a substantial class of borrowers. If markets operate perfectly under laissez-faire, then the increase in loan rates resulting from deregulation is uniformly desirable. True, some borrowers are chased out of the market. However, these borrowers are inefficient; they cannot function profitably when the price of investment funds reflects their true opportunity cost.

Matters change, however, if the true laissez-faire benchmark involves the kind of frictions in the financial process that we have been describing. The rise in interest rates produces a drop in borrower net worth. The market value of collateralizable assets falls. So does the discounted future stream of profits. The drop in net worth forces the premium for external finance to rise, even for borrowers who could operate profitably if markets were perfect. At least in the short run, therefore, deregulation can push investment further below the optimum. We don't mean to suggest that the status quo of financial repression was preferable – rather, only that one must be wary of certain pitfalls when incentive problems hinder the operation of private financial markets.

A second factor involves timing. Typically, it was bad. Many of the liberalizations coincided with aggregate economic downturns. The economic slowdown and high interest rates that plagued industrialized countries in the late seventies and early eighties spilled over to developing countries. The combination of rising interest rates and falling export prices produced a precipitous decline in borrowers' net worth, forcing up the premium for external finance. The absence of substantial equity markets made borrowers in these developing countries particularly vulnerable. As we mentioned earlier, equity markets help cushion borrowers against adverse economic shocks by forcing creditors to share the risk of the downturn. The buildup of foreign debts during the 1970s also increased vulnerability. The poor macroeconomic climate forced many countries to devalue their currencies. Because many loans were denominated in units of foreign currency, the devaluations redistributed wealth from domestic borrowers to foreign creditors, further reducing domestic borrower net worth.

Overall, macroeconomic conditions were independently pressing up the premium for external finance. The liberalizations, thus, were the second part of a double whammy on domestic borrowers. The one notable exception was Korea. There, interestingly enough, liberalization happened in good economic times, during an export boom. The lesson seems to be that, because of the importance of borrower net worth to the sound functioning of financial markets, financial policy cannot be conducted independently of macroeconomic considerations. Our message is not that liberalizations should be delayed indefinitely until macroeconomic conditions are perfect, but rather that they should not be pursued independently of policies designed to directly promote growth and stability of the real sector. Financial liberalization alone is unlikely to turn around an economy in stagnation; and, for the reasons we have discussed, can exacerbate the situation when pursued unilaterally in an environment of economic stagnation.

The third consideration involves the failure in most cases to coordinate adequately liberalization with the design of the financial safety net. In many cases, the government maintained either an explicit or implicit commitment to prevent intermediaries from failing, while at the same time greatly loosening the rein on the kind of investments they could pursue. This kind of policy only served to increase the incentives of financial institutions to abuse publicly provided insurance. For this reason, required along with deregulation was increased supervision and monitoring of banks. But as Diaz-Alejandro (1985) noted, the Latin American countries largely failed to anticipate this need. Lax government monitoring permitted an environment of lax lending policies. What emerged was a vicious cycle of government bailouts and inefficient intermediation, as in the savings and loan crisis in the United States.

2.6   Evidence

We have argued that an important aspect of growth is a decline in the premium for external finance. As economies develop, therefore, an evolution from self-finance to formal credit relationships is to be expected. Indeed, at least since Gurley and Shaw (1955) and Goldsmith (1969), development economists have believed that financial deepening was an important aspect of growth. Much of recent growth theory, however, has ignored financial considerations. In this section, we update the evidence on financial deepening. The general motive is to confirm the potential relevance of the kind of theories we have been describing. One way our analysis differs from much of the previous work is that we make explicit use of panel data techniques: That is, we exploit information from both the time series and the cross section.

Our work is nonstructural in the sense that we do not estimate a formal statistical model. Further, we do not deal with the all-important question of causality, so that the linkages between the financial system and the real economy are not explicitly identified. Rather, we seek, at least initially, to develop robust generalizations at the level of descriptive statistics. As is true of much nonstructural econometric work, our results cannot verify hypotheses, but they are capable of refuting theories. The spirit of our empirical work is to present facts that constitute a benchmark to discriminate between viable and implausible theories.

We take as measures of financial deepening the ratios of various monetary and credit aggregates to income. Our main result, which confirms the thinking of many development economists and which is compatible with the simple theory we outlined, is that financial deepening is an important characteristic of the growth process. A 1% increase in real per capita income is typically associated with approximately a 1.5% increase in the various "financial deepening" measures. Further, this result is robust to a wide variety of perturbations. We also find a positive connection between private external borrowing at per capita GNP within the set of developing countries, as our theory predicts.

Data

Most of our data are taken from the International Monetary Fund's International Financial Statistics (IFS data have been checked for errors and are available upon request). The data are annual, usually spanning 1950 through 1988. We usually focus on a set of 69 developing countries. These countries satisfy the criteria established by Gertler and Rogoff (1990); they are noncommunist and have populations over one million.[42] For purposes of comparison, we have also collected data for 21 developed countries. A virtue of restricting attention mainly to LDCs is that the financial data in the IFS statistics summarize virtually all of the formal credit flows in these countries. Missing are data on stock and bond markets, which are important conduits of credit in many industrialized countries.[43]

Because we are not testing a specific structural model, but rather gathering stylized facts, we take a somewhat eclectic view about our measures of financial depth. We focus on two measures of credit, but also use a variety of other measures to ensure that our statistical generalizations are robust. Given that our theoretical analysis applies to private credit flows (and that publicly provided credit contains a strong subsidy element) the measure of greatest interest is private domestic credit. Combining the claims on the private sector by the monetary authorities and the deposit money banks (IFS line 32d), we usually refer to this variable as "credit." We also concentrate on "quasi-money" (IFS line 35), the difference between M2 and M1. This variable may be viewed as an indicator of the depth of financial intermediation, since it reflects the component of intermediation that is more likely to be driven by lending and borrowing and borrowing considerations than by the demand for a transactions medium. To check our conclusions, we often use variables such as total domestic credit (including claims on central and local governments as well as other banking institutions, IFS line 32) and M2 (the sum of IFS lines 34 and 35) for credit and quasi-money respectively. We also experiment with broader measures of money and credit, but do not report them here since the results are largely unchanged. Finally, we obtained measures of external borrowing from the world debt tables.

We usually convert our variables to real per capita data measured in American dollars. To do this, we use the country-specific period average (nominal bilateral) market exchange rate (IFS series "rf") to convert data into dollars, and subsequently divide the data by the product of the domestic population and the American GNP price deflator. We usually transform all variables by taking natural logarithms.

Results

We attempt to establish a broad empirical characterization of relationship between financial depth and real per capita income. To do so we examine correlations between the (log of the) level of (real per capita dollar income), and the (log of the) ratio of credit to GDP. We find strong evidence of a positive correlation: Countries with higher income have deeper financial systems.

Our empirical results are presented in Table 2.1. As is true of most of our empirical work, the coefficients are estimated in a simple regression of the log of the ratio of credit (or quasi-money) on a constant and the log of real per capita income measured in American dollars. Throughout, our focus is on the slope coefficient. The actual data are displayed in scatterplots of the log of the credit/income ratio against the log of real income per capita (with bordering univariate distributions and box-and-whiskers plots) in the accompanying figure. The data are shown in three ways: (1) pooled across all years and developing countries, (2) pooled only across regions, and (3) pooled only across specific years. Pooled data for the ratio of quasi-money to income also are displayed in the figure.

The first six rows of Table 2.1 describe our benchmark results. The slopes are positive and significantly so, in both economic and statistical terms. We estimate that a 1% increase in real per capita income is associated with an increase in the ratio of private credit to GDP of 0.42%; the comparable increase in the ratio of quasi-money to GDP is similar, 0.56%.[44] The intercepts of both equations are significantly negative at conventional significance levels (this is also true in virtually all perturbations of the basic equations).

These results are quite robust to a variety of perturbations of the basic framework; some of the sensitivity analysis is explicitly tabulated in Table 2.1. For instance, the finding of a positive and significant slope is robust to: the exact measure of credit used; subsampling by region or year; accounting for country-specific "fixed effect" means; and inclusion of year-specific time dummies, a linear trend, or inflation. We have also taken nonoverlapping five year averages of our

Table 2.1 *Income levels and financial depth.*

	Private Credit	Quasi-Money
Benchmark Case		
Slope	.42	.56
	(.02)	(.03)
Intercept	-4.68	-6.57
	(.11)	(.18)
N	2050	2028
e	.686	1.087
Robustness Checks on Slopes		
Aggregate Credit	.24	
	(.02)	
M2		.19
		(.01)
Africa	.42	.47
	(.03)	(.05)
Latin America	.51	.55
	(.04)	(.06)
Asia	.72	.63
	(.06)	(.08)
Developed Countries	.29	.31
	(.03)	(.04)
With Time Dummies	.42	.52
	(.02)	(.02)
With Linear Trend	.41	.63
	(.02)	(.01)
5 year Averages	.40	.57
	(.04)	(.06)
1950 (N=15)	.33	.12
	(.19)	(.24)
1960	.55	.78
	(.15)	(.21)
1970	.45	.75
	(.09)	(.15)
1980	.29	.29
	(.09)	(.11)
1988	.54	.36
	(.11)	(.12)
Growth > 3%	.41	.63
	(.03)	(.04)
Growth < 0	.44	.52
	(.03)	(.04)
Without Country Means	.35	.87
	(.03)	(.05)
With Inflation	.40	.54
	(.02)	(.03)
First Difference Slope	-.17	-.09
(in ECM)	(.03)	(.04)

Standard errors in parentheses.

data to smooth out business-cycle fluctuations and focus on longer-term secular trends, without altering our basic results. In a related check, our results are also insensitive to dividing the sample into high-growth and no-growth observations (a country is said to have experienced high growth if its real per capita income dollar rose by over 3%).

We have also searched extensively for nonlinearities in the relationship between credit and income, using three different types of techniques. First, we tested for threshold effects by allowing the slopes of the relationship between the (log of the) credit/income ratio and (the log of) real per capita GNP to vary at intervals corresponding to $1,000 increments in real income. Second, we incorporated higher polynomials terms in our regressions. Finally, we used more general nonparametric techniques to allow for nonlinearities of a very arbitrary nature. However, while we found results of mixed statistical significance (which seems hardly surprising given the nature of the sample size), we almost never found economically significant or interesting evidence of nonlinearities. That is, a linear relationship between the (logs of the) credit/income ratio and real income appears to be quite consistent with the data. The reason for this is clear from the accompanying scatterplot graph, which portrays the data along with fits from a simple linear regression and a nonparametric data smoother (which can accommodate arbitrarily threshold effects and the like.) The two fitted lines are quite close and never differ by as much as a single standard error in the span of the data.

Our finding of a positive relationship between real income and the credit/income ratio, shown in Figure 2.5, is robust with one exception. When we take first differences of the data, we find a strong negative relationship between the variables of interest. First differencing emphasizes short-run variation in the data and may be inappropriate in our case, since the theory we offer is about the low-frequency relationship between credit and output. That is, our story has little to say about the sign of the high-frequency sign of credit/output correlation (e.g., borrowing might rise to smooth out the impact of a temporary downturn). Simply put, because level variables are likely to be better proxies for the true underlying low-frequency variables than are first differences, we view the "level" regressions as the appropriate representation of the data.

With the short sample size (spanning a maximum of 39 years) it is perhaps unsurprising that one cannot reject the hypotheses that typically the variables are individually integrated but not jointly cointegrated, at conventional significance levels (the test statistics are computed on a country-by-country basis; the signs of the co-integrating slope coefficients linking the levels of income and the credit/income ratio are positive in two-thirds of the cases). Nevertheless, there are no indications of a positive relationship between the growth rate of the credit/income ratio and real income, even if

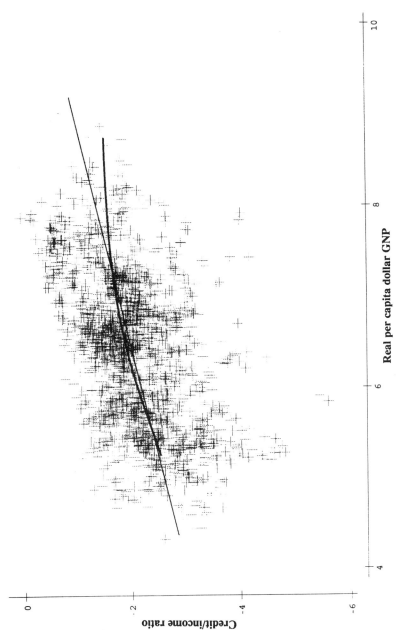

Figure 2.5 The nature of the relationship between credit and income: Linear and parametric (nonlinear) regressions. Natural logarithms of pooled log data; equation RSME = .69

the cointegrating residual is included in a regression of the first difference of the log of the credit/income ratio on the first difference of real income. The slope coefficient is significantly negative, indicating that growth in income is correlated with a decline in the growth rate of the credit/income ratio; the co-integrating residual typically has a positive coefficient (consistent with a negative steady-state relationship between the credit/income ratio and real income). We believe that there are two lessons to be learned from this. First, using excessively high-frequency data is potentially misleading, especially in the presence of data from developing countries which may be measured with error. Second, there may be significant mean-reversion in the relationship between credit and income, so that growing countries experience growth in the credit/income ratio at a declining rate. Both interpretations are corroborated by the fact that there is typically no economically or statistically significant relationship between the growth rates of income and credit/income ratios for developed countries. In the future, we plan to explore our hypotheses further with nonlinear methods. In the meantime, we view this finding as consistent with our essential result of a strong positive relationship between income and financial depth.

Finally, we examined the relation between (the log of) the ratio of private external debt to GDP – call this ratio "external debt" – and per capita GDP. We found that over the entire sample, each percentage point increase in per capita GDP was associated with a 0.12 percentage increase in "external debt." The cross-sectional evidence suggested that the relation was strongest in the 1970s and weakest in the late 1980s (i.e., the coefficient on per capita GNP was 0.36 in a cross-sectional regression in 1970 and 0.15 in 1988). These results reflect the fact that debt overhang became a problem in the 1980s; everything else equal, a rise in net foreign indebtedness reduces domestic borrower net worth, thus placing downward pressure on investment and GDP (see Gertler and Rogoff 1990).

2.7   Concluding remarks

We have sketched a general framework intended to be useful for thinking about the process of financial reform. Many economists have stressed how problems of asymmetric information and contract enforcement impede the functioning of financial markets in developing countries. Our goal here was to flesh out the broad empirical implications of these theories, so as to enhance their relevance to policy. We demonstrated how these theories may be organized around the simple idea that informational and enforcement frictions introduce a premium in the cost of external funds. Factors such as the financial health of borrowers, the efficiency of financial intermediation and the ease of enforcing private financial contracts govern the size of this premium. How financial factors contribute to development may be understood along these lines. One may think also about financial structure: ideally, financial contracts and institutions ought to be designed to minimize this premium.

What are the practical implications for policymakers? As usual, the answers are easiest for the long term. A largely decentralized capital market is optimal. While incentive problems may inhibit the functioning of financial markets, the most direct way for the government to mitigate them is to provide an efficient system of contract enforcement. As we have argued, because of incentive problems inherent in nonmarket credit allocation, publicly managing credit flows is only likely to reduce further the efficiency of investment. To the extent certain sectors merit public assistance, tax credits or subsidies in conjunction with private allocation of credit are preferable to directly regulating credit flows. Other than acting as a lender of last resort in times of a widespread financial crisis, the government should ideally refrain from active involvement in the credit business.

The transition to the long term? Our approach suggests that liberalization alone is not a panacea. Financial and real development are a joint product. While liberalization can ultimately enhance growth, a successful liberalization in turn requires a viable borrowing class, that is, a sufficiently large cohort of borrowers for whom the premium for external finance is not prohibitive. That is, a thriving private capital market depends not only on a prudent regulatory regime, but also on having a thick core of creditworthy borrowers. In this regard, real sector policies – macroeconomic, public finance, and trade policies – which directly stimulate growth and stability should be pursued in concert with financial reform.

NOTES

1 See Gertler (1988) for a survey.
2 This presumes that technology is the same across countries, so that differences in capital explain cross-country differences in output.
3 As an example, the Arrow–Debreu model predicts a risk premium for equity of only about 0.5% (Mehra and Prescott 1985). Part of the reason for this low number is that perfect diversification is possible. The actual equity premium in the United States was about 6% for the 1960s and 1970s.
4 See the *World Development Report* (World Bank 1989) for more detailed statistics on this phenomenon.
5 Gurley and Shaw (1955) outline the stages of financialization.

6 See Gertler and Rogoff (1990) for evidence.

7 Equity markets exist in some developing countries, but typically these markets are not very liquid. See the *World Development Report* (World Bank 1989).

8 Bencivenga and Smith (1991) formalize this point.

9 See Hart and Holmstrom (1986) for an excellent survey of the economics of information, which contains applications to financial markets.

10 In most countries, limits on punishments seem characteristic of financial arrangements. For example, under U.S. bankruptcy laws, consumers can walk away from their debts and still retain their most vital assets – their homes and their human capital. See Kehoe and Levine (1990) for an abstract discussion of how limits on punishments introduce inefficiencies in domestic capital markets.

11 See Bernanke and Gertler (1989, 1990) for explicit calculations of this premium.

12 That paper analyzed markets characterized by severe information asymmetries, as for example the used car market. Buyers in that market have a reason to suspect that sellers are trying to dispose of an inferior car that is prone to breaking down (a lemon, in U.S. parlance); since some of the cars up for sale at any point are sure to be lemons, and if it is costly for buyers to distinguish good cars from lemons, than all sellers will pay a risk – or lemons – premium in terms of a lower price for their vehicle. If uncertainty is very high, Akerlof noted, a Gresham's law of sorts might operate, with bad cars driving out the good. Just as those selling their automobiles have inside knowledge about their quality, so too do borrowers about a host of variables relevant to their ability to repay loans.

13 See Mankiw (1986) and Bernanke and Gertler (1990) for examples.

14 See the costly state-verification models of Townsend (1979), Gale and Hellwig (1985), and Williamson (1987) for examples.

15 Incomplete insurance is a standard approach to mitigating moral hazard problems (see Hart and Holmstrom 1986).

16 Since high-quality borrowers pay higher interest than they would under perfect information, and low-quality borrowers pay lower interest than they would otherwise, the former are more likely to drop out of the market as the riskless rate rises. This reduces the quality mix, making the lemons problem worse. See Stiglitz and Weiss (1981) and Mankiw (1986).

17 Bankruptcy cost could also make the supply curve bend backward, since the probability of bankruptcy is increasing in the loan rate. See Williamson (1987) for an example.

18 A firm's Q ratio equals the ratio of the marginal product of capital to the replacement cost. Under perfect capital markets, firms with Q values exceeding unity should always be investing. The relationship breaks down with imperfect capital markets, however (see, e.g., Fazzari, Hubbard, and Peterson 1988).

19 Q could also be above unity if there is imperfect competition. It could also be temporarily above unity if there are adjustment costs. Gilchrist controls for these factors and still finds an important effect of credit constraints.

20 Recent approaches to motivating debt include Lacker (1990), who emphasizes the inability to observe borrower cash flows (somewhat in the spirit of Townsend 1979), though with an emphasis on collateral rather than costly state verification to resolve the incentive problem. Hart and Moore (1989) emphasize the control right that debt affords.

21 See Gertler and Hubbard (1992) for a formalization of this point.

22 See, for example, Townsend (1988), Green (1987), Stiglitz and Weiss (1983), and Gertler (1988).

23 This is the "delegated monitoring" theory of financial intermediation, developed in Diamond (1984) and Williamson (1986).

24 See Calomiris and Kahn (1991).

25 See also Caprio and Honohan (1991).

26 Diamond and Dybvig (1983) present a model aimed at this issue.

27 Indeed, the papers in Brock (1992) note many of the strong similarities between U.S. and Chilean banking problems.

28 For some interesting perspectives on this issue, see Wallace (1988) and Chari (1989).

29 Diamond and Dybvig (1983) refer to this feature of deposit contracts as "the sequential service constraint." The depositor always bears the risk that, if he is not early enough in line, he can lose everything. This contrasts with equity, for example, where losses are shared equally by creditors.

30 Bernanke and Gertler (1989, 1990) and Calomiris and Hubbard (1990) emphasize this mechanism. See Hubbard and Kashyap (1992) for direct evidence. Greenwald and Stiglitz (1988) offer a related story, which centers on equity rationing.

31 Note that the ex post return on assets serving as collateral need not be certain; the value of the collateral will simply incorporate the effect of the uncertainty. What is important, however, is that the borrower – in this case the farmer – is unable to secretly manipulate the ex post return.

32 If the borrower is risk neutral, it is always optimal for him to invest as much of his wealth as possible in his own project, up to the point where the premium for external finance is driven to zero. If he is risk averse, a trade-off emerges between the need to reduce the premium for external finance and the need to diversify. Incentive considerations dictate that, in general, the borrower is less than fully insured. The text elaborates on this point.

33 Gertler (1990) formalizes how beliefs about future economic conditions affect borrower net worth, in a setting with multiperiod financial arrangements.

34 For an application of this kind of mechanism to growth, see Banerjee and Newman (1991).

35 Bernanke and Gertler (1989) provide a formal – though stylized – analysis of a debt deflation.

36 See Froot and Stein (1991) for an example of how exchange rate revaluations may induce wealth redistributions that have real effects. The example they pursue is foreign direct investment.

37 Figure 2.4 also describes a possible lemons equilibrium: if uncertainty is sufficiently high, as noted above, the market might disappear, meaning the demand curve lies below the supply curve in the first quadrant.

38 See Bernanke and Gertler (1987) for a formalization of this point.

39 See Greenwood and Jovanovic (1990) who emphasize the importance of fixed costs.

40 Unfortunately, it is tough to get good measures of the spread between loan and deposit rates for many LDCs. See Hanson and Rocha (1985) for a discussion. In principle, checking whether loan/deposit spreads are higher and riskless rates are lower in poorer countries would seem to be a good way to test some of our theory. One major difficulty, however, is that factors such as reserve requirements and other legal restrictions will influence the spread.

41 Numerous papers provide excellent descriptions of the financial crisis associated with the liberalizations. Diaz-Alejandro (1983) is a classic reference. See also, for example: Atiyas (1990), Hinds (1988), Tybout (1986), and Veneroso (1986). On the other hand, there is also some evidence of positive effects of liberalizations. See de la Cuadra and Valdés-Prieto (1990), who discuss the case of Chile.

42 The countries are (listed in alphabetical order): Algeria, Argentina, Bangladesh, Benin, Bolivia, Botswana, Brazil, Burkina Faso, Burundi, Cameroon, Central African Republic, Chad, Colombia, Congo, Costa Rica, Côte d'Ivoire, Dominican Republic, Ecuador, Egypt, El Salvador, Ethiopia, Gabon, Ghana, Guatemala, Haiti, Honduras, India, Indonesia, Jamaica, Jordan, Kenya, Korea, Lesotho, Liberia, Madagascar, Malawi, Mali, Mauritania, Mexico, Morocco, Myanmar, Nepal, Niger, Nigeria, Pakistan, Panama, Papua New Guinea, Paraguay, Peru, Philippines, Portugal, Rwanda, Senegal, Sierra Leone, Somalia, Sri Lanka, Sudan, Syria, Tanzania, Thailand, Togo, Tunisia, Turkey, Uganda, Uruguay, Venezuela, Yemen Arab Republic, Zaire, and Zambia.

43 Listed in alphabetical order, the developed countries are as follows: Australia, Austria, Belgium, Canada, Denmark, Finland, France, Germany, Greece, Iceland, Ireland, Italy, Japan, Luxembourg, Netherlands, New Zealand, Norway, Spain, Sweden, Switzerland, the United Kingdom, and the United States of America.

44 The results here are consistent with Hanson and Neal (1986), who found in a cross-section study of 36 LDCs that the quantity of liquid assets relative to GDP varied positively with GDP. Our interpretation of this relationship – which emphasizes the development of intermediation – is somewhat different though. For this reason, we restricted attention to the non-M1 component of M2.

CHAPTER 3

Banking on financial reform? A case of sensitive dependence on initial conditions

Gerard Caprio, Jr.

In the mathematical approach to modeling meteorological phenomena (as well as in other areas amenable to applications of nonlinear dynamics), the importance of initial conditions is taken for granted. Systems formerly thought to be random or "chaotic" now are better understood by applying nonlinear models that highlight, among other factors, the key role played by initial conditions and the effects of infinitesimally small deviations from these conditions on future developments. Unfortunately, the ability to measure and collect data is far less advanced in the analysis of banking than in that of hurricanes. At least in part, this difference has some behavioral origins: Insofar as scientists are aware, air molecules have no incentive to deceive observers as to their natural properties. Unfortunately, life is not so straightforward in the world of banking, nor for that matter, in much of economics. Notwithstanding these measurement problems, it nonetheless is quite plausible that initial conditions matter a great deal in determining the impact of economic reforms on a given system, and in the present case of financial sector reforms.

The preceding chapter shows the effects of information asymmetries and limited enforcement ability on the frictionless and perfect information model in which many economists have been schooled, and was intended to help in the conceptualization of the reform process. The present chapter focuses on banks, the linchpin of most financial systems, and on how their condition at the time reforms are initiated can influence the evolution of the financial sector and the economy thereafter. Although banks can perform many different services and functions, they can be modeled as a mixture of four compo-

I would like to thank Patrick Honohan, Ross Levine, Andrew Sheng, and Mary Shirley for comments on this paper. Responsibility for any errors lies solely with the author.

nents: a portfolio of financial (and some real) assets, a stock of information capital, a stock of human capital – the bundle of skills possessed by the employees and managers – and a system of rules, technologies, and decision-making procedures for applying these inputs to decisions affecting the evolution of their portfolio.[1] Unfortunately, much work on financial reform and bank restructuring only recognizes (part of) the portfolio aspect of banking and often omits the other components of banking or relegates them to lesser importance.

This chapter argues that these elements are likely to be crucial for the evolution of the financial system in reforming economies and demonstrates why financial reform often is such a slow process. Not only might portfolio adjustment take time (and be suboptimal when it does not), but information and human capital require time to accumulate, and incentive systems take time to change, with behavior evolving only slowly once all of these elements are in place. The next sections analyze each of these in turn, and suggest how an understanding of initial conditions in banking at the time of reform can help analysts deduce likely subsequent changes. An appreciation of the various initial conditions in banking and their importance to the evolution of this sector suggests a strategy for reform that differs from the usual choice of pursuing either real or financial sector reform first. Instead, it would appear sensible to begin with those elements – often dubbed institution building – that are crucial for the development of banking and other financial institutions and without which higher profile reforms, such as interest-rate deregulation or bank privatization, will possibly lead to a loss of financial stability.

3.1   Portfolio choice considerations

Bankers have quite a few decisions to make about both assets and liabilities: how to mobilize resources, what types of payments and deposit services to offer, how to price these services, how to allocate resources among a bundle of assets open to them, and how, within regulatory guidelines, to leverage their respective institutions. Many interesting questions relate to interrelationships between asset and liability characteristics, such as the balancing of interest rate and currency risks on both sides of the balance sheet. Although certainly not the first, the U.S. savings and loans association debacle, alluded to in Chapter 2, represented a classic case of interest-rate mismatch, as these institutions held a large fraction of their assets as long-term, fixed-rate mortgages, while their liabilities ultimately proved to be of far shorter term. In effect, S&Ls were deregulated concomitantly with an abrupt ending of a period of negative real interest rates, leaving them with negative net worth (the present value of assets below that of liabilities). Not surprisingly, this portfolio problem influenced their managers to engage in a variety of practices that led to the enormous losses uncovered in the late 1980s.[2] Similarly, many banks in developing countries have encountered difficulties when a devaluation of their home currency led to an increase in foreign currency liabilities unmatched by similar gains on the asset side.

However, abstracting from these interesting questions highlights some simple considerations that will be important in understanding the postreform performance of banks. At the time of reform banks usually begin operating with a new set of external rules, such as greater freedom setting interest rates and choosing portfolios, but they must do so with an existing initial bundle of assets and liabilities. This balance sheet, which may have been appropriate under the previous regime, usually will not be optimal following reforms. If a bank is suddenly given the freedom to make more choices, its overall net worth exerts an important influence on how it will behave, as the U.S. S&L example so vividly illustrates. A bank with substantial capital at stake will likely take different decisions from one with little of its own funds at stake. This point by now is well recognized, hence the importance of examining the financial health of banks prior to reform.

In addition to overall net worth, subsequent portfolio decisions tend to be influenced by the initial mix of assets. This section focuses on the role of banks during periods of adjustment, in a world in which banks have no special information about their borrowers and where there is a substantial asymmetry of information between borrowers and lenders. Following Stiglitz and Weiss (1981), it is assumed that banks, the sole lenders in this setting, unable to distinguish among borrowers, accord all borrowers the same loan amount. Even in this artificial environment, however, the health of the banking sector and its initial mix of assets matters in the determination of subsequent asset choices.

With information asymmetries – borrowers knowing more about their respective projects and their risk–return characteristics than lenders – adverse selection and moral hazard will lead to a situation in which, as the contractual rate of interest rises, eventually the quality of borrowers and their projects diminishes to the point that the effective return to the bank actually falls.[3] Figure 3.1 depicts the loan frontier (LF), which shows combinations of expected return and risk, for variations in contractual interest rates, where the expected return on loans, and the standard deviation of loan returns, σ (a measure of risk), are plotted on the vertical and horizontal axes, respectively. It is assumed that the probability of default rises with increases in contrac-

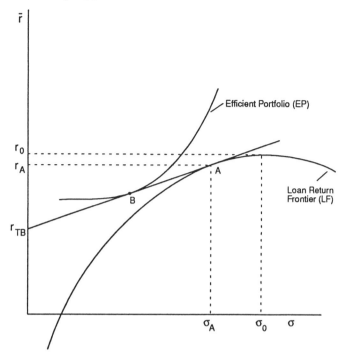

Figure 3.1 Banks' portfolio choice

tual interest rates, so that eventually higher interest rates lead to lower expected returns on loans as the quality of the loan portfolio deteriorates.

Assume first that banks have a simple choice: holding risky loans or riskless Treasury bills that pay a return of r_{TB} without fail. Bankers are taken to be risk averse, with declining absolute risk aversion as net worth rises – that is, with higher (lower) net worth bankers will accept a smaller (higher) return for the same risk or take higher (lower) risks for the same return; this may be termed the "honest banker" assumption. As de Juan has argued, it is quite plausible that as net worth declines – and especially after it becomes negative – bankers whose losses are governed by limited liability will attempt to mobilize more deposits and take ever greater risks in the hope that one of their gambles pays off sufficiently to cover earlier problems. Deposit insurance schemes, either explicit or implicit, help them raise the deposits needed for this gamble with "other people's money."[4] But here it is assumed that more conservative bankers are the norm.

Presume first that there are no controls on interest rates or portfolio

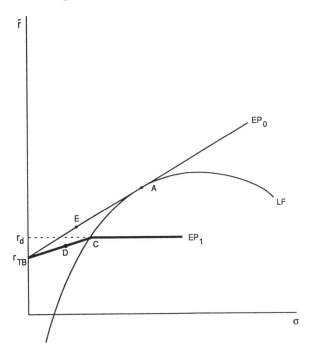

Figure 3.2 Portfolio choice and interest-rate ceilings

decisions. If we suppose that loan demand below r_0 exceeds the lending capacity of banks, then banks will ration credit, as Greenwald and Stiglitz (1990) note, with the efficient investment portfolio (EP) depicted in the figure representing combinations of the riskless asset and risky loans. The interest rate on loans is given by the intersection at point A, while the fraction of bank assets going to loans and Treasury bills is determined at point B. Thus banks would hold a portfolio made up of risky loans paying r_A (with risk σ_A) and riskless Treasury bills paying r_{TB}; the average interest rate and risk of this portfolio is given by the point B. Points to the right of (r_A, σ_A) on LF will never be chosen, as they are dominated by portfolios on the efficient frontier.

In this simple framework, the initial portfolio matters, as shown in Figure 3.2. For example, suppose that prior to reform the government intervened by putting a cap on interest rates. If this ceiling leads to a limit on the expected return by banks, given by r_d, the efficient frontier becomes EP_1, so that banks will operate to the left of point C. Removal of the interest rate constraint would then lead banks to supply more loans (moving from a point like D to E): the substitution effect of higher interest rates will lead to more loans, as will the income effect when there is decreasing absolute risk aversion. The key point is that ending a constraint leads to a *predictable* portfolio shift in favor of the asset effectively discriminated against by the former intervention. The consequent rise in investment illustrates a simple link between financial sector adjustment policies and the real economy. It also argues in favor of examining bank portfolios prior to reform in order to gain an understanding of expected portfolio adjustments and how they might affect the economy.

If instead the prereform environment featured forced allocations of government bonds at below-market interest rates, removing this constraint will also produce a shift toward greater holding of risky loans unless the interest rate on government debt is raised significantly (see Caprio 1992).[5] While an adjustment is necessary, having bankers adjust from strict controls to a large degree of freedom can be dangerous if bankers do not first upgrade their skills in risk assessment and their information about new potential credits, as noted below. Conversely, the larger is the increase in r_{TB} relative to the rate on loans, the more likely it is that banks free of controls will choose to hold larger amounts of the riskless asset and supply fewer loans. That is, reforms characterized by relatively large increases in "riskless" interest rates are more likely to see a substitution away from riskier loans – a flight to government paper, often now described as a credit crunch. Again, the key point is that the manner in which the financial sector was regulated prior to reform and the precise nature of any financial reforms both affects the rest of the economy.

Since the loan frontier reflects bankers' perception of risks, its location changes depending on bankers' views of the riskiness of the environment. Bankers unsure about the direction of policy might well view all loans as riskier, that is, the loan frontier might be viewed as shifting to the right. Thus the slope of the efficient frontier would become flatter, leading banks to shift toward holding more of the riskless asset, other things equal.

Additionally, banks' own profitability might be adversely affected by various structural adjustment measures, especially if they have a large exposure to a sector that is adversely affected by adjustment. In many of the cases examined in Part III, as well as more generally, financial reforms do not occur in isolation but rather at a time when governments are trying to correct other distortions, such as heavy protection, an overvalued exchange rate, or other interventions. General uncertainty usually rises following the announcement of structural reforms, in part because the government's program may not be credible. Assuming that the banks remain solvent following a shock induced by structural measures, they would demand an increase in the interest rate to compensate for a given increment in the risk level or, in other words, a steepening of the indifference curve. Consequently, the tangency with the efficient frontier would shift to the left; in other words, banks would be prone to hold more securities and fewer loans. In the extreme case of former socialist countries, governments are attempting to reform the financial sector where basic market institutions do not exist and policy uncertainty is pronounced, suggesting ever greater likelihood of a credit crunch.

This portfolio framework can be applied to other types of asset constraints. For example, if prereform credit programs effectively limited banks' real estate exposures, ending this constraint will lead to a diversification into property. Furthermore, simultaneous portfolio shifts by banks may be large enough to move asset prices, and if banks see one part of their portfolio rising rapidly in value, they may be tempted to shift even further into this asset. In the case studies presented in later chapters of this book, this type of portfolio shift appears to have been at work in particular in Malaysia and Indonesia with respect to property investments. Indeed, rapidly appreciating asset prices in different sectors – often commodities and real estate – have tended to occur in many countries, leading all but the very best banks to devote more and more of their portfolio to the appreciating asset, at times with disastrous results. The portfolio approach helps to explain the occurrence of real estate bubbles in many reforming economies in the industrial and developing world in the 1980s and suggests an argument for speed limits on the removal of portfolio controls during a reform process.[6] It also shows that "mere" portfolio shifts can affect how financial reforms are judged, as those followed by a speculative bubble may be regarded as evidence of a failure of reform, rather than as an expected consequence of the removal of a prior constraint, in combination with underdeveloped human and information capital and poor incentive and management systems.

3.2   Information capital

In the process of making decisions about the management of assets and liabilities, which is also important for other financial and nonfinancial entities, banks acquire and process information about their clients on the asset side of the balance sheet. Investments in cash and Treasury bills, for example, require less information, in comparison with commercial loans, unless there is the possibility of a government default, either on the value of its currency (hyperinflation) or on its own debt instruments.[7] But loans to the remainder of the economy that are not guaranteed by the government have quite intensive information requirements, with the last chapter clearly demonstrating that financial intermediaries add value precisely because they can reduce information imperfections. These imperfections are likely to be more important in developing countries, in part because of the less developed accounting and auditing systems there. Also, developing countries often have vastly smaller equities markets; because these markets not only consume but also produce company-specific information, they may serve as complements to bank finance.

The absence of developed information sources – audited financial statements, developed equity markets, and so on – leads banks to rely on building long-term relationships with their clients, as noted by Caprio (1992). Information capital is built up over time through these relationships, making it plausible to presume that the supply of bank loans depends not only on the cost and supply of resources at a bank's disposition – its capital, deposits, and the availability of borrowed funds – the rate of return on substitutes, such as government paper, the owners' disposition to risk, and any regulatory constraints, but also on its information capital base, as this will directly affect the expected return and risk of loans.

Returns to investment in information capital can be assumed in general to be positive but diminishing. If so, banks then invest in information capital up to the point where its marginal product equals the cost of additional information. These costs include acquisition of public and client-specific information, and information processing and analysis, in addition to the need to train staff to profit from the added information. Up to some point, banks both improve expected returns and reduce risk by investing in information. In most industrial economies, there are well-established accounting systems, well-developed auditing professions, and an abundance of financial firms who research individual companies and market the results. Banks thus can find it profitable to invest both in information and in information processing, as both are relatively cheap in "normal times" and their cost varies little.

However, in developing countries, without many of these advantages, information routinely is at a premium, and financial repression leads banks to underinvest in information capital. That is, investment in information depends on the incentives facing bankers, in the form of the expected returns to such investments. Artificially low lending rates, characteristic of financial repression, reduce the returns to investment in information. Or, if governments are perceived to be dictating loans through various selective credit programs, through a prior approval process, or especially by giving loan guarantees, then bankers often come to believe that governments will stand behind loans in the event they become nonperforming.[8] In such an environment, it only pays to hire relatively few and unsophisticated loan officers and to invest little in acquiring information. Socialist economies would be an extreme case both of excess intervention into the credit allocation on the part of government and little investment in credit assessment and risk monitoring skills in the so-called banks. Moreover, governments often direct a sizable proportion of bank credit to certain sectors, such as state enterprises and industries producing for the domestic market (often at an overvalued exchange rate), which are rendered uncompetitive when reforms lead to reductions both in public investment spending and in the degree of protection associated with structural adjustment. Last, if the court system is not oriented toward the prompt enforcement of contracts, and if property rights are sufficiently ill-defined, bankers' investments in both human and information capital may be reduced.

Financial reform – a reduction in government intervention in bank decisions – then finds banks with little information (or financial) capital in countries where financial repression has been prolonged and severe. The pullback by the government often means that the banks are responsible for bearing the costs of future losses; thus from the bankers' view, in terms of the model of the last section, the loan return curve shifts out to the right.[9] Moreover, as noted previously and confirmed in the chapters of Part III, financial reforms tend to occur around the time of structural adjustment measures. These measures can render uneconomic much of the information capital that the banks possess. Where, for example large firms, who may be the only clients of commercial banks, produce for the local market and become less attractive for further lending due to a reduction in protection, then banks tend to cut back all lending. In effect, this means yet another rightward shift of the loan frontier, with banks then attempting to shift their portfolio toward government paper or, perhaps, real estate. Banks will also be affected by the impairment of their respective loan portfolios, as many recognize, but the destruction of information capital itself can be important as well, suggesting that even a replacement of nonperforming loans with performing assets (often government bonds) or the writing down of bad assets and an equivalent removal of liabilities from the balance sheet of the banking system may not be sufficient to induce significant bank lending. Where information is in short supply, credit crunches and recessions tend to be deeper and longer.[10]

This point is routinely overlooked in recommendations for developing and reforming socialist economies, where it is often argued that banks should be audited and then cleaned up and left on their own to determine their own lending behavior. But in a high-risk environment, where many if not all of the state enterprises – the only large enterprises in the country – have become decidedly risky businesses (absent a government guarantee), it is all too likely that unregulated banks will choose to hold safe assets as much as possible and to lend relatively little. Yet an abrupt retrenchment by banks may well be inappropriate for macroeconomic reasons; neglect of the importance of information capital likely is one factor behind the overly optimistic investment and growth forecasts typical of adjustment programs.

As time passes, banks build up their information capital, assuming that they face the right incentives. Thus, the loan return curve gradually shifts back in to the left, leading to a diversification away from safer assets. However, this shift may well prove to be a slow process. The more concentrated the prereform banks' portfolios in the dying sectors, the greater the expected destruction of both financial and information capital and the slower is the expected recovery. In economies where investment in all of the large firms is rendered unprofitable, banks are left with smaller – though potentially rapidly growing – firms about which they have little information. That these small firms themselves have little knowledge of how to keep proper records, deal with banks, or fill out loan forms further retards the recovery process. Hence the possibility of "low-lending" traps, even when entrepreneurs insist that there are a number of profitable investment opportunities.

Rebuilding information capital will depend, among other factors, on the

- availability and accuracy of accounts;
- stability of relative prices; and
- returns to investments in information.

If banks suffer from low profitability, then returns to investment in information will be low; limiting entry or not taxing away an exorbitant percentage of bank profits would automatically increase the franchise (or "charter") value of bank licenses and thereby induce a greater investment in information.[11] Note that the implicit model here is more complicated than that of Section 3.1, as we are assuming that bank owners and managers have more complicated choices than just allocating their portfolio in line with a risk–return frontier, but as well have to take actions that will enable them to know better where the frontier lies. Increasing franchise value early in the reform process would help motivate bankers to begin upgrading their staff skills, illustrating an instance in which one type of financial reform should precede real-sector measures. Prior to or early in the reform process, governments also should focus attention on reducing the cost of information capital to the financial sector. One effective way would be to begin building an accounting and auditing profession. Also, eliminating, where relevant, the double or triple taxation of dividends would stimulate the equity market, which not only consumes but produces vast amounts of firm-specific information.

3.3 Human capital: Building, managing, and motivating it[12]

Because the essence of finance is information, the critical importance of human capital and management systems should be evident. The skill base of a bank's employees and its internal incentive system likely are at least as important as its portfolio in the determination of the bank's long-run performance. Without skilled and appropriately motivated staff, even the best portfolio can quickly turn sour. Moreover, if controls during the prereform period were such that most loan decisions were determined by some branch of the government – the planning ministry in socialist economies or the central bank and finance ministry in some developing countries – then banks likely will have underinvested not just in information, but also in a variety of skills in the areas of risk assessment, credit monitoring, and management of assets and liabilities, which are necessary to their survival in a market environment. Often before reform, banking systems are dominated by public institutions or have compensation systems in place with little wage dispersion. So even if employees were all highly trained in precisely the right areas, they still would not be motivated to perform in line with market-oriented institutions in other countries. Prereform bankers in interventionist economies may have responded well to the old incentive system, but it takes a new incentive system to encourage them to seek out and develop the skills needed in a more market-oriented system.

A first step to restoring the health of the financial sector then is to take an inventory of human capital, management, and incentive systems in banks, as is often done in a risk-asset review. This inventory will be essential in economies formerly characterized by heavy intervention in the allocation of credit, in order to reorient banks for a more commercial environment. In many countries' banking systems, it will reveal little systematic evaluation by managers of the risks financial institutions regularly face. Correcting this problem requires the commitment of senior management to change internal incentive systems and train staff, a process that usually takes years to effect. And this commitment cannot be expected unless incentives are pointing in the desired direction, meaning again that unless banks are highly profitable, the incentives to invest in human capital will be muted.

However, internal incentive and management systems are not developed sui generis, but reflect the incentive systems in the economy at large. If contracts cannot be enforced, bank management will not invest much in credit evaluation and will instead deal with only a core of borrowers with an established reputation. If real interest rates have been severely negative for quite some time and remain negative, loans likely will have been allocated by noncommercial methods and investment in loan assessment skills will not become a priority. Depositors will continue to keep their wealth in nonfinancial assets, and bank capital will likely have been eroded to the point that even with an end to negative real rates and government intervention, bankers will have little incentive to perform prudently, as they will have little of their own current or future resources at risk. So authorities have to turn their attention to getting these incentives right, as well as removing restraints on wages and other employment practices in banking. Banks can be employment offices or can allocate capital as efficiently as possible, but there is no hope that they can perform both of these functions. And all other changes will not be effective if banks cannot earn an adequate return. Therefore, even if interest rates cannot be deregulated completely, they should be at least increased in line with inflation rates and sufficiently wide margins should be established so that banks can earn a profit in line with the risks that they face.

In sum, if the essence of finance is information, then the essence of financial reform involves alterations of its collection and processing. These changes demand a revision of internal incentive systems within banks, a change that is unlikely to be made without at a minimum a reexamination of the incentive environment in which banks function. If the first step in a reform process is to deregulate interest rates and recapitalize banks, without first changing incentive systems and giving banks time to respond to new incentives that favor investments in human and information capital, it should be unsurprising that losses result. A better reform sequence would call for beginning with those changes that have a long gestation period and are critical to success. Altering incentive systems and encouraging investment in human and information capital are prime candidates for this early stage of a reform effort.

3.4   Conclusions

The evidence presented in Chapter 4 indicates that the effort to reform finance will pay off in higher efficiency and growth. Given the importance of bank portfolios, their information capital base, the stock of human capital, and nature of incentive systems in banks, authorities determined to reform their financial systems should first take an inventory of their respective banking systems, focusing on each of these elements. If banks have negative net worth, lend only to a few heavily protected clients (who are in the process of losing their protection), have employees that commercial institutions would not hire without much training, and operate with incentive systems designed only to distribute wage payments equitably and without regard to the long-term performance of the bank loans, then abrupt deregulation of banks and financial markets is fraught with danger. Where these elements are impaired, authorities should move fastest in the areas that will take the longest, that is, training and institutional reform, building legal, accounting, and auditing systems and professions – the infrastructure needed for low-cost and reliable information – and revising incentive systems. Banks in most countries need higher capital levels in order to align their incentives with the welfare of depositors. It is doubtful, perhaps ludicrous, to suppose that the current Basle capital guideline (an 8% risk-adjusted capital ratio) is adequate for developing countries; this ratio was devised for diversified industrial economies and U.S. legislation in 1992 already moved to a higher (10%) level. German and American banks held capital/asset ratios of 25% to 35% (at times higher) during their developmental period (the second half of the nineteenth century), and earned commensurately high spreads. This ratio, it should be noted, was not imposed by authorities but a response to the absence of deposit insurance and high franchise value.[13]

The implications of the approach advocated in this chapter to analyzing banks at the time of financial reforms is that in countries with a history of heavily repressed financial systems, which characterized some developing and all formerly socialist economies, the recommended approach to reform is to "make haste gradually." Haste is needed in taking stock of the underdevelopment of the financial system, beginning or accelerating human capital formation in banking, and in establishing market-oriented incentives inside and outside of the banks. But the gradual part is important as well: a wholesale adoption of unbridled competition in banking will be dangerous – perhaps always, but especially after a period of heavy repression – due to the externalities associated with the payments system and the consequent likelihood that the government will intervene to guarantee bank deposits. And complete interest-rate deregulation is inadvisable until some of the conditions noted in Chapter 13 are satisfied, most important, that banks have positive net worth and macroeconomic conditions are stable. Last, some financial sector reforms, such as bank recapitalization, should not run ahead of changes in the real sector; if real-sector distortions persist, even the best banks will encounter problems, offset perhaps if they can easily invest their funds abroad.

So while it is recognized that this cautious approach could be viewed as inimical to change, in all likelihood attempts at rapid reform from a heavily repressed environment will do more damage in the long run to the desire to increase the market orientation of finance. A gradual strategy to reform finance, taking account of the initial condition of the financial and nonfinancial sectors, is adumbrated in Chapter 13, drawing not just from the approach of Part I but also from the practical experience contained in Part III.

NOTES

1 Thus we ignore "off-balance-sheet" business, although conceptually they can be analyzed in the same framework.

2 de Juan (1987) provides an excellent description of how portfolio problems lead even good bankers to engage in increasingly dubious and in some case illegal practices that result in a magnification of losses.

3 See Stiglitz and Weiss (1981) and Greenwald and Stiglitz (1990). This section borrows from Caprio (1992), which includes a fuller description of the framework.

4 The quotation marks refer to the book by Louis Brandeis, *Other People's Money*, written in condemnation of unsafe banking practices of the 1920s in the United States.

5 To be sure, when banks are required to hold a given percentage of assets or deposits in government paper, the demand for this paper is being artificially stimulated.

6 Political factors occasionally dictate moving rapidly on financial reform, in which case the government may wish to use bank supervision to slow down portfolio shifts. However, in practice this is likely to be difficult, as some bankers, inclined to see only greater safety in an environment of rising real estate prices, will be inclined to ignore moral suasion and will complain that supervisors are preventing "sure" investments. Higher capital requirements, or a variable risk-weighting of capital requirements to increase the capital needed when portfolio concentration rises, or both, are more promising as solutions.

7 However, all but the shortest term Treasury bills carry interest-rate risk, which must be managed.

8 In a prior approval process, potential borrowers must first obtain approval from some government department or agency, most often the central bank or the finance

ministry, before they can secure access to – or in some case, even apply for – credit. This process is open to abuse. Bankers uniformly argue that when a loan with government approval has become nonperforming it is the government's responsibility.

9 The initiation of a structural adjustment program (or any potentially severe macro shock) can render worthless a good portion of information capital by reducing the attraction of lending to large, established firms (often public enterprises, at times the only large firms in the economy), pushing the loan return curve further to the right (Caprio 1992). The result of such a shift can be to lead banks to attempt to hold more of the riskless asset; although the shift may be welcomed – far better for the banks to hold Treasury bills than to lend to the "losers" – the resulting retrenchment by the banks can make the postadjustment period a good deal longer than forecast. Gertler and Rose (Chapter 2) emphasize the importance of borrower net worth in affecting the success of liberalization efforts. This approach suggests that even if economywide net worth is unimpaired by reforms or other shocks, a contraction of credit might still be expected if the declining sector is the main one on which banks have information.

10 Bernanke (1983) makes a similar argument about the U.S. banking system in the 1930s; as he puts it, uncertainty rose because much of the firm-specific information was wiped out when thousands of banks failed. In developing countries banks may remain open but insolvent for long periods of time because of an implicit government guarantee, especially if they are state-owned, or in some instances because the public doubts that they would be repaid if they attempted to withdraw their funds. But information capital, if not destroyed, is clearly rendered worthless at times of major swings in relative prices.

11 Caprio and Summers (1993) argue that franchise value – the present value of expected future profits – will explain a good deal about how banks perform. If bank franchise value is high, then managers will invest more in making their bank safe and sound, in order to ensure that they be able to remain in the banking business. Their research is consistent with an implication of Calomiris (1992), namely that countries with more numerous and less diversified banks will experience greater loan losses from sector shocks than those with fewer and more diversified institutions.

12 This section is a brief and cursory treatment of an involved subject by an economist. For a thorough treatment of the subject by an experienced banker, see the two-volume study by McNaughton (1993), especially the chapter on human resource management in commercial banks.

13 Caprio and Summers (1993) argue that, since governments today will stand behind (at least) their large banks, and that bank supervision cannot be depended on as the first line of defense against unsafe and unsound banking practices, then increasing the franchise value of bank licenses may be the best way to ensure that bank management improves its performance in this area.

CHAPTER 4

Credit where it is due? A review of the macro and micro evidence on the real effects of financial reform

Fabio Schiantarelli, Izak Atiyas, Gerard Caprio, Jr., John Harris, and Andrew Weiss

The relatively recent drive for financial reform in most countries has been spurred by the belief that the existing financial structure was not adequate to promote and assist growth in the real economy. Although specific arrangements differed from country to country, many systems were characterized by interest-rate controls that had led to low, often negative real interest rates. Moreover, there was a high degree of interference by the government in the allocation of credit, with designated priority sectors enjoying privileged access to credit. It has become common to use the label of financial repression to characterize the state of the financial systems under these circumstances. Many developing countries have moved away, in different degrees, from this model, and have introduced liberalization measures designed to leave to the market a greater role in the determination of interest rates and in the allocation of financial resources.

Together with the practical dissatisfaction with the existing structure of the financial systems, the move to liberalization was also influenced by the intellectual challenge to financial repression that started with the seminal contributions by McKinnon (1973) and Shaw (1973). Although the details of the analysis differ, the basic idea is that lifting the ceiling on interest rates and eliminating other interventions into the credit allocation process will increase the amount of financial savings, as well as the quantity and quality of investment, and stimulate growth. Much has been written since on the role of the financial system in promoting growth, but there has been relatively little convincing empirical evidence on the real effect of financial liberalization, in part because in many cases reform programs did not take hold until the 1980s. Until very recently, one had either to rely on country-by-country case studies or on mostly aggregate econometric evidence.

The objective of this paper is twofold. First, after a critical discussion of the channels through which financial development may influence the real economy, we review what we learn about the effects of financial liberalization from studies based on aggregate data. Second, and most important, we provide a survey of recent empirical evidence based on firms' panel data. The access to firm-level panel data makes it possible to investigate the micro effects of financial reform on the allocation of credit and changes in sources of funds. This is particularly important if, as it is likely to be the case, the impact of the latter varies according to a firm's characteristics such as size, age, and market orientation. Moreover, the availability of both the time series and cross-section dimension enables us to identify more precisely the importance of regime shifts following the liberalization measures.

In Section 4.1 we touch on the general issues involved in the comparison between a system of directed credit with a free market regime, critically appraise the arguments in favor of financial liberalization, and discuss some recent theoretical contributions on the relationship between financial development and growth. In Section 4.2 we review the aggregate evidence on the effects of financial reform, and in Section 4.4 we summarize the more recent evidence from firms' panel data.

4.1   What are we comparing and what can we learn from the theory?

When we compare a system of directed credit with a free market regime we are not necessarily comparing a regime governed by the whims of government bureaucrats with one determined purely by economic efficiency. A free market banking system has many problems. Because of information imperfections and contract enforcement problems, free market economies might not allocate investment funds to areas where the marginal product of investment is greatest. Also, in no country today is all credit allocated by the market; all governments have some mechanism to set aside some portion of credit for various and sundry groups – farmers, small and medium enterprises, exporters, and others. Indeed, recent data for the United States, often argued to be among the more market oriented, put the government's direct and indirect share of credit of 25% of the total. (See Schwarz 1992.) Moreover, even in developed countries, the larger fraction of financing for investment comes from internally generated funds, although there are marked differences between countries. For instance, during the period 1970–85 retentions accounted for 102.4% of total sources in the

United Kingdom and 85.9% in the United States, at the top of the range. The corresponding figure for Italy was 51.9% and for Japan 57.9%, at the bottom of the range (see Mayer 1990).[1] In developing countries, a sample of 20 countries showed that firms' own internally generated funds accounted for about 60% of investment financing. For both developed and developing countries most of external finance is accounted for by bank loans and in no country do firms raise a substantial part of their finance in stock markets (Honohan and Atiyas 1989).

Thus we can take as the benchmark for comparing directed credit regimes, a market-based financial system characterized by informational imperfections and in which internally generated funds are of great importance in the allocation of investable funds. If we look at outside credit, it is not at all clear that in a free market for credit, lenders will finance those investments with the highest expected gross returns. Lenders will care about the probability of loans being repaid, not about the expected gross returns on projects. Some of the factors that determine which firms get loans in a competitive banking system are degrees of leverage, liquidity, collateralizable wealth, and long-term relationships with the lender.[2] These factors, which tend to favor large, well-established firms and to discriminate against start-ups, may outweigh the profitability of investments in determining which firms get loans.

Of course firms – at least those with the intention of repaying – generally apply for loans only if they think that the private return from the project they wish to have financed will outweigh their interest rate costs. This positive selection effect mitigates some of the problems discussed in the previous paragraph. However, while selectivity on the part of potential borrowers is a mitigating factor, there are still many potential borrowers who are either turned down for loans, or who do not apply, even though their projects have positive expected net returns. One reason they do not apply may be because they know that given their assets and liabilities they have little chance of obtaining outside finance. On the other hand, directed credit programs in some countries appear to have encouraged an attitude that loans do not have to be repaid, thereby limiting efficiency gains associated with self-selection.

For all these reasons comparing a system of directed credit with a market-based allocation of funds involves a comparison between two imperfect systems.[3] In general, liberalization will not *necessarily* lead to efficiency gains, or to the relaxation of financial constraints faced by firms in the presence of informational and enforcement problems.

Ultimately, only an empirical investigation of the consequences of financial liberalization in those countries where it has occurred will allow researchers to assess the overall effect of reforms. However, in order to evaluate the relevance and importance of the empirical evidence discussed in the next two sections, it is useful to start from a brief review of the theoretical arguments in favor of financial liberalization.

The intellectual challenge to government interventions in the financial system, which keep interest rates artificially low and, possibly, replace market with administrative allocation of funds, is contained in the seminal contributions by McKinnon (1973) and Shaw (1973). There are three main ingredients of the McKinnon and Shaw position.[4] First, low interest rates on deposits may discourage total savings. Second, even if the amount of total saving is not affected, the composition of saving – and how it is intermediated – is. In particular, potential lenders may prefer unproductive assets (commodity stocks, gold, etc.) to bank deposits. This limits the supply of loanable funds and has adverse effects on investment. Finally, when there are interest rate ceilings, the quality of investment suffers: When banks cannot charge a risk premium, they become unwilling to finance high-yielding but risky investment projects. Also, interest ceilings usually imply that some part of available credit will not be allocated according to economic criteria. All these effects result in lower growth compared to that which could be achieved if the constraints impeding the development of the financial system were removed. It should also be noted that, even if not mentioned by McKinnon or Shaw, reducing financial repression might boost savings because the types of financial instruments offered would increase and bank branches would proliferate. However, this last effect has thus far not been fully examined.

The consequence of an increase in interest rates on the total amount of savings, a popular subject of economic research, is obviously theoretically ambiguous, and only empirical evidence can help in assessing whether financial liberalization can have favorable effects on savings. Similarly, as we have remarked, even in a free market it is not clear that lenders will finance investment projects with the highest expected returns. The issues concerning the total amount of savings and the quality of investment projects, however, were not at the center of the theoretical debate that followed the McKinnon and Shaw contribution. The main discussion concerned portfolio composition effects, and the supply-side consequences of an increase in interest rates. It has been argued that it is not necessarily true that financial liberalization will unambiguously increase the real supply of credit available to firms.

The Neo-Structuralist critique of the McKinnon and Shaw approach (see Van Wijnbergen 1982, 1983a,b, 1985; Taylor 1983; Buffie 1984; Khosaka 1984; Lim 1987; Morisset 1993) emphasizes the existence of informal (curb) credit markets that satisfy the residual demand for credit by firms and are not subject to reserve requirements. In this setting, the effect of an increase in the deposit rate on loanable funds depends upon whether households substitute out of curb market loans or out of cash (or unproductive assets held as inflation hedges). If time deposits are closer substitutes for curb market loans than for cash, than the supply of funds to firms will fall, given that banks are subject to reserve requirements and curb market institutions are not. Moreover the resulting increase in the interest rate on curb market loans may lead to a cost-push increase in prices and to a decline in output.

The view of informal credit markets as an efficient channel to intermediate funds from lender to borrowers may, however, not be an accurate description of reality; informal lenders may have lower costs than formal intermediaries because they are avoiding taxes, hence this cost structure may imply little about their efficiency. Whereas it is true that the use of local knowledge may decrease information costs on certain type of loans, the informal market is often characterized by a high degree of segmentation with limited possibilities of exploiting economies of scale in risk pooling and information processing or economies of scope. Indeed, curb markets are frequently regionally specialized, making them less safe – more exposed to local shocks – than more diversified banks. It is moreover not clear that all the resources intermediated by the informal markets will be channeled to firms. They may be employed instead to finance consumption or may be appropriated as monopoly profits by lenders, or put to other unproductive uses. Ultimately the result of liberalization will depend upon the comparative efficiency of the banking sector and of the informal sector in the process of intermediation.[5] Also in this case the controversy cannot be solved at a theoretical level, but will require empirical evidence in order to discriminate between alternative models. This debate is similar to that in U.S. banking history regarding trade-offs between unit banks – one office with no branch network – compared with larger, more diversified branching banks, or the similar controversy between adherents of local and nationwide banking. Calomiris (1992) reviews the evidence and finds that large, more diversified banks were less prone to fail and experienced smaller losses than smaller, unit banks. However, most observers appear to agree that at some point diseconomies of scale take over as the superior information at the local level is ignored or lost.[6] (In the United States the degree to which diseconomies of scale take over may only become clear when limits on interstate banking are completely removed.)

A very recent set of papers has attempted to formalize, in the context of endogenous growth models, the idea contained in the work of McKinnon and Shaw, and Goldsmith (1969) before them, that the development of the financial system is essential for economic growth. The mechanism through which this may occur differs in the various papers. In Bencivenga and Smith (1991) the existence of financial intermediaries reduces the investment in liquid assets with low rates of return, and prevents the unnecessary liquidation of investment by entrepreneurs in order to satisfy liquidity needs. Under appropriate assumptions about the value of structural parameters (for instance, if risk aversion is high enough), the equilibrium with intermediation can be shown to yield higher growth rates than the equilibrium without financial intermediaries, although this is not true in general. Greenwood and Jovanovic (1990) stress instead the role that intermediaries play in collecting and in analyzing information, making it possible for investors to put funds to better uses. Cooley and Smith (1991) emphasize the idea that financial markets may promote specialization (especially entry into entrepreneurial activity), technological innovation, and learning by doing. The importance of financial markets in allowing a greater specialization of resources is also discussed in Saint-Paul (1992). Roubini and Sala-i-Martin (1992) suggest that financial development can be seen as reducing the transaction costs of converting nonliquid into liquid assets.

Finally, some of the papers stress the fact that the relationship between financial and real development runs both ways (for instance, see Greenwood and Jovanovic 1990 and Levine 1992 in the context of an endogenous growth model, but see also Gertler and Rose in this volume). Financial intermediaries may promote growth, and economic growth, in turn, stimulates changes in financial markets. Although all these theoretical contributions are very helpful in giving us insights into the relationship between financial and real development, they do not provide a complete and unambiguous answer as to the consequences of financial liberalization. Typically the models are very stylized, and fail to capture fully the issues that arise in economies characterized by informational imperfections, and with different types of financial intermediaries (banks, curb market institutions).[7] Ultimately, an assessment of the real effects of financial reform must rely on the empirical analysis and testing of the various hypotheses suggested by the theoretical contributions discussed in this section.

4.2   The effects of liberalization: Evidence from aggregate data

Until recently most of the empirical evidence on the effects of liberalization has been based on aggregate data. We will provide here a brief critical review of the main results obtained thus far.[8]

A first group of papers presents direct empirical evidence on the relationship between aggregate growth rates for different countries and financial development, using cross-section data or pooled cross-section time-series data. The growth rates are regressed either on measures of financial deepening, like the ratio between widely defined money aggregates and GDP or on real interest rates.[9] Higher real rates are seen as the consequences of the process of financial liberalization. The standard result is that growth rates are positively and significantly associated both with measures of financial development and real interest rates. King and Levine (1993a,b) do the most thorough empirical investigation of finance and growth to date and find a significant positive relationship for a sample of 119 countries during the 1960–89 period.[10] They regress the average real per capita growth on the logs of initial income and school enrollment, the ratio of trade to GDP, that of government spending to GDP, and average inflation, as well as four financial indicators – financial depth, as measured by liquid liabilities to GDP, the ratio of commercial (deposit money) bank assets to total bank assets (including those of the central bank), the proportion of credit to private sector firms to total credit, and the ratio of claims on the private sector to GDP. All four financial sector indicators are significant at the 5% level and the size of the coefficients is indicative of an important impact. An interesting feature of the King–Levine study is the finding that countries with more lending intermediated by the commercial banking sector (compared with those with much central bank credit, a proxy for directed credit programs) grow faster.

Moreover, using extreme bounds analysis, they (and Levine and Zervos, 1993) show that the links between finance and growth are quite robust. King and Levine (1993b) also find that when predicting growth over the 1960–89 period using the aforementioned nonfinancial variables, indices of civil liberties, numbers of revolutions and coups, and of assassinations, as well as indicators of monetary, fiscal, and trade policies, the residual – the unexplained part of growth – is closely related to the financial depth at the start of the period. In other words, finance appears to be an important component of the economy, in particular in the way in which the financial sector helps to allocate resources.

Although the King–Levine evidence certainly is more persuasive than most of the literature, as it appears to find a link between initial financial development and subsequent growth, most of the empirical literature cannot be read as evidence that financial liberalization necessarily *causes* faster growth.[11] For instance, the financial system might develop and prosper to a greater extent in faster growing countries. The existence of a class of good borrowers with collateralizable assets is instrumental to the development of intermediation, as argued in Chapter 2. The value of collateralizable assets depends upon future profit prospects and these will be more favorable when growth rates are higher. Moreover, the positive correlation between growth rates and interest rates could reflect the fact that in macroeconomically stable countries with lower inflation the demand for money as a proportion of income is higher, stock markets are more prosperous, and the real growth rate is higher. Indeed, Jung (1986) finds that Granger causality tests confirm that causation runs both ways between finance and growth, for a sample of 56 countries with at least 15 annual observations each; however, he offers some hope: Causation runs somewhat more often from financial development to growth rather than in the opposite direction.

Another approach to testing the effects of financial liberalization has focused on the effect of interest rates on savings. The basic idea is that financial liberalization should lead to higher real interest rates, stimulating in this way national savings, which provide the major part of resources for investment. In the context of endogenous growth models (Romer 1986 and Lucas 1988), the increase in the savings rate permanently affects the real growth rate. Apart from the obvious observation that the effect of the real rate of interest on savings is theoretically ambiguous, the econometric results obtained on aggregate data suggest that there is not a robust and strong correlation between interest rates and saving behavior. Fry (1978, 1980, 1988) finds a significant positive effect of the interest rate in a traditional aggregate saving equation, using panel data for Asian countries. However, the statistical significance of the interest rate coefficient is not robust to changes in the time period used or the countries included in the regression (Giovannini 1983, 1985). The latter paper by Giovannini estimates the Euler equation for consumption for a consumer that faces a perfect capital market. Rossi (1988) estimates the appropriate Euler equation for liquidity-constrained consumers on aggregate panel data for a large set of developing countries from all regions of the world. With the exception of countries in Sub-Saharan Africa and in South America, the effect of the rate of interest on consumption is not only negative, but also significant.

Whatever the significance level, the magnitude of the effect of interest rate changes on saving is rather small for most countries (see also Fry 1988). The general conclusion is that there is no convincing empirical support for the proposition that a higher real interest rate leads to substantial increases in domestic savings in less developed countries. Jappelli and Pagano (1992) have suggested that lack of financial development that results in consumers' liquidity being constrained, may lead to higher saving rates. When the maximum loan to value ratio for the purchase of a house is used as an inverse proxy of liquidity constraints for households, estimation of an aggregate saving equation on a panel of (mainly) OECD countries suggests that indeed this is the case. They also show that in the context of an endogenous growth model, liquidity constraints may enhance growth. Econometric results from standard growth regressions on a sample of 30 countries provide some empirical support for this contention, since the maximum loan to value ratio is significantly and negatively associated with growth. Note, however, that the regressions do not include other proxies for financial development that capture the effect of different degrees of sophistication of the intermediation system on investment, and hence no overall conclusion can be reached about the overall effect of financial development. Moreover, liquidity constraints may also have negative effects on growth, since individuals' inability to borrow against future income reduces the incentives for human capital accumulation.[12]

Returning to the effect of the interest rate on saving, another strand of the literature looks for nonlinear effects. Tests of changes in interest rates within the narrow band of slightly positive or slightly negative rates that have held for most industrial economies may be precisely the range within which interest rate variation has no impact. Yet it remains possible that increases in rates from substantially negative levels to the neighborhood of zero may well induce greater saving (not just the proportion of saving intermediated by the financial sector), as this change amounts to the elimination of a heavy tax on saving, especially on financial saving. Once inflation reaches a certain point, the emphasis is devoted to spending funds as fast as possible, and it is in rapidly inflating economies where substantially negative real interest rates are found. Reynoso (1989) presents some evidence (also hinted at in Dornbusch and Reynoso 1989) suggesting that the relationship between saving and real interest rates may be a parabola, with saving increasing most significantly when rates rise from sharply negative to just below zero, then leveling off, and finally declining as real rates become highly positive. Since saving and interest rates are both endogenous variables, it may be important to examine the specific causes of higher rates. Last, one approach to test for noninterest components of liberalization is to investigate empirically the effect on saving of greater accessibility to depository institutions in rural areas. There is some evidence that greater proximity may lead to an increase in savings from a limited sample of five countries over time (Fry 1988). However it is unclear if this result holds up for a broader sample.[13]

Instead of looking at the effect of financial liberalization on savings, another set of papers directly analyzes its effect on investment. The basic idea here is that financial liberalization will increase credit availability (because of the hypothesized, although questionable, positive effect of higher real deposit rates on savings), and relax the severity of credit constraints faced by firms. All of the studies use aggregate data and estimate ad hoc flexible accelerator types of investment equations containing proxies for the availability of credit, typically the stock of real domestic credit. The latter variable tends to be significantly and positively related to investment. However, the econometric techniques used in estimating these equations are often not appropriate, either because endogeneity problems of the regressors are disregarded, or because country-specific effects are not sufficiently accounted for, when using pooled time-series cross-section data. Moreover, one may want to allow the effect of variables capturing the stringency of financial constraints to vary in the periods before and after liberalization. With aggregate data, however, there are not many degrees of freedom to estimate separate coefficients, given that the process of financial liberalization in most countries is a rather recent phenomenon.

A last strand of the literature attempts to investigate the impact of financial reform by looking at economywide measures of efficiency. The most sensible way of rationalizing the work in this area is to think of a production technology with a fixed capital/output ratio under the assumption that the supply of labor is infinitely elastic (as in the stripped down version of the Harrod–Domar model). The efficiency of investment is then measured by the incremental output capital ratio (IOCR) that is meant to capture the technical (or organizational) ability to transform the capital input into output. The empirical work in this area is vast. Just to mention one of the more recent contributions, Gelb (1989) finds evidence from a cross section of 34 countries over the 1965–85 period for which reliable interest rate data were available that increased interest rates are associated with greater efficiency, as measured by the IOCR, and with higher growth through this channel.

The channel he finds runs from higher real rates to a greater share of savings intermediate by the formal financial sector to increased efficiency, by his measure. And for the countries investigated in this study there are some signs of an upturn of the IOCR following the onset of financial reforms.[14] However, these ratios in practice are not straightforward in their measurement, being sensitive to the method by which the deflator for capital goods is estimated. Moreover, short-term comparisons of the IOCR are extremely sensitive to business-cycle fluctuations, so it is premature to place much emphasis on this upturn.

King and Levine (1993b) also find cross-section evidence of a relationship between different indicators of financial development and efficiency, using a measure similar to the IOCR. Briefly, they find that efficiency gains are associated both with a higher ratio of liquid liabilities (broad money) to GDP and also with increases in the proportion of credit intermediated by commercial banks instead of central banks, in systems relying heavily on directed credit. In other words, freeing up the financial system – letting banks have control over their resources and lend them to the private sector – appears to contribute to gains in this measure of efficiency.

A serious reservation about IOCR-based estimates of efficiency relates to the simple underlying Harrod–Domar view of technology. The reciprocal (IOCR) can be interpreted generally as a proxy for the (marginal) capital intensity of production. Any formal investment model with standard neoclassical technology with flexible production coefficients implies that the capital intensity of production will decrease (and with it the IOCR) if the real interest rate increases, everything else equal.[15] A lower IOCR is therefore not informative about efficiency, since efficiency could be the result of technical progress, better utilization of capital, or changes in factor proportions. Moreover, the links between such a change in factor proportion and the efficiency of investment is unclear, if efficiency is taken to mean profitability of the investment project, as it is sometimes the case in this literature. Perhaps a way to rescue the relevance of the empirical work described is to argue that in countries with an abundance of labor, it is reasonable to assume that the use of more labor-intensive techniques is a good thing. Insofar as financial liberalization removes a price distortion that favors highly capital-intensive projects, it may therefore have beneficial effects.

Another approach that has been advocated by some economists to assess the effect of financial liberalization on the efficiency with which resources are allocated is to measure whether the cost of capital becomes more nearly equal across firms and industries after liberalization. They assume that the cost of credit is a good proxy for the unobserved marginal productivity of capital. Cho (1988) shows that the variance across industries of the average cost of credit in Korea is reduced after liberalization and concludes that this is an indication of an improved locative efficiency. Unfortunately a serious problem arises from differences between the shadow value of capital and the interest rate paid by borrowers who get credit. Suppose a government decreed that all loans must be made at a 1% real interest rate. We would find that in that economy all borrowers paid the same interest rate; however, there would be vast differences in the availability of capital. Besides great reliance on internally generated funds, there would likely be great differences in the marginal product of capital across firms. Even if all firms have an equal cost of funds and equal access to those funds, that cost may be so high or the access so limited that firms rely mainly on cash flow as a source of investment funds. Again in that case a great disparity in the productivity of investment across firms could result. In conclusion, it is not possible to infer much about allocative efficiency from changes in the dispersion of the observed averaged cost of credit.

4.3   New empirical evidence from firm panel data

In this section we will discuss new empirical evidence on the effects of financial liberalization obtained using firm-by-firm panel data for developing countries. The use of panel data for individual firms presents a set of potential advantages. First, it allows researchers to investigate the effects of financial liberalization on the sources and uses of funds. It is in fact likely that firms were treated differentially in a regime of financial repression, but it also likely that the effects of liberalization differ across firms according to their size, age, market orientation, and other factors. This is so because, as explained earlier, the alternative to a financially repressed system is not a perfect capital market, but a market for funds characterized by informational asymmetries and less than complete contract enforceability, giving rise to agency problems, whose severity varies for different types of firms.

Second, the availability both of the time-series and the cross-section dimension for a large number of firms provides us with the possibility of identifying more precisely the effects of liberalization. As emphasized in this volume, especially in Chapter 3, financial reform is not an act, but a process, so a conclusive answer concerning its effects will require more years of observation. It takes time for institutions to adapt and for practices to change. However, the availability of panel data for countries that have liberalized during the 1980s permits us to draw some tentative conclusions.

Firm-level panel data can be used to compare the efficiency of the allocation of credit before and after liberalization. There are several approaches for measuring this allocative efficiency. A production function can be estimated with a firm-specific, time-invariant component that measures the distance of each firm from the production possibility frontier. This has been defined in the literature as "technical efficiency."[16] Technical efficiency (inefficiency) captures the degree of X inefficiencies or the access to the best practice technology. We can then estimate whether the more efficient firms according to this component get a greater or smaller share of investment funds after liberalization.

Using a panel of 420 Ecuadorian firms in the manufacturing sector, Jaramillo, Schiantarelli, and Weiss (1992a,b) provide evidence that, ceteris paribus, there has been an increase in the flow of credit accruing to technically more efficient firms, after liberalization, controlling for other firms' characteristics. This result is robust to different specifications of the production function and to different estimation methods.[17] An advantage to using this definition of technical efficiency to explain the allocation of capital is that it is less likely to be open to objections concerning endogeneity and reverse causation. For instance, if one uses the rate of profits from operations as an explanatory variable to explain the allocation of credit, a significant association between debt allocation and efficiency can be found simply because firms that had access to external funds could invest in better technology and become more efficient and profitable. Note that the econometric results for Ecuador also suggest that efficiency correlates *directly* with size and age. In particular, there is a shift of resources from smaller firms to larger firms, which are both more efficient and more profitable after liberalization. The econometric analysis is consistent with the simple observation that the degree of leverage decreases for all firms after financial liberalization, but there is evidence that the decrease is more substantial for small firms. It is also consistent with the fact that the share of new debt, relative to value added, decreases for small firms after liberalization. This shift is not surprising, if one considers carefully the initial conditions. In Ecuador a subsidized credit program for small firms was basically eliminated after liberalization. More generally, it is quite possible that in a world of asymmetric information, small firms may find it hard to obtain credit from financial intermediaries because they are riskier and have not yet accumulated "reputation capital."

Indonesia, another country that went through a process of financial liberalization, reveals both differences and similarities (see Harris, Schiantarelli, and Siregar 1992 and Siregar 1992). Econometric estimation of the determinants of changes in the allocation of new credit in Indonesia on a panel of 524 establishments in manufacturing confirms the results obtained for Ecuador of a positive and significant association between the latter variable and measures of firms' technical efficiency based on production function estimates (see Siregar 1992).[18] Also for Indonesia there is evidence therefore that the process of financial liberalization has helped to direct resources to more efficient firms. However, it appears that the degree of leverage increased for small firms after liberalization, contrary to what happens in Ecuador. Leverage also increased for large firms and decreased for medium-size firms. Looking at the distribution of debt before and after liberalization, it appears that both small and large firms increased their share of new domestic debt relative to value added, while medium firms experienced a decrease. The data also suggest that in the period following liberalization, larger firms are successful in obtaining foreign credit.

The empirical evidence described so far in this section has concentrated on the issue of the efficient allocation of resources. The availability of panel data also allows us to investigate whether financial liberalization has succeeded in relaxing financial constraints faced by firms. Jaramillo, Schiantarelli, and Weiss (1993b) develop a model in which they allow both for the interest rate paid by firms to be an increasing function of the degree of leverage, and the existence of a ceiling on the maximum degree of leverage that lenders are willing to accept. Estimation of the appropriate Euler equation for capital on the panel of Ecuadorian firms suggests that both forms of capital market imperfections affect small firms, although not larger ones. If one believes that banks are more efficient in screening and monitoring borrowers than the curb market, one may expect a decrease of the premium for external finance after liberalization. The shift from a curb market to one dominated by efficient banks would lead to an outward shift of the supply curve for funds and to a lower premium for external finance, for a given level of borrowing and collateralizable wealth.

Ultimately, however, it is an empirical question whether this hypothesis is correct. Moreover, swings in borrower net worth could dominate the results of a change in the form of financial intermediation on the premium paid by a firm at each level of borrowing. It is also an empirical question whether financial liberalization decreases the degree of rationing. The econometric results for Ecuador suggest that there was not a significant decrease in the premium for external finance paid by small firms after liberalization at each level of the debt-to-capital ratio. Similarly, there was not a relaxation of the maximum degree of leverage allowed. These results should be interpreted with caution, because of the short nature of the panel, and because of the macroeconomic conditions in Ecuador (the 1987 earthquake shock and the concomitant episode of fiscal instability led to high inflation and to a reduction in the supply of credit to the private sector). However, they are consistent with the results obtained on the allocation of credit, that suggest that small Ecuadorian firms were not the gainers in the process of financial liberalization.

Estimation of an ad hoc investment equation for Indonesian firms (Harris, Schiantarelli, and Siregar 1992) confirms the basic message that had been obtained for the allocation of credit flows. When investment is regressed on output growth, cash flow, and the degree of leverage, investment by small firms is more sensitive to cash flow than for larger firms. If cash flow is taken as an indicator of differential access to outside funding, and of the necessity to use internal funds, the results imply that small firms are more financially constrained. Moreover, investment for small firms is negatively related to the degree of leverage, as one would expect if the degree of leverage is a proxy for the premium to be paid on outside finance. After liberalization, the coefficient for cash flow for small firms decreases, and the one for the degree of leverage becomes closer to zero. This suggests that small firms are less financially constrained after liberalization and enjoy a better access to outside funding.

The use of cash flow as an indicator only of financial constraints is open to criticism. Cash flow is, in fact, also a proxy for future profitability. When future profits are added as an additional regressor, cash flow remains significant for small firms, although with a smaller coefficient that now does not change significantly after liberalization. The interesting fact is that future profits matter much more for larger firms than for smaller firms, particularly before liberalization. After liberalization, the response to future profits becomes more similar across firms. Also in this case, the coefficient on leverage decreases after liberalization. All this is consistent with a scenario in which smaller firms can respond better to profit prospects after financial reform, perhaps because they have better access to outside funding.

The effect of financial factors on investment behavior was also analyzed for the case of Korea; although the data did not permit an investigation of efficiency, an examination of the impact of reform on financing decisions was possible. A Q-model of investment was estimated for about 180 firms in the manufacturing industries, over the period 1984–8 (Atiyas 1992). Lagged investment, degree of leverage, output, Q-ratio, and a stock measure of liquidity were used as independent variables.[19] Results show that over the sampled period, and for the entire sample of firms, the effect of debt on investment is not significant, whereas liquidity does enter significantly. Moreover, the estimated coefficients do not exhibit any significant change between the earlier and later years of the reform period.[20] When the sample is split according to size, however, a different picture emerges. Investment behavior of small firms is affected by both liquidity constraints and debt; however, the impact of both is reduced in the late 1980s. Hence small firms' access to external finance seems to have improved after liberalization. For large firms, however, while the impact of financial variables was insignificant in the early 1980s, the effect of both liquidity and indebtedness becomes significant in the late 1980s, suggesting that financial reform actually *decreased* the access of this group to external finance. At least until the late 1980s, then, the main effect of financial reform was to change cross-sectional patterns of access to finance.

These results are not surprising, given the change in targeted credit policy during the reform period. Even though most preferential interest rates applied to directed-credit programs were abolished, and the volume and scope of directed credit were reduced, directed credit nevertheless was not eliminated. More important, the target of directed credit was switched from large companies in heavy and chemical industries to small and medium firms. Therefore, the empirical results at least partially seem to reflect this reorientation of credit policy.

4.4   Conclusions

The empirical results on the effects of financial liberalization obtained from firms' panel data for developing countries are a very useful addition to the macro evidence available. On the one hand, microeconomic evidence can address problems that cannot be usefully tackled using more aggregate data, such as the differential effects of financial liberalization on different types of firms. On the other hand, results from macroeconomic studies are sometimes inconclusive, and often subject to serious problems of interpretation, or at least courageous assumptions (like the lack of substitutability among factors of production in studies using the IOCR as a measure of efficiency). In general the evidence that financial reform has positive efficiency effects appears supported from the micro studies reviewed here. Firm-level data show clear evidence of credit flowing to more efficient firms following the adoption of financial reforms in Ecuador and Indonesia. Interestingly, the financing constraint was relaxed for small firms in Korea and Indonesia. While in the former case this likely was not a result of liberalization but merely a different credit rule favoring small firms, in Indonesia it appears to be the result of less government interference with credit allocation and pricing.

An important difference that may explain the different effect of financial liberalization on financial constraints faced by small firms in Indonesia and Ecuador concerns the pace of credit expansion. Credit in Indonesia has been growing at a rapid rate since reforms began (averaging close to 25% a year between 1983 and 1991 in real terms), in sharp contrast to the decline in real credit in Ecuador (approximately 7% a year). So one could argue that small firms in Indonesia faced less tight financial conditions also because of the easier credit policy. This may explain why the evidence from investment equations suggests that there has been a relaxation of financial constraints for small firms in Indonesia, but not in Ecuador. However, since Indonesian authorities achieved and maintained single-digit inflation rates over the second half of the 1980s, it is *not* clear that from a macro standpoint credit growth was excessive.

Of course these conclusions must be viewed as preliminary: Ideally a longer time span of postreform data and data from more countries would be desirable. However, the initial micro results discussed here should give some encouragement to those who think that finance matters. With the passage of time, more and better data sets should help us see which types of prereform controls were the least efficient, and which types of liberalization paid the largest returns.

NOTES

1 These figures are calculated on a net basis, with accumulation of equivalent financial assets subtracted from liabilities. The figures on a gross basis are lower. The general point that retentions are in most cases the most important source of financing remains true.

2 This point is important both because of better information flows and because those long-term relationships generate good incentive effects.

3 Following Stiglitz and Weiss (1981), Cho (1986) has indeed argued that removing an interest rate ceiling will not lead to a fully optimal allocation of capital, in the absence of well-functioning equity markets.

4 See Fry (1988) for a more extensive discussion of the McKinnon and Shaw position.

5 See Owen and Solis-Fallas (1989) for an attempt at incorporating these considerations in Van Wijnbergen's model.
6 This debate is important for small developing countries, where banks with nationwide branches may have as concentrated portfolios as U.S. unit banks in the 1900s. Restrictions on holding foreign assets make small economies' banks inherently fragile, since if the local economy is highly specialized, a bank that holds only local assets will have an excessively concentrated portfolio.
7 See Bencivenga and Smith (1991) for an endogenous growth model that allows for an informational friction that makes it difficult to distinguish high- from low-quality investment, and may give rise to credit rationing.
8 Fry (1988, ch. 6) provides additional references and a more detailed discussion of some of the empirical issues addressed in this section.
9 See Gertler and Rose (Chapter 2 of this book), the World Bank's *World Development Report* (1989), and the papers quoted in Fry (1988).
10 Similar results are also obtained by Roubini and Sala-i-Martin (1991) and by Atje and Jovanovic (1992), whose proxy for financial development incorporates measures of stock market size.
11 For most of the literature, as we have already discussed, it is possible to argue that causation runs also in the opposite direction.
12 See De Gregorio (1992) for a theoretical and empirical contribution in this area.
13 One reservation about Fry's results is that he regressed savings rates that are generally trending on several stationary variables and branching per capita over a 25-year period. However, since branching in the countries covered likely increased more or less steadily over time, any explanatory power may have been picking up a time trend.
14 This ratio rises in five of the seven countries examined in Chapter 6, and indeed in Malaysia, one of the two cases in which the ratio clearly declines, the comparison is biased, as the base period dates from before the generalized decline in productivity at the time of the first oil shock. Since the mid-1980s (1984–5), when Malaysia was adjusting to the decline of real commodity prices, the incremental output-investment ratio has increased by 34 percentage points. Indonesia, a heavy oil- and nonoil-commodity exporter, saw a gain of 14 percentage points from the same period. All of the ratios reported here use data for nominal GDP and nominal gross investment, or, which is the same, deflate numerator and denominator by the same GDP deflator.
15 Even if the technology were putty-clay we would expect that the capital output ratio on the last vintage decreases if new machines become more expensive relative to labor.
16 See the seminal contribution by Aigner, Lovell, and Schmidt (1977), and the one by Schmidt and Sickles (1984) on the estimation stochastic production frontiers, when panel data are available.
17 Different methods employed included least squares dummy variables, GLS, and GMM estimators.
18 As for Ecuador, the efficiency measure is positively related to size.
19 The data did not allow the calculation of an accurate measure of cash flow. Hence, a stock measure of liquidity was used instead to capture the effect of the availability of internal funds.
20 Financial reform in Korea is characterized by its gradualism; hence no single year in the 1980s can be identified as the one in which financial reform took place. Instead, it was assumed that the impact of financial reform was revealed in the last two years of the sample period.

PART II
THE REFORM EXPERIENCES

CHAPTER 5

An overview of financial reform episodes

Izak Atiyas, Gerard Caprio, Jr., and James A. Hanson

Financial reform usually entails a variety of steps to ease portfolio controls and directed credit, as well as to limit government intervention in the determination of interest rates. Reducing barriers to competition in the financial sector, scaling back government ownership of financial intermediaries, allowing new financial products to appear, limiting excessive taxation of banks and other intermediaries, and reducing restrictions on financial dealings of domestic households and businesses with counterparts abroad also may be a part of reform efforts. The success of these steps, though admittedly difficult to define (see Chapter 13), may depend on the order in which reforms are undertaken and especially on the initial conditions both in the financial sector and in the economy at large. This chapter reviews the state of the economies and their financial systems on the eve of reform, provides an overview of the path of reform chosen by the authorities, and briefly reviews some of the features of the period following the onset of reforms. It represents a very brief summary of the reform stories, aimed especially at those who do not have the time for the individual cases that are analyzed in much greater detail in subsequent chapters or who first want an overview of some of the main elements of the reform episodes. In keeping with a guide's brief, no grand conclusions are ventured here. But we don our analysts' hats again in Chapter 13, where we attempt to draw lessons from the analytical papers and case studies, and to construct a reform strategy for authorities contemplating financial reform.

5.1   Macroeconomic background

Pinpointing the start of financial reform is usually not possible, especially where reforms are introduced gradually. Malaysia and Korea

moved over a period of years, beginning some changes in the 1960s
and early 1970s. New Zealand, in contrast, poses no classification
problem, having moved instantaneously, by policy-making standards,
to abandon a wide array of controls on domestic and international
financial intermediation within a nine-month period in 1984–5. Most
other countries, including some of those in this study, fall somewhere
in between. The starting date for the reforming cases examined here
has been picked as that point at which experts appear to agree that the
pace of change picked up. Table 5.1 presents the prereform dates as
well as some summary macroeconomic indicators for the countries
covered.

A fairly clear demarcation appears between the three Asian economies, where financial reform took place in relatively good economic
times, and the other countries shown in the table. *Korea* enjoyed an
excellent real growth performance at the start of the reform period,
having already advanced on a real sector adjustment program, including an exchange-rate devaluation and a reduction of both the budget
deficit and inflation, before making many changes in the financial
sector. Moreover, reforms in the Korean financial sector were in many
ways the most cautious of the cases surveyed in this volume.

Malaysian authorities also began financial reform in an exceptionally favorable macro environment, both in the early 1970s, when some
longer-term interest rates gradually were deregulated, and in 1978,
when complete interest-rate decontrol was (briefly) attempted.[1] Although Malaysia had the lowest per capita income at the start of the
reform period, it also enjoyed the lowest inflation rate, by a wide
margin, and the deepest financial system, as measured by M2 relative
to GDP. These two economies thus began financial reforms with an
invaluable advantage: Because they were not forced into reform by
unfavorable external or internal circumstances, any difficulties caused
by reform in the financial or real sectors for the health of financial
institutions could easily have been offset by robust macro developments.

Indonesia's export prices for oil and other commodities were historically high but declining on the eve of reform. Although real growth
averaged 5% immediately before the onset of the 1983 reforms, it had
slowed to a mere 2.2% in the year preceding reform. Also, Indonesia
began reforms with the shallowest (onshore) financial system, with M2
less than 17% of GDP, a level below that in many of today's low-
income countries. This figure undoubtedly is influenced by the extent
of offshore intermediation being conducted then in Singapore. Moreover, Indonesia only began to allow private domestic banks in 1981.

Table 5.1 Economies on the eve of reform: Macro indicators

Country	Pre-reform period	Population	Per Capita GDP	Average GDP growth, pre-reform	Growth in year prior to/of reform	Average inflation rate	Current Account Deficit	Budget Deficit	Broad Money
		(millions)	dollars	(% per annum)	(%)	(% per annum)	% GDP	% GDP	(M2/GDP)
Chile	1971-73	10	1102	-1.9	-5.7/1.0	260.1	4.0/2.9	4.1	21.0
Indonesia	1980-82	154	584	4.9	2.2/4.2	13.2	0.8	2.1	16.7
Korea	1979-81	39	1721	3.6	6.7/7.3/ 11.8	22.7	7.2	2.4	32.5
Malaysia	1970-72	11	442	8.2	7.8/6.7	2.2	2.4	7.2	37.1
New Zealand	1981-83	3	7060	2.7	2.9/5.0	12.9	5.4	8.2	26.7
Turkey	1977-79	44	1590	2.1	-0.9/-0.7	43.1	3.67	5.6	26.2

* *Note* that the figures for GDP growth and inflation are 3-year compound averages, those for current accounts, budget deficits, and broad money are simple averages, and that for population and per capita GDP (and for Chile, the M2 figure) is the latest year in the pre-reform period. For the purpose of comparison, the average M2/GDP ratios over the 1965-87 period for high growth, medium growth, and low growth developing countries were, respectively, 43%, 31.2%, and 23.9% (World Bank, 1989).

However, the authorities had several potentially offsetting advantages. First, they had devalued the currency before beginning reforms, thus starting with realistic prices and a pickup in the export sector. Second, though not nearly as low as in Malaysia, inflation was under control and, at least as important, the internal and external accounts were near balance. Indeed, in reaction to the Sukarno years, domestic government debt was banned; by thus limiting the gains from inflation, this ban increased the credibility of government policy announcements. Third, Indonesia already had a fairly high savings rate, as did Korea and Malaysia; initial investment rates in these three Asian countries also were generally above those of Chile, New Zealand, and Turkey (Figures 5.3 and 5.4). These high savings and investment rates were part of the growth advantage enjoyed by the Asian economies.

At the opposite extreme, *Chile* and *Turkey* began their reform efforts with decidedly poor growth and inflation, low savings rates, and relatively shallow financial systems. Both countries also had experienced long periods of relatively severe financial repression: Real deposit rates in Chile were significantly negative since at least the 1940s (Figure 5.1), and in Turkey government intervention into the credit process also was substantial. According to the argument advanced in Chapter 3, these shocks plus repression of this magnitude most probably left the balance sheets, human capital stock, and incentive systems in these countries' banks in poor condition. Malaysia had a diametrically opposite experience, with real interest rates mostly positive in the 1970s (Figure 9.1), and Korea (Table 8.2) saw only modest interest-rate repression relative to that seen in the Southern Cone area, although there was significant directed credit.

New Zealand represents a mixed picture, in terms of the prereform environment. The immediate prereform macro setting, shown in Table 5.1, was more positive than a longer view suggests. New Zealand had the lowest rate of real economic growth in the OECD region over the 1960–84 period and experienced little or no growth in the decade immediately before reforms began. Its saving rate had dwindled steadily to under 22% of GDP, inflation (at 13%) was high by OECD standards, and the budget and current account deficits had reached alarming proportions by the early 1980s. Real interest rates on deposits had been modestly negative for virtually all of the 1970–83 period, fluctuating for the most part between −2% to −10%. And its monetary depth put it little ahead of today's low-income developing countries.

To summarize, then, the Asian countries began reforms in generally more favorable macroeconomic environments, which in the Gertler–Rose framework was a key advantage in that it led to a favorable

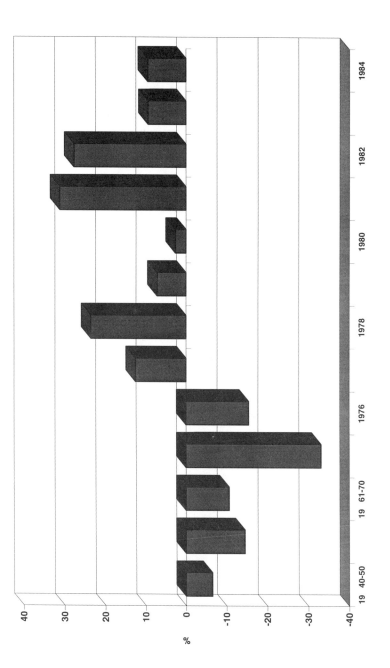

Figure 5.1 Chile: Real interest rates, 1940–84

evolution of borrower net worth. This advantage likely accounts in part for the apparently successful aftermath to the reform programs.

5.2   Initial conditions in the financial sector

Table 5.2 describes some of the prereform characteristics of the banking systems in each of the six countries. In addition to a categorization of the interest-rate regime, portfolio requirements, the supervisory system, ownership of banks, and the subsidization of credit, the table also describes the openness of the capital account, inasmuch as this characteristic often is linked to the sophistication of the financial system. Although all of these governments engaged in significant financial sector intervention by present-day industrial-country standards, *Malaysia* stands out as having the most market-oriented financial system at the start of reform, with relatively little effective de jure intervention into the allocation of credit. For the most part guidelines on credit allocation, which were only imposed in the mid-1970s, were quite broad and were not very binding (see Chapter 10).[2] Broad-based programs – for example, lending to native Malays – leave credit decisions to individual banks and, consequently, do less damage to incentives compared with programs that steer credits to individual firms.

Also, Malaysian authorities at least allowed banks to charge for their cost of funds, plus a markup (reportedly as high as 4 percentage points), whereas in many countries priority borrowers are granted rates far below prime (and then may not pay); as in Japan, Malaysian authorities appear to have left responsibility for credit assessment in the hands of the banks. More extensive subsidization was done through the budget, but even then government directed credits bore interest rates between 50% to 100% of the full cost of funds; with Malaysia's low inflation and interest rates, the resulting wedge between priority and nonpriority rates was generally small or nil. The absence of severe repression prior to reform likely is an important factor behind Malaysia's relatively benign reform experience. Also the openness of the capital account and the proximity of Singapore limited the extent of interest-rate repression in Malaysia (and Indonesia), and the presence of a significant foreign banking community likely contributed to the skills base in the banking sectors.

Although facing similar external competition, *Indonesia* had a far less developed financial system at the outset of the reform process, with very little competition among mostly public sector banks; five public sector banks accounted for 83% of total bank assets. Monetary policy was enforced by bank-by-bank credit ceilings, which contrib-

Table 5.2 *Prereform characteristics of the banking system*

Country	Interest Rate Repression	Portfolio Requirements	Supervisory System	Ownership of Banks	Subsidized credit	Openness to Capital Flows
Chile	Substantially negative for decades	Extensive	Weak; rules only	Nationalized in 1971-3, Privatized in 1975-6	Extensive	Closed
Indonesia	Modestly negative in 1970s	Modest	Mostly rules oriented	No private domestic banks until 1981	Moderate	Extremely open since early 1970s
Korea	Modestly negatively	Substantial: Policy loans of 41 to 51% of bank assets in 70s, 39-48% in 90s	Mostly rules oriented	Significant public ownership until 1981-83	Mild in 1970s, essentially absent in 1980s	Essentially closed in 1970s and 80s
Malaysia	Near zero or slightly positive	Relative small or non-binding	Relatively well developed	Large banks publicly owned	Minimal in 1970s and 1980s	Relatively open, but with ad hoc intervention
New Zealand	Modestly negative	Extensive until 1984, minimal after	Informal, only 4 banks	Private	Extensive until 1984, minimal after	Closed until late 1984, open thereafter
Turkey	Substantially negative	Substantial	Mostly rules oriented	Mixed system, approximately 50% state owned.	Extensive until 1985	Closed until 1988

uted to the weakness of competitive forces; coupled with branching restrictions, these controls effectively constrained the size of nonstate banks, as well as limiting the development of money markets and liquidity management skills. Deposit and lending rates were tightly controlled. In addition to these factors, the incentive to mobilize deposits also was low because refinancing was liberally available for the central bank.

The *Korean* banking system also was largely public-owned and public-controlled. In fact, the government continued to appoint the heads of the large banks throughout the 1980s. Government intervention into the credit process was marked: The strategy of developing extremely large-scale heavy industry and chemical industry with directed credit necessarily entailed effectively allocating credit to specific firms.[3] Also in contrast to Malaysia, in Korea there were somewhat wider spreads between priority and nonpriority credit. For example, as Nam notes in Chapter 8, bank rates for some preferred credits during the latter half of the 1970s averaged between 8% and 13%, respectively, compared with 17% for general bank loans and the wholesale price index (WPI) inflation rate of 16%. So Malaysian banks both had more influence and responsibility in making loans and effectively were less "taxed" for making priority loans.[4] While Indonesian authorities ultimately allowed easier entry and branching by private domestic and foreign banks as a way to encourage greater efficiency in banking, Korean authorities, facing a large nonperforming loan (NPL) problem related to the directed credit program, instead allowed nonbanks greater powers but kept the banking sector more controlled.

Chile, New Zealand, and *Turkey* had a much higher prereform degree of intervention in the financial sector, as is demonstrated especially by high portfolio requirements. In each of these cases subsidized credit was relied on more extensively than in the Asian countries examined here. Chile by far had the most distorted interest rate structure, as noted above.[5] New Zealand experienced less distortion, with average real lending rates between -2% and -3% for most of the 1970s after being modestly positive in the 1960s, while Turkey fell somewhere in between these two cases. Turkey's financial system was not too distant from that seen in reforming socialist economies, having functioned for two decades in a planning-based system.[6] In both New Zealand and Turkey, there were strict ceilings on deposit and lending rates and entry was restricted. In New Zealand the commercial banks constituted a captive market for government paper, issued at below-market rates, while in Turkey the Central Bank was a passive financier of the budget deficit through automatic advances. Neither country's banking system was well prepared for the abrupt changes that were to come.

Banks' supervisory systems are difficult to rate, inasmuch as their results often are not perceived unless an institution is being closed; given the lack of transparency of bank earnings statements, outsiders rarely know of an individual bank's problems before a run or other obvious sign of distress becomes evident. Still, anecdotal evidence indicates that the Malaysian supervisory system, especially by the late 1970s when financial reform picked up pace, was very advanced relative to that of other developing countries, in terms of its orientation more toward at least attempting to evaluate the health of banks. Most of the other countries' systems were oriented more toward verifying compliance with detailed credit-allocation and interest-rate rules, as is often the case in financial systems that view banks as a tool for enforcing the government's credit decisions.

5.3   Approaches to reform

From different starting points the various countries covered in this volume took different approaches to reform of the financial sector. Table 5.3 provides a thumbnail sketch of the main actions taken in the six countries. *Chile* and *New Zealand* opted for a big bang approach, following in both instances a change in government in favor of decidedly more market-oriented reforms. Both political urgency and economic arguments were advanced to explain the rapid pace of reform. In both cases, as in reforming socialist countries today, financial markets were identified as a quick means of making visible reforms that would improve the efficiency of resource allocation.[7] However, it is important to emphasize that even with a big bang approach, New Zealand authorities waited three years before allowing new entry, giving existing banks some time to adjust to the changing rules. This learning period, in which the four commercial banks were sheltered from competition, may have prevented some of the damaging postreform excesses of, for example, the U.S. savings and loan industry. New Zealand authorities have persisted with their program despite the difficulties in achieving greater labor flexibility in a highly unionized setting, for it was not until 1991 that major labor legislation was able to be passed. In Chile in 1976–7, the lack of supervision or regulation contributed to bankruptcies in a number of formal and informal finance companies and then to the government's takeover of a major bank. This in turn led to some tightening of regulation on nonbank intermediaries.

Table 5.3 *Summary of financial reforms*

Chile	Big Bang:complete interest rate deregulation in 1975, privatization of all banks by 1978, reserve requirements reduced 1974 onwards. Capital controls on nonbanks lifted within 2 years, on banks within 5 years; all financial institutions given "universal" banking powers. Simultaneous dramatic reforms of real economy, with average tariffs reduced from nearly 100% in 1973 to below 30% in 1976, and budget deficit eliminated by 1975, with large surplus by 1979.
Indonesia	Eliminated bank-by-bank credit ceilings, reduced subsidized credit program, decontrolled most deposit and lending rates, and ended subsidies on deposit rates. Second stage (5 years after start) saw lifting of ban on new entry into banking, easing of branching restraints on domestic and foreign banks, sharp reduction in reserve requirements (15% to 2%). Later strengthened prudential regulation and abolished remaining subsidized credit lines from central bank. In 1990 partially reversed reforms by requiring that 20% of lending go to small firms. Concomitant with real sector reform program: 2 large devaluations, reduction of tariffs, shift away from commodities, especially oil.
Korea	Began relaxing regulations of branching and management in early 1980s, transferred ownership of banks to private sector by 1983. Most preferential interest rates on policy loans abolished by mid-82, restrictions on non-bank financial companies eased. Selected interest rate controls gradually abandoned 1988-91, but tacit intervention continued. Non-performing loans remained large through most of the 1980s. Controls on international capital flows maintained during 1980s.
Malaysia	Gradually lifted controls on long term deposits and opened capital account in early 1970s, full liberalization of deposit and lending rates in 1978, then re-introduced administering of rates through mid-1980s; complete deregulation again in 1991. Reduced scope of priority lending program from mid-1970s, with no bank credit below banks' cost of funds. Active central bank role in developing money and securities markets throughout period. Non-performing loans rose in mid-1980s but declining by end of decade. Major budget deficit reduction program in the early 1980s.
New Zealand	Big Bang in 1984-5: interest rate controls and bank-by-bank credit guidelines removed, currency devalued then floated, all capital controls lifted, portfolio requirements and reserve asset ratio dropped, tariff reductions announced. Allowed new entry into banking in 1987, began selling state-owned firms and commenced tariff reductions in manufacturing sector. Also eased restrictions segmenting various financial institutions. Reserve Bank bill legislating price stability goal passed in 1989; tightening of monetary and fiscal policy from 1987 onwards.
Turkey	Phase 1: abolishment of interest rate ceilings on deposits and loans, introduction of CDs in mid-1980; entry into non-bank financial sector eased significantly. Crisis led to re-regulation and limits on entry. Phase 2: introduction of partial deposit insurance, new banking law (1985) with higher capital requirements, strengthening of supervisory system and development of on-site supervision, requirement of external auditing. Development of interbank money market. Heavy portfolio requirements on banks continued, and interest ceilings continued until 1988.

Turkish authorities also started with a rapid approach, under the assumption, notwithstanding the previously high degree of financial repression, that prompt interest-rate deregulation would allow for a rapid improvement in the efficiency of financial intermediation. However, this approach led to a financial crisis and the government reregulated lending rates, limited entry, and generally took a more gradual approach to reform. Also, the Turkish reforms were slowed by the continued heavy reliance on the banks to finance the large public sector borrowing requirement. This effectively limited the proportion of their portfolio over which banks had control and, especially until 1985, these forced purchases clearly constituted a tax on the banks and thus forced up the unregulated lending rate.

Financial reform in *Malaysia* and *Korea* was the most gradual of the cases studied. Both countries had already attained a measure of macro stability before beginning reforms, but differed in that Korean authorities reformed gradually behind the barrier of capital controls, which were maintained throughout the 1980s, whereas Malaysian authorities began reforms with an already quite open capital account. Malaysia began in the early 1970s – as the Japanese authorities did in the 1980s – by gradually deregulating interest rates, starting with very-long-term deposits and then to shorter-term ones. A Treasury bill auction began in 1973, while some industrial countries, notably Japan, still were financing government debt by forced allocations to a captive cartel of banks.[8] Concentration in the Malaysian banking system remained fairly high throughout the period, though there were a large number of institutions. Korean authorities were not able to proceed as quickly on banking reforms due to a large nonperforming loan problem. Instead, they moved to liberalize the nonbank financial sector, thereby greatly increasing the proportion of finance intermediated by this subsector, partly at the expense of the banks in the system but especially away from the curb market. Korean authorities have been criticized as having moved especially slowly on financial reform, especially as pertains to the banking sector (Amsden and Euh 1990).

Indonesian authorities took an explicitly multistage approach toward financial reform, beginning first with an easing of interest-rate controls and, importantly, abandoning the system of bank-by-bank credit ceilings that restrained competition. It was not until after five years had passed that they then liberalized entry and branching. Directed credit programs were greatly reduced. Private banks expanded dramatically at the expense, in terms of market share, of the state banks; foreign banks also gained somewhat after their ability to branch was eased in 1988.

5.4   Adjustment issues

In keeping with the argument of Chapter 13, no attempt is made here to assess the success or failure of reform programs. Briefly, the instances are too few, the postreform period has been too short, and many other factors likely had an important role to play in the recent evolution of the financial sectors in these countries, not least of which is the shocks experienced by their real sectors. But a few issues stand out in the years since reforms began. Undeniably, there has been a sizable increase in financial depth, especially in the ratio of quasi-liquid liabilities/GDP, roughly a measure of the nontransaction demand for money (Figure 5.2). This measure of financial depth rose significantly in Korea and Malaysia, with Korea seeing even more rapid deepening of even broader financial indicators (not shown), reflecting the concentration of reforms in the nonbank sector.[9] From a lower base, compared with Korea and Malaysia, Indonesia experienced rapid financial deepening following the beginning of reforms in 1983 and even faster expansion after the ending of entry and branching restraints in 1988.[10] As Johnston (1991) has argued, a temporary bulge of credit growth might well be expected following the elimination of direct controls on credit, and Indonesia's rapid growth of credit might reflect the binding nature of these controls in the prereform period, or the transfer of intermediation from offshore to onshore locations. Chile's comparable boom in quasi-liquid liabilities (from 5% of GDP to 30% over a seven-year period) was equally dramatic but was halted in the early 1980s by a financial crisis. New Zealand's gains have been smaller and more erratic, in part because of the beginning in 1987 of electronic funds transfer.[11]

Financial deepening occurred concomitantly with a broadening of financial markets, as all of the economies saw an expansion of the financial instruments open to households and businesses. Even in the relatively controlled reform effort in Korea, Nam (Chapter 8) cites an impressive broadening of the available asset menu, much of it offered by commercial banks, in part to relieve the competitive pressures on them resulting from the nonbanks' lighter regulation. The expansion of asset choice in all of these countries also was accompanied by a general rise in the structure of real interest rates, to levels generally somewhat above those seen in the industrial world. In Korea, the average cost of funds in manufacturing in the last half of the 1980s averaged 8%, compared with an average of just under −1% for the 1976–9 period. In Malaysia, the increase was far smaller, as the average lending rate for the same two periods increased from about 5.5% to 7.8%. Most of the other economies experienced larger increases, with New Zealand at the opposite extreme, as real rates rose from zero to −5% in the earlier period to 5% to 15% in the latter. Turkey saw slightly larger swings. Figure 5.1 gives an indication of the dramatic increases in Chilean interest rates.

In general, although higher real rates may have caused difficulties, there were not the dislocations that occurred in the Southern Cone

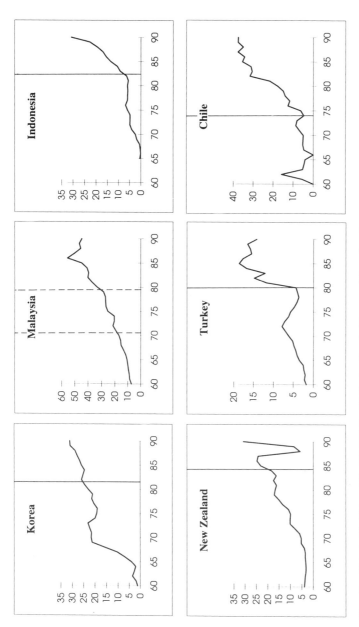

Note: Quasi-Liquid Liabilities = M2 - M1 (IFS, line 35).Vertical line signifies start of financial reform.

Figure 5.2 Quasi-liquid liabilities/GDP, 1960–90

context. Indeed, as seen in Figure 5.3, investment/GDP ratios by the end of the 1980s were at or near their 20-year peak in all of the countries except New Zealand, again likely at least in part reflecting that country's dramatic monetary policy tightening. Even in Indonesia, where real interest rates topped 10%, investment has risen smartly, in line with arguments that, within some limits, credit availability, rather than its price, is more important to investment behavior. Although some observers have argued that financial reform may lead to an increase in credit to consumers, at the expense of savings and investment, the cases examined here generally refute that presumption.

As seen in Figure 5.4, savings rates have also performed well recently, again outside of New Zealand. As summarized in Chapter 4, broad evidence suggests that any effect of real interest rates on savings likely will be small, especially if the change in interest rates is not from severely negative levels to modest positive rates. However, other noninterest components of reforms, such as increased branching or a greater menu of financial products, may help to raise savings rates, and this effect may help explain the evolution in Figure 5.4.[12] Alternatively, of course, this evolution may be merely a cyclical phenomenon.

Despite generally improved savings and investment rates and visible broadening and deepening of the financial system, postreform adjustment could have been marred by increased asset price volatility. *New Zealand,* for example, saw two major equity market collapses – in May and October of 1987 – only one of which can be easily blamed on external factors. However, in view of the many policy changes being made in the 1980s, it is difficult to sort out the effect of financial reforms from those of other policy shifts, in particular the move to tighten both monetary and fiscal policies and achieve a low rate of inflation. Moreover, volatility tests of various asset prices for New Zealand (Chapter 7) actually show less volatility in the second half of the 1980s than in the first part of the decade; volatility of stock and bond prices (but not exchange rates) in particular seems to have lessened since the adoption in March 1988 of the price stability goal. *Turkey* also experienced difficulties following the first phase of its reforms as noted, and the ensuing crisis was sufficiently severe to delay some reforms until the late 1980s.

In the Asian economies, volatility of financial markets was not an issue, most likely because of their greater inflation stability. However, these countries did experience some postreform adjustment problems. In *Malaysia* the reduction of the budget deficit (from 19% of GDP in 1981 to 8% three years later and 4% by 1988) contributed to a slow-

Figure 5.3: Gross Domestic Savings
(% of GDP)

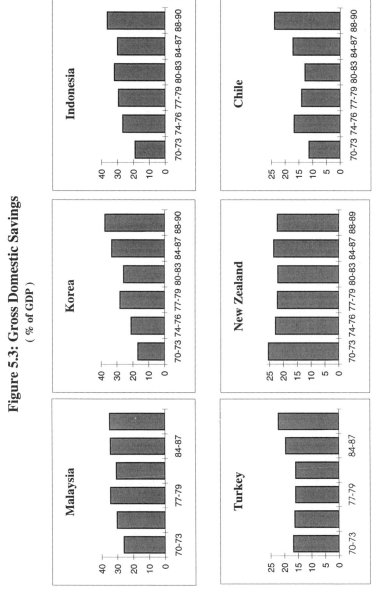

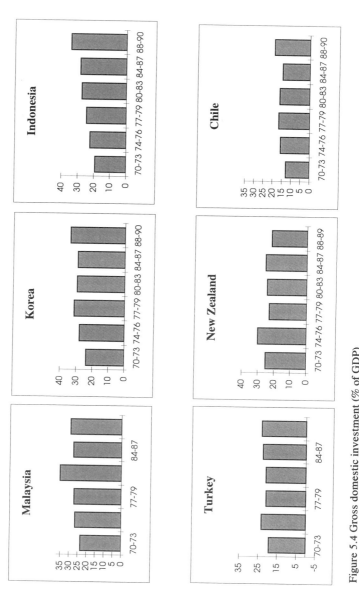

Figure 5.4 Gross domestic investment (% of GDP)

down of growth in the mid-80s. At the same time, banks had been increasing property lending at an excessively rapid rate (as in other developing and industrialized countries; see Chapter 10), and the macro slowdown put a sudden end to this real estate bubble. The resulting rise of nonperforming loans (NPLs) led to a modest widening of interest rate spreads for several years (Figure 10.3), but by the end of the decade spreads were on the decline and banks' earnings appeared more favorable.

Korea also underwent a NPL problem, less related to macro problems but more linked to the very large directed credit program of the 1970s to the heavy and chemical industries (HCIs). While Amsden and Euh (1990) have cited partial data purporting to suggest that NPLs were less concentrated in the HCIs, Nam casts doubt on this data and clearly argues that directed credits were likely the factor behind the banks' difficulties. Both would agree that NPLs have been the major reason behind the government's reluctance to extend reform measures to the banking sector.

Indonesia's adjustment problems have been the least in evidence. Chant and Pangestu (Chapter 9) find some isolated signs of distress, and also find the very rapid growth of credit disquieting. Indeed, the latter factor, perhaps along with some concerns about individual banks and a small rise in nonperforming loans, led the government to raise capital requirements and thereby rein in bank credit expansion last year. This slowdown may have exposed some sloppy lending practices, as is often the case after a long period of rapid growth. But even if significant problems arise, it is clear that the Indonesians have enjoyed a high savings and investment rate, in addition to more efficiently allocated capital following their reforms (as shown in Chapter 4), both of which may help to offset any mistakes associated with rapid growth. Indeed, a key question for future research would be whether the efficiency gains from a more rational allocation of credit – the long-term goal of financial reform – were sufficient to pay for any losses stemming from rapid credit growth.

In sum, the adjustment issues encountered by the reforming economies have been fairly diverse. Turkey and New Zealand suffered some serious problems, though by the early 1990s, like Chile, their financial system appears to be much improved and more stable than it was in the immediate aftermath of reform. For Indonesia, all of the evidence is not yet in on growing problems with NPLs, but thus far the difficulties appear manageable. We now turn to a careful assessment of the reform efforts in detail, and then attempt to derive some lessons from the cases and in light of the preceding chapters.

NOTES

1 The apparent stop-and-go and gradual nature of the reforms makes determining a starting date particularly difficult, but most observers would pick either the early or the late 1970s.

2 Countries might have unofficial methods of intervening in credit decisions, for example by suggestions from government officials, and in fact it is difficult to find any countries for which such intervention is not alleged. However, such informal methods of intervention are difficult to detect or quantify, and are not dealt with here.

3 This specific targeting also occurred to some extent in Indonesia.

4 The only implicit tax on Malaysian banks was to the extent that priority credits were riskier than nonpriority credits, in which case the interest rate could have been insufficient to cover possible losses. Unfortunately, data on nonperforming loans are not available on a desegregated basis for either country, so it is not possible to verify how losses on the two types of credit compared. Nor are there good data on commissions and other charges.

5 An informative view of the Chilean and other Southern Cone episodes on the domestic side can be found in Corbo, de Melo, and Tybout (1986) and sources cited there. On Chile, see also Edwards and Edwards (1987).

6 All three countries were turning from such a significant involvement in the financial and real sectors that they represent the closest approximation in this sample to the economies of Eastern Europe and the former Soviet Union. But still they had more institutions at least familiar with markets and many more individuals experienced in banking, as well as stronger traditions of contract enforcement.

7 Financial sector reform also is attractive in countries that have previously repressed finance heavily, as it will then likely be an expanding sector and thereby help lower unemployment.

8 Note, however, that all policy changes were not in one direction: Between the deregulation of interest rates in the early 1970s and removal of all such controls briefly in 1978, the authorities had initiated a directed-credit program! Indonesia more recently has imposed some directed guidelines after seven years of a reform program.

9 The vertical lines in Figure 5.2 indicate the starting date of financial reform, with the two lines for Malaysia indicating the lifting of interest controls on four-year time deposits and the "complete" if temporary deregulation of deposit and lending rates in 1978.

10 As noted in Chapters 9 and 13, the pace of expansion of bank credit in Indonesia raises some cause for concern as to the ability of banks to manage themselves when real credit has been doubling on average every three years since 1983.

11 Electronic Funds Transfer Point of Sale accounts were begun in 1987, leading many time deposits to shift into M1. However, in 1989 the main banks pulled out of the scheme and the accounts shifted back into M2.

12 For example, Fry (1988), in attempting to explain the savings/GDP ratio by real deposit rates, the terms of trade, the dependency ratio, rural population per branch, and GNP growth, finds all variables to be significant in a pooled cross-section time series for six Asian countries. This finding suggests then that branching matters, but would need to be confirmed in a broader sample. Also, it is possible that the population per branch is picking up the influence of time, so it would be useful to rerun the equations with a time trend.

CHAPTER 6

The impact of financial reform: The Turkish experience

Izak Atiyas and Hasan Ersel

Financial liberalization, along with trade reform, was at the core of the comprehensive economic reform program launched in 1980 in Turkey. The purpose of this chapter is to examine the impact of financial liberalization on the behavior of financial-sector agents as well as on the corporate sector. In the first section, the history of the Turkish financial liberalization program is briefly summarized. The second section addresses the changes in the structure of the financial system and examines the behavior of banks. The corporate sector is then examined, while the final section is devoted to conclusions and lessons that can be derived from the Turkish experience.

6.1 A brief history of financial reform in Turkey

Financial development during the prereform period: From statism to planned development.

As demonstrated in Akyuz (1984), the Turkish financial system during the 1970s was relatively underdeveloped even when compared to countries at similar levels of industrialization. Historical factors such as the rather centralized character of the government apparatus in Turkey, as well as the statist growth and industrialization strategy adopted in the 1930s in response to economic crisis considerably enhanced the role of government in economic life. Economic policies

Izak Atiyas is from the World Bank and Hasan Ersel, currently with Yapi Kredi bank, was Director of Research and the Deputy Governor of the Central Bank of the Republic of Turkey when this study was done. The views expressed in this paper are those of the authors and should not be attributed to either of the institutions. The authors are grateful to Gerard Caprio, Asli Demirguc-Kunt, Ercan Kumcu, and Emin Oztark for helpful comments.

103

in the 1950s, which initially attempted to increase the role of the market mechanism, were unsuccessful and led to a more drastic, albeit uncoordinated, increase in the level and extent of government intervention. The search for coordination led the post-1960 regime to adopt a planned development strategy, which seemed to fit the country's statist traditions. It was hoped that such a planned approach to development would prevent inconsistencies that arise from shortsightedness in economic decision making. The planned development model adopted in the early 1960s placed a heavy emphasis on the real sector.

The planning strategy in Turkey can be interpreted as assuming either the existence of a centralized mechanism to allocate financial resources or a perfectly accommodating financial system. However, in Turkey there was no central mechanism to allocate financial resources, and whether the financial system was accommodating to the imperatives of development plans was also highly questionable. Akyuz (1984) examined the performance of the Turkish economy for the 1971–81 period and concluded that the workings of the financial system was an important impediment in allocating savings into investments according to the requirements of development plans.[1]

Until the first oil crisis, Turkey succeeded in sustaining a relatively high rate of growth in a stable economic environment. However, starting from 1974, and particularly after 1977, the need for reforming the existing growth strategy as well as the allocation mechanism became evident. After two unsuccessful attempts in 1977 and 1978, a comprehensive reform program was launched in 1980. The main features of the program were a switch from import substitution to export promotion, trade reform, and the liberalization of the financial sector.

The strategy of financial reform

The Turkish reform strategy was to promote financial market development through deregulation and inducing competition by easing entry into the banking sector. Opening up the banking system to foreign competition was seen as an important element of enhancing competition. The reformers paid much less attention to promote nonbank financial institutions. In this sense, the Turkish reform strategy was overconfident in its reliance on competition among banks in developing the financial markets.

This strategy left the considerable dominance of banks in the financial sector unchallenged, and in fact, strengthened it by allowing them to function in the newly emerging financial markets. The reforms broadened the spectrum of the activities of banks and consolidated and strengthened the existing universal banking system. Within this system, banks were allowed to collect deposits, extend loans, underwrite securities, trade in securities, establish and manage mutual funds, manage their own as well as their customers' securities portfolios, participate in corporations and engage in foreign exchange transactions. The reasons for relying exclusively on the banking system and completely neglecting problems of conflict of interest is mainly attributable to, first, popular confidence in banking institutions, which increased especially after the so-called bankers' crisis of 1982, and second, the political strength of these institutions.[2]

Being the only type of financial institution available, banks were successful in exploiting opportunities offered by the liberalization program and diversified their activities into the newly emerging financial markets, particularly securities markets, which enabled them to broaden the domain of their dominance. The existence of an inherited universal banking system and complete absence of fire walls between various financial activities, even in the postliberalization regulations, enabled banks to impede the emergence of nonbank competitors in the financial markets.

*Main institutional elements and implementation of
financial reform*

Prior to the reform initiative, the Turkish financial system was characterized by features typical of financial repression: There were ceilings on interest rates for deposits and credits; real interest rates were negative; liquidity and required reserve ratios were high; and preferential credits existed and were subject to subsidies. The public sector deficit was financed, to a great extent, by monetization, that is, by direct advances from the Central Bank. Entry into the banking system was restricted. Foreign exchange operations were constrained.

The liberalization program was launched in January 1980 by the then ruling Justice Party government. However, the program became effective almost one year later, under the military rule.

Deregulation in the financial markets began with the abolition of interest rate ceilings on loans and deposits and the introduction of certificates of deposits (CDs) in July 1980.[3] Simultaneously, in order to curb inflation, a tight monetary policy was followed. The reduction in aggregate demand caused a deep decline in corporate earnings. Distressed borrowing by financially fragile companies further deteriorated their balance sheets and put an upward pressure on interest rates. Meanwhile, especially smaller and financially weaker banks engaged in a fierce competition for deposits to finance nonperforming loans. Accompanied by a persistent reduction in the rate of inflation, real interest rates on deposits reached 20% in 1982. Neither the policymakers, nor the financial intermediaries and corporations were ready to deal with the dynamics of competition in an unstable environment. In particular, the regulatory bodies of the government, especially the Central Bank, were not capable of monitoring closely the behavior of banks.[4] The developments in the financial markets led to a major crisis in 1982, and the liberalization process was partly reversed. The government intervened in and closed down five small private banks, the majority of whose assets and liabilities were taken over by state-owned banks. In 1983 the Central Bank reregulated the deposit rates.

The 1980-2 period can be considered the infancy of the Turkish liberalization program. In this phase, the main dynamic element behind the liberalization efforts was deregulation. The authorities, naively, hoped that the competitive economic environment created through deregulation would, in a relatively short time, increase the efficiency of the financial system in allocating resources. The 1982 crisis ended these hopes and the reformers shifted their emphasis to the creation of the institutional framework necessary for the working of a market system. Consequently, the second phase of the liberalization program (1983-7) was more consistent in the sense that policymakers recognized the need for laying the institutional foundations of the financial system.

In this framework, the Capital Market Board (CMB) was established in 1982 and became operational in 1983 to promote and develop securities markets. The Capital Market Law of 1981 empowered the CMB to regulate primary markets for equities and bonds. The law envisaged a merit system rather than a disclosure system for the issuance of securities; that is, it authorized the CMB to reject an issue whenever its analysis concluded that the financial soundness of the issuer was unsatisfactory. In 1983, secondary market operations were regulated by a decree, and within this framework the Istanbul Stock Exchange was reopened in 1985 and became operational in 1986.

There are two distinguishing features of the securities market regulation in Turkey; the first is the role of the banks. The regulations did not attempt to restrict banks from engaging in any type of activities either in the primary or in the secondary markets. On the contrary, in some instances, such as in the case of establishing and managing mutual funds, banks were granted a monopoly position. The second feature is that it created a central authority (CMB) to control and monitor effectively developments in the securities markets. It is evident that this choice was not in line with the general attitude of the reformers since it granted the CMB discretionary powers. This divergence can be explained, partly, by the shocking experience of the 1982 crisis, which caused a deterioration in popular confidence for nonbank financial institutions.

The second important development was the enactment of a new banking law in 1985. That law was aimed at improving the structural weakness of the banking system which abruptly manifested itself during the 1982 crisis. The new law introduced a provision for a minimum capital base for banks. In addition, the law established a capital adequacy ratio (5% in 1989, to reach 8% in 1992). The ratio is calculated under the (BIS) Bank for International Settlements guidelines for determining primary and secondary capital and risk weights. Credit extended to a single customer was limited to 10% of bank equity capital. Investment in participations are limited to 100% of capital. The law also obliges banks to use a uniform chart of accounts.

In 1983 a Savings Deposit Insurance Fund was introduced to prevent the reemergence of the liquidity problems faced by the banks in the 1982 crisis. However, the coverage of the insurance system is limited, (currently 100% of the first 25 million Turkish lira (TL) and 60% of the next 25 million). Deposits over TL50 million are not covered, and the insurance fund is not authorized to assist the liquidation and rehabilitation of financially weak banks. Such authority lies with the Treasury. The current banking law does not allow the government to take over the bank, inject new capital when necessary, or buy the nonperforming assets of the bank. The law does authorize the government to change the management of problem banks, and to implement measures to improve their liquidity.[5]

Another novelty of the law was the introduction of the definition of nonperforming loans. The law forced banks to report nonperforming loans separately and required them to cover the defaulted loans through provisions. Finally the law introduced a standard accounting system and obliged external auditing of the banks.

The banking law also authorizes Sworn Bank Auditors (SBA) associated with the Treasury to examine banks' legal compliance and financial standing. SBA carry out on-site examinations once every two years, though the frequency is higher for problem banks. In addition, the Banking Department within the Treasury monitors the financial performance of banks through quarterly financial statements.[6] The Central Bank also has a role in supervision. The Bank Supervision unit in the Central Bank, established in 1986, carries out off-site supervision by following about 50 quarterly and monthly reports. The Central Bank's analysis concentrates on capital adequacy, asset quality, profitability, and liquidity.[7] Finally, banks are required to have an external audit every year by independent auditing firms authorized by the Treasury and the Central Bank.[8]

The Central Bank established an interbank money market in 1986. Until 1987 the Central Bank acted as a blind broker. Later, however, the Central Bank started to get involved in transactions as a dealer, in order to solve short-term liquidity problems.[9] In May 1985 government securities began to be auctioned on a weekly basis by the Central Bank. In 1987 the Central Bank started open market operations.

In the area of foreign exchange, residents were allowed to hold foreign-currency-denominated deposits in 1984. Banks were allowed to keep foreign currency abroad. In 1984 banks were allowed to set their exchange rates within a margin around the Central Bank rate. Further steps to liberalize exchange rate determination were implemented during this period.

The third phase of the liberalization episode, 1988–90, was characterized by a reform fatigue. There were some major developments during this period, especially in the area of foreign exchange and the capital account. The Central Bank established a Foreign Exchange and Banknotes Market in 1988. Exchange rates are determined in the market with the participation of banks and other relevant financial institutions.[10] In 1989 foreign exchange operations and international capital movements were liberalized entirely and the TL became convertible. In 1990 banks were left completely free to determine their exchange rates. However, these interventions were mostly realizations of previous decisions. In fact, during this period there was a noticeable decline in the appetites of the reformers for consolidating the achievements of the previous attempts, which manifested itself in the postponement of the much needed regulatory changes such as in the capital market law, banking law, corporate law and (except for minimal amendments) bankruptcy law.

6.2   Developments in financial markets

Although the financial liberalization measures were announced as early as 1980, their impact on the structure of the financial system became effective after 1986 – that is, after the establishment of the fundamental institutional framework necessary for the operation of financial markets. In this section, we review several important features of developments in the financial system during the reform period.

Financial deepening

During the 1980–90 period the Turkish financial system grew considerably. In order to describe the characteristics of the development of financial markets, a single summary measure is not sufficient. The traditional measures of financial deepening such as M1 (currency in circulation + sight deposits) or M2 (M1 + time deposits) underestimate the growth of the financial system, since they do not take into account the developments in the securities markets and the emergence of foreign-currency-denominated deposits. On the other hand, the sum of all financial assets (currency in circulation + total deposits + total securities) exaggerate the development in the financial system since a bulk of public sector securities are held by banks. Tables A.1 and A.2 in the appendix to this chapter present data relevant for the two measures. A closer inspection of Table A.2 reveals that the share of total securities (private and public) in total financial assets (i.e., sum of currency in circulation, total deposits, and total securities) increased first at a mild rate from 22% in 1982 to 25% in 1986, then climbed sharply to 43% in 1990.

Foreign exchange deposits

The second important feature of the liberalization policies was the role played by the foreign exchange and foreign-exchange-denominated financial assets. In 1984 Turkish citizens were allowed to hold foreign exchange deposits in banks, and these became an important financial saving instrument after 1986. This is reflected in Table A.1 as a considerable divergence between two monetary aggregates M2 and M2Y (M2 + Foreign Exchange Deposits).[11] The government's policies concerning foreign-exchange-denominated financial instruments were somewhat mixed. On the one hand, at various times, the policymakers supported such instruments by allowing them (as in the case of foreign exchange deposits) or by introducing them (as in the case of foreign-exchange-denominated public sector securities); on the other hand, authorities tried to prevent the widespread use of such instruments for fear of institutionalizing the indexation and therefore currency substitution.

The dominance of the public sector

The course of development of financial markets in Turkey was shaped not only by the policies aimed at promoting these markets but even more by the financing needs of the public sector itself. One of the main

Table 6.1 *Public sector borrowing requirements*

Year	PSBR/GNP (%)
1980	10.5
1981	4.9
1982	4.3
1983	6.0
1984	6.5
1985	4.6
1986	4.7
1987	7.8
1988	6.3
1989	7.1
1990	9.4

Source: State Planning Organization and the Undersecretary of
Treasury and Foreign Trade.

targets of the reform program was to reduce the public sector deficits.
It was also thought that in order to minimize the inflationary impact
of the deficits as well as to introduce an enduring fiscal discipline to
the public sector, the deficits should be financed from the financial
markets at the competitive rates.

Economic policies followed during the 1980–90 period were not
successful in curbing the public sector borrowing requirement (PSBR).
Indeed, as can be seen from Table 6.1, the average PSBR/GNP ratio
was higher (7.1%), in the second half of the 1980s, from its already
high level (6.4%) in the first half.

The persistence of relatively high public sector borrowing requirements, when coupled with the stated objective of the authorities in
relying more on domestic financial markets for their financing, induced
a series of measures to enhance the marketability of public sector
securities. The first type of measures were aimed at forcing banks to
allocate a portion of their portfolio to public sector securities. In order
to achieve this aim, banks were obliged to hold public sector securities
against their liquidity requirements.[12] Therefore, a demand for such
securities, closely related to the expansion of deposits, was created.
The second type of measures were implemented to enhance the attractiveness of these securities. Their yields became market determined
after the introduction of the auction system in 1985. Finally, the fact
that returns from these securities were free from income taxes (they

were still subject to a 10% withholding tax) contributed to the dramatic shift in the demand.

As a result of these measures, the public sector enjoyed the advantages offered by the developments in the securities markets. It can be seen from Tables A.3 and A.5 that the public sector dominated the primary and secondary markets. Although the share of the public sector started to decline in both markets toward the end of the decade, it is still above three quarters. Finally, as can be seen from the figures in Table A.4, the yields of public sector securities were indeed competitive with domestic private sector paper; also, rates on savings deposits are higher than the contemporaneous rate of inflation until 1988. After 1988 yields on government securities lagged behind those on savings deposits and the rate of inflation.

Starting from 1986, the Treasury became the major supplier of securities. However, the persistence of large public sector deficits and the thinness of financial markets situated the Treasury in a disadvantageous position despite its monopoly status and kept interest rates high.

The introduction of the auction mechanism for government securities institutionalized this phenomenon. Even though, at least in 1987 and 1988, it was common to blame buyers' collusion for high interest rates, in his analysis of auctions between 1987–9, Alkan (1990) has argued that banks may actually enjoy high interest rates without attempting to collude, once they are sophisticated enough to follow the trends in the auction market and aware of the desperate need of the Treasury to sell public securities.

Persistent high public sector deficits exerted pressures on the already thin financial markets. The first consequence of this phenomenon was the crowding out of the private sector. In spite of efforts to promote capital markets and induce the corporate sector to change its financing pattern by relying more on securities markets, particularly through equities, the results were far from satisfactory. The second effect of the high public sector deficits and their financing pattern was on the banking system. Banks considered placing their funds in public sector securities a safe investment.[13] Since the borrowing needs of the public sector seem to be countercyclical, the permanent existence of the Treasury in these markets also cushioned the banks against fluctuations in earnings from their loan portfolio.

Interest rates

When the government intervened following the crisis of 1982, the Central Bank was authorized to fix interest rates on deposits, which were lowered from 50% to 45% in January 1983. Regulation of interest rates continued until 1988 and adjustments were made according to movements in the rate of inflation so as to keep them positive in real terms.

Inflation started to pick up toward the end of 1980s. In the fall of 1988, inflation figures were higher than the expectations of the government and a run out of the Turkish lira into foreign exchange ensued; parallel market exchange rates shot up. While intervening into both the parallel market and the foreign exchange market by selling foreign exchange, the Central Bank also announced the liberalization of deposit interest rates. Banks responded frantically and announced one-year deposit rates varying between 70% and 88%, up from a uniform rate of 65%. Compared to the seemingly similar episode in 1982, the banks' response was possibly driven by the uncertain and speculative economic environment rather than widespread financial distress. Nevertheless, banks offering lower rates were besieged by depositors trying to switch their funds to those offering higher rates. There was also a severe competition in the interbank market. The Central Bank reintervened by advising a temporary informal but uniform ceiling of 85% on one-year deposit interest rates. Monetary authorities also required banks to report desired changes in interest rates in advance. Both the foreign exchange market and the market for the Turkish lira were stabilized as a result of the intervention, despite several inconsistencies and reversals in policies. However, except for a few exceptional periods in December 1988 and the first few months of 1989, real interest rates on deposits remained negative (Table A.4).[14]

Even if temporary, high deposit interest rates resulted in a large inflow of deposits into the banking system. In the following period, especially in 1989, the banking system was characterized by an excess supply of funds and faced substantial difficulties in placing them. Again, compared to 1980–2, there was no comparable increase in demand for credit; as discussed in the next section, the increase in interest rates did not generate a vicious cycle of distress borrowing in the corporate sector. The banking system suffered a temporary reduction in profitability in 1989 (see Table 6.11).

Developments in the banking system

The Turkish banking system's response to the implementation of the financial liberalization program was generally considered as quite accommodating. Banks, which immediately adapted themselves to the

Table 6.2 *Ratio of bank assets to GNP*

Year	(%)
1980	28.5
1981	34.4
1982	38.2
1983	41.5
1984	41.3
1985	40.9
1986	48.6
1987	54.0
1988	51.0
1989	46.3
1990	43.2

Source: Total assets figures are obtained from *Banks in Turkey*, various issues, The Banks' Association of Turkey. The GNP figures are from the State Institute of Statistics.

new conditions, started to modernize themselves by switching from manual methods to computerized systems and by recruiting qualified personnel to extend their activities beyond their traditional markets.

However, a closer examination of the developments in the banking sector reveals that its growth was nevertheless neither smooth nor completely in line with the expectations of the reform program.

Under the liberalization program the Turkish banking system demonstrated a rather peculiar development pattern. The characteristics of this development pattern may be summarized as follows:

1 Until 1987, the Turkish banking industry expanded. On the one hand the new banks entered into the market, on the other, existing banks followed an expansionary policy to secure their market shares. As can be seen from the Table 6.2, bank assets/GNP ratio climbed from 28% in 1980 to 54% in 1987. However, starting from 1987 this trend was reversed. After reaching its peak level in that year, the rate of growth of the banking system slowed down and the bank assets/GNP ratio declined steadily to 43% in 1990.

The enactment of the new banking law in 1985, which put the banking system under more serious prudential regulation and supervision, the increase in uncertainty due to the resurgence of inflation, and

Table 6.3 *Three-bank concentration ratio (measured as % of total assets accounted by three largest banks in each category)*

Year	Commercial Banks	
	Private Banks	All National Banks
1980	70	51
1981	67	48
1982	69	49
1983	72	56
1984	74	57
1985	73	53
1986	68	50
1987	65	48
1988	62	45
1989	54	46
1990	52	44

Source: The 1980-89 figures are reproduced from Pehlivan (1991), Table 8.11. The data are from *Banks in Turkey*, various issues, The Banks' Association of Turkey. The 1990 figures are own calculations based on the 1990 issue of the same publication.

Table 6.4 *Average rate of growth of commercial bank assets 1986–90 (%)*

No. of Branches	State-Owned	Private	Foreign	Total
1-30	-	63.3	51.1	59.2
31-100	50.6	72.8	26.7(*)	52.2
101+	47.0	42.4	-	44.8

Source: Data collected by the Banking Department of the Central Bank of the Republic of Turkey.

loss of credibility in the economic policies followed, were the major factors behind the reversal in the growth trend.

2   A second dimension of structural change in the banking sector manifested itself as a decline in concentration, measured by the share of three largest banks in total assets (Table 6.3).[15]

Table 6.5 *Share of state-owned commercial banks in total assets (%)*

1986	47.0
1987	47.0
1988	46.2
1989	48.9
1990	48.2

Source: Data collected by the Banking Department of the Central Bank of the Republic of Turkey.

Table 6.6 *Share of securities in total assets (%)*

1980	3.7
1983	3.4
1987	13.2
1990	11.2

Source: Central Bank of Turkey.

These figures clearly show a decline in concentration in Turkish banking.[16] Note that concentration ratios for private banks decline faster than those for the commercial banking system as a whole. This can be attributed to two factors. The first is that the growth rates of Turkish private commercial banks varied considerably, and dynamic medium-sized or small banks grew faster than large banks. The former found opportunity to expand relatively rapidly, whereas for large banks, restructuring implied slower growth. The average rate of growth of total assets of various categories of commercial banks given in Table 6.4 for the 1986–90 period supports this view.

The second factor is the continuation of the dominance of the large state-held banks in the banking system, which explains the relatively slow decline in the three-bank concentration ratio for all commercial banks. In fact, the share of total assets held by state-owned commercial banks was almost constant in the 1986–90 period (Table 6.5).

3 Another major change was the increased share of securities in banks' portfolio. The share of securities in the total assets sharply increased in the second half of the 1980–90 period (Table 6.6).

This sharp increase in the securities portfolio can wholly be attributed to the increase in holdings of government securities.

Table 6.7 *Share of income from credit and securities market orientations in bank earnings*

		Number of Branches			
		1-30	31-100	101+	Total
1986	a/	48	56	62	61
	b/	13	5	16	15
1987	a/	41	39	60	57
	b/	17	9	15	14
1988	a/	37	36	54	52
	b/	16	12	18	17
1989	a/	50	40	50	49
	b/	20	17	24	23
1990	a/	54	43	55	54
	b/	21	12	22	21

Note: Total earnings includes net rather than gross income from foreign exchange operations.

a/ Share of income from credit operations.
b/ Share of income from securities market operations.

Banks' obligations to hold government securities against high liquidity requirements created a rather large and expanding market for these papers. In addition, the high yields of public sector securities, especially after taking the tax advantages into account, made them attractive for banks and to a lesser degree for corporations to hold them in their portfolios.

This change in the asset structure of the banking system was also reflected in its earnings structure. Table 6.7 shows that the share of credit-related income (interest and commissions) in total earnings declined over the 1986–90 period whereas that of income from securities market operations increased. While this trend is apparent in banks of all size categories, medium-sized banks seem to be less involved in securities market operations.

4   During the 1980–90 period, banks also increased their capitalization. The ratio of capital (defined as the sum of paid-up capital reserves, revaluation fund, and profits) to total liabilities considerably increased from an average of 7.6% in 1980–84 to 9.0% in 1985–90 (Table 6.8).

5   The opening up of the Turkish economy also affected the structure of the Turkish banking system. As can be seen from Table 6.9, the share of claims on and liabilities to nonresidents of the commercial banks increased sharply after 1986.

Table 6.8 *Capital structure in the commercial banking system*

Year	Share of Equity Capital in Total Liabilities (%)
1980	5.2
1981	6.3
1982	6.9
1983	7.7
1984	9.1
1985	8.0
1986	8.9
1987	8.2
1988	9.1
1989	9.4
1990	10.1

Source: *Banks in Turkey*, various issues, The Banks' Association of Turkey.

Table 6.9 *Commercial banks' exposure to nonresidents (% of balance sheet total)*

Year	Claims on nonresidents	Liabilities to nonresidents
1981	0.1	0.1
1982	0.4	0.3
1983	0.9	0.8
1984	1.8	2.0
1985	0.2	0.2
1986	6.4	3.8
1987	6.6	3.9
1988	9.8	4.9
1989	8.0	4.5

Source: Iskenderoglu, Ozturk, and Temel (1991).

6   During the 1980–90 period, total domestic credits as a percentage of GNP declined (Table 6.10). The relatively high level of credits in the beginning of the decade was mainly the result of the existence of direct medium- and long-term credits of the Central Bank. The Central Bank was acting in a dual capacity, both as an official semidevelopment bank and as a central

Table 6.10 *Credits as percentage of the GNP*

Year	Central Bank credits	Commercial Bank credits	Other credits	Total credits
1980	7	15	3	25
1981	6	16	3	26
1982	5	17	3	25
1983	4	17	3	24
1984	2	14	2	19
1985	3	15	2	20
1986	2	19	2	24
1987	3	21	2	26
1988	2	17	2	21
1989	2	16	2	19
1990	1	17	2	20

Source: *Quarterly Bulletin*, various issues, Central Bank of the Republic of Turkey.

Table 6.11 *Bank profitability (as % of total assets)*

Year	GEM	OC	NEM	PBT
1983	5.0	3.6	1.3	1.0
1984	5.7	3.3	2.4	1.9
1985	3.8	2.9	0.9	0.6
1986	5.4	2.8	2.6	1.9
1987	7.3	2.8	4.5	3.0
1988	8.5	3.3	5.2	3.5
1989	7.4	3.8	3.6	2.4
1990	6.3	5.1	7.2	3.6

GEM: Gross Economic Margin = Interest Received - Interest Paid + Other Income (Net)

NEM: Net Economic Margin: GEM - OC.

PBT: Profits Before Taxes = NEM - Other Expenses (Net).

OC: Operating Costs.

Total Assets: Arithmetic averages of the year-end values.

Source: Iskenderoglu, Ozturk and Temel (1991); calculated from data compiled by the Banking Department of the Central Bank.

bank. In the 1980s, in line with the policy of curbing directed credits, the Central Bank's credit lines were first reduced and then phased out, thereby ending the peculiar dual identity of the Bank, and creating an opportunity to transform itself into an institution solely responsible for central banking.[17] However, the rest of the banking system was not able to fill the gap created by the elimination of directed credit. After 1987, decline in the ratios of commercial bank credits also contributed to the reduction of the credit/GNP ratio.

7 The profitability of the Turkish banking system increased considerably in the second half of the 1980s. Data in Table 6.11, tabulated for the commercial banks only, reveal a significant increase in bank profitability, despite accompanied increase in operating costs.

The increase in operating costs in the 1988–90 period is noteworthy. A closer examination of income statements reveals that personnel expenses remained relatively stable during the period, except for an increase in 1990 due to labor agreements signed by big private banks and a new wage-setting system introduced by public banks which also led to sharp pay raises. By contrast, there was a sharp increase in other administrative expenses. As discussed in Akkurt et al. (1991), these trends may be attributed to banks' tendency to prefer investing in computerization over employing more staff. This is especially true for larger banks which have established ATMs and on-line connections among branches.

Nevertheless, the increase in bank profitability was not uniform among various categories of banks. Small domestic and foreign commercial banks are in general more profitable than larger banks and state-owned banks in Turkey (Table 6.12). The profitability of the foreign banks declined sharply after 1988, and, in contrast to national banks, did not recover in 1990. The worst-performing category of banks was medium-sized state-owned banks, which declared losses in 1987 and 1989.

The increase in bank profitability is especially noteworthy in view of the decline in the degree of concentration in the banking system.[18] The differences in the profitability and patterns of growth of the various categories of banks indicate that small domestic commercial banks were the most dynamic elements in the banking system.

8 Contrary to the expectations of policymakers, the role of foreign banks in enhancing competition in the Turkish banking

Table 6.12 *Profits before taxes/average total assets for commercial banks*

	1987	1988	1989	1990
Private domestic banks				
1-30 Branches	4.1	7.1	5.1	5.3
31-100 Branches	2.7	3.5	2.8	4.1
101 + Branches	3.3	3.7	2.9	3.9
State-owned banks				
1-30 Branches	-	-	-	-
31-100 Branches	-2.1	3.9	-1.1	0.2
101 + Branches	2.5	2.4	1.6	2.3
Foreign banks				
1-30 Branches	5.8	8.1	5.0	4.3
30-100 Branches	4.4	8.6	4.7	4.4(*)
101 + Branches	-	-	-	-
(*) One bank only				

Source: Data collected by the Banking Department of the Central Bank of the Republic of Turkey.

Table 6.13 *Ownership composition of the banking system*

	1980	1986	1990
Private domestic banks			
(a)	26	26	29
(b)	45.7	46.7	44.5
State-owned banks			
(a)	13	12	11
(b)	51.5	50.1	52.0
Foreign banks			
(a)	4	18	26
(b)	2.8	3.7	3.5

(a)   Number of banks.

(b)   Share in total assets of banking system.

Source: *Banks in Turkey*, various issues, The Banks' Association of Turkey.

system remained negligible. As shown in Table 6.13, foreign banks are relatively small and their share in the total assets of the banking system is not significant. A closer inspection of their activities also reveals that foreign banks never had the intention of becoming major players in the Turkish banking system. They concentrated their activities on foreign-trade-related areas where they had, especially in the first half of the period considered, absolute advantage due to their know-how in these areas and their international connections and, in general, did not attempt to compete with domestic banks in traditional banking activities. Pehlivan and Kirkpatrick (1991) argue that this resulted from restrictions placed on foreign banks. Nevertheless, some foreign banks did play an important role in training a new generation of middle-level bank managers, who were subsequently employed in domestic banks.

Bank behavior in Turkey: Evidence from survey results

The liberalization measures had a dual effect on banks. On the one hand, by broadening the spectrum of financial markets and opening them to banks, the liberalization program enabled banks to diversify their activities. On the other hand, the uncertainties inherent in the liberalization programs, aggravated by the inconsistencies in the implementation of economic policies, induced banks to follow rather conservative strategies.

In this section we attempt to gain some additional insights into bank behavior in Turkey and report results of a questionnaire distributed to the bank managers and the accompanying interviews made during the summer of 1991. A complete set of results are reported in Atiyas, Ersel, and Ozturk (1992).

The main idea behind the survey was to understand the relationship between banks and their clientele in loan markets and the mode of competition. The questions were inspired by the recent theoretical literature on imperfections in financial markets that result from problems of information and costly contract enforcement. In particular, based on the theoretical exposition in Calomiris and Hubbard (1990),[19] priors about the structure of credit markets in Turkey, the relationship between banks and their clientele, and the nature of competition, the questionnaire hypothesized a pool of potential borrowers segmented into a group for which banks have more complete information ("blue chip companies") and others for which banks have little or no information.

The survey found that banks' customer patterns displayed significant variation. The majority of small and midsized banks concentrated their activities on predominantly "blue chip" companies in large cities. Banks with an extensive network of branches, on the other hand, had a much wider customer base. In general, an overwhelming majority of bank managers confirmed the suggestion that whereas there is a fierce competition among banks for blue chip companies, in the non–blue chip sector competition is among firms requesting those services. Moreover, banks were found to be reluctant to expand their customer base.

It is well known that bank loan rates exhibit wide variation in Turkey. It is also generally believed that, contrary to practices in economies with developed financial markets, many banks in Turkey prefer to announce a "maximum" lending rate rather than a prime rate. Survey results suggest that all large and multibranch banks prefer announcing a maximum rate and then negotiate it downward during bargaining for a loan package. The basic reason for this preference is that with borrowers that are perceived to be risky, negotiating lending rates downward is easier than asking for premiums over a prime rate. Small banks, on the other hand, are more likely to work on the basis of a prime rate,[20] but are very reluctant to announce it to the general public. A possible explanation for banks' aversion to announcing a prime rate is that it reflects their reluctance to expand their customer base.[21]

Only a small number of blue chip companies as well as companies that belong to the same conglomerate groups as the banks are able to obtain credit without collateral. In general, roughly 80–90% of all bank lending is made against collateral.

Banks were asked about their primary concern in lending to a firm that has not yet established a reputation. They were asked whether their primary concern would be not being able to distinguish firms' risk and return characteristics or not being able to monitor borrowers once loans are made. Banks' responses depended very much on their organizational structure. Small banks dealing with blue chip companies indicated that neither problem was a major concern; that response reflected to a large extent that they would not attempt to include new borrowers into their clientele. Large banks' responses differed according to their institutional capabilities. Those that had established a well-functioning information-gathering network indicated monitoring as a major problem. Some banks indicated that they had units that undertake the monitoring function and therefore are more concerned with ex-ante information gathering.

Another question inquired what would make banks more willing to lend to borrowers currently not in their customer base: The options were reduction in macroeconomic instability and uncertainties, establishment of an efficient legal system, establishment of a well-functioning information-gathering system or credit subsidies. Only one bank indicated that subsidies would help. Reduction of macroeconomic uncertainties and establishment of an information-gathering system to collect necessary data to make loan decisions were the options chosen by the majority of banks.[22] Regarding establishment of an efficient legal system, it turned out that banks had almost complete mistrust of the legal system and based their lending strategies so as to keep recourse to the legal system at a minimum. Improvements were seen as either irrelevant or improbable.[23]

Almost all bank managers favored making package deals with their customers. This can be interpreted as an indication for banks' desire to operate as multiproduct firms – that is, diversifying their activities among various financial services.

All bank managers distinguished credits from other bank services and stressed that their securities, money, and foreign exchange market activities cannot be considered as substitutes for credit. Although the managers seem to draw such a complementarity between credit services and banks' operations for liquidity and foreign exchange management, most of them also added the qualification that "under exceptional conditions," such as those that prevailed in 1989 when the high cost of loanable funds created difficulties in placing loans, these activities may certainly become substitutes for loans. Therefore, it can be concluded that there is an asymmetric relationship between these activities, which is conditional upon the state of the credit market.

6.3   Developments in corporate finance

This section focuses on patterns of financing in the corporate sector and reviews trends during the financial reform period. The main source of data is the balance sheets and income statements of a sample of 81 firms registered at the Capital Markets Board. The data set is not representative of the corporate sector in Turkey. It consists of large, financially relatively healthy firms that possibly have better access to external financing than an average Turkish firm.[24]

Table 6.14 *Composition of corporate debt I[a]*

	Size	1982	1983	1984	1985	1986	1987	1988	1989
Debt/Asset Ratio	S	0.63	0.52	0.46**	0.45**	0.48	0.48	0.50	0.49
	L	0.58	0.56	0.55	0.55	0.54	0.52	0.50	0.49
Short Term Debt	S	0.76**	0.74**	0.76**	0.78*	0.83**	0.81**	0.78	0.72
	L	0.65	0.64	0.66	0.69	0.68	0.70	0.69	0.65
Long Term Debt	S	0.24**	0.26**	0.24**	0.22*	0.17**	0.19**	0.22	0.28
	L	0.35	0.36	0.34	0.31	0.32	0.30	0.31	0.35
Bank Loans	S	0.40**	0.40**	0.37**	0.39**	0.37**	0.33**	0.37**	0.36
	L	0.54	0.54	0.56	0.56	0.58	0.45	0.49	0.40
Short Term Bank Loans	S	0.24	0.21*	0.19**	0.22	0.25	0.19	0.22	0.22
	L	0.28	0.27	0.29	0.28	0.33	0.24	0.25	0.20
Long Term Bank Loans	S	0.17**	0.19*	0.19*	0.17**	0.12**	0.14*	0.15*	0.14
	L	0.26	0.27	0.27	0.28	0.25	0.22	0.24	0.20
Finance Bills	S	0.00	0.00	0.00	0.00	0.00	0.00	0.00*	0.00**
	L	0.00	0.00	0.00	0.00	0.00	0.01	0.01	0.03
Other Liabilities	S	0.57**	0.57**	0.60**	0.59**	0.60**	0.63**	0.61**	0.60
	L	0.40	0.42	0.41	0.42	0.37	0.47	0.47	0.55
Short Term Other Liabilities	S	0.52**	0.54	0.57**	0.56**	0.58**	0.61**	0.56**	0.50*
	L	0.36	0.37	0.37	0.40	0.36	0.45	0.43	0.41
Long Term Other Liabilities	S	0.04	0.04	0.03	0.03	0.03	0.01	0.05	0.10
	L	0.04	0.05	0.04	0.01	0.02	0.02	0.04	0.14

Note: Stars indicate significance levels at which the null hypothesis of equality of means is rejected. A single star denotes 10% and a double star denotes 5% level of significance, respectively.

a/   Shares in total debt. Tax and insurance premium liabilities are excluded.

S: Firms with total assets smaller than TL 78 billion in 1984.

L: Firms with total assets larger than TL 78 billion in 1984.

Trends in the composition of liabilities

Some indicators for the composition of corporate debt are provided in Table 6.14. In order to assess whether access to external finance varies across groups of firms differentiated by size, the sample has been split into two groups of equal number of firms on the basis of the value of total assets in constant prices. Specifically, firms where the value of total assets (in constant 1985 prices) were below TL78 billion in 1984 were classified as small. Table 6.14 reports the mean value for each variable for the group of small (S) and large (L) firms, along with indicators of whether the difference in the means is statistically significant or not.

The main components of debt (excluding liabilities in the form of taxes and insurance payments) are short- and long-term bank loans, direct financing (finance bills), and other liabilities. Other short-term liabilities include borrowings from owners, but mainly consist of trade credits.

The following patterns emerge: If debt is measured as a percentage of total assets, large firms are generally more indebted than small firms, but the difference is often insignificant and is completely eliminated by the end of the sample period. This is mainly due to a steady reduction in the degree of indebtedness of large firms. In general, the composition of debt differs across the two size categories; however, the differences decrease over time. A larger proportion of total debt consists of short-term debt in the case of small firms, however in 1989 the difference is no longer statistically significant. Regarding the breakdown of sources of debt, large firms use more bank loans whereas small firms rely more heavily on other liabilities. However, by 1989, the share of bank loans in the two subsamples is no longer significantly different. Closer inspection reveals that this is primarily due to an impressive reduction in the share of short-term bank loans in the liabilities of large firms. By contrast, large firms continue to be dominant in the use of long-term bank loans throughout the period. However, the share of long-term bank loans decreases over time for both large and small firms, suggesting that financial reform failed to increase the availability of long-term loanable funds.

The share of other short-term liabilities is significantly higher in small firms' liabilities, most likely reflecting the importance of trade credit. Finally, the share of finance bills is very small, and close to zero in the case of small firms. Hence, direct borrowing plays an insignificant role in corporate finance. Nevertheless, their importance seems to show an increasing trend in 1987–9 in the case of large firms.

With the exception of long-term bank loans and trade credit, the liability structure of small and large firms exhibits a pattern of convergence during the 1980s. There may be two reasons for this increasing similarity. The first is structural changes in financial markets that generate more uniform treatment of large and small firms. An alternative reason may be that firms in the data set grow over time; if after a certain threshold the impact of size on liability structure diminishes, then firm growth would explain the increased similarity. In order to

Table 6.15 *Composition of corporate debt II[a]*

	Size	1982	1983	1984	1985	1986	1987	1988	1989
Debt/Asset Ratio	S	0.65	0.52	0.44**	0.42**	0.53	0.50	0.50	0.54
	L	0.57	0.56	0.55	0.54	0.50	0.50	0.50	0.47
Short Term Debt	S	0.76*	0.76**	0.77**	0.79*	0.90**	0.81	0.79	0.82**
	L	0.67	0.65	0.67	0.70	0.71	0.73	0.71	0.64
Long Term Debt	S	0.24*	0.24**	0.23**	0.21*	0.10**	0.19	0.21	0.18**
	L	0.33	0.35	0.33	0.30	0.29	0.27	0.29	0.36
Bank Loans	S	0.41*	0.39**	0.37**	0.36**	0.37**	0.40	0.35	0.34
	L	0.51	0.52	0.53	0.53	0.51	0.39	0.46	0.39
Short Term Bank Loans	S	0.22	0.21	0.19*	0.21	0.30	0.23	0.21	0.26
	L	0.29	0.26	0.27	0.27	0.29	0.21	0.24	0.19
Long Term Bank Loans	S	0.19	0.18*	0.18	0.14**	0.07**	0.17	0.14	0.07**
	L	0.23	0.26	0.26	0.26	0.22	0.18	0.22	0.20
Finance Bills	S	0.00	0.00	0.00	0.00	0.00	0.00	0.00	0.00*
	L	0.00	0.00	0.00	0.00	0.00	0.00	0.00	0.02
Other Liabilities	S	0.05*	0.58**	0.60**	0.60**	0.62**	0.58	0.62*	0.64
	L	0.44	0.44	0.44	0.45	0.44	0.54		

Note: Stars indicate significance levels at which the null hypothesis of equality of means is rejected. Single star denotes 10% and double star denotes 5% level of significance, respectively.

a/   Shares in total debt. Tax and insurance premium liabilities are excluded.

S: Observations with total assets smaller than TL 50 billion.

L: Observations with total assets larger than TL 50 billion.

see whether this was the case, the data set was split on the basis of observations rather than firms and a lower cutoff point for size was established. Accordingly, observations where the value (in constant 1985 prices) of total assets were below 50 billion Turkish lira were classified as small. In this classification, the number of observations in the S category change between one third (in the earlier period) and one fourth (later period) of the data set. The results are displayed in Table 6.15.

The main difference between Tables 6.14 and 6.15 lies in the fact that in the latter the share of short-term debt remains significantly higher in observations that correspond to small firms, and mainly due to a higher share of short-term "other" liabilities and lower share of long-term bank loans. This underscores the importance of trade credit for small firms and suggests a pattern of development where firms switch away from trade credit as they grow and find long-term bank loans more accessible.

The decline in the use of short-term bank loans by large firms in the 1988–9 period deserves further comment. As discussed in Ersel and Ozturk (1990, 1993), especially large and healthy firms started reducing their use of short-term bank loans in 1989. The emergence of this trend can be traced back to 1988, when the cost of bank credit increased sharply, following the complete deregulation of deposit interest rates. At the same time, the increased risk of default made banks more cautious in selecting their customers. The coupling of self-restraint by prime borrowers and cautious behavior of banks resulted in a surplus of funds. This reduction in intermediation in response to the interest rate shock contrasts sharply with the experience of the early 1980s. Then, the interest rate shock was accompanied with a rapid deterioration of corporate earnings. Firms, finding themselves illiquid, resorted to distress borrowing, further deteriorating their balance sheets positions. The crucial difference between the two periods is that in 1989 firms could rely on relatively high earnings to reduce their exposure to short-term loans.

Variations in corporate indebtedness and the impact of financial reform

We now focus in more detail on variations in corporate indebtedness with a view to examine the impact of financial reform on firms' financial behavior. Following the literature on the determinants of capital structure, we attempt, first, to explain cross-section variations in corporate indebtedness by firm-specific variables. Second, to gauge the impact of the process of financial reform, we test whether the importance of these variables in explaining cross-section variations in indebtedness has changed over time. In particular, we would like to examine whether there have been any changes in (i) the importance of size in accessing external finance, (ii) firms' reliance on internally generated funds, (iii) the role of collateral, and (iv) the role of firm investment opportunities that are difficult to monitor by creditors.

Because we expect that the impact of these variables should vary across different types of financial instruments, several indicators of corporate indebtedness are used. There are three types of short-term debt: Short-term bank loans (excluding long-term bank loans maturing in the current year); other short-term debt (most of which consists of trade credit); and total short-term-funded debt (that is, bank loans, other short-term liabilities, and finance bills, excluding debt in the form of taxes and social security premiums). The measures of long-term debt are long-term bank loans (including those that are due in the current period) and total long-term debt (consisting of bank loans and bonds, excluding other long-term liabilities).

The variables used in the analysis are the following. SIZE measured as the logarithm of total assets in constant prices, reflects existence of transaction costs in the provision of external finance. If fixed transactions costs are important, then size should be positively related to indebtedness. Profitability, measured as operating income per unit assets (OITA), captures the importance of internal finance. It has been argued that because of imperfections in financial markets, external finance is more expensive than internally generated funds; in other words, firms pay a premium for external finance. If that is the case, then, everything else equal, profitability should have a negative impact on indebtedness since increased profitability implies higher availability of retainable internally generated funds. When firms produce unique products, their bankruptcy and eventual liquidation imposes costs on suppliers, customers, and workers. Since higher debt ratios imply higher probability of bankruptcy, these costs are relevant to capital structure decisions. Hence uniqueness is expected to be negatively related to indebtedness. Following Titman and Wessels (1988), we measure uniqueness by the ratio of selling expenses to sales (SES). Equity-controlled firms have a tendency to invest suboptimally to expropriate wealth from the firms' creditors (Myers 1977). Rational creditors are aware of this possibility and request an "agency premium" that increases the cost of debt. Hence, firms with high growth opportunities are likely to face higher costs of debt. This is especially true with long-term debt. In fact, it has been suggested that short-term debt may be relatively free of this agency problem, since creditors have the option of terminating their commitment whenever the investment behavior of firms jeopardizes the value of debt claims. Growth opportunities are measured by the percentage change in total assets in constant prices (GTA). Assets that can be used as collateral reduce the cost of debt and therefore are expected to be positively related to indebtedness. Collateralizable assets are measured by the ratio of inventories and net fixed assets to total assets for (INPTA) long-term debt, and by the ratio of accounts receivable to total assets (ARTA) in the case of short-term debt. The degree of indebtedness is also expected to be related to the existence of nondebt tax shields, although the direction of the relation is in principle ambiguous (Dammon and Senbet 1988). Nondebt tax shields are measured by the ratio of the change in accumulated depreciation to total assets (DTA).[25] Finally, volatility of firm's earnings, measured by the standard deviation of the ratio of operating income to total assets (SOITA), is expected to be negatively related to indebtedness.

As in most of the literature, the variables are averaged over time. However, in order to test for the stability of the coefficients, the sample period was divided into two: 1984–6 and 1987–9. A dummy variable (T) which is equal to 1 for the 1987–9 period and zero otherwise was used both by itself and interactively with the explanatory variables. The results are reported in Table 6.16.

Short-term bank loans are positively affected by collateral assets and negatively affected by profitability and growth opportunities. The coefficient on size is positive but not significant. The effect of growth opportunities diminishes in the second period. Other liabilities, on the other hand, are not affected by size, growth opportunities, or collateral assets but negatively related only to profitability. Moreover, no significant structural change is detected in the second period. These results uncover an interesting contrast between short-term bank loans and trade credit, namely that at least in the 1984–6 period, trade credit was less subject to agency problems than bank loans. This may be because trade creditors have better information than banks about firms that they do business with and they are better able to monitor borrowers' behavior in the course of business. However, firms still prefer to use internally generated funds to trade credit, as reflected in the significant coefficient on the profitability variable. The coefficients in the equation for total short-term-funded debt display a pattern similar to those in the equation for short-term bank loans except that nondebt tax shields also appear significant.

Contrary to components of short-term debt, size does play a significant role in explaining variations in long-term bank loans. Moreover, the importance of size is not diminished in the second sample period. As expected, assets that can be used as collateral are also positively related to long-term debt. Surprisingly, the agency cost variable has a significant but positive coefficient; fast-growing firms carry a higher share of long-term bank loans.[26] Finally, profitability is negatively related to long-term bank loans. Another interesting result is that the negative sign on T*INPTA (collateral assets) becomes insignificant in the second period. One of the survey results reported earlier in this chapter indicated that blue chip companies were able to borrow without collateral. Given that the data set consists mainly of

Table 6.16 *Determinants of corporate indebtedness*

	Short-term bank loans	Other short-term debt	Total short-term debt	Long-term bank loans	Total long-term debt
Intercept	-0.000 (-0.000)	0.446 (2.431)	0.384 (2.018)	-0.323 (-2.088)	-0.233 (-1.453)
SIZE	0.012 (1.030)	-0.013 (-0.893)	0.006 (0.402)	(0.030 (2.784)	0.027 (2.459)
OITA	-0.214 (-1.791)	-0.347 (-2.413)	-0.054 (-3.853)	-0.185 (-1.843)	-0.235 (-2.248)
SES	0.133 (0.587)	-0.078 (-0.287)	0.132 (0.466)	0.174 (0.910)	0.313 (1.581)
DTA	0.201 (-1.424)	-0.277 (-1.633)	-0.466 (-2.625)	-.0.079 (-0.662)	-0.102 (-0.826)
ARTA	0.503 (5.255)	0.164 (1.426)	0.675 (5.668)		
INPTA				0.200 (2.392)	0.153 (1.777)
GTA	-0.202 (-2.792)	-0.010 (-0.120)	-0.236 (-2.625)	0.199 (3.155)	0.176 (2.697)
SOITA	-0.250 (-0.882)	0.264 (0.774)	0.039 (0.110)	-0.019 (-0.081)	-0.157 (-0.659)
T	0.298 (1.312)	0.040 (0.145)	0.475 (1.678)	0.329 (1.504)	0.361 (1.593)
T*SIZE	-0.024 (-1.337)	-0.006 (-0.257)	-0.038 (-1.679)	-0.020 (-1.308)	-0.023 (-1.443)
T*OITA	0.036 (0.226)	-0.171 (-0.896)	-0.155 (-0.784)	0.001 (0.004)	0.070 (0.501)
T*SES	-0.237 (-0.730)	-0.124 (-0.319)	-0.484 (-1.202)	-0.280 (-1.023)	-0.381 (-1.344)
T*ADTA	-0.141 (-0.766)	0.156 (0.712)	-0.054 (-0.234)	0.181 (1.190)	0.108 (0.681)
T*ARTA	-0.129 (-0.992)	0.119 (0.767)	-0.023 (-0.143)		
T*INPTA				-0.207 (-1.820)	-0.209 (-1.778)
T*GTA	0.241 (1.905)	0.189 (1.243)	0.426 (2.710)	-0.187 (-1.766)	-0.101 (-0.925)
T*SOITA	-0.001 (-0.003)	0.307 (0.716)	0.157 (0.355)	-0.009 (-0.029)	0.088 (0.290)
Adj.R²	0.368	0.220	0.553	0.085	0.072

large firms, the significance of both INPTA and T*INPTA suggests that the ability to borrow without collateral developed in the late 1980s.

We can now summarize the main results of this section. First, it seems that financial reform did little to reduce firms' preference for internally generated funds over external finance. This finding is valid for all types of financial instruments. Second, the importance of size in obtaining long-term loans is also not diminished in the 1980s. The fact that the data set is biased and consists of large firms makes interpretation difficult. In particular, it is not possible from these results to make inferences about the impact of financial reform on enterprises that are smaller than those in the data set. However, coupled with the sluggish increase in financial deepening and banks' reluctance to expand their customer base, both reported earlier in this chapter, one is tempted to conclude that financial reform did not yet result in increased availability of long-term investment funds to smaller firms. On the other hand, empirical results also suggest that collateral requirements and the adverse impact of agency problems generated by growth opportunities on acquiring short-term bank loans decreased in the late 1980s. This may reflect an increase in banks' ability to monitor borrowers as a result of financial reform. Alternatively, it may also reflect that as a result of long-term relations with banks, firms in the sample became better able to rely on their reputation to gain access to bank loans.[27]

6.4   Lessons of the Turkish experience

After the crisis of 1982, Turkey adopted a more cautious approach to financial reform. Efforts were made to develop a legal and institutional framework for the functioning of financial markets and for the supervision of financial institutions. Any lessons that can be derived from the Turkish experience need to be qualified; financial reform is likely to require more time before its impact can be fully evident. With these caveats, this section attempts to draw some preliminary lessons from the Turkish experience.

The new literature on the link between finance and real activity emphasizes the importance of borrowers' net worth in determining the availability of external finance. In their exposition of the recent theory, Gertler and Rose (Chapter 2) argue that a decline in borrowers' net worth is likely to reduce the extent of financial intermediation. More generally, the financial condition of the borrowing sectors is seen to be a critical determinant of the degree of efficiency in the allocation of loanable funds. The experience in Turkey, especially the response of the financial and corporate sectors to interest shocks, confirms this view. In 1982, when the corporate sector was experiencing a decline in gross margins, liberalization of interest rates created a vicious cycle whereby distress borrowing by an illiquid corporate sector and accommodation of especially troubled banks resulted in unsustainably high interest rates and overborrowing.[28] By contrast, in response to the interest-rate shock of 1988, the corporate sector could rely on internally generated funds to reduce their stock of short-term loans and adjust their balance sheets. The absence of distress borrowing is closely linked to the absence of a separate gross-earnings shock. The lesson is that any potential adverse effect of interest rate liberalization is smaller when the corporate sector is financially strong.

The major shortcoming of the Turkish financial reform was macro-economic uncertainty and the burden that public sector borrowing placed on financial markets. Concern with macroeconomic uncertainty is evident in bank managers' responses to survey questions, where uncertainty is identified as a major deterrence to increased intermediation toward firms that are perceived as risky.[29] In addition, the government's recourse to the financial system to finance the budget deficit crowded out financial flows to the private sector. Hence, the potential positive impact of financial reform was considerably hindered by a lack of discipline in government finances. In fact, it can be said that the government has been the main beneficiary of developments in financial markets. The lesson is that fiscal policies may limit the benefits of financial reform.

The analysis of firm-level data reveals that firms' reliance on internally generated funds did not change over the reform period. The importance of size in accessing long-term bank loans is also not diminished. These findings are consistent with the limited impact of financial reform on the financing of the private sector. Nevertheless, there is also some evidence that the importance of agency problems and collateral requirements were reduced over the reform period, at least for the firms in the sample.

The Turkish strategy of financial reform emphasized institutional development insofar as authorities tried to establish a regulatory environment for the development of foreign exchange and interbank money markets. However, overwhelming focus on the banking system led to the neglect of the development of nonbank financial institutions and instruments. Even though company data reveal the slow emergence of finance bills as a new instrument of corporate finance, development of alternative sources of funds, including the stock market, has lagged behind significantly.[30]

Finally, it also seems that a more efficient judicial system may play an important positive role in expanding the benefits of financial reform. The problem is not only one of reforming the legislation that governs financial transactions, but perhaps more important, one of increasing the processing capacity of courts. Strengthening the confidence of financial intermediaries in the judicial system may enhance their willingness to expand into new types of clients or areas of business, and develop more complex financial contracts.

Appendix 6

Table A.1 *Financial deepening*

	M1/GNP	M2/GNP	M2Y/GNP
1982	11.6	22.8	-
1983	12.6	23.9	-
1984	9.6	22.4	23.1
1985	8.9	24.1	25.8
1986	9.0	24.5	27.5
1987	9.6	23.0	27.4
1988	8.2	19.7	25.1
1989	7.8	20.3	25,3
1990	8.1	20.3	25.3

Source: State Institute of Statistics, Central Bank of the Republic of Turkey.

Table A.2 *Stocks of financial assets (% of GNP)*

	1982	1983	1984	1985	1986	1987	1988	1989	1990
I. Currency in circulation	4.2	3.9	3.6	3.4	3.4	3.6	3.1	3.2	3.6
II. Total deposits	18.6	20.0	19.5	22.4	24.1	23.8	22.0	22.1	26.7
Sight deposits	7.4	8.7	6.0	5.5	5.6	6.0	5.1	4.6	5.6
Time deposits	11.2	11.3	12.9	15.2	15.5	13.4	11.5	12.5	12.4
Foreign exchange deposits	-	-	0.7	1.7	3.1	4.4	5.4	5.0	5.0
III. Total securities	6.5	6.1	7.0	8.1	9.4	12.8	12.4	13.6	23.2
III.1 Total private securities	2.6	2.5	2.2	2.1	2.5	3.6	4.0	4.6	9.4
Private debt instruments	0.6	0.5	0.4	0.4	0.5	0.9	0.9	0.7	1.0
Shares	2.0	2.0	1.8	1.8	2.0	2.8	3.1	3.9	8.4
III.2 Total public securities	3.9	3.5	4.8	6.0	6.9	9.2	8.4	9.0	13.8
Government bonds	2.1	3.1	2.9	3.7	3.8	4.1	4.9	6.3	10.4
Treasury Bills	1.7	0.5	1.9	1.8	2.1	3.3	2.5	2.1	3.1
Revenue sharing certificates	-	-	0.1	0.5	0.9	1.8	1.0	0.6	0.3
Total	29.3	30.0	30.1	33.9	36.9	40.2	37.5	38.9	53.5

Table A.3 *Primary issues (sales volume, billion TL)*

	1982	1983	1984	1985	1986	1987	1988	1989	1990
Bonds	10.7	14.8	12.1	33.3	75.0	338.0	177.5	545.5	793.8
Commercial Paper	-	-	-	-	-	55.8	271.0	465.3	215.1
Bank Bills	-	-	-	-	48.6	66.1	182.0	173.9	
Shares	9.10	34.7	63.8	96.4	102.0	187.2	364.5	971.5	4106.6
Mutual Fund Participation Certificates	-	-	-	-	-	45.0	53.0	161.5	855.0
Total Private Securities	19.7	49.5	75.9	129.7	225.6	692.1	1048.0	2317.7	5970.5
Government Bonds	59.2	199.9	199.4	673.0	1269.4	2045.4	3816.2	9061.0	12458.4
Treasury Bills	257.6	78.2	495.1	1217.0	1787.9	3954.5	5114.9	7643.3	8442.7
Revenue Sharing Certificates	-	-	10.0	140.0	220.0	660.0	-	400.0	600.0
Total Public Sector Securities	316.8	278.1	1032.1	2030.6	3277.3	6659.9	8931.1	17104.3	21501.1
Total Securities	336.5	327.6	1108.0	2160.3	3502.9	7352.0	9979.1	19422.0	27471.6
Memo Item: The Share Public Sector Securities in Total (%)	94.2	84.9	93.2	94.0	93.6	90.6	89.5	88.1	78.3

Source: Capital Market Board, Annual Report 1990, Tables 42, 43, and 45.

Table A.4 *Yields of financial assets (net %)*

	1980	1981	1982	1983	1984	1985	1986	1987	1988	1989	1990
Savings deposits a/	26.5	50.0	50.0	42.5	45.0	50.0	51.8	48.1	69.3	65.1	57.3
Private sector securities b/											
Bonds	25.6	36.0	37.4	38.6	47.2	49.9	49.9	48.3	67.1	65.4	55.3
Commercial paper	-	-	-	-	-	-	-	50.0	54.9	64.8	53.3
Shares	12.0	30.4	79.9	110.2	-5.2	46.8	86.5	295.8	-37.3	511.2	55.6
Mutual fund participation certificates	-	-	-	-	-	-	-	-	68.3	67.8	46.2
Public sector securities b/											
Government bonds	29.0	34.0	34.0	31.8	43.0	50.6	51.0	47.0	62.4	52.2	48.2
Treasury bills	28.0	30.6	-	-	51.0	50.7	49.6	45.2	57.9	47.5	43.8
Income sharing certificates	-	-	-	-	-	43.0	50.1	59.1	95.6	95.2	61.4
Foreign exchange c/											
Nominal appreciation of U.S. dollar	155.0	44.0	35.6	47.0	53.4	27.1	29.1	32.7	75.4	25.7	25.8
Nominal appreciation of Deutschemark	123.3	25.4	30.2	26.2	34.7	36.2	63.1	62.1	57.7	32.2	41.9
Fx-deposits U.S. dollar	-	-	-	-	-	40.4	41.5	44.5	89.2	51.7	34.7
Fx-deposits Deutschemark	-	-	-	-	-	46.5	73.9	71.3	65.3	50.2	48.3
Memo item:											
Inflation rate d/	110.2	36.6	29.9	31.4	48.4	45.0	34.6	38.9	75.4	69.6	63.6

Source: State Institute of Statistics, Capital Markets Board, Central Bank of the Republic of Turkey.

a/ Quarterly average of the highest after tax rate on saving deposits when compounded. **Akkurt et al.** (1991, table 4).

b/ 1980-1985 figures are obtained from Ada (1991, table 2.5), 1986-1990 figures are from Capital Market Board *Annual Report 1990*, table 39.

c/ 1980-1985 are obtained from Ada (1991, table 2.5), 1986-1990 figures are from Capital Market Board *Annual Report 1990*, table 40.

c/ Inflation rate is measured by consumer price index (yearly average).

Table A.5 *Secondary market volume (billion TL)*

	1986	1987	1988	1989	1990
(1) Bonds	104.5	394.9	1032.2	1463.3	3006.0
(2) Commercial paper	-	51.7	175.7	856.9	670.8
(3) Bank bills	36.4	95.6	170.3	188.3	196.7
(4) Private debt instruments (1+2+3)	140.9	542.2	1378.2	2508.5	3873.5
(5) Shares	8.7	105.4	148.4	1735.9	15313.0
(6) Private sector securities (4+5)	149.6	647.6	1526.6	4244.4	19186.5
(7) Government bonds	546.3	1520.1	2630.9	10828.0	61742.9
(8) Treasury bills	1411.9	3219.8	7320.7	18762.8	32023.3
(9) Income sharing certificates	289.2	329.5	394.6	1098.1	1078.3
(10) FX-Indexed bills	-	86.4	13.7	1558.4	1631.9
(11) Public sector securities (7+8+9+10)	2247.4	5185.8	10359.9	32247.3	96476.4
(12) Total securities (6+11)	2397.0	5833.4	11886.5	36491.7	115662.9
Memo item: Share of public sector securities traded in the secondary markets (%)	93.8	88.9	87.2	88.4	83.4

Source: Capital Market Board, Annual Report 1990.

NOTES

1 Fry (1972) reaches a similar conclusion for the First Five Year Plan period, 1963–7.
2 Some attempts were undertaken to create competition through diversity in the early 1980s, by promoting nonbank financial institutions, or "bankers" as they were called in Turkey. These institutions were much less regulated than banks, and played an active role in precipitating the financial crisis of 1982. See Atiyas (1990).
3 For more details on this period, see Akyuz (1990) and Atiyas (1990).
4 Besides raising deposit rates, banks attracted funds by issuing CDs through nonbank financial institutions. The Central Bank had no means of keeping track of the volume of CDs issued.
5 A draft Banking Law envisages to replace the Savings Deposit Insurance Fund with a Deposit Insurance Corporation, and endows it with wider powers to deal with problem banks.
6 As of 1990, there were 36 active SBA and 9 assistant SBA.
7 As of 1991, there are 5 inspectors and 20 examiners at the Central Bank, excluding data processors and clerical staff.
8 Banks are usually invited every year to the Central Bank to review the findings of examiners and external auditors. In case financial weaknesses are identified, the Central Bank sends follow-up letters to banks; whenever necessary, the Treasury is also informed with views on necessary measures to be taken.
9 Even though maturities available in the market include overnight, 1–4 weeks, and 1–3 months, most transactions undertaken are overnight. The market grew rapidly and the average volume of daily transactions increased from TL6.4 billion in 1986 and TL200 billion in 1987 to TL2.2 trillion in 1990.

10 Participants in the market are commercial banks, special finance houses, and institutions authorized by the Treasury. The Central Bank both acts as a blind broker and trades in the market.

11 The increased popularity of the foreign exchange deposits can be explained by the currency substitution phenomenon. In Turkey, traditionally gold and, for the last decades at an increasing rate, foreign exchange are held as hedges against inflation. The introduction of foreign exchange deposits no doubt had a promotional effect on currency substitution, since it legalized foreign exchange holdings. However, its main consequence was in the manifestation of the phenomenon, rather than a radical change. For empirical evidence on high elasticity of substitution between domestic and foreign currency deposits, see Kumcu (1989) and Iskenderoglu (1989).

12 In 1983 the previously complicated structure of reserve and liquidity requirements was simplified by unifying rates at 10% and 25% respectively, for all deposits. In 1985 the reporting frequency was changed from one month to one week and the compliance lag was shortened from six to two weeks. In 1986 legal requirements were extended to foreign exchange deposits. The liquidity requirement ratio was divided into two components according to which banks were required to keep 5% of their liabilities as free reserves at the Central Bank and vault cash and 12% as government securities. The ratios increased gradually over time, reaching a total of 35% (with 30% in the form of government securities). For more details, see Akkurt et al. (1991) and Bayazitoglu, Ersel, and Ozturk (1991).

13 According to survey results reported in Alkan (1990), in 1989 about one-half of banks' purchases of government paper was to meet legal liquidity requirements. Most of the rest were resold either directly or through repurchase agreements. The share of purchases as an asset alternative to credit was only about 5%. Results of another survey, reported in Atiyas, Ersel, and Ozturk (1992) and summarized in more detail below, indicate that in general bank managers perceived the nonobligatory portion of government securities as instruments of short-term liquidity management. Only under exceptional circumstances were these instruments perceived as substitutes to credit. Finally, Ersel (1992) also provides evidence that the nonobligatory holding of government securities by banks and the nonbank public was more than 50%.

14 Data on bank loan rates are not available. However, there is ample anecdotal evidence that banks apply a wide range of lending rates, depending on the perceived quality of borrowers. See below.

15 Data collected by the Banking Department of the Central Bank of the Republic of Turkey. The figures in Table 6.3 are computed only for national banks. As demonstrated below, the share of foreign banks in total assets remained negligible throughout the period.

16 As can be seen from the following table, a similar picture emerges if one computes the concentration ratio on the basis of total deposits (i.e., the sum of TL and FX denominated sight and time deposits). Note, however, that the ratios decrease at a slower rate in this case. See the table on p. 138.

17 In 1989 the Central Bank's practice of extending medium- and long-term credits in the form of advances against bonds was terminated. It was decided that rediscount credits would be extended only against short-term company paper and their use as tools of selective credit policy came to an end.

18 Denizer (1991) finds econometric evidence that bank profits are positively related to concentration. Hence it seems that profitability increased despite a reduction in the degree of monopoly power in the banking system.

Three- and four-bank concentration ratios				
	Private banks		All national banks	
1980	71.7	78.1	53.2	64.3
1981	69.4	77.2	50.6	63.1
1982	72.5	79.6	55.3	65.2
1983	75.8	82.5	56.5	65.9
1984	74.6	80.2	57.3	66.0
1985	74.8	80.8	54.5	64.8
1986	71.0	77.5	53.0	62.8
1987	58.8	62.5	49.6	59.3
1988	66.5	75.5	47.4	56.9
1989	59.8	69.5	45.3	53.2
1990	57.0	66.6	43.3	51.3

(Measured as % of total deposits accounted by the three and four largest banks in each category.)
Source: Data collected by the Banking Department of the Central Bank of the Republic of Turkey.

19 Calomiris and Hubbard (1990) develop a model where the credit market is divided into a "Walrasian" segment, where borrowers' relevant characteristics are costlessly identified, and an "information-intensive" segment, where borrowers' characteristics are private information unavailable to lenders.
20 This is not surprising since most small banks were found to concentrate their business on blue chip companies.
21 An alternative explanation could be that announcing a prime rate would increase the degree of competition in the banking system.
22 The emphasis on macroeconomic uncertainty as a determinant of bank's exposure to risky borrowers is consistent with predictions in the literature. See Caprio (Chapter 3 and 1992) for the importance of the degree of uncertainty in bank's choice between risky and riskless assets.
23 The legal system in Turkey is notoriously slow and overburdened. Courts in Istanbul are sometimes loaded with 70–80 cases per day. There is also anecdotal evidence of an increase in "economic crimes," especially bounced checks (see, for example, the weekly Nokta, August 4, 1991). Perhaps unsurprisingly, in the 1980s a "check mafia" emerged in large cities, which specialized in debt collection through intimidation and use of force. The mafia functioned mainly in settling debts among smaller businesses.
24 For more details on the data set, see Ersel and Ozturk (1993). The analysis that follows is subject to two qualifications. First, financial liabilities are expressed in

terms of stocks rather than flows. Data on sources and uses of funds, which would help provide a more complete picture of financing patterns, are unfortunately unavailable. Second, the analysis of patterns of external financing does not take into account external equity, due to lack of firm-level data on issues of new shares to the market for the sample period. However, only a small portion of increases in equity (on average 14–15% in 1990–1 according to CMB data). The CMB currently requires firms to realize at least 15% of capital increases through market issues.

25 Annual flows of depreciation expenses were not available from the income statements; hence the first difference of accumulated depreciation was used to approximate the flow.

26 What may be captured here is the special institutional features of long-term bank loans in Turkey. Most of these funds are loans from development banks or, at least until the late 1980s, preferential credits from the Central Bank. As reported in Ersel and Ozturk (1990), access to such loans requires a time-consuming process of project evaluation that is costly for borrowers. The positive relation between long-term bank loans and GTA may therefore reflect a self-selection process whereby only firms with large investment projects apply for these loans. Hence, GTA may be a bad proxy for agency problems in the case of long-term loans. Alternatively, in the case of loans from development banks, it may also reflect development banks' ability to monitor borrowers after a loan is made.

27 In a model where firms build reputation over time, Diamond (1989) predicts that older firms will find it optimal to choose safer projects because they have incentives to maintain their reputation capital.

28 The fact that the crisis involved excessive (and quite likely inefficient) intermediation rather than disintermediation is possibly explained by expectations of a de facto deposit insurance.

29 Ersel and Ozturk (1993) provide further econometric evidence on the impact of macroeconomic uncertainty, in their case identified with variability in inflation rates. Their analysis of firm-level data shows that greater uncertainty increases the share of short-term debt and especially short-term other debt (mainly trade credits) and reduces the share of bank loans.

30 The most striking contrast would be with Korea, where direct financing became a major component of sources of funds in the 1980s. See Cho and Cole (1992).

CHAPTER 7

Financial policy reform in New Zealand

Dimitri Margaritis, with Dean Hyslop and David Rae

7.1 Introduction

A major program of economic reform was undertaken in New Zealand in the 1980s. The process of transformation of the economy started with a number of changes in the late 1970s, in particular a closer economic relations agreement with Australia and the start of an import licensing liberalization process. The changes were greatly accelerated after a change in government in July 1984, with the majority of reforms being either implemented or announced in the period between July 1984 and March 1985.

The restructuring of New Zealand's economy was based on a strategy of economic and financial liberalization, supported by macroeconomic policies intended to provide a stable and more efficient financial system and a low rate of price inflation (Spencer 1990). The removal of all interest-rate, ratio, and credit regulations, the lifting of controls on capital flows in international markets, and the floating of the exchange were, along with the reduction of border protection, the principal components of the reform program.

Economic liberalization is a continuous process. This study analyzes and discusses the New Zealand experience from 1984 to 1992 recognizing the problems encountered in the derivation of definitive conclusions. The process of liberalization of the New Zealand economy has not been easy nor without significant social and economic

Dimitri Margaritis is a Reserve Bank Senior Research Fellow and Associate Professor of Economics, University of Waikato. We are grateful to Jerry Caprio, Arthur Grimes, and Michael Reddell for helpful comments. All remaining errors are our own. Furthermore the views expressed in this paper are those of the authors and do not purport to represent the views of the Reserve Bank of New Zealand.

costs. However, the benefits of the economic revolution that has taken place in New Zealand should not be overlooked. This process of transformation not only has created a more modern, efficient, and open economy but also has contributed significantly to a number of important cultural and social changes in the New Zealand society.

It is interesting to note that economic reform programs in other countries, and especially the countries of the Southern Cone, have been the subject of extensive analysis and discussion in the international literature. Yet, the recent New Zealand experience with financial and other economic reforms has attracted very little attention. This is surprising since the reforms have been more radical, extensive, and rapid than anywhere else in the Pacific region or the OECD countries.

The paper begins with a brief review of the major problems facing the economy in 1984 and discusses how the financial regulatory framework had contributed to the development of those problems. A presentation of the sequencing of reforms follows. The main financial and other economic reforms are outlined and their consequences are discussed. Particular attention is paid to issues concerning volatility in financial and foreign exchange markets under deregulation as well as the relationship between monetary aggregates and nominal income or inflation in the formulation of monetary policy in the new environment. Also discussed are the effects of liquidity constraints in the monetary policy transmission mechanism and the impact of nominal shocks on the performance of the real sector under a policy of disinflation. Issues arising from New Zealand's experience of deregulation and disinflation are presented in the concluding section of the paper. An important finding, especially for governments interested in embarking on financial reforms, is that the authorities were able to maintain monetary control despite financial reform, though volatility of interest rates and exchange rates may have been exacerbated in the process. Also, the slower implementation of trade and labor market reforms may have increased the costs of reducing inflation during the adjustment process.

7.2   Initial conditions

This section presents some information on the state of the New Zealand economy at the time the financial and other economic reforms were undertaken.[1] This information is useful to understand the nature of the problems facing the economy and to identify the objectives and scope of the changes. It also serves as a background to an analysis and discussion of the range and order of the specific measures and reforms undertaken.

In the period 1960–84 New Zealand's economy had been characterized by the lowest average rate of real economic growth among all OECD countries (e.g., the country's per capita income had slipped from 4th to a ranking of 19th in the OECD during this period). Actually, in the decade prior to 1984, New Zealand's economic performance was even more disappointing. During this period the country had experienced little or no economic growth, the current account deficit had reached record levels and had been financed mainly through the accumulation of a sizable amount of foreign debt. Unemployment was slowly but constantly rising and actual or underlying inflation was high for most of the period.

A long period of border protection had largely insulated the economy from international competition and a wide range of market interventions had distorted price signals and prevented adaptation of business activity to changes in market conditions. The manufacturing sector was highly diversified but very inefficient. The agricultural sector, which was the major source of export revenue, became supported by an expensive system of subsidies that discouraged greater efficiency on farms and in the processing sector.

The government had undertaken or guaranteed a large part of the country's capital formation with an unimpressive performance in terms of rates of return. The fiscal deficit varied to some extent in relation to the electoral cycle but its trend since the mid-1970s was strongly upward. Monetary policy was for most of the period highly constrained by the exchange rate system and the extensive interest and other financial controls. Interest rate controls, entry restrictions into the financial sector, and segmentation among financial institutions reduced sustainable national income levels by lowering the efficiency of the financial intermediation services, and encouraged the development of less efficient fringe financial intermediaries (Spencer and Carey 1988).

In summary, the financial market and other controls that existed in 1984 were, broadly, of: (1) interest-rate controls; (2) regulations affecting credit allocation and activities of financial institutions; (3) foreign exchange capital transactions controls and a fixed (crawling peg, 1979–82) exchange-rate regime; and (4) nonfinancial industry economic policies, including price, wage, and rent controls.

    1   *Interest rate controls*
       Deposit rate controls – applied to bank and nonbank institutions:

a No interest on checking accounts
b A 3% interest-rate restriction on "ordinary" savings accounts
c Minimum 30-day maturity for interest-bearing deposits at trading banks
d Term-deposit rate levels restricted until June 1984
Loan rate controls
a Widespread ceilings on loan rates of banks and non-banks (real lending rates were often negative – see Figure 7.1)
b Lending rate controls applied to mortgage loans in 1983
c Non–mortgage-lending controls applied to nontrading banks in 1984

All interest rate controls were removed in July–August 1984.

2 *Regulations affecting credit allocation and activities of financial institutions* (See also Table 7.1.)
a Regulations required both banks and nonbank institutions to purchase government securities at government-set (presumably below-market) interest rates (e.g., short-term government security yields rose from 10.40% in July 1984 to 14.28% in August to 20.00% in March 1985, and long-term yields went up from 10.25% to 15.12% to 17.52% during the same period) (repealed February 1985).
b Credit growth guidelines issued to all institutions (1983–4 formal 1% per month growth guidelines) (removed August 1984)
c Guidelines to trading banks regarding credit allocation by sector (relaxed in early 1984 and subsequently repealed at the end of 1984)
d Trading banks reserve asset ratio – with seasonal variations in the range of 10–30% (abolished February 1985); also public sector securities ratios for other institutions
e Restrictions on types of activities different institutions may undertake. (This applied especially to trustee savings banks and other nontrading banks.)
  i Foreign exchange dealing by trading banks only (nonbank dealers authorized September 1983)
  ii Building societies and trustee savings banks could offer only "mortgages and a narrow range of deposit-taking activities" (Harper and Karacaoglu 1987, p. 207) (restructuring/relaxing 1985–6 onward;

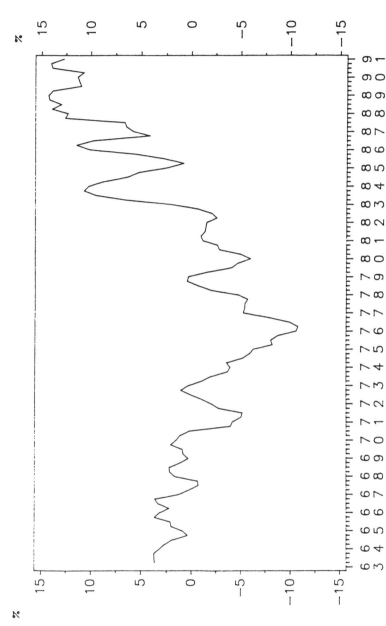

Figure 7.1 Real trading bank lending rate

Table 7.1 *Ratio requirements abolished as of February 11, 1985*

Institutional group	Type of ratio(s)	Ratio Base
Private savings bank	Government securities (GS)	Deposits, less statutory cash and low start mortgages
	Statutory cash ratio (SC) requiring 5% of the first $m in deposits and 2.5% of additional deposits to be held in the form of certain liquid assets.	Deposits
Trustee savings banks	GS ratio of 38% (with special 15% ratio on outstanding housing bonds)	Deposits, less statutory cash. Low start mortages and housing bonds.
Life insurance Offices	Public sector (PS) securities ratio of 31% of which minimum GS of 20% and 11% optional GS or local authority securities (LA)	Total assets, less bank overdraft
	Minimum housing/farming investments ratio (HF) of 20%	
Private superannuation funds	Overall ratio of 41% of which minimum GS of 20% optional or LA ratio of 11% and optional GS or HF ratio of 10%	Total "residual" assets
Finance companies	GS ratio of 30%	Invests
Building societies	PS ratio of 19% of which minimum GS of 14%. Also special GS ratios of 30% for holdings of "savings bank" deposits and 50% for home/farm ownership account deposits	Total assets (less some exclusions)
Trading banks	Reserve asset ratio of 27% set at beginning of February 1985 (virtually all held in GS)	Average reserve asset holdings for month as proportion of average total deposits through previous month

Source: Reserve Bank of New Zealand.

different restrictions applied to institutions in different market segments)
Entry barriers to financial services industry, especially into "Banking," via statutory law in which each institution type affected by different legislation. (The 1986 Reserve Bank Amendment Act enabled the Reserve Bank to register an unlimited number of banks.)
3   *Foreign exchange transactions controls*
   a   Restrictions on private overseas borrowing (removed October 1984)

    b Restrictions on access to domestic financial markets of foreign-owned companies operating in New Zealand (removed November 1984)

    c Restrictions on New Zealand financial institutions borrowing overseas (removed November 1984)

    d Restrictions on New Zealand residents purchasing foreign exchange for investment purposes (removed December 1984)

4 *Nonfinancial industry economic policies*

    a State/public-owned enterprise pricing often did not reflect production costs (The Treasury 1984).

    b Restrictive labor market practices included the wage controls of the period 1982–4, a centralized wage-setting system, and compulsory unionization (which became voluntary briefly in 1984 and once again compulsory in 1984–91).

    c Variable assistance to industry included subsidies for agricultural export producers; import controls/quotas/customs duty to protect domestic manufactures. (Tariff and import licenses were reduced in 1985, import licenses ended in 1986, tariffs were restructured in 1987 setting 52% of tariff items duty free and 20% with duties of less than 15%. In 1991 a review of remaining tariffs recommended that they will be cut by one third between 1992 and 1996. Agricultural subsidies and export incentives were phased out from the mid-1980s.)

    d Many products were subject to price controls prior to 1984 but have since been phased out. A wage and price freeze was also in place between 1982 and 1985.

5 Related to item (a) was the noncompetitive operating environment for state/public owned enterprises, which also received assistance via low debt costs, subsidized equity finance, and absence of taxation – in comparison with private sector enterprises (The Treasury 1984).

6. A nominal-based tax system and the absence of a capital gains tax provided incentives for investment in nominally appreciating real assets.

General economic effects of these controls

Interest-rate controls had the effect of allocating too high a proportion of loan funds to low-risk investment projects. This occurred as a result

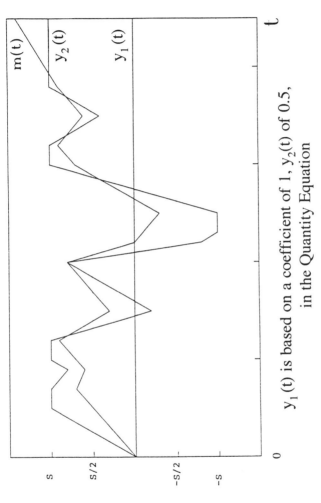

Figure 7.2 State-dependent pricing: Dynamics of money and output

of the low level of domestic savings funds available (in part because of low deposit-interest rates) and the absence of incentives to make loans available to high-risk-adjusted investment projects (because of controls on loan rates). Official guidelines for the allocation of loan funds to "favored" activities irrespective of earnings or their riskiness made resource allocation less responsive to market price signals. Interest-rate controls also tended to reduce price competition in financial markets. Noncompetitive tactics such as product tie-ins existed – for example, requirements of savings records in order to obtain mortgages enabled institutions to offset their low loan rates with low deposit rates.

The segmentation of the financial industry on the basis of type of financial activities available, caused by regulatory controls, tended to reduce the scope of financial services offered. This was due to institutions being unable (through regulation in many instances) to exploit economies of scope in offering a variety of services. The absence of competition was strengthened also by the legal barriers to entry into the financial services industries. Consequently, the overall view of the financial services industry in 1984 is one of an industry divided into protected but strictly controlled segments where price signals and allocative efficiency were of secondary importance.

Widespread price controls and the effects of the state-owned enterprise environment severely distorted relative price signals, thus affecting the efficient allocation of resources within the economy (The Treasury 1984). Such regulatory factors also inhibited the economy's ability to adapt in response to the changing circumstances it faced. For example, the economy maintained reliance on protected primary product industries in spite of the steady deterioration in New Zealand's terms of trade and the difficulties in finding export markets. However, encouraged in part by direct incentives, manufacturing exports had been increasing relatively rapidly since the early 1970s.

The combination of interest-rate controls and foreign exchange transactions controls had severe effects on New Zealand's economic prosperity. The low domestic interest rates, together with the inability of residents to take advantage of higher foreign interest rates and invest overseas, discouraged domestic savings. The nominal-based tax regime also discouraged savings by the taxation of nominal interest earnings, reducing the real rate of return on savings in an inflationary environment. At the same time domestic investment in inefficient projects was encouraged via artificially low domestic interest rates. With the addition of an accommodating monetary policy there existed an expansion in aggregate demand relative to output, a steadily increasing current account deficit, and high domestic inflation. The requirement of capital inflows to balance the current account deficit (with little success at attracting foreign investment) necessitated increasing levels of official and private overseas borrowing. Such overseas borrowing essentially served to support the low domestic interest rates, and subsidized domestic investment by the amount of the difference between the low domestic interest rates and the higher costs of overseas borrowing.

Thus the effect of the financial sector controls, together with other distorting economic regulations and expansionary macroeconomic policies, largely contributed to the high level of overseas debt but extremely poor growth record of the New Zealand economy. In the decade to 1984 New Zealand's average current account deficit as a fraction of GDP was 4.8%, compared with the OECD average of 0.3% for the same period (see Spencer and Carey 1988, p. 2). Over the same period New Zealand's average inflation rate of 13.8% was considerably higher than the OECD average of 8.8%. Additionally, New Zealand's average per capita growth rate of 0.3% per annum was the lowest of the OECD countries and compared with the OECD average of 2.0%. Rather than contributing to any significant productive investment growth, the increasing level of external public debt (from 10.7% of GDP in March 1975 to 36.7% in March 1984) had supported high levels of government and private consumption expenditure, which could not be sustained by the economy. Much of the debt was also devoted to financing a series of state-backed energy-intensive development projects in the early 1980s, most of which subsequently have proved to be uneconomic.

7.3   The reforms

In its initial stages the reform agenda was strongly influenced by the economic situation surrounding the election of the government in July 1984. Expectations of a possible currency devaluation driven by rising fiscal and current account deficits, in combination with frozen interest rates, had created a foreign exchange crisis. In just four weeks prior to July 1984, the Reserve Bank sold as much foreign exchange as it would normally have expected to sell in one year (Deane 1986). Despite extensive overseas borrowing and the official writing of a large volume of forward exchange contracts, foreign reserves dropped to a very low level.

The new government immediately devalued the exchange rate by 20%, removed all interest-rate controls and imposed a temporary price freeze to facilitate the introduction of its program of economic policies. An extensive package of major microeconomic and macroeconomic reforms was soon introduced. A chronology of the sequence of reforms is given in the Appendix 7.1.

The primary aims of the structural reforms that have occurred in New Zealand since 1984 are, at the microeconomic level, to achieve more efficient resource allocation; and at the macroeconomic level, to achieve low inflation and a balanced budget. Pursuing the former objective involved the removal of regulations to allow and encourage decision making on the basis of market-determined price signals. The latter involved developing a monetary policy, carried out by the Reserve Bank, with the primary goal of achieving and maintaining price stability, free from the obligation to finance fiscal deficits.[2] It also involved pursuing a fiscal policy to eliminate the fiscal deficit.

Although some liberalization had occurred, such as the removal of some products under price control and credit-allocation guidelines, the foreign exchange crisis around the time of the general election in July 1984 immediately preceded, and perhaps precipitated, the start of an extensive series of financial and broader economic reforms in New Zealand. A combination of factors – the Labor Party's substantial lead in preelection polls and its promise to devalue the currency by 20%; the incumbent government's refusal to adjust policy; and the fixed exchange rate regime – resulted in a massive run on foreign exchange reserves. This crisis served to highlight the problems of the regulatory financial environment, and in particular the risks to which the government was exposed in supporting such an environment.

The removal of interest-rate controls may not have significantly aided the subsequent inflow of foreign reserves in 1984, but it may be seen as the first step in the process of reform of the financial sector. By the end of the year all interest-rate controls had been removed, along with restrictions on overseas borrowing and investment by New Zealand residents and institutions, restrictions on foreign companies access to domestic financial markets, and credit growth guidelines to financial institutions.

In early 1985 the Reserve Bank began paying interest on trading bank settlement account balances; reserve asset requirements on trading banks and similar requirements on other financial institutions to purchase government securities were removed; in March the exchange rate was floated. By this stage financial sector controls not requiring complex legislation had largely been removed.

The legislation changes that followed were designed to ensure a more uniform environment for all financial institutions to operate in, and a contestable environment for activities. The Reserve Bank Amendment Act of 1986 enabled an unlimited number of banks to be registered at the discretion of the Reserve Bank, provided they satisfied minimum standards in the areas of capital adequacy, individual borrower exposure, open positions in foreign exchange, and exposures to borrowers that are connected to the bank (see White 1991). Thus the number of registered banks increased from four, their number during the 1980–6 period, to 14 in 1987 and leveled off in 1989 at their present level of 21. Legislation also has been introduced which removed restrictions on Trustee Banks' and Building Societies' activities.

In association with the increasingly deregulated nature of the financial industry, the Reserve Bank's role in prudential supervision was formalized.[3] In its prudential supervision role, the Reserve Bank monitors the assets and liabilities of major financial institutions in order to assess their risk exposure. If an institution is at risk of failing and the Reserve Bank assesses that such a failure would destabilize the financial system, it can appoint a statutory manager to facilitate an orderly restructuring or exit from the market. The Reserve Bank has established a policy on large individual exposures and requires banks to meet specified capital adequacy requirements.

Other economic reforms were being implemented in a short time and had different impacts on various sectors of the economy. In the export sector, the major form of assistance, export performance taxation incentives, were phased out between 1985 and 1987. The phasing out of agricultural subsidies began late 1984.

Since the late 1970s there had been a progressive move to replace import licensing (traditionally the principal mechanism for closing the New Zealand economy) with tariff-based protection for import-competing industries. Import licensing ended in 1986. In 1987 a four-year tariff-reduction program began to reduce the level of tariffs with the aim of increasing the exposure of the import-competing sector to internal and external competition. The level of tariffs was reduced in this period to a maximum of 20% (except for 'plan' industries, e.g., cars, carpets, clothing, footwear, textiles, and tires). The fourth Labor government planned to reduce tariffs to a maximum of 10% by 1996 – however, the current National government intends to reduce them by only one third in that period.

In 1986 a comprehensive value-added tax on goods and services (GST) was introduced. This largely replaced the existing system of variable sales taxes on a range of products, reducing the distortionary price effects it caused. The introduction of GST was associated with a reduction in the level of personal income taxation and represented a move to a broader based taxation system.

The changes in the structure of the public sector have been dramatic. They are probably the most radical reform of government attempted by any OECD country thus far. The focus of the reform has been twofold: to achieve efficient use of resources with pricing decisions in trading areas to reflect underlying costs and other commercial factors, and to improve accountability and decentralized decision making. Under this system, the efficient supply of outputs rather than the monitoring and control of inputs is the criterion for evaluating government activity.

In 1985 moves to make public sector enterprises more efficient began with road user charges being increased to cost-recovery levels, and electricity and coal prices increased gradually to reflect the full cost of supply. In 1987 corporate structures were introduced for state-owned enterprises (SOEs). Under the new structures the SOEs are required to finance activities by market borrowing and are expected to pay tax and dividends to the government. The organizations also lose special privileges they had previously received in legislation (e.g., monopoly status) and practice (e.g., subsidized finance).

Major benefits were expected in the structure of incentives to perform functions efficiently and a clear identification of the underlying resource costs of such functions. Following the corporatization of trading organizations, a privatization program began in 1987 with the dual aim of retiring one-third of the public sector debt and removing essentially private sector enterprises from the public sector umbrella.

Importantly, little had been done to deregulate the labor market between late 1984 and 1991. In the 1987 Labor Relations Act there were some legislation changes designed to strengthen the democracy and accountability of unions and remove unnecessary restrictions in the wage-fixing process. Under this legislation the national award system of collective bargaining was maintained and unions were required to have a minimum number of members (1,000) in order to be registered. The extent of labor market flexibility under the national award system is debatable. For example, a given dispersion of wage settlements would often be interpreted by employer groups as indicating a lack of flexibility, while unions claim it represented substantial flexibility (Easton 1987, pp. 196–7).

The Employment Contracts Act of 1991 (ECA) has radically changed the law with regard to industrial relations. The main thrust of the ECA is to allow the negotiation of individual contracts between employers and employees to be extremely flexible. The extent to which it will enhance labor market flexibility is an issue for the future. However, after a year of the new regime there are already significant signs of change; for example, almost all collective agreements are now enterprise of site agreements; very few multiemployer agreements remain.

The sequencing of the reforms

In the economic liberalization literature there are two opposing views on the optimal sequencing of reforms. The conventional wisdom (see, e.g., Frenkel 1983) is that distortions in domestic goods and capital markets should be removed and fiscal balance achieved first, before liberalization of the trade balance, and only in the final stage should the capital account be opened up. The opposing belief, in sum, is that liberalization in general is in the public interest. The main argument in support of this belief is that "in view of political constraints and vested interests which inhibit change, any opportunity to implement a desirable set of reforms in a coherent way should be seized even if other more desirable changes have not yet been achieved" (Institute of International Finance 1990, p. 5). The case of New Zealand, in addition to demonstrating political commitment to reforms, included other reasons for early financial deregulation (Deane 1986). Reform of the financial sector was seen as a significant method to improve the effectiveness of monetary policy in achieving disinflation. A floating exchange rate would give the Reserve Bank greater control over monetary aggregates and better insulate the domestic economy from external shocks. As the foreign exchange crisis in July 1984 showed, under the previous regime of financial controls the government was the major bearer of risks. A deregulated financial sector with free capital flows and a floating exchange rate would highlight any domestic policy problems and therefore encourage the implementation of a credible policy regime.

The removal of the wages and prices freeze in 1984 and the July 1984 devaluation of the exchange-rate-generated inflationary pressures. The removal of interest-rate and other financial sector controls led to an increase in interest rates and to strong growth in financial services and private sector credit. The high interest rates and returns on real and financial assets first attracted an inflow of capital and then, following the exchange-rate float, led to an appreciation of the domestic currency. The early growth in financial services and credit and capital inflows also drastically increased the inflationary pressures in the economy. Further, the decision to fully fund the budget deficit in domestic financial markets pushed domestic interest rates higher.

The increase in interest rates and the exchange rate (from July 1985), the reduction of export subsidies and import protection, and weak overseas demand for New Zealand's export products eliminated any encouragement to the export and import-competing sectors provided by the initial currency devaluation. This constrained the extent to which the Reserve Bank could raise interest and exchange rates in pursuit of the disinflation objective.

In terms of assessing where the pressures lay and which sectors were most affected by the reforms and the disinflationary monetary policy, the post-1984 era needs to be split into two subperiods characterized by the stock market crash in 1987. The precrash period was dominated by high inflation, weak export prices, and booming foreign and domestic equity markets. In this period, with financial deregulation stimulating financial sector growth, the tight disinflationary monetary policy focused pressure on the tradeable goods sector. High interest rates, which caused an appreciating nominal and real exchange rate, meant that the exchange rate was not able to provide appropriate price signals to the tradeable goods sector. According to Blyth (1987, p. 10), "instead of the exchange rate reflecting real cost advantages, it now reflects interest rate differentials. . . ."

Following a brief loosening in 1986, monetary policy was tightened in late 1986. The postcrash period was characterized by significant progress in the disinflation process, stronger world prices for exports, and a somewhat lower exchange rate from mid-1988. *Tight monetary policy increased pressure on the financial sector and resulted in massive falls in real and financial asset values as well as a significant number of corporate failures.* The Reserve Bank's and the government's view was that the majority of business failures were "the inevitable result of over-ambitious balance sheet expansions during the boom period" (Spencer 1990). There was also an element of policy credibility at stake as the Reserve Bank had already warned that excessive borrowing would not be bailed out once asset markets fell.

The performance of fiscal policy has been erratic in the post reform period. Despite some progress in deficit reduction since 1984,[4] New Zealand's net public debt to GDP ratio is still high by international standards. Most of the debt reduction has been achieved via large asset sales and not through significant fiscal discipline. Further, the progress in deficit reductions has mainly been achieved through revenue increases rather than expenditure reductions, although in 1991 and 1992 some progress has been made in lowering the ratio of government expenditure to GDP.

High debt levels and large budget deficits raised the exposure of the economy to adverse interest-rate and exchange-rate movements and added significant pressure to monetary policy.[5] In addition, fiscal policy lacked orientation toward achieving its social objectives. The institutional characteristics that impede job creation were not considered carefully. Less money was spent on programs to discourage long-term unemployment and thus improve the much needed quality of the country's human capital. Inevitably, welfare support became the budget's major burden.

7.4   Domestic savings

One of the main objectives of the reforms discussed in the previous section was to improve the allocation and mobility of capital and the efficiency with which savings are used. Some evidence on the inefficiencies in resource allocation may be obtained from a comparison of saving ratios and growth trends between New Zealand and the OECD countries. Although New Zealand's ratio of savings to GDP has not differed much from the OECD average over the last three decades, the country's economic growth rate has been much lower than the corresponding OECD average.

According to Spencer and Carey (1988) expansionary monetary policies contributed to the distortion of savings and investment decisions in New Zealand:

(1)   by creating high and variable inflation rates and thus distorting the role of the price mechanism in the allocation of resources;

(2)   through their interaction with exchange controls and a fixed exchange-rate system that encouraged overspending, overinvestment at marginal rates of return and discouraged saving.

Financial market regulation and nonfinancial economic policies also contributed to the distortion of savings and investment decisions in ways that have already been discussed in the previous sections. Removal of the price distortions and the artificial (dis)incentives structure for savings and investment were expected to increase domestic savings relative to domestic investment and reduce the current account deficit.

Table 7.1 shows that the balance-of-payments current account deficit as a percentage of nominal GDP has declined steadily since 1985. Much of this reduction in the current account deficit has come from government savings and a fall in import prices, not from an increase in private savings. The failure of private savings to rise significantly following the increase in real interest rates after deregulation is due to household savings behavior. The household savings ratio (see Table 7.2) fell during the second half of the 1980s to a level that is among the lowest in the OECD countries.

Several factors have contributed to the dramatic decline in the household savings ratio (see Barry 1991 and Ord Minnett Securities-NZ-Ltd. 1991). One is the effect of lower fiscal deficits, which reduce the chance of future tax increases. Ironically, financial deregulation, which increases households' access to credit as well as their ability to diversify their portfolios, may lower savings by reducing the uncertainty in future income. Another factor was the redistribution of income and wealth from the higher- to the lower-saving households (e.g., the share of wage and salary earners in the total disposable income declined by 5% in the years 1983 to 1989).

Prior to the share market crash of 1987, both real estate and the share market boomed, which resulted in a substantial increase in wealth and reduced the households' need to save. The fall of wealth following the share market crash and the real estate crisis did not increase saving as real incomes were declining at the same time and households attempted to preserve their consumption levels. The result of this behavior was a fall in the household saving ratio. The government's superannuation policy may have also contributed to the low household saving rate by creating a moral hazard problem. People will have a lower incentive to save if they are guaranteed a minimum retirement income. More recent changes in the superannuation system combined with medium-term demographic changes and increasing uncertainty over future government social policies may have a positive effect on household saving.

The decline in household saving has been offset by higher government and corporate saving (the corporate saving rate is the highest in the OECD). In this respect New Zealand's saving as a percentage of GDP has been quite stable in the 1980s, in contrast to the general trend in the OECD of falling saving rates. Overall the outlook for national saving in New Zealand appears to be quite positive.

Financial deregulation may not have boosted the saving performance, but with the help of disinflation and trade liberalization has certainly resulted in a much more efficient use of it. This is evident from the significant productivity gains that have been achieved in the New Zealand economy over the last five years (see Table 7.2 and the September 1990 Reserve Bank of New Zealand Monetary Policy Statement, p. 26). Some of these productivity gains have come from

Table 7.2 *New Zealand economy: 1980s at a glance – Annual percentage changes of annual totals or averages*

	Real Expenditures of GDP[1]				
	March Years (base 1982/83)				
	1980/81	1981/82	1982/83	1983/84	1984/85
Final Consumption					
- Private	0.5	1.7	-0.4	2.5	3.9
- Public Authority	0.9	1.8	0.5	2.3	2.3
- Total	0.6	1.7	-0.2	2.5	3.5
Gross Fixed Capital Formation;					
- Private: Residential	0.9	12.6	-3.4	14.9	5.9
Business	0.6	21.7	-1.1	-0.8	21.8
- Public Authority	-4.9	15.9	19.4	9.8	-16.0
- Total	-1.1	18.3	4.7	5.4	5.5
Final Domestic Expenditure	0.3	5.1	0.9	3.2	4.0
Stockbuilding[2]	-1.9	0.9	0.4	0.2	1.7
Gross National Expenditure	-1.5	6.0	1.3	3.3	5.6
Exports of Goods & Services	3.8	2.7	5.1	4.8	7.8
Imports of Goods & Services	-5.3	8.5	1.6	-0.1	13.3
Expenditure on GDP	1.3	4.2	2.3	4.9	3.9
Government Accounts[3]					
GFS Financial Balance ($m)	-925.0	-1322.0	-1673.0	-2384.0	2464.0
- As a % of Nominal GDP	-4.0	-4.8	-5.4	-6.9	-6.3
Primary Balance	-516.0	-378.0	-565.0	-925.0	-212.0
- As a % of Nominal GDP	-2.2	-1.4	-1.8	-2.7	-0.5
External Accounts					
Balance on Merchandise Trade ($m)	505.0	-14.0	0	79.0	-734.0
Balance on Invisibles ($m)	-1328.0	-1614.0	-1914.0	-1995.0	-2554.0
BOP Current Account Balance ($m)	-823.0	-1628.0	-1914.0	-1916.0	-3288.0
As a % of Nominal GDP	-3.6	-5.9	-6.2	-5.6	-8.5
Terms of Trade (SNA)	-10.6	0.6	-3.3	1.0	-1.6
Real TWI (level, CPI basis)	94.9	93.6	97.0	91.3	82.7
Incomes and Prices					
Real Household Disposable Incomes	-1.9	1.6	-4.1	0.3	2.8
Savings/Disposable Income Ratio	9.4	10.0	8.1	6.2	4.8
Consumers Price Inflation[4]	15.2	15.9	12.6	3.5	13.4
Monetary					
90 Day Bank Bill Interest Rate (level)	13.1	14.8	15.9	12.5	16.5
Nominal M3[4]	12.8	16.5	13.4	14.6	26.5
Nominal TWI Exchange Rate (level)	94.0	86.7	82.8	77.3	65.9
Labor Market					
Employment[4,5]	0.1	1.1	-1.6	0.9	1.8
Registered Unemployment Rate (%)[6]	4.3	4.3	6.5	6.6	4.9
Labor Productivity Index (Private Sector)	6.0	-2.0	0.7	14.5	-1.2
Unit Labor Costs (Private Sector)	12.0	21.9	10.7	-10.8	6.9

[1] GDP figures are RBNZ estimates from 1980/81 to 1982/83.

[2] Percentage point contribution to growth rate in GDP

[3] 1989/90 is a June year - other figures are March years.

[4] Annual percentage change: March quarter to March quarter percentage changes.

[5] Employment figures for 1980/81 to 1985/86 are an RBNZ series based on the QES. Figures for 1986/87 onwards are based on the HLFS.

[6] Rate as at March quarter.

Table 7.2 (continued)

| | Real Expenditures of GDP[1] | | | | |
| | March Years (base 1982/83) | | | | |
	1985/86	1986/87	1987/88	1988/89	1989/90
Final Consumption					
- Private	0.7	3.3	2.5	1.7	0.9
- Public Authority	1.3	2.0	0.8	0.9	0.3
- TOTAL	0.9	3.0	2.1	1.6	0.8
Gross Fixed Capital Formation;					
- Market Sector Investment:					
- Residential[7]	0.5	-3.8	1.8	6.0	9.1
- Business[8]	5.8	-4.9	11.6	-5.6	13.8
- Non-Market Government Investment[9]	22.6	-1.5	-6.5	9.3	2.1
- TOTAL	6.1	-4.4	8.2	-2.5	11.9
Final Domestic Expenditure	2.2	1.1	3.6	0.5	3.5
Stockbuilding[2]	-2.6	0.9	-1.8	-0.1	3.1
Gross National Expenditure	-0.4	2.0	1.8	0.5	6.6
Exports of Goods & Services	1.2	4.5	5.2	2.3	-3.0
Imports of Goods & Services	1.5	2.5	11.6	0.2	15.0
Expenditure on GDP	-0.6	2.6	-0.6	1.2	0.0
Government Accounts[3]					
GFS Financial Balance ($m)	-1397.0	-1866.0	-1147.0	-1332.0	-894.0
- As a % of Nominal GDP	-3.1	-3.5	-1.9	-2.1	-1.3
Primary Balance	1090.0	1027.0	2168.0	2510.0	3142.0
- As a % of Nominal GDP	2.4	1.9	3.6	3.9	4.5
External Accounts					
Balance on Merchandise Trade ($m)	-651.0	709.0	1697.0	3319.0	1373.0
Balance on Invisibles ($m)	-3363.0	-3587.0	-4203.0	-4025.0	-3568.0
BOP Current Account Balance ($m)	-4013.0	-2878.0	-2506.0	-707.0	-2195.0
- As a % of Nominal GDP	-9.0	-5.3	-4.2	-1.1	-3.1
Terms of Trade (SNA)	0.0	6.4	10.8	9.4	4.3
Real TWI (level, CPI basis)	88.6	88.3	99.6	98.4	95.1
Incomes and Prices					
Real Household Disposable Incomes	0.7	2.7	0.1	1.8	-1.9
Savings/Disposable Income Ratio	3.8	4.4	4.0	2.0	-0.8
Consumers Price Inflation[4]	12.9	18.2	9.0	4.0	7.0
Consumers Price Inflation (Excluding GST)[4,10]	12.9	11.8	8.0	4.0	5.0
Monetary					
90 Day Bank Bill Interest Rate (level)	23.4	19.4	19.0	14.6	13.6
Nominal M3[4]	29.4	19.0	13.7	3.4	1.4
Nominal TWI Exchange Rate (level)	64.9	60.1	64.4	62.8	61.0
Labor Market					
HLFS Employment[4,5]	0.2	0.8	-1.9	-4.1	0.4
HLFS Unemployment Rate (%)[6]	4.2	4.1	5.0	7.4	7.3
Labor Productivity Index (Private Sector)	-4.2	3.2	-0.7	8.8	3.0
Unit Labor Costs (Private Sector)	17.9	13.6	11.6	0.2	3.0

[7] Market sector residential investment comprises private and government residential investment.

[8] Market sector business investment includes all private sector and SOE investment.

[9] Non-market government investment comprises core central and local government investment.

[10] CPI figures excluding GST are RBNZ estimates.

Source: Reserve Bank of New Zealand, December 1991.

| | Real Expenditures of GDP | | | |
| | *March Years* | | | |
	1990	1991	1992	1993
Final Consumption				
- Private	0.9	-0.2	-0.8	-0.3
- Public Authority	0.3	-0.2	-1.1	-2.4
- Total	0.8	-0.2	-0.9	-0.7
Gross Fixed Capital Formation:				
- Market Sector:				
- Residential	9.1	-0.2	-17.7	2.4
- Business	13.8	2.8	-21.6	0.9
- Non-Market Government Sector	2.1	-12.3	0.4	-2.7
- Total	11.9	1.1	-19.3	0.8
Final Domestic Expenditure	3.5	0.1	-5.9	-0.4
Stockbuilding[1]	3.1	-0.4	-1.2	0.9
Gross National Expenditure	6.6	-0.3	-6.8	0.5
Exports of Goods & Services	-3.0	8.8	8.0	4.9
Imports of Goods & Services	15.0	3.5	-6.7	1.3
Expenditure on GDP	0.0	1.0	-1.7	1.8
Government Accounts[2]				
Financial Balance ($m)	-943	-2342[3]	-2750	-2050
As a % of GDP	-1.4	-3.2[3]	-3.8	-2.7
Primary Balance as a % of GDP	4.4	2.4[3]	1.6	2.4
External Accounts				
BOP Current Account Balance ($m)	-2195	-2820[4]	-1305	-750
As a % of GDP	-3.1	-3.8	-1.8	-1.0
SNA Terms of Trade	4.3	-3.6	-3.4	1.3
Incomes				
Real Household Disposable Incomes	-1.9	-1.8	-1.0	-0.1
Prices[5]				
Consumers Price Inflation	7.0	4.5	1.6	2.4
Labor Market[5]				
HLFS Employment	0.4	-0.5	-1.8	0.4
HLFS Official Unemployment ('000s)	115.7	160.4	205.7	216.9
HLFS Official Unemployment Rate (%)	7.3	9.9	12.5	13.1

[1] Percentage point contribution to growth rate of GDP.

[2] June years.

[3] Excludes proceeds from the sale of Crown Forestry Assets.

[4] RBNZ estimate: differs from official Dept. of Statistics estimate due to assumptions about investment income flows.

[5] March quarter to March quarter % changes or rate/level as at March quarter.

Source: Reserve Bank of New Zealand, December 1991.

Table 7.3 *Ratios of money supply (M3) and personal sector credit (PSC)*

	To nominal GDP (YN)	
Year	M3/YN	PSC/YN
1980	2.35	1.83
1981	2.20	1.83
1982	2.19	1.95
1983	2.28	2.00
1984	2.38	2.19
1985	2.63	2.40
1986	2.68	2.55
1987	2.79	2.70
1988	2.77	2.77
1989	2.70	2.76
1990	2.69	2.86

OLS Results

(1) LM3/YN = 0.717 + 0.149 D + 0.005 T R^2 = 0.918

(5.343)   (4.047)   (0.787)

(2) LPSC/YN = 0.120 + 0.134 D + 0.034 T R^2 = 0.999

(1.322)   (5.779)   (9.189)

Notes: D is a shift dummy = 0   1980-1984
                                       1985-1990
LM3/YN = log of M3/YN
LPSC/YN = log of PSC/YN
T = time trend
Numbers in parentheses are t-ratios

the introduction of new technologies, but most of the gains over 1988–9 in particular have resulted from layoffs.

There is also evidence of greater intermediation by the financial system, as indicated by the rise in the ratio of M3 to nominal GDP and the significance of the shift dummy variable *(D)* in equation (1) of Table 7.3. There is evidence of easier access of households to credit markets [as seen by the rise in the trading bank lending to the personal sector – PSC – and the significance of D in equation (2)]. Further, there is evidence of increased flexibility of the intermediation process (e.g., the share of finance and insurance in sectoral capital formation has grown from 10% to 25% in the last six years).

7.5   The role of monetary aggregates

Monetary policy has played a very important role in New Zealand's economic reform program. Its focus from the beginning of the program has been the task of permanently lowering inflation. This section discusses the role of monetary aggregates in the formulation of monetary policy under financial liberalization, a topic of great interest given widespread concerns that liberalization might be inconsistent with monetary control. The role of the liquidity constraints in the monetary policy transmission mechanism is the subject of the next section.

The float of the dollar and the removal of financial controls enabled the Reserve Bank, for the first time, to pursue monetary policy effectively. The monetary control mechanism since the float in March 1985 has been centered on quantities rather than prices. The float ensured that settlement cash balances held by banks at the Reserve Bank would be the key instrument for short-term monetary control. Should the banks fall short of settlement cash, further cash is available from the Reserve Bank by discounting Reserve Bank bills of short maturity at a penalty margin. The Reserve Bank restricts, however, the supply of both cash and Reserve Bank bills.

While the Reserve Bank of New Zealand operates a daily quantity target, it does not attempt to achieve direct control over the measured money and credit aggregates. Various attempts were made to directly control the growth of money (M3) and credit (Private Sector Credit) aggregates in the period up until 1985 in spite of the conflicting demands placed upon the monetary policy mechanism. A widely held view in 1985, and which has not changed since, was that financial deregulation would hinder any money or credit targeting strategy by strongly affecting the behavior of the monetary aggregates. It would also affect their relationship with nominal income or the ultimate inflation target as well as the relationship between the aggregates and the policy instruments. This was basically the experience that most central banks had with the effects of financial deregulation. It has also become evident that the observed rates of growth in money and credit had been or were expected to be significantly affected by the process of financial reintermediation following removal of financial controls. The behavior of the private sector in the face of a boom in property and equity values is also expected to affect the growth of money and credit.

Eclecticism has marked the approach to monetary policy in New Zealand from 1985 to present. Monetary conditions are assessed using the following indicators:

- The exchange rate
- Level and structure of interest rates
- Inflation expectations and forecasts
- Growth of money and credit
- Trends in the real economy

The relative importance of interest rates and the exchange rate has varied over time, but these two indicators have consistently played a much greater role in guiding policy over 1985–91 than the money and credit aggregates.

The purpose of this section is to evaluate the relationship between monetary aggregates and nominal GDP in New Zealand under financial liberalization. Financial policy reform in OECD countries often has been associated with less emphasis in the use of monetary aggregates as indicators or intermediate targets of monetary policy. The evidence presented by Blundell-Wignall, Browne, and Manasse (1990) is that financial liberalization has undermined the use of monetary targeting in some OECD countries, thus lending support to the view that monetary policy should focus directly on the ultimate objective of inflation.

Two major aspects of the relationship between money and policy targets are assessed. First, the long-run relationship between money, prices, and real GDP is empirically estimated using cointegration techniques. Restrictions on this relationship are tested within this framework. A stable relationship between money, prices, and output is a precondition for the use of monetary aggregates as targets or indicators in policy. Second, the short-run dynamic relationship between money and nominal GDP is investigated. For a monetary variable to be a useful target, the goal variable should be caused by the target in a predictable manner.

The data used in this analysis are quarterly seasonally unadjusted observations of the log of real GDP (y), the log of the M3 measure of money (m), and the log of the GDP implicit price deflator (p). The sample period for this data is the third quarter of 1964 to the first quarter of 1991. The deterministic dummies are used to proxy the effects of seasonal variations and the start of the reform program in the third quarter of 1984.

Cointegration test results are shown in Table 7.4.[6] The hypothesis of nonstationarity without cointegration ($r = 0$) is rejected at the 5% significance level against the alternative of possible stationarity ($r \leq 3$) and the alternative of at most one cointegration vector ($r \leq 1$).[7] Estimated coefficients of the cointegrating vector are shown in Table 7.5. The estimated price coefficient is close to 1, while the coefficient of

Table 7.4 *Cointegration tests: Money, prices, output*

	95% Critical Values[1]			
	H_1^2	H_2^3	H_1	H_2
$r \leq 2$	.141	.141	8.083	8.083
$r \leq 1$	11.452	11.311	17.844	14.595
$r = 0$	38.055	26.603	31.256	21.279

[1] Critical values are taken from Johansen and Juselius (1990).

[2] H_1 tests the restriction that there are at most r cointegrating vectors in the series against the alternative that all series are stationary. This is Johansen's trace statistic.

[3] H_2 tests the restriction that there are at most r cointegrating vectors in the series against the alternative of r+1 combinations. This is Johansen's maximum eigenvalue statistic.

Table 7.5 *Cointegrating vectors*

Vector	m	p	y
Normalised Coefficients	1.000	1.039	0.637

	Hypothesis	
		95% critical
P = 1	y = 1	value of $\chi^2(1)$
1.818	3.927	3.841

output is much smaller than 1. The Johansen procedure was also used to test the unity restrictions on the coefficients of price and output. The test results are also shown there. The hypothesis that money and prices are proportional cannot be rejected at the 5% level. Proportionality between money and output is, however, rejected at the 5% level. This suggests that the stationary long-run relationship among the levels of money, prices, and output is not the velocity of money circulation per se, since stationarity of velocity requires that the coefficients of prices and output be equal to one (Orden and Fisher 1990).

On the basis of these results, it is possible to conclude that there is reasonable evidence to support the hypothesis that financial reform has not undermined the long-run relationship between money, prices, and output. This is consistent with the Reserve Bank's long-run view of the relationship between money and prices. This view is reflected in the monetary policy's action of applying consistently firm pressure to monetary conditions with the aim of reducing the underlying rate of monetary expansion and hence, eventually, the rate of price inflation (Spencer 1990).

To assess the short-run role of the monetary aggregates as leading indicators of excessive nominal demand and inflation pressures in the economy, a causality analysis of the M3 aggregate as a candidate for an intermediate target or indicator of policy is performed. This analysis is based on the construction of an error correction model (ECM) for M3 and nominal GDP. The objective of the analysis is to see whether financial deregulation has permanently distorted the relationship between money and nominal income, or alternatively that this relationship has reverted back to stable forms. If a stable relationship has been reestablished, then there is a case for increasing the indicator weight of M3 or even return to monetary targeting. On the other hand it is possible that the dynamic nature of financial liberalization and the increased competitiveness of the financial markets would discourage the use of money as an intermediate target or indicator for monetary policy. The presence of cointegration has two important implications for causality inferences, namely:

1   The appropriate short-run model is the error-correction model. The absence of the error correction term in conventional causality regressions could lead to a misspecification bias problem.
2   There must be causality in at least one direction between the variables. For two variables to reach dynamically a long-run equilibrium there must be some causation amongst the variables to provide these dynamics (Cruse 1990).

The causality analysis results are given in Table 7.6. They are based on vector error correction models for changes in nominal incomes (yn), money and (short-term) interest rates (i). (The interest rate equation is not reported.) Recursive Wald χ^2 tests indicate that nominal GDP causes (or leads) M3 for all regressions recursively estimated throughout the postliberalization period. Nominal GDP also causes M3 through the error correction term (ec). There is no significant impact of interest rate changes on money growth immediately following the 1984 deregulation. However, this situation changed subsequently. Starting in 1988:1 interest rates are shown to lead monetary growth. This finding probably reflects the increased aversion of policy to the high volatility of interest rates in the post-1984 period.

Recursive tests reveal an interesting pattern in the indicator role of

Table 7.6 *Money and nominal income equations*

Dependent variable	Δm_{-1}	Δm_{-2}	Δm_{-3}	Δyn_{-1}	Δyn_{-2}	Δyn_{-3}	Δi_{-1}	Δi_{-2}	Δi_{-3}	ec_1	R^2
Δm	-.016	.484	-.094	-.145	-.091	-.014	.096	-.247	0.285	-0.213	0.858
	(.163)	(5.240)	(.937)	(2.587)	(2.092)	(.368)	(1.087)	(2.427)	(3.404)	(3.890)	(3.890)
Y	.547	.238	.342	-.288	-.548	.014	-.227	.155	.018	.200	.627
	(2.163)	(.970)	(1.280)	(1.931)	(4.716)	(.134)	(.962)	(.574)	(.082)	(1.372)	

Recursive Y:(3)Tests 1985:1-1991:1

Money Equation Nominal Income Equation

$\Delta yn_{-1} = \Delta yn_{-2} = \Delta yn_{-3} = 0$ $\Delta i_{-1} = \Delta i_{-2} = \Delta i_{-3} = 0$ $\Delta m_{-1} = \Delta m_{-2} = \Delta m_{-3} = 0$

t-values in brackets.
95% Critical value of] (3) = 7.815

M3 in relation to nominal income. The tests show no causality from M3 to nominal GDP in the immediate postliberalization period. There is, however, evidence that the role of M3 as a leading indicator of nominal GDP was restored around 1989:3. M3 does not appear to cause nominal GDP through the error correction term.

The results thus indicate that M3 causes nominal GDP without feedback through the traditional causality route of the lagged regressors. On the other hand, nominal GDP causes M3 via both the feedback and lagged regressors route. In conclusion, the results indicate that there is still not enough evidence to support the targeting of M3 in the short run, although its usefulness as an indicator of nominal GDP has probably increased recently. This finding could be of some relevance for the weight placed on the monetary aggregates in the Reserve Bank's eclectic approach to monetary policy.

7.6   Liquidity constraints

The previous section examined the use of monetary aggregates in the formulation of monetary policy. If financial liberalization has distorted the relationship between money and nominal income, then this could be linked with the undermining of the old monetary policy transmission mechanisms through liquidity constraints (Blundell-Wignall et al. 1990). The use of various credit and financial controls can enhance the ability of monetary policy to influence consumption and the rate of price inflation, thus contributing to a close relationship between monetary aggregates and inflation or nominal income.

In the event that financial liberalization and innovation ease liquidity constraints, the ability of monetary policy to affect consumption via current income/liquidity constraints is likely to be weakened. In this situation the effectiveness of monetary policy will become increasingly dependent upon permanent income and intertemporal substitution in credit demand, which is influenced by variations in interest rates (Blundell-Wignall et al. 1990). Evidence concerning the changing nature of liquidity constraints is examined in relation to consumption expenditure. More specifically, an econometric investigation is performed to examine whether permanent income has become more important relative to current income over time, via reduced liquidity constraints, as financial liberalization has proceeded. The procedure used here is based upon the benchmark Hall (1988) model further extended by Campbell and Mankiw (1991).

Campbell and Mankiw (1991) built a model that assumes that not all households consume according to the permanent income hypothesis.

They argue that many of the stylized facts that are seemingly inconsistent with the permanent income hypothesis can in fact be explained if a portion of households follow a rule of thumb of consuming their current income, with the remainder being orthodox forward-looking optimizing agents. They also argue that households whose liquidity is constrained will consume their current income (that is, follow the rule of thumb) and so interpret their model as one in which a portion of households are liquidity constrained whereas the others are not. They suggest further that the importance of liquidity constraints has eased since the deregulation of the financial system.

The results of estimating the model (described in Appendix 7.2) with unadjusted data are summarized in Table 7.7. The table shows only the results from the model in which consumption growth depends on current income growth. The expanded model, in which the change in current income is replaced with a weighted average of current and lagged income growth, gave poor statistical results. Also, the level of the real interest rate was insignificant and has been omitted from the estimated equations.

The key result is that the parameter λ is only marginally significant on a one-tailed test at the 5% level, and only for some specifications of the model. The first line of the results in Table 7.6 suggests that in over 80% of the households liquidity is constrained, although this figure is very uncertain. This is due to the large size of its standard error and also the difficulty in giving an exact interpretation of the coefficient λ in terms of the fraction of current income consumers in a log-linear model.

There is no evidence in any of the regressions of a change in the importance of liquidity constraints over time or since deregulation. The coefficient of the dummy variable or the time trend (λ_1) is always insignificant. Two variables are consistently significant: changes in nominal interest rates and the error correction term. The error correction term is expected to be significant as consumption is cointegrated with disposable income. However, the persistent significance of the nominal-interest-rate term can be interpreted as evidence in favor of liquidity constraints. It appears that, other things constant, a 1 percentage point drop in the nominal interest rate will boost consumption 0.2%.

The lagged change in consumption (which represents quadratic adjustment costs) is consistently positive as expected and has a fairly stable coefficient value across different specifications but is insignificant at any level more demanding than 10%. A major caveat to these results is that they depend crucially on the instruments used to form

Table 7.7 Seasonally unadjusted data, 1975:1–1990:3

Model: $\Delta_4 C_t = \mu + (\lambda_0 + \lambda_1 \times \text{Dummy}) *[\alpha\Delta_4 Y_t + (1-\alpha)\Delta_4 Y_{t-5}] + \theta_2\Delta_4 C_{t-5}$
$$+ \theta_3(c-y)_{t-5}$$

Where $c = 1/4(C + C_{-1} + C_{-2} + C_{-3})$ and $y = 1/4 (Y + Y_{-1} + Y_{-2} + Y_{-3})$

λ_0		λ_1		α	$\Delta_4 i$		ΔC_{t-5}		$(c-y)$		$\bar{R}^2$
0.831	(1.7)	-0.289	(0.3)	1	-0.002	(2.0)	0.19	(1.4)	-0.055	(2.3)	0.125
0.798	(1.7)	-	-	1	-0.002	(2.0)	0.17	(1.4)	-0.055	(2.4)	0.140
0.660	(1.5)	-	-	1	-0.002	(1.9)	-	-	-0.045	(2.0)	0.123
0.640	(1.4)	0.250	(0.3)	1	-0.002	(1.9)	-	-	-0.046	(2.0)	0.108
1.953	(1.1)	-.0015*	(0.7)	1	-0.002	(2.1)	0.19	(1.5)	-0.057	(2.4)	0.131

* Indicates coefficient estimate of time, not shift dummy variable.

t-value in brackets.

the change in current income. Changes to the instruments lead to large swings in the estimated value and significance of λ, although the results for the nominal interest rate and error correction terms are reasonably robust.

Table 7.8 summarizes the results for the seasonally adjusted data. Here the evidence is even less in favor of Campbell and Mankiw's (1991) model, although the results must be treated with caution as the X11 procedure may bias the tests against the theory (see Wirjanto 1991). The key coefficient λ is never significant, and is in fact sometimes negative. As before, there is little evidence that consumers follow the rule of thumb of consuming their current income and no evidence that there has been any change in this tendency over time. However, the nominal interest rate term is again significant with the same coefficient value, providing evidence for some form of liquidity constraints. But notice also that the coefficient on the lagged dependent variable, despite being consistently significant, has the "wrong" sign. This suggests that the equation may be misspecified when using adjusted data. Setting $\alpha = 1$ so that the expanded model collapses down to the basic model does not alter the conclusions.

In summary, it seems that the evidence is against Campbell and Mankiw's (1991) theory that a portion of consumers follow the simple rule of thumb, with the remainder being forward-looking utility maximizers. This counts against the interpretation that a certain fraction of the households are liquidity constrained whereas the remainder are not. Lagged changes in disposable income have only a marginal impact on current changes in consumption, indicating that, once the impact of nominal interest rates is taken into account, most households are free to vary consumption in line with changes in their permanent income. However, the persistent importance of nominal interest rates in the equations points to a source of liquidity constraints on households, even if it does not persuade them to follow the rule of thumb.

This result may appear at first sight to be quite surprising since financial deregulation resulted in a big increase of credit demand in New Zealand. Private sector credit almost doubled from 1984 to 1986 and grew another 20% in 1987. However, one needs to bear in mind that part of this explosion simply reflects reintermediation in which the main financial groups regained market share previously lost under market regulation. This is particularly true for the "private-to-private" mortgage market facilitated through solicitors (see Ord Minnett Securities- NZ-Ltd. 1991). It is also possible that other factors, such as the equity and real estate crisis or the rise in unemployment, have worked to offset the effects of financial deregulation on λ. Finally, it is possible

Table 7.8 Seasonally adjusted data, 1975:1–1990:3

Model: $\Delta C_t = \mu + (\lambda_0 + \lambda_1 * Dummy) * [\alpha \Delta Y_t + (1-\alpha) \Delta Y_{t-1}] + \theta_1 \Delta i_1 + \theta_2 \Delta C_{t-1}$
$+ \theta_3 (C-Y)_{t-1}$

λ_0		λ_1		α		$\Delta_4 i$		ΔC_{t-1}		$(C-Y)_{t-1}$		R^2
-0.3	(1.4)	0.65	(1.5)	.0623	(3.1)	-0.002	(2.0)	-0.41	(3.6)	0.010	(0.2)	0.185
-0.97	(1.1)	0.010*	(1.0)	0.53	(1.5)	-0.002	(2.0)	-0.38	(3.3)	0.002	(0.1)	0.181
0.008	(.04)	-		7.04	(0.1)	-0.002	(1.9)	-0.37	(3.1)	-0.012	(0.3)	0.145
0.04	(0.2)	0.18	(0.6)	1	(-)	-0.002	(1.9)	-0.38	(3.2)	-0.02	(0.2)	0.138
0.166	(0.8)	0.164	(0.5)	1	(-)	-0.001	(1.3)	-		-0.02	(0.5)	-0.004

* Indicates coefficient estimate of time, not shift dummy variable.

t-values in brackets.

that the use of a model that treats the preferences of consumers for nondurable goods and services as separable from the service flows of durable goods including housing will understate the significance of liquidity constraints and will not fully account for the impact of financial deregulation on households' access to credit.

7.7   Asset-price volatility

Financial deregulation increases the flexibility of the market, which allows investors to move more freely to their desired positions, thus reducing transaction costs through the increase in competition. It also improves the efficiency of resource allocation through the greater effectiveness of the process of financial intermediation (Hunn et al. 1989). The removal of financial controls and the more flexible operation of the market tends also to increase the volatility of asset prices. This is expected to increase the number of transactions investors undertake to cover their risk, thereby increasing their costs. Higher asset-market volatility may also be associated with a negative influence on investment and hence growth. And protracted periods of high volatility may interfere with the financial markets' clearing and settlement activity, causing a loss of investor confidence and thus reducing market participation and liquidity when it is most needed (Kupiec 1991). In addition, excessive volatility increases required rates of return, and thus lowers asset values and increases the cost of capital.

High exchange-rate volatility interferes with business marketing and planning decisions. It increases the amount of resources businesses need to spend on minimizing exchange-rate risk, thereby leading to a lower level of participation in both export and import activities. It facilitates unnecessary movements of resources between the tradeable and nontradeable goods sectors of the economy. Further, high exchange rate or interest-rate volatility restrains the ability of policymakers to pursue effectively a policy of constraining inflation with a narrow inflation band.

In the period immediately following the float of the exchange rate, the Reserve Bank operated a policy that allowed substantial interest rate volatility, with open market operations only undertaken when liquidity projections indicated large movements in cash balances (Spencer 1990). The Reserve Bank's interest in reducing fluctuations in exchange rates and interest rates was greatly raised in 1988 when the price-stability policy was more closely defined. This section pre-

Table 7.9 *Averages and volatilities of stocks, bonds, and the exchange rate*

	Monthly averages		Volatilities
		Stock Returns	
1960-69	.69%		2.32%
1970-79	.09		2.90
1980-84	2.35		3.65
1985-91:1	-.07		5.59
		5 Year bond yields	
1962-69	5.13%		.12%
1970-79	8.50		.22
1980-84	14.65		.56
1985-91:9	13,31		.40
1980:1-1984:6	11.98%		.34%
1984:7-1988:2	17.03		.74
1988:3-1991:9	12.31		.32
		TWI Changes	
1985:3-1988:2	.41%		1.69%
1988:3-1991:9	-.26		1.71

sents historical movements in financial market volatilities and also investigates the effects of the volatility on the real economy through its influence on investors' expectations.[8]

Table 7.9 reports monthly average levels of stock-index returns and their volatilities for different periods. The trend is for stock return volatility to increase over time. There is also evidence that stock return volatility is higher during the period of the floating exchange rate. This period includes the two 1987 share market crashes. The table also reports monthly averages of bond yields and their volatilities. A first examination of the results suggests that the period of financial deregulation and floating exchange rate (1985–91) is characterized by lower volatility than the first half of the 1980s. A closer examination, however, reveals that the period from the deregulation up to the time of the more formal adoption of the price stability goal in March 1988 is actually the period characterized by the highest interest-rate volatility.

Results for exchange-rate return volatility are also presented there.

Table 7.10 *Investor confidence equations, 1968:2–1991:2*

Dependent variable	Stock return	Volatility	R^2
Expected profits	.542	-2.680	.49
	(2.248)	(3.273)	
Business Confidence	2.045	-5.891	.65
	(4.268)	(2.774)	
Investment Intentions	.460	-3.229	.75
	(2.380)	(2.687)	

t-values in brackets.

It is interesting that there is no significant volatility change after March 1988, when a period of greater general price stability commenced. This is probably attributed to significant increases in exchange-rate volatility in recent months associated with the easing in monetary conditions and the substantial progress toward price stability.

Financial market volatility may have indirect effects on the real economy through its effects on consumer and investor expectations. Increased financial market volatility could induce a loss of consumer or investor confidence and indirectly affect real consumption and investment decisions. Table 7.10 reports the results of regressions of the New Zealand Institute of Economic Research surveys of business confidence, investment intentions, and profit expectations on stock market returns and return volatility, using quarterly data for the 1968:2 to 1991:2 period. The estimates have been obtained with a correction for first-order serial correlation. The results indicate that in all cases there is a strong link between financial market volatility and investors' confidence. This finding has important implications for the analysis of financial shocks on the real sector of the economy under a policy of disinflation that is presented in the next section.

7.8   The share market crash

Up until the share market crashes of 1987 the New Zealand economy had followed a relatively smooth process of transition from a highly regulated to a market-driven economy. This process of transition was not painless. The time of the liberalization coincided with high inflation and rising foreign debt. The combination of rising interest rates, a strong exchange rate, falling export prices, and a weak export sector had a negative effect on borrowers' net worth, forcing up the premium for external finance, which is an important deterrent to economic growth (see Gertler and Rose, Chapter 2 of this book). The booming equity and real estate markets helped cushion borrowers against adverse economic shocks and helped smooth the adjustment of the economy. They also helped maintain the strong level of aggregate demand that took most of the pressures off the exposed parts of the manufacturing sector – pressures resulting from reduced rates of import protection and the strong exchange rate.

The world stock market crash of October 1987 was preceded in New Zealand by another major downfall (of 10%) in May of the same year. The May fall appears to be largely associated with the rise in interest rates following a tightening of monetary conditions in late 1986 (interest rates rose steadily from October 1986 and then sharply further in April–May 1987). The stock market reached a low in June 1987 and then reached a new all-time high in September before it crashed. It then carried on falling (unlike other world markets), not reaching a low before 1990.

The October fall (47%) was one of the most severe among the world financial markets. The main reason for the severity of the New Zealand crash was the high-geared, interconnected nature of many of the large listed companies. A large number of new investment companies appeared in the 1984–6 period (they made up about one quarter of the top companies in the New Zealand stock market). These companies reported high profits only by asset trading, which was profitable in a rising market. They were high-geared, with most of their assets being investments in other listed companies. The degree of high exposure was thus the critical factor of this major downturn.

In the postcrash period the situation changed dramatically from that which prevailed during the first three years of the reforms. The vulnerability of the investment and financial markets soon spread to the property markets. The weakening state of the economy added to the manufacturing sector's problems arising from increased foreign competition and continuing low returns in export markets. Falling profitability and increasing risk aversion on the part of both manufacturers and financial institutions created an environment of extreme business caution. Loss of business confidence and an increased level of restructuring led manufacturers to reduce employment well in excess of output. The Reserve Bank and the government did not come to the rescue of business failures. Their view was that the majority of business failures were the inevitable result of overambitious balance sheet expansions during the boom period (Spencer 1990). In this respect, the effect of firms' overreaction to deteriorating business conditions may not have been accounted for by the direction of government policy.[9]

The Reserve Bank eased policy somewhat in early November 1987. Yet its major concern was to maintain downward pressure on inflation at a time when progress on disinflation was only just beginning to show through Spencer (1990). In spite of growth in world demand, a downward trend in unit labor costs, and a rise in commodity prices in 1988–9 and their positive effects on the export sector, a prolonged period of recession began in New Zealand.

Equilibrium recessions

Two recent papers, (Frank 1990) and (Caplin and Leahy 1991), provide an interesting theoretical framework for the analysis of recent (post-crash) macroeconomic events in New Zealand. The main policy implication of these models is summarized by Frank (1990):

> Policymakers cannot assume . . . that they can marginally change employment in the economy to ease inflationary pressures, but rather that any deflationary move may well lead, as firms adjust their expectations to a new equilibrium, to a discrete fall in employment – a recession.

Frank considers a model with monopolistic competition, diminishing returns, risk aversion, and multiple equilibria. In this model production is a risky activity. A risk premium is added to the standard marginal cost of production. The size of the risk premium depends upon the state of the economy. In this respect its effect on supply decisions will differ with the state of the economy. If aggregate demand is low, firm profitability will in general be low, and the risk premium will be high. The overreaction (due to decreasing relative risk aversion) to an anticipated fall in aggregate demand will cause firms to behave in an extremely cautious manner in their employment decisions, and that will sustain a recession. Similarly, in Caplin and Leahy's approach monetary disturbances have real effects. The impact of these nominal shocks depends critically on the state of the economy. In addition, the fluctuation in output (or employment) can be shown to be accentuated in situations where the coefficient of the output variable in the quantity equation is less than 1, which is precisely the finding reported in Section 7.5.

In summary, it is evident from recent theoretical models that the consequences of financial and monetary shocks on output and employment can be quite significant, especially in economies dominated by risk-averse firms which are price setters. Deregulation and liberalization are not sufficient to generate sustained growth unless they can stimulate sufficient growth in knowledge and investment. This requires a favorable investment environment (in terms of access to finance, low real interest and exchange rates, and, more important, a positive outlook of business conditions). Improvements in business confidence and anticipations of an increase in aggregate demand is the mechanism by which a high level of employment is achieved. Government programs to get the unemployed on the job are also required to ensure that the quality of the human capital is not worsened by long-term unemployment.

7.9   Conclusion

A number of issues arise from the New Zealand experience with financial and other economic reforms. As in other countries, economic reforms in New Zealand were combined with a monetary policy of disinflation. Because disinflationary and reform policies interact, it is very difficult to separate the effects of liberalization on the real sector of the economy from those of monetary tightness. Unlike other countries, New Zealand did not abandon or reverse changes at any stage of the reform process.

New Zealand's experience confirms that under a combined policy of disinflation and liberalization the deregulation of the real goods and labor markets should proceed as rapidly as possible in order to ease policy pressure on the most exposed sectors of the economy (Spencer 1990).

It has been argued that the upward pressure on the exchange rate exerted by the disinflation policy and the slow adjustment of the real goods and labor markets could have been avoided under a different sequencing of reforms. However, political and economic considerations implied that it would have been unwise to delay the opening up of the financial markets and the capital account until after substantial progress had been made in liberalizing trade flows and deregulating the labor market (Spencer and Carey 1988). Indeed, much less progress in total might have been made if advantage had not been taken of the opportunity presented in mid-1984 to liberalize financial markets. Moreover, for a Labor government it might well have proved impossible to have begun the reform program with the labor market.

Even if the real goods and labor markets had been freed up early in the reform program, the inherently slow adjustment in these markets would have unavoidably led to transitional price distortions (Spencer and Carey 1988). Real exchange pressures on the export- and import-competing sectors of the economy would not have been avoided.

It was apparent from the beginning of the reform process that early momentum was necessary to overcome pressures from political groups and special interest groups. The credibility of the overall program relied quite heavily on the ability of the authorities to pursue an effective monetary policy.

In this respect, the long waiting period for the float of the exchange rate in March 1985 following the deregulation of interest rates in July 1984 and the opening of the capital account in December 1984 helped prolong the exchange-rate adjustment period and limited the effectiveness (and credibility) of monetary policy in the early stages of the disinflation program. In addition the excessive focus on primary liquidity in the monetary control mechanism led to high volatility in interest rates. Both seasonal and structural shifts in the demand for primary liquidity meant that primary liquidity was not an appropriate instrument for monetary control (Spencer 1990). In late 1985 the quantity of settlement cash balances – the cash component of PL – became the key instrument for short-term monetary control.

The distortionary effects of the stock market and real estate market shocks could have been lessened if banking supervision had been stricter, especially with respect to large bank exposures before the crash. Increased risk aversion by banks (and other companies) following the 1987–8 financial and real estate market crisis limited investors' access to finance and contributed to the severity and persistence of the economic recession.

Fiscal deficits also affected the economy by applying extra pressure on monetary policy. Fiscal deficits do not always have a negative impact on the economy. In the United States, for instance, expansionary fiscal policies helped the economy to overcome the recessionary pressures of the disinflation policy of the early 1980s and contributed to the strength of the economy throughout the 1980s. However, the effect of fiscal deficits in the New Zealand case has been different. One explanation is the asymmetry between U.S. and New Zealand fiscal policy with respect to movements in the exchange rate. U.S. fiscal deficits have tended to appreciate the U.S. dollar, whereas New Zealand's (like other countries') fiscal deficits have tended to depreciate the domestic currency. To combat the inflationary effects of currency depreciation, the Reserve Bank of New Zealand was forced to apply extra tightness in the economy.

Recent developments in the labor market are expected to ease the pressure from the exposed sectors of the economy and reduce the costs of relative price distortions. The recent national award round gave clear evidence of restraint in the movements of wages which is expected to continue in the near future. The Employment Contracts Act of May 1991 signaled a major change in industrial relations and the expectation for increased flexibility in the labor market.

Progress in trade tariff reductions continues but at a recently announced slower than expected pace. This will further delay improvements in the real goods sector, but it will probably give a psychological boost to the tradeable-goods sector of the economy.

The process of transforming the New Zealand economy is far from complete. Significant progress has been made in achieving the microeconomic conditions necessary to obtain a better resource allocation and monetary conditions for achieving price stability (New Zealand's inflation rate is currently the lowest in the OECD). In this respect, the basic requisites have been put in place to allow for increased productivity, increased international competitiveness, and investment growth, which should eventually lead to real economic growth.

A word of caution: Macroeconomic and structural reform imbalances (e.g., labor market rigidities, slow progress in fiscal consolidation, and the lowering of border protection) mean that rapid output and especially employment growth are unlikely to occur immediately (see the forecasts section of Table 7.1). The severity of the unemployment problem and its social consequences (increases in crime and violence) should not be underestimated. This situation could affect the political sustainability of the reform program and lead to a reversal in policy. Such a temptation should be resisted. At the same time, improvements in human capital and government programs to get the unemployed in the workplace are essential for the viability and success of the economic reform program.

Appendix 7.1: Chronology of reforms

1984:   Increase in import license tendering
              Removal of product price controls begins (two product
              groups removed from price controls)
July   Exchange rate devalued 20%
July–August   Interest-rate controls removed
August   Credit-growth guidelines removed (credit-allocation
              guidelines removed early 1984)

	Reserve Bank begins open market operations in government securities
October	Restrictions on private overseas borrowing removed
November	Restrictions on foreign-owned companies' access to domestic financial markets removed
	Wage and price freeze ends
December	Restrictions on New Zealand residents purchasing foreign exchange for investment purposes removed
	Reserve Bank announces a number of changes in monetary and financial sector policies

1985:

January	Reserve Bank begins paying interest on trading bank settlement account balances
February	Reserve asset ratio requirements on trading banks removed
	Requirements for financial institutions to purchase government securities removed (government servicing its debt through the market at market rates)
March	Exchange rate floated
September	Schedule for tariff reductions and phasing out import licensing announced
1985–6	Relaxation of financial institutions' legislation begins
1986	Import licensing ended
	Reserve Bank Amendment Act enables unlimited increase in the number of banks, at the discretion of the Reserve Bank
	State-owned enterprise (SOE) legislation introduced
	Repayment of subsidized state loans and refinancing at market rates required
	Shift toward indirect taxation with the introduction of GST

1987:

April	Incorporation of SOEs begins (nine corporations formed)
May	New Zealand share market suffers largest one-day fall
October	A record fall on Wall Street: New Zealand market one of the worst affected
December	Sale of state assets begins. The Bank of New Zealand (part sale), New Zealand Steel, Petrocorp, Air New Zealand, Development Finance Corporation (DFC), Rural Bank, Government Printing Office, PostBank, Telecom are among the companies sold between 1987 and 1992

	Start of tariff reduction program to reduce manufacturing tariffs from up to 40% to about 18% by 1992 and to below 10% by 1996
1988:	
June	DFC sold to National Provident Fund and Salomon Bros
1989:	
May	Reserve Bank (price stability) Bill introduced
October	DFC statutory managers appointed
October	Bank of New Zealand announces provision for bad debts
	Government and Fay, Richwhite inject capital
December	Reserve Bank Act passed to become effective February 1990
1991:	
May	Employment Contracts Act passed

Appendix 7.2

The basic permanent income hypothesis assumes that the change in consumption equals the change in permanent income:

$$\Delta C_t = \Delta YP_t$$

In contrast, the model of Campbell and Mankiw assumes that consumption is a weighted average of current and permanent income, with weights λ and $(1-\lambda)$:

$$\Delta C_t = \lambda \Delta Y_t + (1-\lambda)\Delta YP_t$$

They also assume that changes to permanent income cannot be forecast, so

$$\Delta C_t = \lambda \Delta Y_t + (1-\lambda)\epsilon_t$$

Where ϵ_t is white noise. The preceding equations have been derived from the basic permanent-income model using the assumption that the real interest rate is constant. However, a rise in the real interest rate is expected to affect consumption by shifting more of the consumption into the future. To take account of this effect Campbell and Mankiw add the real interest rate to the equation. This gives a basic equation to estimate:

$$\Delta C_t = \mu + \lambda \Delta Y_t + \Theta r_t + \epsilon_t$$

They also try the alternative of using a weighted average of current and lagged changes in income in case consumers take account of last

period's income as well as today's. That is, the term $\alpha\Delta Y_t +$
$(1-\alpha)\Delta Y_{t-1}$ is used in place of ΔY_t. As tests of model misspecification
several other variables are added. Changes in nominal interest rates
are added as a further source of liquidity constraints, as consumers
who face an upper limit on the ratio of their nominal debt servicing to
their nominal income must cut back consumption when nominal interest rates rise (Wilcox 1989). Because consumption and income are
cointegrated an error correction term $(C - Y)$ is also included in the
model. Finally, the model is modified to include a shift dummy or
time variable to test whether the proportion of liquidity constrained
consumers has dropped since deregulation.

Because the real interest rate and the change in disposable income
may be correlated with the error term, the model is estimated using
instrumental variables. Also, the model is estimated with both seasonally adjusted and seasonally unadjusted data. The seasonal adjustment
method is the X11 procedure in SAS.

As in Campbell and Mankiw (1991), all instruments are lagged at
least two periods. There are two reasons for this. First, this procedure
overcomes the first-order serial correlation problem associated with
the use of time-averaged data, data that may be subject to measurement errors, or data classified as nondurable consumption although
they may be subject to durability. The second reason for using at least
a two-period lag is that delays in the publication of aggregate data
mean that consumers may know their own consumption and income
but not the aggregate numbers. If so, the aggregates are not valid instruments.

The income variable is real quarterly disposable income. Consumption is the sum of consumption of nondurables and services. Both
consumption and income are divided by the total population, and are
estimated in logs. The nominal interest rate is the nominal 90-day
interest rate, the real interest rate is the real short-term interest rate
(which is the nominal short-term rate less the rate of producer price
index-output inflation). Also used are registered unemployment (divided by the population), the nominal wage rate, and real exports of
goods (over the population). The sample is 1975:1 to 1990:3.

For the seasonally unadjusted data, the instruments used are lagged
changes in income (lag 4), lagged changes in consumption (lag 4), and
lagged changes in the unemployment rate (lags 4–7). (All changes
when dealing with unadjusted data are annual changes.) Together
these gave an adjusted R^2 of only 7% in explaining growth in disposable income.

For the seasonally adjusted data, the instruments were lagged changes in income (lags 2–4), lagged changes in consumption (lags 2–4), and lagged changes in the unemployment rate (lags 1–4). These instruments explain 6% of disposable income growth.

NOTES

1 The initial discussion draws heavily upon the work of Reserve Bank of New Zealand (1986), Bollard and Buckle (1987), Spencer and Carey (1988), Hunn et al. (1989), and Institute of International Finance (1990), who are the major contributors to the literature on the New Zealand experience thus far.

2 The operation of monetary policy involved a shift away from direct controls over interest rates and toward the targeting of *primary liquidity* (PL). Primary liquidity refers to the liquid reserve base of the financial system – i.e., those assets that are available to the private-sector financial institutions for settlement with the Reserve Bank.

3 The focus of the prudential supervision role of the Reserve Bank is to preserve the stability of the financial system and encourage prudentially sound behavior by individual institutions. It is not to provide government insurance for depositors or to prevent bank failure.

4 In inflation- and cyclically adjusted terms, the government was actually able to run a small surplus in the years 1987–8 to 1989–90.

5 Fiscal policy over the years 1987 until mid-1990 was probably a source of significant upward pressure on real interest rates or the real exchange rate. Success in monetary and fiscal policy was mutually reinforcing, and the domestic and overseas credibility of the reform and stabilization programs grew during this period. However, the outcome of the 1990 budget was a source of considerable disappointment to the financial markets, as a lot of ground was lost, not only in terms of balancing the fiscal position but also in terms of lost credibility for the direction of the reform program. As a result, pressure came on interest rates and the exchange rate, and prospects for a sustained recovery in investment and growth were set back.

6 Cointegration analysis is performed using the Johansen (1988) maximum-likelihood procedure. This analysis is undertaken with a fourth-order model of money, prices, and output. The cointegration and stationarity tests suggest that the logs of all individual time series are nonstationary with a single cointegrating relationship among the money, price, and output series provided that a single deterministic shift variable is included in the model to account for the effects of financial deregulation. These results provide further support to the results reported by Orden and Fisher (1990).

7 It is worth pointing out that Orden and Fisher (1990) could only establish a cointegrating relationship between the smoothed money, prices, and output series but not the adjusted series with the seasonal constants. The difference in the results is that their sample was smaller (1965–89), the GDP series they used is not the recently revised series, and the shift variable in their study was defined to start at 1984:1 not 1984:3.

8 The data used for the volatility analysis consists of monthly observations on stock prices, five-year government bond yields, and the trade-weighted exchange-rate index (TWI) of the New Zealand dollar. Monthly estimates of asset-return volatility are calculated using the Schwert (1989) volatility estimator. The Schwert volatility estimator is calculated by first regressing monthly returns on monthly dummy variables and 12 lagged return values. The absolute values of the estimated residuals from this regression are then regressed on monthly dummy variables and 12 lagged values of

the transformed residuals. The predicted values from the second step regression scaled by a constant (1.2533 under the assumption of monthly returns normality) are then estimates of the standard deviation of monthly returns.

9 Firm overreaction to falling aggregate demand can be the result of a change in attitudes towards risk (e.g., the possibility of significant bankruptcy costs may lead an otherwise risk-neutral firm to behave in a risk-averse manner (Frank 1990)). In this framework a low-level equilibrium is sustainable. Unlike other countries (e.g., Australia, the United Kingdom), New Zealand did not ease monetary policy immediately after the crash. Note that policy easing is not expected to stimulate the economy in an environment where credit demand exceeds its supply. The price inflation adjustment process was thus a lot faster in New Zealand compared to other countries whose expansionary macroeconomic policies kept them off the disinflation path for more than a year.

CHAPTER 8

Korea's financial reform since the early 1980s

Sang-Woo Nam

8.1   Introduction

The second oil shock in the late 1970s exposed the extreme weakness of the Korean economy. Inflation accelerated, and many heavy and chemical industrial projects suffered from weak export competitiveness, overcapacity, and large operating losses. These economic difficulties were, to a large extent, attributable to extensive government intervention in resource allocation and the ensuing rapid monetary expansion. Against this background, the 1980s saw a series of liberalization programs in many sectors of the economy. Industry-specific incentives were mostly phased out, import restrictions were significantly eased, and substantial progress was made in financial liberalization.

Financial liberalization efforts included the elimination of many administrative controls on banking, privatization of nationwide commercial banks, reduction of entry barriers, and diversification of financial services. Because of these measures, along with the efforts to curb inflation and improve the industrial incentive system, interest rates have been less repressed, financial development has accelerated, and the efficiency of credit allocation has increased. In this course, the Korean financial market did not experience any major instabilities such as bankruptcy of financial intermediaries, undesirable shifts in bank portfolios, a large jump in real interest rates, or destabilizing capital flows. Absence of these side effects often accompanying financial deregulation in other countries, however, does not necessarily mean that Korea's financial liberalization was a success. Financial liberalization in Korea is a very cautious, slow, and still ongoing process. Despite the slow pace of deregulation, rapid growth of non-

184

bank financial institutions has contributed to making Korea's overall financial market much more liberal. In the process of liberalization, Korea has also avoided complications that might result from the opening of the capital account or ownership concentration of major banks.

This chapter describes the background, scope, and sequence of Korea's liberalization policies in the 1980s. Then, in order to examine the effects of financial liberalization, financial market developments are reviewed and compared with the prereform period. As one of the major constraints to financial liberalization in Korea, attention is paid to the accumulation of nonperforming bank loans, government bailout policy and its consequences. Finally, the chapter presents the main features of the Korean financial reform.

8.2   Legacies of the 1970s: The prereform state

By the end of 1970s, the Korean economy was suffering from serious internal and external macroeconomic imbalances. Inflation had accelerated despite extensive price controls and substantial real appreciation of Korea's currency, the *won*. The second oil price shock was a fatal blow to the balance of payments, which had been already deteriorating due to weak exports.

It is not too difficult to trace the sources of these troubles. After the successful takeoff of the economy on the basis of light manufactured exports, Korean policymakers in the early 1970s were concerned about continued export growth. Following the first oil price shock, industrialized nations raised protectionist barriers against light manufactured goods from developing countries. The emergence of China and other second-tier newly industrializing economies (NIEs) was also seen as a serious potential threat to Korea's continued export-led growth. Earlier, in 1971, under the Nixon Doctrine, the United States pulled out one-third of its troops stationed in Korea, leading Koreans to believe that the United States would eventually withdraw altogether.

Government intervention in resource allocation

Under these circumstances, the government believed promoting heavy and chemical industries (HCIs) could kill two birds with one stone by developing indigenous defense industries and restructuring the export composition in favor of more sophisticated and high-value-added industrial goods. The overriding objective of tax, credit, interest-rate, and trade policies in the 1970s was to promote HCIs, including iron and steel, nonferrous metals, shipbuilding, general machinery, chemicals, and electronics.

While tax incentives for exports were actually reduced in the early 1970s, tax incentive policy began to receive increasing emphasis as a means of affecting resource allocation among industries. Trade policy was also geared to protect favored industries by limiting imports of competing goods. For the manufacturing sector as a whole, the import liberalization ratio declined slightly to 40% during the first half of the 1970s before rising to 57% by 1980.[1]

The government used credit allocation through the banking system as its most powerful means of supporting favored industries. In order to finance large-scale investment projects in the HCIs, a National Investment Fund was set up in 1974 by mobilizing public employee pension funds and a substantial share of banking funds. However, as these funds proved insufficient, banks, practically owned by the government, were directed to make loans to "strategic" industries on a preferential basis. During the latter half of the 1970s, the share of policy loans in domestic credit for deposit money banks rose steadily from 40% to a 50% level.[2] A more significant aspect of the policy loans might be interest rate differentials. During the latter half of the 1970s, bank rates for export-related loans and equipment investment loans in key industries averaged 8% and 13%, respectively, compared with 17% for general bank loans and the WPI inflation rate of 16%.

Consequences of intervention

Owing to this strong and concerted support in the tax, trade, and credit policies, almost 80% of all fixed investment in the manufacturing sector during the late 1970s is estimated to have been directed to the HCIs. Such disproportionate incentives together with overoptimistic assumptions regarding world trade prospects led to excessive investment in some areas. In order to correct the situation, in 1980 the government had to intervene and coordinate negotiations among participating firms for relinquishing some projects or reducing their capacity.

In addition to investment inefficiency, the HCI promotion policy gave rise to serious sectoral imbalances and complications in macroeconomic management. First, as the government-favored HCI projects preempted limited financial resources, credit to other industries was unduly squeezed. Moreover, because of the huge capital requirement and weak business position of small and medium-sized firms, the new

HCI projects were "granted" to large business groups, contributing to the serious concentration of economic power.

Furthermore, due to credit expansion to the HCIs as well as the boom in Middle Eastern construction activity, the latter half of the 1970s saw a rapid growth in the money supply. Inflationary pressure was aggravated further by the sectoral imbalance in the allocation of resources. Not only did inflation accelerate, but speculation in real assets was rampant. It became increasingly evident that the growth potential of the economy was being wasted as the nation's entrepreneurial talent and other valuable resources were drawn out of socially productive activities. Accelerating inflation made financial savings unattractive because real interest rates remained low. With the subsequent disintermediation and stagnation of the financial sector, small and medium-sized firms became pinched for funds and the informal money market grew.

8.3   Economic liberalization in the 1980s

Dealing with internal and external macroeconomic imbalances in the early 1980s

The second oil price shock in 1979 exposed Korea's striking macroeconomic imbalances (Table 8.1). With the overvalued exchange rate, fixed to the U.S. dollar from 1975–9 despite a large disparity in inflation rate, exports in real terms in 1979 recorded negative growth. Faced with both high inflation and widening deficits in the balance of payments, Korea chose to tackle the problem of external imbalance by depreciating the exchange rate by 20% and by adopting a flexible exchange-rate system in early 1980. This did not mean that curbing inflation was given a lower policy priority. On the contrary, in the spring of 1979, prior to the second oil price shock, Korea had already adopted a comprehensive stabilization package comprising restrictive fiscal and monetary policies together with investment adjustment in heavy industries.

In the early 1980s, top priority in economic policies was given to fighting inflation. Fears that restrictive demand management, relying on monetary and fiscal policies alone, would be overly depressive, led the government to use income policy as well. Such policies included setting informal wage guidelines, stabilizing government purchase prices of major grains, and controlling interest rates and dividend payouts. Realistic exchange-rate management had a favorable effect,

Table 8.1 *Major macroeconomic trends*

	71-73	74-75	76-78	79-81	82-85	86-88	89-90
GNP Growth (%)	8.9	7.3	10.9	3.0	9.0	12.6	7.9
Current Account Balance (US$	-0.5	-2.0	-0.5	-4.7	-1.6	9.5	1.4
billion)							
CPI Inflation (%)	9.5	24.8	13.2	22.8	3.8	4.3	7.2
Wage Increase (%)	14.8	30.7	34.2	24.1	11.1	11.3	20.0
Exchange Rate	398	484	484	701	890	684	716.4
(won/$, period-end)							
M2 Growth	30.1	27.6	35.1	36.7	17.4	18.1	19.8
(%, year-average)							
Unified Budget Balance	-2.8	-4.3	-2.7	-3.1	-1.8	0.6	-0.5
(% of GNP)							

reducing the current account deficit from an average of $4.7 billion per year during 1979–81 to $2.6 billion in 1982. At the same time, consumer price inflation dropped substantially from an annual rate of 25% during 1980–1 to 7% in 1982.

Process of economic liberalization

There is no denying that economic liberalization increases efficiency by promoting competition and eliminating distortions in the allocation of resources. After the problems caused by the government's overzealous promotion of HCIs in the 1970s, Korean policymakers strongly felt the need for trade and financial reforms as well as the realignment of other industrial incentives.

Realignment of industrial incentive system

In the early 1980s, promotion of strategic industries with preferential credit and tax treatment gave way to a more indirect and functional support of industries. The tax reform of 1981 substantially reduced the scope of special tax treatment for key industries, keeping 100% special depreciation as the only available option required for most beneficiaries. In order to further streamline the industrial incentive system, the Industrial Development Law became effective in July 1986. The Law replaced existing individual industry promotion laws, and defined how the government might intervene for industrial rationalization in areas where market failure occurred.[3]

One such area comprises industrial sectors whose international competitiveness is vital to the economy yet not expected when left to the market. In this case, the government encourages specialization through indirect incentives designed to promote technological advancement. The other area is declining industries, for which the government may intervene in the phasing-out process. In this selective intervention, minimizing government discretion and seeking wide consensus are considered critical. Thus, deliberations of the Industrial Development Deliberative Council play an important role in formulating a rationalization program. Under the law, eight industries have been designated for rationalization for two or three years.[4] The rationalization packages included subsidized credit for upgrading capital equipment, mergers, barring entries, and long-term supply contracts.

It was not until 1983, when Korea had nearly corrected the severe external imbalance caused by the second oil shock, that a serious import liberalization program for 1984–8 was adopted. With the completion of the five-year liberalization program, the import liberalization ratio has steadily risen to over 95% from 80% in 1983.[5] Together with reduced quantitative import restrictions, the average nominal tariff rate has been gradually lowered from 24% in 1983 to 18% in 1988 and 13% in 1989. By 1993, tariffs on industrial products are slated to be brought down to 6.2% through annual cuts. As for agricultural products, import restrictions covering 28% of all agricultural products in 1989 are to be reduced to 15% by 1991, and tariffs will also be lowered from 21% in 1989 to 17% by 1993.

Import liberalization has not caused any major industrial dislocations so far. This might be explained by the policy of providing advance notice and liberalizing first the items in which Korea has a competitive edge. Korean firms have yet to be seriously affected as the liberalization of the least competitive products coincides with the appreciation of the won and large wage hikes. On the other hand, there are indications that Korean firms have responded to import liberalization with stronger efforts for technological development, quality improvement and the deepening of vertical intraindustry international specialization.

Opening of capital account

In Korea capital flows in and out of the country have been tightly controlled. It has resulted from concern about capital flight, monetary expansion, and inefficient use of foreign borrowing and foreign exchange. Foreign capital has been introduced, but only under strict government guidelines with a view toward maximizing the efficiency of foreign borrowing in both its cost and use. For nonfinancial private corporations, foreign borrowing has mainly been confined to financing imports of capital goods and raw materials, while that of financial intermediaries has been primarily restricted to funds for relending to firms in foreign currencies.

Because of current account surpluses in the latter half of the 1980s, Korea has gradually relaxed controls on capital outflows. At the same time, the fear of massive capital inflows attracted by relatively high domestic real interest rates and anticipated appreciation of foreign exchange has prompted the authorities to tighten controls on capital inflows. In the absence of market-determined interest and exchange rates, balancing the demand and supply of funds and foreign exchange, only discretionary controls could prevent excessive capital flows in one direction.

Process of domestic financial liberalization

Financial liberalization efforts started with the lifting of many restrictions on bank management in order to promote competition and efficiency. Detailed regulations governing the organizational, budgetary, branching, and business practices of banks, not furthering prudential supervision, were relaxed. More significantly, between 1981 and 1983, the government divested its equity shares in all nationwide city banks, transferring ownership to private hands.

In order to promote competition in the financial market, entry barriers were lowered. Financial services provided by different intermediaries were diversified and made increasingly to overlap.[6] Two additional nationwide city banks were opened in 1982 and 1983, and many short-term finance companies and mutual savings and finance companies were established. Entry barriers into financial markets were further lowered during 1988–9, when the government approved establishment of many new financial institutions mostly outside Seoul. They include commercial banks specializing in small and medium-sized firms, securities investment companies, leasing companies, and life insurance companies.

Progress has also been made in the area of monetary and credit management. By June 1982 most preferential interest rates applying to various policy loans were abolished, making it easier to scale down policy loans. The relative share of policy loans has declined since the authorities have reduced the National Investment Fund (NIF) and, more recently, automatic short-term export credit. Another significant step taken in early 1984 was to allow financial intermediaries, within a given range, to determine their own lending rates according to the creditworthiness of borrowers. The range of lending rates initially started at 0.5 percentage point but later widened to 1.5 percentage points.

With controlled interest rates, financial development is critically limited. Fortunately, the changing economic environment was believed to provide favorable conditions for interest rate deregulation in Korea. First, low and stable inflation since 1983 and high national savings in excess of domestic investment have narrowed the disparity between regulated and free market rates. Second, with successful industrialization leading to the recent current account surpluses, Korean industries were generally believed to be competitive enough to remain strong without the effective subsidies of interest rate controls.

Third, as Korea allows freer external capital flows, such flows would undermine domestic monetary stability more seriously in the presence of interest rate controls. Freer international capital transactions mean that Korean interest rates will be more closely related to international rates through the market mechanism. Finally, as wages increase with the growing strength and number of labor unions, continued interest rate controls could mean relative underpricing of capital, which would wrongly encourage capital-intensive technologies.

Against this background, most bank and nonbank lending rates and some long-term deposit rates were decontrolled in December 1988. Deregulated interest rates or yields also include those on financial debentures, corporate bonds, asset management accounts and funds, and such money market instruments as commercial paper (CP), certificates of deposit (CDs), and large repurchase agreements (RPs). Rates on some policy loans were not deregulated, and short-term deposit rates are still controlled for fear of excessive competition among financial intermediaries. To prevent any massive transfer of funds to liberalized financial assets, restrictions were imposed in the form of a minimum transaction unit (CP) and ceilings on the handling of some businesses (CDs and asset-management accounts and funds).

The results of interest rate deregulation have so far fallen short of expectations. Bank lending rates and most rates in the primary

Table 8.2 Regulated and market interest rates

	Regulated Rates		Market Rates		Average Borrowing Cost[1] (manufacturing)	Consumer Inflation Rate	Real GNP Growth	M2 Growth Rate
	Bank 1-Year Time Dep.	General Bank Loans	Corp. Bond Yield	Curb Rate				
1970	22.8	24.0	-	49.8	14.7	15.4	7.6	-
1975	15.0	15.5	20.1	41.3	11.3	25.4	6.4	27.0
1976	15.5	16.5	20.4	40.5	11.9	15.3	13.1	29.2
1977	15.8	17.3	20.1	38.1	13.1	10.0	9.8	37.0
1978	16.7	17.7	21.1	41.2	12.4	14.5	9.8	39.3
1979	18.6	19.0	26.7	42.4	14.4	18.2	7.2	26.8
1980	22.7	23.4	30.1	44.9	18.7	28.7	-3.7	25.8
1981	19.3	19.8	24.4	35.3	18.4	21.6	5.9	27.4
1982	10.9	12.5	17.3	30.6	16.0	7.1	7.2	28.1
1983	8.0	10.0	14.2	25.8	13.6	3.4	12.6	19.5
1984	9.1	10.6	14.1	24.8	14.4	2.3	9.3	10.7
1985	10.0	11.5	14.2	24.0	13.4	2.5	7.0	11.8
1986	10.0	11.5	12.8	23.1	12.5	2.8	12.9	16.8
1987	10.0	11.5	12.8	23.0	12.5	3.0	13.0	18.8
1988	10.0	11.5	14.5	22.7	13.0	7.1	12.4	18.8
1989	10.0	11.5	15.2	19.1	13.6	5.7	6.8	18.4
1990	10.0	11.5	16.4	18.7	12.7	8.6	9.0	21.2
June 1991	10.0	11.5	18.6	-	-	10.1	-	18.4

Note 1) Calculated by dividing interest payments of the year by the average outstanding of borrowings including corporate bonds.
Sources: Bank of Korea. *Monthly Bulletin* and *Financial Statements Analysis*, various issues.

securities market are still very rigid and unresponsive to market conditions, indicating that the Korean financial market is still far from being fully integrated and operating purely on a competitive basis. Concerned with a drastic rise of interest rates, the government has also given a tacit consent to, and even encouraged, collusion on interest rates by financial institutions. In many of the primary securities markets, the issuing rates have deviated from the market rates, resulting in various irregularities associated with the underwriting and underdevelopment of secondary markets.

8.4   Effects of financial liberalization

Interest-rate movements

Regulated interest rates

The bank deposit (one-year time deposit) interest rate in the latter half of the 1970s was mostly negative in real terms (Table 8.2). Despite high nominal interest rates (20–21% on the average) on one-year time deposits and on general bank loans, real interest rates (using the consumer price inflation rate) were about 2% negative on the average during 1979–81. As inflation slowed dramatically thereafter, interest rates became significantly positive. During 1984–7, the real interest rate on one-year time deposits ranged between 7% and 8% and that on general bank loans between 8% and 9%. With accelerated inflation and rigid official rates during 1988–90, average real rates dropped to a 3–4% level. It is noteworthy that nominal bank deposit rates did not change at all in spite of deregulation of lending rates effective in December 1988.

Market-determined rates

Corporate bond yields determined in the secondary market were 3–5% points higher than the general bank loan rate during 1975–8. The rate difference rose to 7–8% points during the second oil shock of 1979–80, before it dropped steadily to 1–2% points by 1986–7. With accelerated inflation thereafter, the gap widened again to 5% points by 1990. The average real bond yield, which stood at 7.6% during 1976–9, rose to 10.7% during 1982–7 when inflation decelerated significantly, but returned to 8.3% during 1988–90.

Another market interest rate is the curb loan rate that is typically applied to discounting corporate bills by individual money lenders.

The rate is fairly high because the borrowers are usually not sufficiently creditworthy to have an easy access to organized financial markets and because of other risk factors derived from the illegal nature of the transaction. Compared with corporate bond yield, the curb loan rate was about 20 percentage points higher during 1975–8. The gap dropped to 15 percentage points during 1979–80 and stabilized within a range of 10–13 percentage points during 1981–7. Thereafter, the gap narrowed sharply to a 2 percentage point level by 1990. The real curb rate has also showed a steady drop, falling on average from 26% during 1976–9 to 10% by 1990.

Average borrowing cost

The weighted average borrowing cost of corporations may be lower than the general bank loan rate because of policy loans extended at subsidized rates. Actually, during 1975–80, the average borrowing cost for manufacturing firms was 4–5 percentage points lower than the general bank loan rate (Table 8.3). However, the situation turned around quickly. During 1982–4, the average borrowing cost of manufacturing firms were 3–4 percentage points higher than the general bank loan rate (and 1–2 percentage points higher during the latter half of the 1980s). This development resulted mainly from the elimination of preferential interest rates given to policy loans, fast growth of nonbank financial institutions whose interest rates are generally higher than bank rates, and time lags between bank rate changes and the adjustment of other rates applied to existing as well as new liabilities of firms.

Growth of financial markets

Financial development more or less stagnated during the 1970s due to the negative interest rates throughout most of the period as a result of the two oil shocks (Table 8.4). The M2/GNP ratio, which stood at 32% in 1970, remained the same 10 years later. During the 1980s, the ratio rose from 32% to 41% thanks to the deceleration of inflation and the resulting positive real interest rates on deposits since 1982. However, the growth of M2, the major monetary target, has been constrained by the restrictive monetary policy particularly during the first half of the 1980s and introduction of new financial assets such as CP, RPs, variants of trust deposits, and CDs (which are not part of M2).

The ratios of M3/GNP and domestic financial assets/GNP thus grew much faster. This rapid growth of nonbank financial intermediaries can

Table 8.3 *Average cost of borrowing by manufacturing sector*[1]

	1974	1975	1976	1977	1978	1979	1980	1981	1982	1983	1984	1985	1986	1987	1988	1989	1990
Total Manufacturing	10.5	11.3	11.9	13.1	12.4	14.4	18.7	18.4	16.0	13.6	14.4	13.4	12.5	12.5	13.0	13.6	12.7
Large Firms (A)	10.5	11.2	11.8	11.9	11.9	14.4	18.4	18.3	16.1	13.7	14.5	13.3	12.3	12.1	12.7	13.4	12.3
Small Firms (B)	11.4	13.9	14.4	13.8	15.6	14.2	20.7	18.8	15.4	13.0	14.1	14.4	14.0	14.3	14.1	14.5	14.4
(B)-(A)	0.9	2.7	2.6	1.9	3.6	-0.3	2.3	0.5	-0.7	-0.8	-0.3	1.1	1.8	2.1	1.4	1.1	2.1
Export Sector (C)	9.8	9.8	11.3	12.9	12.7	15.7	16.0	15.8	13.6	12.4	12.9	13.0	11.4	11.4	12.4	14.1	12.6
Domestic Sector (D)	10.9	12.6	12.3	13.2	12.3	13.8	21.0	20.4	17.6	14.4	15.2	13.6	13.3	13.4	13.4	13.4	12.8
(D)-(C)	1.1	2.8	0.9	0.4	-0.4	-1.9	5.0	4.6	4.0	2.0	2.3	0.6	1.9	2.0	1.0	-0.7	0.2
Heavy Industry (E)	10.4	10.2	10.1	11.5	10.1	12.5	17.6	17.5	15.3	12.9	14.4	12.7	12.0	12.1	12.7	13.5	12.5
Light Industry (F)	10.6	12.2	13.7	14.3	15.9	16.6	20.1	19.6	16.9	14.6	14.5	14.8	13.5	13.4	13.6	13.8	13.1
(F)-(E)	0.2	1.9	3.6	2.8	5.8	4.1	2.5	2.2	1.6	1.7	0.1	2.0	1.6	1.3	0.9	0.2	0.5

Note: (1) The interest paid plus the discount, divided by total borrowing, which includes all sources, i.e., bank, NBFI, bond, foreign, etc.
Source: Bank of Korea, *Financial Statement Analysis* (various issues).

Table 8.4 *Trend of financial deepening*

	M2/GNP	M3/GNP	Domestic Financial Assets/GNP	National Savings Rate (%)
1970	0.32	0.37 ('71)	2.12	18.0
1975	0.31	0.39	2.17	18.2
1976	0.30	0.38	2.05	24.3
1977	0.33	0.42	2.12	27.6
1978	0.33	0.43	2.14	29.7
1979	0.32	0.43	2.16	28.4
1980	0.34	0.49	2.40	23.1
1981	0.34	0.51	2.57	22.7
1982	0.38	0.59	2.90	24.2
1983	0.37	0.61	2.94	27.6
1984	0.35	0.65	3.09	29.4
1985	0.37	0.70	3.28	29.1
1986	0.37	0.78	3.31	32.8
1987	0.38	0.87	3.51	36.2
1988	0.39	0.94	3.59	38.1
1989	0.41	1.06	4.10	35.3
1990	0.41	1.15	4.22	35.3

Note: Stock of financial assets is on a year-end basis.
Sources : Bank of Korea, *Monthly Bulletin* and *National Accounts*, various issues.

be explained by lower entry barriers to these markets, introduction of new financial instruments, and more attractive interest rates offered to depositors (often circumventing interest rate controls by the authorities). This favorable environment for the growth of nonbank financial intermediaries can be attributed to the desire of the government to absorb curb market funds and thus maximize the mobilization of financial resources through organized markets. Rapid growth of nonbank financial intermediaries has mainly been represented by short-term finance companies (corporate bills discounted and resold), securities of investment trust companies (sales of beneficial certificates), money in trust offered by banks, life insurance companies (reserves), and deposits in mutual savings and finance companies and mutual credit of agricultural cooperatives.

The role of the securities market in Korea's total financial savings has increased steadily throughout the 1970s and the 1980s. The share of securities issues in the outstanding of total financial assets rose from 13.2% in 1972 to 21.3% in 1979 and to 31.1% in 1989. Although the role of the equity market declined upon entering the 1980s, it was more than compensated by the increasing role of public and financial debentures and corporate bonds. As the stock market recovered strongly in the latter half of the 1980s, this market accounted for more than 13% of total outstanding financial assets during 1988–90.

The ratio of total domestic financial assets to GNP, the broadest

Table 8.5 Composition of financial savings (year-end, % of GDP)

	Bank Time & Savings Deposits Including CDs		Nonbank Deposits	Securities	(Public Debentures)	(Stocks)	(Corporate Bonds)	Inter-sectoral Transactions (-)
1972	70.0	(82.2)¹	22.2	13.2	9.3	3.1	0.8	5.4
1975	60.2	(65.8)	27.6	15.6	5.6	8.1	1.9	3.4
1976	57.7	(63.2)	31.3	18.0	4.6	10.4	3.0	4.2
1977	54.9	(60.1)	30.0	18.7	4.8	9.5	4.4	3.6
1978	53.1	(57.6)	20.0	4.0	9.9	6.1	3.1	
1979	48.9	(53.3)	32.0	21.3	4.2	8.8	8.3	2.3
1980	45.9	(51.5)	37.8	21.8	4.8	7.2	9.8	5.4
1981	44.2	(49.8)	40.8	22.1	5.9	6.3	9.9	7.1
1982	41.4	(46.2)	45.7	24.1	8.1	5.8	10.2	11.2
1983	38.4	(42.6)	47.8	24.8	8.2	5.8	10.8	11.0
1984	36.4	(40.9)	50.7	25.1	8.5	5.8	10.8	12.1
1985	36.3	(42.3)	53.6	24.4	8.5	3.7	12.2	14.3
1986	34.5	(41.3)	56.9	25.0	8.3	5.3	11.4	16.4
1987	32.6	(41.8)	59.0	24.4	7.9	6.1	10.3	16.0
1988	30.2	(41.0)	59.9	26.8	6.8	10.8	9.2	16.9
1989	25.5	(38.4)	59.4	31.1	6.5	15.6	9.0	16.1
1990	25.6	(38.8)	60.3	29.9	6.3	13.3	10.3	15.8
June 1991	25.5	(38.7)	59.7	29.9	6.8	12.3	10.8	15.1

Note: Securities = (Public Debentures) + (Stocks) + (Corporate Bonds).
Note: 1) In the parentheses are bank time and savings deposits including both CDs and money in trust (the latter being formally classified as nonbank deposits).
Source: Ministry of Finance, *Fiscal and Financial Statistics*, various issues.

indicator of financial development, also stagnated during the 1970s, but showed a rapid growth during the 1980s, rising from 2.16 in 1979 to 4.22 in 1990. Significantly positive interest rates, introduction of new financial assets, more extensive network of financial services, development of the securities market, and sustained economic growth during the 1980s all contributed to this rapid financial development. A growing share of savings came to be held outside banking deposits (Table 8.5). Net accumulation of financial assets, however, does not find an exact parallel in the national savings rate. As analyzed by Nam (1989), although positive real interest rates certainly help, the national savings rate is dominated by the growth of income.[7] This is clearly shown by the substantial drop in the national savings rate in the early 1980s and a drastic rebound since 1986.

Korea has experienced a rapid rise in real estate prices, which can raise serious issues for financial development. During 1981–90, land prices rose at the annual rate of 14.1% nationwide, while consumer inflation averaged 6.3%. Whenever real estate prices soared, the government strengthened antispeculation measures, but the efforts usually faded with price stabilization. It was only recently that the government launched an all-out attack on housing and land problems in the midst of acceleration of real estate prices during 1988–90. A comprehensive and progressive land tax together with a new system of land assessment were introduced; new laws are in effect limiting residential land ownership and imposing the development gains charges and the excess land profits tax; and housing supply is substantially increased by relaxing regulations controlling residential construction and developing several new satellite cities around Seoul, which helps trigger reduction in housing prices since mid-1991.

Portfolios of financial intermediaries

Share of policy loans

Autonomy of financial intermediaries in asset portfolio management is one of the key elements of financial liberalization. The ratio of policy (government-directed) loans in total domestic credit may serve as such an indicator. The share of policy loans for deposit money banks, which jumped to over 50% at the end of the 1970s from a 40% level in the mid-1970s, declined back to below 40% in the mid-1980s. The share, however, rose again to a 47.5% level during 1988–90. Since 1987 export financing has been phased out to a large extent, but increased credit to the Korea Development Bank (KDB) and the Export-Import

Bank of Korea (KEXIM) has more than compensated. Policy loans to the agricultural and housing sectors and temporary subsidized credit for facility investment have also contributed to the expansion of policy loans.

The share of policy loans for nonbank financial intermediaries, which declined from over 50% in the mid-1970s to a 45% level at the end of the 1970s, accelerated its decline during the 1980s. By 1990, policy loans of nonbank financial intermediaries accounted for only 12.7% of their domestic credit. This decline mainly reflects the shrinking importance of development institutions among nonbank financial institutions; it contributed to the steady fall in policy loans in the combined domestic credit of both banks and nonbank financial institutions peaked during 1978–9 at about 49%, and has declined steadily to 28% by 1990.

Industrial composition of bank credit

The latter half of the 1970s saw a gradual decline in the share of credit extended by deposit-money banks to the manufacturing sector (Table 8.6). During the 1980s, the shares for both heavy and chemical industries and especially light manufacturing industries declined, notwithstanding the HCIs' greater share of GDP, compared with that of the mid-1970s. The fairly rapid drop in credit share for the manufacturing industry in the first half of the 1980s was matched by increased shares for the services industry during 1981–3 and for the utilities and construction sector during 1984–6. Reflecting growing political pressure to help farmers who are hit hard by the opening of the domestic market, the share of deposit-money bank credit for agriculture, forestry, and fisheries has also increased from 8–9% during 1979–86 to over 10% since 1987.

Share of total financing and financial accumulation by government, business firms and individuals

Financial liberalization since the early 1980s resulted in greater access to credit by individuals at the expense of the business sector. The individuals' share in total financing of the nonfinancial sectors rose steadily from a 12% level during 1978–80 to 31% during 1988–90. Part of this increased credit access for individuals reflects a reduction in government borrowing since 1984. Sustained high economic growth and the subsequent improvement in corporate liquidity during 1987–8 contributed to the easier access to credit by individuals, while strong corporate borrowing needs due to the dull stock market situation and

Table 8.6 *Industrial composition of loans by deposit money banks (%)*

	Agriculture, Forestry and Fisheries	Mining	Manufacturing	(Light Industries)	(Heavy & Chemical)	Utilities and Construction	Services and Other
1970	12.0	1.7	45.8	22.1	23.7	8.2	32.3
1975	10.4	1.2	57.1	30.0	27.1	8.9	22.4
1976	10.3	1.4	57.3	29.2	28.1	8.5	22.5
1977	10.8	1.1	56.6	28.3	28.3	8.3	23.2
1978	10.0	1.2	54.4	26.1	28.3	9.3	25.1
1979	9.1	1.4	54.3	24.2	30.1	11.5	23.7
1980	8.5	1.1	54.1	23.0	31.1	12.4	23.9
1981	8.1	0.8	52.2	21.9	30.3	12.8	26.1
1982	7.6	0.9	47.6	19.4	28.2	10.5	33.4
1983	8.1	0.6	45.5	18.4	27.1	12.4	33.4
1984	8.8	0.6	43.9	17.8	26.1	14.9	31.8
1985	8.5	0.5	43.3	17.2	26.1	16.4	31.3
1986	8.6	0.4	45.8	17.9	27.9	17.0	28.2
1987	10.1	0.3	45.4	17.2	28.2	17.2	27.0
1988	10.6	0.5	44.2	16.5	27.7	17.1	27.6
1989	9.8	0.4	41.4	15.3	26.1	16.8	31.6
1990	10.0	0.4	42.0	14.6	27.4	16.7	30.9

Note: Manufacturing = (Light Industries) + (Heavy and Chemical Industries).
Source: Bank of Korea, *Monthly Bulletin*, various issues.

increasing demand for facility investment amid weakening competitiveness of exports reduced the credit share for individuals from 36% in 1988 to 27% in 1990. The share of total financial accumulation for business firms has also decreased since the early 1980s. The business sector accounted for over 50% of total financial accumulation by the nonfinancial sectors during 1979–80, but the share declined to less than 30% in 1990. It may be explained by the declining share of credit to business firms as well as corporate effort to economize on fund holdings as interest rates on these funds relative to their borrowing cost have become less attractive. Net financing (total financing minus financial accumulation) by the business sector relative to the total financing or financial accumulation of the nonfinancial sectors also dropped in the early 1980s. It fell from 36% during the latter half of the 1970s to below 30% during 1980–3, before showing a slow rising trend until 1988–9, when corporate liquidity improved substantially.

Corporate capital structure

With subsidized credit available, business firms are expected to borrow more than otherwise. Real interest rates may also affect corporate investment and financing decisions. The ratio of net worth to total assets for manufacturing firms ranged between 21% and 21.5% during 1976–9, but declined to a 17–18% level during 1980–1 when the second oil shock brought about a severe recession. The net worth ratio, however, rose to a 22–23% level during 1984–7, and jumped to over 28% by 1989 mainly due to improved corporate liquidity and a boom in the stock market.

Another development during the first half of the 1980s was a shift in the composition of liabilities toward more current liabilities. This weak liability structure has improved somewhat since the mid-1980s. On the other hand, liabilities with subsidy elements are mainly represented by foreign loans and bank borrowings. The share of these loans in total liabilities and net worth has fallen sharply since the early 1980s, declining from an average of over 38% during 1978–81 to 27% during 1987–9. The capital structure of small- and medium-sized manufacturing firms has undergone a similar trend. Their capital structure, however, is still very weak with a high current-liabilities ratio – 55% of total assets – notwithstanding a fairly steady share for bank borrowings.

Maturity structure of bank deposits

Last, the 1980s saw a shortening of the term of bank liabilities; the share of long-term (with maturities of two years and over) deposits in total deposits of deposit-money banks fell drastically from 29.4% in 1979 to 20.5% in 1982, and subsequently has remained rather stable within the range of 21% and 24%. The general tendency of shorter maturity for bank deposits since the early 1980s seems to reflect the increased availability of other financial assets with more attractive returns in the money and capital markets. Demand deposits have averaged just over one third of total deposits for most of the 1980s, despite the introduction of preferential savings deposits.

Efficiency of credit allocation

It is generally believed that the Korea's financial system saw a fair degree of liberalization and integration in the 1980s without much real liberalization of banks. This was possible due to the relatively rapid growth of the more liberalized nonbank financial sector. Nonbank financial intermediaries (NBFIs) have been much less constrained than banks in terms or their expansion and sectoral allocation of credit. They were often allowed to easily circumvent interest-rate ceilings, which were already set at higher levels than those on bank deposits and loans.[8] This differing degree of government control toward banks and toward NBFIs seems to have originated from the differing perceived externalities associated with the failure of financial institutions as well as from the desire to maximize the mobilization of financial resources through organized markets while still retaining some institutions (banks) providing low-cost funds.

Cho and Cole (1992) note that this liberalization and integration of the Korean financial markets in the 1980s was accompanied by a sharp reduction in the spread of borrowing costs across 68 different manufacturing industries. They also observed more equal access to bank loans enjoyed by different sectors of the economy as well as narrower disparities in rates of return across different sectors. They interpret this as an unmistakable indication of a liberalization (and higher efficiency) of credit allocation.[9]

Amsden and Euh (1990), however, argue that a smaller variance in borrowing costs across different industries is not necessarily good and indicative of greater allocative efficiency. The more highly developed the industrial sector, they maintain, the fewer new industries requiring special treatment (preferential loans). Basically, the reduced interindustry variance of borrowing costs is viewed as a result of industrialization, and not necessarily an input into it. They also believe that the policy of promoting heavy and chemical industry was far from being a failure. The share of heavy and chemical products in total exports rose from 24% in 1977 to 54% in a 10-year period, and heavy industry developed as Korea's new leading sector. Meanwhile, the manufacturing sector was observed to account for only a small share of total nonperforming loans, with the share for HCIs being far lower than their share of total outstanding credit. However, the industrial distribution of NPLs provided by Amsden and Euh is hardly a good indicator of investment efficiency by industry. First, as already mentioned, there was major government-initiated investment in 1980 in several HCIs, so many potential problems were addressed early on. Second, their NPL data include only those involved in the government rationalization operation during 1986–8, producing a bias since not all firms with NPLs were rationalized. The 1986–8 industry rationalization was undertaken, in part, as a supplementary measure to the 1984–6 restructuring of the shipping and overseas construction industry. Many other restructured firms were also in declining industries. Third, many inefficient HCI projects launched in the late-1970s must have become viable after 10 or more years, as comparative advantages were to shift toward HCIs with the lapse of time.

These results strongly suggest that cheap capital in the 1970s led to excessive (inefficient) investment in the HCIs. Notwithstanding Amsden and Euh's (1990) argument that government efforts to promote HCIs were not a failure, it seems evident that HCI promotion in the 1970s was pushed too far. As investment in the favored HCIs slowed and wages rose sharply around the end of the 1970s, it appears that other manufacturing industries made vigorous efforts to substitute capital for labor. However, already high wages in these labor-intensive industries together with accumulation of capital stock much faster than value-added growth resulted in relatively low measured capital efficiency during 1979–85.

Nonperforming loans and government bailout policy

The government effort to promote strategic industries in the 1970s produced mixed results. After the second oil shock, some industries, like electronics and passenger cars, grew into leading industries in the 1980s, while some other heavy industries, such as Korea Heavy Industries, shipbuilding, overseas construction, and shipping became seriously ill.

Nonperforming loans of banks have mainly been rooted in government-directed credit allocation at subsidized interest rates. With such government backup, lending banks had little incentive for serious credit evaluation or ex post monitoring. Availability of cheap credit and tax benefits caused many firms to neglect appraising their investment projects. These overly leveraged firms were very vulnerable when the industry experienced recession.

Very often, the government and creditor banks delayed appropriate actions against nonperforming loans, keeping the borrowing firms alive and allowing the NPLs to prolong and snowball. Liquidation of large firms was often out of the question because of concerns over massive unemployment and visible losses to domestic financial institutions which might trigger a chain reaction of defaults and extreme instability in financial markets. There was also concern that such a situation would threaten confidence in domestic firms and financial institutions in the international market, perhaps bringing about requests for early repayment of foreign debts as well as reduced availability of foreign borrowing and a sharp rise in country risk. There were, however, no guidelines concerning the identification of industries eligible for government-initiated restructuring.

As was the case for overseas construction and shipping industries, restructuring (rationalization) programs in Korea typically entailed reduction of the number of firms, with troubled or insolvent firms absorbed by healthier firms. Usually, the debts of absorbed firms were rescheduled and additional credit was even infused.

Because of its central role in initiating and shaping restructuring programs, the government failed to impose market discipline. The government continued to be viewed as an implicit risk partner, since creditor banks were largely excluded from the major restructuring decision making even though they generally had the best information about the prospect of the loans. As bank losses were to be assumed partially by the government, banks had no alternative but to accommodate whatever packages the government came up with. In addition, the banks, which had been under government control for a long time, did not have enough expertise to work out such restructuring programs completely on their own. The uncertainty surrounding the government's continuing role as risk partner failed to eliminate the moral hazard. The restructured firms were reluctant to reduce capacity and tended to pursue risky strategies in anticipation of another government rescue in the case of failure.

Certainly, the government's role as a restructuring promoter with all the tax and financial incentives helped impose on the firms restructuring measures that they otherwise would not be willing or able to undertake. As such, agency problems caused by conflicts of interest between creditors and debtors and the associated cost in the process of prolonged negotiations could be reduced. If the Korean government and banks had reacted more quickly to the problems, cost of restructuring could have been much smaller.

Nevertheless, speediness is not all that counts. The government-imposed industry restructuring in Korea put the major emphasis on mergers rather than industrial exit or conversion, which tended to delay needed adjustments and entail inefficient resource allocation. Furthermore, the troubled firms were mostly taken over by large business groups, contributing to the concentration of economic power. Absence of clear criteria related to takeovers as well as little information made available to the public about the performance of those acquired sick firms has weakened credibility toward government policy on industrial restructuring.

With the second oil shock, several Korean industries suffered severely from declining orders, overcapacity, and financial distress. Thus, the Korean government attempted investment adjustment in 1980 in areas where duplicative and excessive investment was most evident. In the areas of heavy power-generating equipment and heavy construction equipment, through negotiations among participating firms and the government, merger arrangements were worked out. Attendant supports were provided such as blanket orders related to the construction of nuclear power plants, conversion of Korea Development Bank loans into equity investment, and additional bank credit. In motor vehicles, division of labor was agreed among participating firms by product line. In vessel diesel engines, electronic exchangers, heavy electrical equipment, and copper smelting, the government imposed its restructuring program including mergers, acquisitions and designation of product lines, after the 17 involved firms failed to reach any agreement.

During 1984 and 1985, the two major ailing industries, shipping and overseas construction, were rationalized. In the case of shipping, the government imposed its rationalization program, reducing the number of firms from 63 to 17 through mergers, cutting their shipping capacity, and lowering tax and financial burden in this process. By the end of 1985, about 3 trillion won of loan principal and interest owed by shipping companies was rescheduled to be repaid over a 20-year period after a 10-year grace at 3% interest rate per annum. Restructuring of the overseas construction industry was not very successful in spite of financial support including that associated with imports and disposal

Table 8.7 *Financial assistance to 78 restructured firms, 1986–8 (trillion won)*

	Shipping Industry Rationalization (6 firms)[1]	Overseas Construction Rationalization (10 firms)[1]	Others	Total
Grace period for principal repayment	0.8	0.5	0.4	1.6
Long-term loans with interest subsidy	-	-	4.2	4.2
Seed money: loans for loss compensation	-	-	0.5	0.5
Writeoff of principal	-	-	1.0	1.0
Total assistance (principal)	0.8	0.5	6.0	7.3
Total credit by financial institutions	1.8	1.1	6.8	9.8

Note: 1) Includes survivors only, while those merged with other firms are included in 'others.'
Source: Bank of Korea (Bank Supervisory Board).

of idle construction equipment. Only five firms were either merged with financially healthier firms by the persuasion of their main banks or entered into management consignment.

Another round of industry restructuring occurred between 1986 and the first half of 1988 under the guidelines of the Industrial Development Deliberative Council created by the Industrial Development Law. Of the 78 corporations involved, 21 firms were restructured as a supplementary measure to the earlier restructuring of shipping and overseas construction industry. Forty-nine of the remaining 57 firms restructured were those formally designated for rationalization.

In the restructuring process, financial support played a critical role and was provided using grace periods for principal repayment of 5–30 years with normal interest payments, loans with subsidized interest rates (ranging from 2% to 10% per annum) payable over 5–30 years,[10] seed money (loans with interest rate of 10% payable over 10 years following a 10-year grace period, extended to compensate for the estimated loss from acquisition of defaulted firms) and writeoffs of principal (Table 8.7). When a firm was encouraged to take over a sick firm, the guiding principle in working out a package of financial support was that the implicit subsidy should equal the estimated excess of liabilities over assets of the acquired firm.

According to the Bank Supervisory Board, at the end of March

1988, commercial bank loans to firms designated for rationalization (5.3 trillion won) amounted to 11.9% of their total loans. Of the total loans to "rationalization firms," those on which interest was regularly received did not exceed 15%, while those on which interest payments were deferred or reduced accounted for 76%, with the remaining 9% written off.

Between December 1985 and May 1987, the Bank of Korea provided 1.7 trillion won of special credit, carrying a low interest rate of 3% per annum, to banks in order to alleviate their financial burden due to corporate restructuring. Other central bank loans to banks extended in connection with industrial rationalization have usually carried an interest rate of 6%. By the end of 1987, the total central bank credit to commercial banks related to industry rationalization programs reached 3.0 trillion won, which was almost equivalent to the total increase in reserve money during 1985–7. The estimated annual subsidy associated with the central bank credit amounted to 189 billion won, equivalent to 42% of a total annual loss of 451 billion won arising from financial assistance for rationalization.

On the other hand, tax exemptions given to the 1986–8 industry restructuring amounted to 241 billion won. Corporate income tax and acquisition tax (81 billion won) were exempted in connection with the sale of real estate held by the troubled firms and takeovers of such real estate and equity stock. Withholding tax (160 billion won) on presumptive donated income of the acquiring firms was also exempted.

Nonperforming loans and bank profitability

The rate of return on total assets of nationwide commercial banks was relatively high (0.80%) during the second half of the 1970s, when the financial regime had been very repressive. Pyung Joo Kim (1990) ascribes this rather paradoxical phenomenon to large increases in foreign capital inflow during this period (which provided banks with profitable foreign exchange businesses) and to central bank credit associated with policy loans (with its generous interest margin).

A sharp drop in bank profitability since 1981 seems to have been due mainly to a large cut in bank lending rates in June 1982, as well as snowballing NPLs. The rate of return on total assets was as low as 0.20% during 1984–7. Since 1988, however, bank profitability has improved significantly, raising the rate of return to 0.66% in 1989. This improvement in bank profits has been accompanied by a steady drop in the share of NPLs, noticeable increases in the shares of total income

Table 8.8 *Share of NPLs^a and bank profitability,*
1971–89 (%, seven nationwide commercial banks)

	1971-75	1976-80	1981-83	1984-86	1987	1988	1989
Net Profit/ Total Assets	0.44	0.80	0.34	0.20	0.19	0.36	0.66
Share of NPLs^2	1.3	2.4	7.6	10.5	8.4	7.4	5.9

Notes:
  1) Nonperforming loans (NPLs) are defined as those against which actions of collection or other measures are needed, regardless of whether they are secured by collateral (classified as Fixed) or not (Questionable), or are judged to be uncollectible (Estimated Loss).

  2) The figures are the ratio of NPLs to total credit outstanding, including acceptances and guarantees. For 1971-75, the share represents the ratio of narrowly-defined NPLs (classified as Questionable and Estimated Loss) to total loans.
Source:
  Bank of Korea. Quoted from Pyung Joo Kim, "Financial Institutions: Past, Present, and Future," presented at the Honolulu Workshop on Korea's Political Economy, August 6-11, 1990, East-West Center, Hawaii.

by securities holding and miscellaneous operating incomes, including those from trust and credit card businesses, and increased interest on reserve deposits.

It is obvious that the accumulation of NPLs has been one of the major determinants of bank profitability. The share of NPLs in the total credit of seven nationwide commercial banks showed a steep rise from 2.4% during 1976–80 to 10.5% during 1984–6 (Table 8.8). This rise reflects the aggravated industrial situation given the worldwide recession following the second oil shock. The situation was most serious for shipping, overseas construction, shipbuilding, and other heavy and chemical industries, where drastic expansion of supply capacity met shrinking overseas demand.

The impact of the financial burden, incurred by commercial bank support for industry rationalization, on profits was obviously large. In 1987 total uncollected interest for five nationwide commercial banks amounted to 653 billion won, of which 415 billion won, or 64%, came from loans to firms designated for rationalization. Total uncollected interest accounted for as much as 78% of operating profit in 1987, and must be held mainly responsible for the drop in the average deposit/ loan interest margin from 4.4% to 2.3% between 1985 and 1987.

By bringing the long-covered-up NPLs into daylight, thereby writing off some of them, and through the benefits of a favorable external environment, the seven nationwide commercial banks managed to rapidly reduce the share of NPLs from 10.5% in 1986 to 5.9% in 1989.

The stock market boom during 1986–9 enabled the banks to write off some of the NPLs with the funds raised through recapitalization. The accumulated write-offs by commercial banks (except for foreign banks) during 1986–9 amounted to 620 billion won, equivalent to 1.0% of their total credit outstanding. The net worth of the seven nationwide commercial banks grew dramatically from 3.5% of their total assets to 11.0% during the 1987–9 period. This addition to net worth represented 26% of the increase in total assets of these banks during this period. Additional reduction of the NPLs was possible as they were upgraded thanks to a cyclical upturn for some of the rationalized industries and the increase in the price of land offered as collateral.

8.5   Main features of the Korean financial reform

Slow pace of financial liberalization

Despite privatization and the greater managerial autonomy of commercial banks, the banking system is still subject to heavy government intervention. First of all, the government continued to play a role in banking because of the heavy burden of nonperforming loans, for which government intervention in bank lending in the 1970s was held responsible. Many firms were saved from bankruptcy for fear of enormous financial losses to the banking sector and the ensuing social and economic repercussions. The government played a key role in the bailout decisions and helped the banking institutions by providing subsidized central bank credit, exempting capital gains tax on collateral supplied by the troubled firms, limiting competition, and delaying financial deregulation.

Given the deteriorated loan portfolios of Korean banks, drastic financial liberalization could threaten the soundness and safety of banks. Complete interest-rate deregulation, for example, was out of the question, because banks would be in a critically disadvantaged position in competing with nonbank financial intermediaries. In other words, the cost of imprudent government intervention has been paid by continued financial repression as well as consumers and taxpayers. It is, however, an open question whether or not a different approach such as relieving banks of the burden of nonperforming loans and exposing them to vigorous competition was a better solution, if only it were politically feasible.

Second, in the absence of effective tools for indirect monetary control, credit ceilings and other direct controls have been imposed on Korean financial intermediaries. The discount window plays only a limited role, because much of central bank loans are automatic redis-counts of policy loans by the banking sector. Because banks have long suffered from a chronic shortage of reserves, changing the required reserve ratio has generally been difficult and ineffective. Also, open market operations have been constrained by the underdeveloped money market, inadequacy of traded securities, and the absence of a secondary market, all of which are largely attributable to interest rate regulation.[11] An efficient money market will have to be promoted by improving the call market, introducing interbank deposit and bills markets, and fostering specialized money market dealers and brokers.

Third, policy loans by banks still account for almost half of domestic credit. Such loans include credit by development institutions like Korea Development Bank, credit to the housing and agricultural sectors, loans to small and medium-sized firms, and foreign currency loans mainly for capital goods imports. Until commercial banks are freed from the obligation of extending policy loans, financial liberalization necessarily must be limited. Preferential policy loans may be needed in order to complement imperfections of the market, as is the case for risky projects with a long gestation period and anticipated externality to the economy. Subsidized credit may also be provided with social consideration. This obligation, however, is desired to be fulfilled by the government budget rather than commercial banks.

Finally, the major motivation of still regulating most interest rates in Korea is to keep lending rates from rising too high and to avoid any financial panic for business firms whose capital structure is generally very weak. As such, further interest rate deregulation is constrained by the low level of financial development, a legacy of the 1970s. However, prolonged control of interest rates would result in a vicious circle of interest rate regulation and financial retardation. In spite of widening gap between regulated and market interest rates in recent years, bank and other regulated rates have been little adjusted. Because the government hopes to see strong corporate investment, which would accelerate structural adjustment of the Korean industries, it has been reluctant to raise interest rates. The government's desire to borrow cheaply by itself as it issues public debentures must also have affected its interest rate policy.

The consequence of continuing government intervention in asset management, setting interest rates, and limited competition among financial intermediaries has been clear. Korea's financial deepening, measured as the ratio of domestic financial assets to GNP, compares poorly with other countries: The ratio remained at 4.4 for Korea in 1989, while it reached 6.1 for Taiwan and 7.6 for Japan.

Table 8.9 *Level of financial deepening: Korea,*
Taiwan, and Japan (ratio to nominal GNP)

	Broadly-Defined Money (M2)			Domestic Financial Assets		
	Korea	Taiwan	Japan[1]	Korea	Taiwan	Japan
1970	.322	.411	.722	2.12	2.14	3.74
1975	.311	.568	.823	2.17	2.82	4.41
1980	.341	.640	.852	2.39	3.40	4.94
1985	.366	1.047	.980	3.27	3.88	5.99
1989	.416	1.429	1.201	4.40	6.10	7.55

Note: 1) M2 + CD.

Korea's relative performance is far weaker when measured by M2, a more banking-related variable (Table 8.9). Furthermore, operational efficiency of Korean banks is very poor (Table 8.10). In 1990, interest-rate margins between loans and deposits for Korean banks averaged 4.5 percentage points, compared with 1.2 percentage points for Japanese nationwide banks (1989) and 2.4 percentage points for U.S. banks. Labor productivity of Korean banks was roughly one-tenth of Japanese banks' in terms of the size of assets, deposits, or loans per employee.

Rapid growth of nonbank financial intermediaries

Korea used to have a relatively large informal curb market where private short-term funds are invested outside the organized, formal market. In response to the highly dualistic structure of the national financial market, the government froze outstanding curb loans in 1972 and introduced several formal sector nonbank institutions to take the place of the curb market. They include short-term finance companies, mutual savings and finance companies, and credit unions. Even though they were subject to prudential regulation and other operational restrictions, nonbank financial institutions were, in general, allowed to offer relatively attractive interest rates and to operate under more lax regulations so that they might absorb the curb market funds. For one thing, except for development institutions such as Korea Development Bank and KEXIM Bank, they were rarely asked to provide policy loans. Even though a couple of troubled mutual savings and finance companies were taken over by banks, concern over the healthiness of nonbank intermediaries has been minimal.

The short-term finance company's own bills and corporate bills

Table 8.10 Selected statistics on Korean, Japanese, and U.S. bank management

	Return on Assets (%)		Interest Rates (%)			Productivity (million won/emp)			
	Including Trust Account	Excluding Trust Account	Loans	Deposits	Margins	Assets	Deposits	Loans	A/W[1]
Korea (1990)									
5 largest NCBs[2]	0.54	0.68	10.37	6.10	4.27	1325	892	721	-
All NCBs	0.55	0.68	10.48	6.23	4.25	1387	907	733	174
Regional Banks	1.11	1.33	11.94	6.15	5.79	925	679	480	108
All Commercial Banks	0.63	0.77	10.74	6.21	4.53	1285	857	677	160
Japan (1989)									
City Banks	0.22	-	6.13	5.25	0.88	19454	12110	8280	380
Regional Banks	0.23	-	5.21	3.24	1.98	10857	5025	3575	160
Trust Banks	0.33	-	6.39	5.83	0.56	15407	7595	5470	275
All Nationwide Banks	0.23	-	5.89	4.69	1.21	17125	8000	5650	268
U.S.A. (1990)									
9 Money Center Banks	-	0.37	11.19	9.22	1.97				-
Large Banks[3]	-	0.35	9.16	7.43	1.73				-
Medium Banks[4]	-	0.54	9.43	7.00	2.43				-
Small Banks[5]	-	0.80	10.67	6.94	3.73				-
All Banks	-	0.50	9.92	7.54	2.38				64

Notes:
1) A/W: Total Assets/Annual Employment Cost.
2) NCBs: Nationwide commercial banks.
3) Large Banks: More than $5 billion in assets excluding 9 Money Center Banks.
4) Medium Banks: Between $300 million and $5 billion in assets.
5) Small Banks: less than $300 million in assets.

Sources: The Bank of Korea, Bank Supervisory Board, *Bank Management Statistics.*
Ministry of Finance (Japan), *Banking Bureau Annual Financial Report*, 1990.
Federal Reserve Bulletin, July 1991.

Table 8.11 *Interest rate trends of banks and nonbanks (%)*

		Banks			Investment and finance companies (60-90 day bills)	Mutual saving and finance companies
		3-month time deposits	Over 1 year time deposits	Savings deposit	Bills sold without recourse	Mutual Install-ment deposit (15 months)
1974	Dec.	15.0	15.0	n.a.	-	-
1975	Jan.	-	-	n.a.	17.9	-
	Jul.	12.6	-	n.a.	-	-
1976	Aug.	15.0	16.2	n.a.	-	23.0
1977	Feb.	-	-	n.a.	19.6	-
	Jul.	-	-	n.a.	-	-
	Aug.	-	-	15.0	-	-
	Oct.	13.2	14.4	13.2	-	-
1978	Jan.	-	-	12.6	-	-
	Jun.	15.0	18.6	-	20.5	-
1979	Feb.	-	-	-	20.9	-
	Jul.	-	-	-	24.5	-
1980	Jan.	19.2	24.0	-	29.2	27.0
	Apr.	-	-	16.8	-	-
	Sept.	17.2	21.9	14.8	25.4	-
	Nov.	14.8	19.5	12.3	23.1	24.0
1981	Apr.	-	-	-	21.6	-
	Jul.	-	-	14.4	-	-
	Nov.	-	17.4	-	-	-
	Dec.	14.4	16.2	-	-	23.0
1982	Jan.	-	15.0	-	18.6	21.0
	Feb.	-	-	-	17.6	-
	Mar.	12.0	12.6	12.0	-	-
	Apr.	-	-	-	15.5	18.6
	Jun.	7.6	8.0	8.0	11.0	13.0
1983	Jun.	-	-	-	10.5	-
1984	Jan.	6.0	9.0	6.0	-	-
	Nov.	-	10.0	-	-	-
1985	Apr.	-	-	6.0	-	-
1987	May	-	-	-	10.0	-
1988	Dec.	-	-	5.0	-	-
1990	Jul.	-	-	-	9.0	-

Source: Bank of Korea.

discounted and resold by them emerged as an attractive money market instrument (Table 8.11). The money market became more diversified when commercial paper (CP) and cash management accounts (CMA) were introduced in the 1980s by short-term finance companies and merchant banking corporations. With the rapid growth of the capital market and household income, the business of securities investment trust companies and life insurance companies has also expanded substantially. Mutual savings and finance companies have also grown fast by providing deposit and financing services to small and medium-sized firms and individuals who have limited access to banks.

The government's promotion of nonbank intermediaries to bring about financial deepening, diversification of financial assets, and an easing of the dualistic financial structure, however, led to an erosion of the banks' intermediation role. Disintermediation out of banks was particularly pronounced after substantial interest-rate reductions in June 1982. The lagging growth in the banking sector constrained the government's practice of using bank credit as a major incentive in its industrial policy. In an effort to correct this situation, the government sometimes responded to narrow the interest rate differentials between banks and nonbank intermediaries. For instance, selective bank interest rates were twice adjusted upward in 1984, a Liberal Savings Deposit facility, with very attractive rates, was introduced by banks in 1985, and a slight downward adjustment was made in nonbank interest rates in 1987.

A more important way of helping the banking sector by the government, however, was to introduce new businesses for banks (Table 8.12). During 1982 and 1983, banks newly added such services as credit cards, the sale of discounted commercial bills, selling government and public bonds on repurchase agreements, factoring, and trusts. Trust business (money in trust) has shown a substantial growth, as attractive rates have been given to longer-term trusts and the Corporate Trust Account was introduced in 1987 designed for short-term investment in the money market. In 1984, negotiable certificates of deposit were reintroduced by banks with interest rates higher than those of ordinary time deposits in the hope of strengthening the banks' position in mobilizing short-term funds. The secondary market for CDs was provided by short-term finance companies, merchant banking corporations, and large securities companies.

The government opted for this strategy of assisting the banking sector rather than higher bank interest rates for two reasons. First, the government wanted to maintain stable bank interest rates, as it viewed that high bank rates, without much narrowing of rates between banks and nonbanks, would have adverse effects on industries. Second, high bank-deposit rates would increase bank time and savings deposits and put pressure on the expansion of M2, which has been used as the major monetary aggregate for monetary policy. With rather restrictive M2 targets set for an anti-inflation purpose, a practical solution was offering attractive deposit rates not to ordinary bank deposits but to such new bank deposit facilities as CDs and trusts, which are not included in M2. In spite of these government efforts, nonbank interme-

Table 8.12 *Newly introduced financial services in the 1980s*

	Money Market Businesses			Peripheral Services		
	Banks	IFCs and MBCs	SCs	Banks	IFCs and MBCs	SCs
1980			(2) RPs officialized	(9) Credit card (CNB)	(10) Factoring (MBCs)	(1) Workers securities savings
1981		(6) CP			(4) Factoring (IFCs)	
1982	(9) Sales of commercial bills (11) RPs (government & public bonds)			(1) Credit card (nationwide commercial banks)		
1983				(2) Factoring (4) Mutual installment deposits (5) Trust (local banks)		(7) Short-term credit on securities deposited
1984	(6) CD issuing	(3) Guaranteed CP (4,7) CMA (6) CD brokerage	(4) CP (6) CD brokerage	(2) Trust (nationwide commercial Banks)	(3) International factoring (IFCs)	(4) Guarantees for corporate bonds (4) Overseas securities business
1985				(3) Money in Trust for Households (7) Trust (foreign banks)		
1986						
1987	(9) Corporate Trust Account		(8) Bond Management Fund	(1) Pension-type savings trust		

Notes: Figures in parentheses are months of the year.
IFCs: Investment and finance (short-term finance) companies; MBCs: Merchant banking corporations; SCs: securities companies; CNB: Citizens National Bank.

Table 8.13 *Deposit shares in banks and nonbank intermediaries (%)*

	1972	1975	1980	1985	1990
Banks	91.4	80.0	66.0	52.4	45.8
Deposits (CD included)	81.0	74.7	60.1	43.6	30.6
Money in Trust	10.4	5.3	5.9	8.8	15.2
Nonbank Intermediaries	8.6	20.0	34.0	47.6	54.2
Insurance Companies	4.5	4.6	6.5	11.9	15.0
Short-term Finance Companies	0.3	7.2	11.8	11.9	10.9
Mutual Credit	1.6	3.6	5.5	5.3	7.1
(Agricultural Cooperatives)	-	1.2	2.3	4.8	4.4
Mutual Savings and Finance Companies	-	1.1	3.6	3.4	4.8
Credit Union	-	-	3.6	9.9	11.1
Securities Investment Trust	2.2	2.3	0.7	0.5	0.9
Others					
Total	100.0	100.0	100.0	100.0	100.0

diaries have grown much faster than banks (Table 8.13), though these new financial products may have slowed the erosion of the banks' position, and contributed to the financial choices available to firms and households.

Delayed opening of capital accounts

It is generally believed that international capital controls should be lifted only after the domestic financial market has been reformed and domestic interest rates have been deregulated (see Chapter 11 for a summary of the pros and cons, and Chapters 9 and 12 for different sequencing decisions). Korea has more or less followed the conventional wisdom, postponing the deregulation of external capital transactions for the last phase of economic liberalization. Given the rapid growth of exports, Korea could pursue import liberalization more aggressively than domestic financial deregulation in the 1980s. Delayed opening of the capital accounts has prevented its interference with the process of import liberalization. Actually, liberalization of external capital transactions is in its initial stage, which may be justified given the slow progress toward domestic financial liberalization.

Since 1985 many Korean companies have issued convertible bonds in overseas markets. As large disparities exist in the cost of borrowing between domestic and foreign markets, however, it has been inevitable to limit foreign borrowings to specified uses with priorities given to activities not resulting in a liquidity buildup in the domestic market, and to imports in such preferred areas as high-tech industries.

As an initial step toward opening the capital market, international trust funds were established in the early 1980s, which was followed by the launch of several corporate-type funds. Only beginning in 1992 and subject to a ceiling, were foreign investors allowed to buy individual Korean stocks in the domestic market. In conjunction with the opening of the domestic capital market, the government plans to gradually liberalize overseas securities investment by Korean investors. It is an import complement that helps avoid possible macroeconomic complications following the opening of the capital market.

Finally, before fully opening the capital market, it is essential that domestic interest and exchange rates are deregulated and stabilized on the basis of an efficient market system. It has already been mentioned why interest-rate deregulation is a slow process in Korea. Korea adopted a market-average exchange rate system in March 1990, which allows the exchange rate to be market determined within a specified upper and lower range, where the base rate is set at the weighted average interbank rate on the previous day. For the exchange rate to reflect the true demand and supply situation, foreign exchange controls should be relaxed in a way that will broaden the base of the market.

Government control of NCB management with dispersed ownership

Before nationwide commercial banks (NCBs) were privatized between 1981 and 1983, the government owned 20–30% of total shares of these banks. Furthermore, the voting power of any one private shareholder was limited to a maximum of 10% regardless of their equity shares. As the government-held shares were sold to the private sector, there was a great concern over the possibility of large business groups controlling these banks. This concern led to a new provision that limits the maximum equity share of a NCB that can be held by a stockholder (including those with special relations to the stockholder) to 8% of the total.

Contrary to this concern, no attempt to control these banks by any business groups has been reported. Initially, there were many large business groups purchasing NCB shares, mostly their main banks, probably in anticipation of some favors. This initial interest, however, seems to have been largely lost. The number of business firms with equity shares of over 1% in any of the five NCBs declined from 19 in 1986 to 10 in 1989, and ownership is dispersed (Table 8.14).

Tight control over credit to large business groups since 1984 might be partly responsible for their declining interest in holding NCB

Table 8.14 *Ownership structure of financial intermediaries*[1] *(end of 1989, %)*

	Five NCBs	Provincial Banks	Investment & Finance Cos.	Securities Companies	Merchant Banking Corps.	All Listed Companies
Securities Companies	3.4	2.8	1.4	2.7	9.6	5.1
Insurance Companies	14.2	3.5	0.8	2.8	0.4	2.6
Other Financial Intermediaries	3.2	1.9	6.2	7.5	35.4	3.2
Nonfinancial Corporations[2]	17.2	20.7	18.3	24.8	14.2	20.6
Foreigners	0.0	2.7	0.7	1.8	23.8	2.1
Domestic Individuals	61.8	68.5	72.4	60.3	16.4	54.6
Total	100.0	100.0	100.0	100.0	100.0	100.0[3]
Small Shareholders	77.7	76.0	66.6	65.5	55.1	-
Corporations	14.5	11.2	10.5	14.2	40.3	-
Individuals	63.1	64.8	56.1	51.4	14.7	-
Largest Stockholder	5.8	9.4	16.1	26.2	17.6	-
Other Shareholders	16.5	14.6	17.3	8.3	27.2	-
Corporations	16.0	11.5	7.7	6.8	25.2	-
Individuals	0.5	3.0	9.5	1.6	2.0	-

Notes: 1)   Includes listed companies only: 10 provincial banks, 29 investment and finance companies, 22 securities companies, and 3 merchant banking corporations. And the figures are simple averages.
2)   Includes securities investment companies.
3)   Includes 11.8% held by government-invested companies.

shares. The share of NCB loans extended to the largest five business groups dropped from 12.4% in 1987 to 7.2% in 1989, and the share for the largest 30 groups declined from 20.8% to 14.7% during the same period. As the government continues to intervene in the management of NCBs in credit allocation as well as selection of bank presidents, business groups seem to find little interest in holding NCB shares for the purpose of controlling these banks.

The average equity holdings of the largest shareholder for each of the five NCBs dropped from 8.7% in 1986 to 5.8% in 1989. Combined equity shares for those stockholders owning more than 1% of the total (excluding trust property) decreased from 33.2% to 18.9% during the same period. Among these stockholders, the combined shares for business firms and individuals dropped from 16.3% to 3.5%, while the share for institutional investors (mainly insurance companies) dropped only marginally.

This dispersed ownership structure of NCBs and appointment of their presidents by the government were frequently blamed for inefficiency of bank management. However, allowing large business groups to control these banks is certainly not a solution. As entry into banking is restricted and bank loans have a subsidy element (while the burden of nonperforming loans is alleviated by the government), allowing business groups to hold controlling shares of banks would be an unjustifiable favor to the business groups and would lead to concentration of economic power.

Even when financial markets are competitive with free entry, the mix of financial and nonfinancial products within a business group increases the probability of abuses involving conflicts of interest as long as the involved firms have market power in the nonfinancial products. Tie-in sales are a common means of exploiting conflicts of interest. Given the highly oligopolistic Korean market structure where business groups have market-dominating power in many industries, the room for abusing conflicts of interest is potentially great.

In this connection, however, there is no strong rationale for applying the 8% ownership restriction for NCBs in an indiscriminate way, if concerns about the concentration of economic power and abuses involving conflicts of interest are the major reasons for restriction of bank ownership. Limiting the restriction only to large business groups, which are so extensively diversified as to have high potential for abusing conflicts of interest, may be an alternative. It will be much easier to monitor and regulate any abuses by relatively small business groups doing business in limited industries. Furthermore, the fact that ownership restrictions apply only to NCBs among financial intermediaries is rather unfair, since NCBs no longer dominate the financial market and the uniqueness of commercial banks will be weakened in the future.

Even granting that large business groups should not be allowed to hold controlling shares of NCBs, government appointment of their presidents is not desirable for managerial efficiency of these banks. During a transition period, top management of NCBs may be selected by a committee composed of large shareholders, the current president, and representatives of small shareholders, consumers, and other public interests. Large shareholders should not be excluded because they have the strongest incentive to monitor bank management. In order to check them from seeking their own interest at the sacrifice of others, representatives from small shareholders, consumers, and other public interests should be important participants. Opinion of the current president should also be respected to give him more sense of responsibility for bank management.

8.6   Summary and conclusion

Korea's financial reform since the early 1980s may be characterized as cautious. Curbing inflation was the top economic management priority in the early 1980s. This policy was viewed as critical not only for the maintenance of economic growth potential by inducing resources to more productive sectors, but also for deregulation of interest rates and other liberalization efforts.

Stabilization efforts were accompanied or followed by a process of economic liberalization. Industry-specific promotion measures were gradually replaced by a more indirect and functional support of industries, and a significant progress was made in trade liberalization. Financial liberalization emphasized relaxing administrative controls over bank management, privatization of banks, lowering entry barriers, and diversifying financial services. Delayed opening of the capital accounts in Korea has prevented major interferences from occurring with the process of import liberalization and monetary management.

Domestic financial liberalization in Korea has been rather slow in such areas as deregulation of interest rates, reduction of policy loans, and enhancement of autonomy in bank management. This slow pace was, to a large extent, due to the legacy of extensive government intervention in resource allocation during the 1970s. Snowballing NPLs as well as inertia and incompetence of banks prevented any bold financial liberalization programs, which would have driven banks to compete with much healthier NBFIs. The continued role of the government in bailout decisions as well as in selecting the top management of the major nationwide commercial banks have perpetuated the delay in financial liberalization. Splitting the nonperforming loans from the creditor banks for special treatment while inducing them to vigorous competition was another solution, but was ruled out because of its political sensitivity.

Another big obstacle to financial liberalization has been government efforts to keep investment activities vigorous for sustained economic growth. A drastic increase in corporate financing cost, which may result from interest-rate deregulation, would certainly be a heavy burden for most Korean firms with highly leveraged capital structure. However, high market-interest rates may be inevitable given the strong investment needs. Frequently forgotten is that delaying deregulation will make the situation even more difficult to tackle. The government's desire to save its own borrowing cost is another factor that has contributed to its cautious approach to interest-rate deregulation.

Reduction of policy loans has also been slow for the similar reason as well as with growing concern over social equity.

Another feature of the Korean financial reform is the rapid growth of NBFIs, which have not been subjected to such strict government regulations as it has applied to banks. NBFIs have been favorably treated in regard to interest-rate control, burden of providing policy loans, entry barriers, and ownership regulation. This differential treatment between banks (including development banks) and NBFIs has been the result of the government's efforts to redress the dualistic financial market structure by absorbing informal curb market funds into the organized credit market. The Korean financial market as a whole has become fairly liberalized, simply because the share of NBFIs, which operate in a relatively free environment, has risen significantly. Promotion of NBFIs has proved to be a pragmatic way of deepening the financial market while maintaining government-controlled credit allocation through the banking system. The consequences of this policy have been inefficiency in banking, various government assistance to banks, slow progress toward a universal banking system, lack of competition in the financial market, and delayed financial liberalization.

Finally, Korea's cautious approach to financial liberalization and the differential treatment between the banks and NBFIs were no exceptions in ownership restriction for financial intermediaries. Concern over the possibility of large business groups controlling the newly privatized nationwide commercial banks led to a new provision that sets the maximum a shareholder can hold to 8% of the total equity. This concern is justified given that the banks still provide a substantial portion of their credit at subsidized rates to large business groups in return for various government assistance, and that these groups usually operate in very oligopolistic markets allowing them to easily abuse conflicts of interest. The ownership restriction coupled with tighter credit control to large business groups since 1984 and the continued government appointments of bank top management have discouraged business firms to making equity investments in these banks.

NOTES

1 The import liberalization ratio represents the proportion of items out of 7,915 at the eight-digit level of the Customs Cooperation Council Nomenclature (CCCN), for which import approval is automatic under the regular trade notice.
2 Policy loans include those lent to earmarked sectors at preferential or nonpreferential

rates and unearmarked loans extended at preferential rates with policy considerations.

3 Individual industry promotion laws covered machinery, electronics, textiles, iron and steel, nonferrous metals, petrochemicals, and shipbuilding.

4 They include textiles, ferro-alloys, dyeing, and fertilizer as declining industries; and automobiles, diesel engines, heavy electrical equipment, and heavy construction equipment as emerging industries.

5 Import licensing, however, has also been restricted by means other than the regular trade notice. There are 39 special laws, serving various public interest objectives, under which relevant ministries can designate commodities requiring their import approval. An import surveillance system has also been operating in order to prevent excessive importing. Furthermore, an import-source diversification program is in effect with a view to easing excessive bilateral trade imbalances by providing infant-industry protection.

6 Financial services now provided by commercial banks include sales of discounted commercial bills and public debentures under repurchase agreements (RPs), issuing of negotiable certificates of deposit (CDs), and handling of trusts. In the nonbank financial sector, a commercial paper (CP) market and various asset-management funds have been established through short-term finance companies and merchant banking corporations.

7 According to the analysis of Nam (1990), a 1.0 percentage point sustained increase in bank interest rates results, with a one-year lag, in a 0.27 percentage point rise in the household savings ratio and a 0.17 percentage point rise in the national savings ratio.

8 The banks required a large portion of borrowing as a compensating deposit balance to circumvent interest rate ceilings.

9 See Chapter 4 for a discussion of this point.

10 During 1986–8, corporate bond yields averaged 13.4% per annum. Using this yield as a representative market rate (instead of the curb loan rate, which was almost 10 percentage points higher), interest subsidies ranged from 3.4% to 11.4% a year.

11 The Monetary Stabilization Bond issued by the central bank has recently been the major tool for sterilizing liquidity. However, these bonds have been issued at below-market rates and sold mainly to financial institutions by coercion. The ever increasing issues of these bonds have seriously affected the liquidity position of financial intermediaries and the resulting crowding out in the shallow market has often depressed the corporate bond market drastically.

CHAPTER 9

An assessment of financial reform in Indonesia, 1983–90

John Chant and Mari Pangestu

In March 1983 the Indonesian government introduced a program of financial measures that would transform the country's banking system as part of a broader program including reform of taxation, regulations governing international trade, and other areas of financial markets. The measures were a response to deteriorating economic conditions especially in the market for Indonesia's primary export, petroleum products, and were intended to strengthen the economy by diversification. This chapter provides the macroeconomic and financial background to these measures, presents and explains the various reforms, and analyzes their costs and benefits.

9.1 Economic background to deregulation

After the oil boom

The macroeconomic climate in Indonesia at the start of the reforms was not encouraging. It was nearing the end of its second oil boom in less than a decade, and its dependence on oil during the boom years had been substantial: at the peak of the boom, 80% of exports and 70% of government revenues came from oil. Indonesia's industrialization up to the early 1980s followed the pattern of import substitution behind protection. During the boom years (1973–82), state intervention increased with trade and industrial policies influencing the pattern of industrialization through protection of domestic industries. State intervention also guided financial sector development (see Section 9.2).

Even during the boom there was a recognition that diversification from oil was needed. Policy measures to increase nonoil exports began as early as 1978 when the government devalued the rupiah by 50% to offset the appreciation of the real exchange rate. An export certificate program intended as a duty drawback scheme for exporters was also introduced.

Inflation in the postdevaluation period and the lack of deregulation to reduce the high-cost economy meant that nonoil exports were still not competitive. In the wake of the devaluation, further attempts to reduce trade barriers were made. In April 1979 tariffs and import taxes on 1,000 goods and services were significantly reduced. After the promising start, the subsequent increase in oil prices in 1979 dampened the urgency of further trade liberalization.

As oil prices began to fall in 1981–2, the nonoil export drive began again with the introduction of the subsidized export credit scheme. The central bank, Bank Indonesia, provided liquidity credits to administering banks of up to 75% of the loan amount and the banks provided exporters with credit at below-market rates. Both the export certificate and export credit schemes led to some increase in nonoil exports. However, with the presence of other factors in the high-cost economy, the policies were insufficient to sustain growth in nonoil exports.

Initial phase of oil price decline: 1982–5

From the beginning of the New Order, Indonesia had pursued a conservative macroeconomic policy. During the oil boom, foreign debt was kept under control through an implicit rule of thumb limiting the debt service ratio at around 20%. Thus, when oil prices began to decline, the impetus for economic adjustment and reforms began to be felt. Following the conventional wisdom of correcting macroeconomic imbalances prior to reforms, beginning in 1983, the government undertook several macroeconomic adjustment measures including the first steps in its program of financial reform.

A devaluation of the rupiah in March 1983 immediately preceded the first step of the financial reform. While the devaluation was precipitated by the rapid weakening of the economy, the measure was taken with a view to longer run considerations (Lane, Cole, and Slade 1991). The devaluation succeeded in placing the economy back onto a firm footing. Woo and Nasution (1989) report

> The response of the non-oil export sector was impressive, as in the previous devaluation – exports expanded 26 percent in physical volume and 58 percent in local purchasing power. . . . Manufacturing exports grew especially rapidly, jumping from $850 million in fiscal 1982 to $1,480 million in fiscal 1983, and then to $2,166 million in fiscal 1984. (p. 109)

Thus, the financial reform initially would have less chance of being complicated by distorted prices with an overvalued exchange rate.

Still, following some tariff reductions in 1979, protectionist policies were on the rise. Tariff rates remained high and the effective rates of protection had the usual high variance. Beginning in 1983, increased protection was undertaken with the justification of conservation of foreign exchange. In addition, there was renewed support for industrialization through import substitution aimed at intermediate and upstream products such as iron, steel, synthetic fibers, cement, chemicals, fertilizers, and motor vehicle engines. As a result, there was an increase in nontariff barriers and in domestic component or localization policies. Instead of increasing tariffs, which were already high, less visible nontariff barriers were increased.

Despite the trend toward increased protection during the early 1980s, two important trade reforms did occur. In 1985 the tariff system was rationalized substantially by an across-the-board reduction in the range and level of nominal tariffs. The range of tariffs declined from 0–225% to 0–60%, with some exceptions. The number of tariff levels was also reduced from 25 to 11.

A more significant move was the customs and shipping reforms. In April 1985, all operations relating to the import and export of goods by the customs department were totally disbanded in one bold sweep. The reform was undertaken to reduce the discretionary powers of customs officials, a long-recognized problem and important element in Indonesia's high-cost economy. Customs officials were replaced by a private Swiss surveying company, Société Générale de Surveillance (SGS). It is widely accepted that the average time spent on customs procedures has been cut by several weeks and that the cost of shipping exports and imports has fallen substantially. These measures were important symbolically because they signaled the seriousness of the government's intent to undertake the necessary reforms.

Second phase of oil price decline: Substantive reforms

The dramatic decline in oil prices in 1986 marked the turning point in the economic reform process. The price of oil reached a low of $12/barrel in 1986. The decline in oil prices and appreciation of the yen led to the deterioration in the balance of payments and government budget situation that provided the political will for substantive deregulation. These reforms were the background for the second stage of financial reform which began in October 1988.

Once again, the reform process started with macroeconomic stabilization in the form of continued austerity in government spending and a 50% devaluation in September 1986. Moreover, exchange-rate policy shifted after 1986 toward maintenance of competitive real effective exchange rates by allowing the rupiah to depreciate when necessary to offset any inflation differential. Despite shifting to a managed floating exchange rate in 1978, the rupiah had remained more or less fixed up to then. Since 1988, the rupiah has depreciated at about 5% per annum and the real effective exchange rate has been maintained to ensure competitiveness of nonoil exports.

Trade liberalization

More significantly, various trade liberalization and deregulation measures were subsequently undertaken, especially targeted at offsetting the effects of the high-cost economy on exports. The sequence of trade reforms in Indonesia is in accordance with conventional wisdom: initially to offset the bias against exporters from the system of protection; to move from nontariff to tariff barriers; to rationalize the tariff system and to reduce protection by reducing tariffs.

To offset the high cost of imported inputs, the duty drawback system was improved in May 1986, partly in response to international pressure to remove the subsidies and partly due to the inefficient and less than transparent procedure of the system. The institutional change and effectiveness of the policy, added to the government's credibility.

The next stage of deregulation followed the September 1986 devaluation in an attempt to stimulate further nonoil exports, given the favorable real effective exchange rates achieved by the devaluation. Trade reform packages followed almost annually from 1986 to 1991, all aimed at removing nontariff barriers and replacing them with equivalent tariffs. The November 1988 package strengthened the government's credibility by removing two controversial import monopolies – steel and plastic raw materials – which are crucial inputs for downstream industries. Beginning with the May 1990 package, tariffs were also reduced with the ceiling on tariffs lowered to 40% in May 1990 and again to 30% in June 1991.

Reforms to facilitate and promote investment

In May 1986, along with the improvement in the duty exemption scheme, several important changes in foreign investment policy were undertaken. Export-oriented investments could have up to 95% foreign equity (compared with 80% previously) where export oriented is defined as exporting 80% of production, later modified to 60%. For other firms in Indonesia, the divestment requirement of 51% in 15 years still holds, although it is not monitored closely. In the May 1986 reforms, foreign firms were also allowed for the first time to distribute their own products in a joint venture setup.

Investment licensing was relaxed in July 1987. Renewals of licenses no longer were necessary, expansion of capacity less than 30% no longer required approval, and expansion to related product lines was permitted without specific approval. The simplification was intended to reduce the bureaucracy involved in operating in Indonesia.

The context of financial sector reform

In terms of the conventional wisdom, the Indonesian financial reforms were not introduced in the most favorable conditions. They started just as the slumping oil market was reflected in growing fiscal and current account deficits. In addition, Indonesia reversed the recommended textbook sequence, beginning with the financial sector reforms prior to completing the real sector. Indeed, at the beginning of the reforms, protectionist policies were also on the rise. Finally, the absence of foreign exchange controls, especially on the capital account, meant that Indonesia could be vulnerable to capital flight.

Several favorable features increased the chances of success. In March 1983, just two months before the start of financial reform, the rupiah had been depreciated by almost 40% against the U.S. dollar. Further, unlike other developing economies, the government of Indonesia did not have any domestically held debt. These two factors combined to remove an important constraint on Bank Indonesia. It could direct monetary policy toward maintaining domestic stability without the need to consider the government's financing requirements or, in the short run, external balance. To the extent Bank Indonesia pursued domestic stability as its primary goal, its policies would more likely be viewed as credible by the public and have greater chance of success.

9.2   Financial background to banking reform

Financial reform has been a continual process in Indonesia from the time of independence onward, following two distinct cycles.[1] From independence though 1965, the last year of the Sukarno regime, successive reforms displaced market processes by placing more of the financial sector under government control. With the beginning of the New Order, the direction of the reforms reversed.

The most useful starting point for the present analysis is the extreme degree of government control which was reached in 1965. As Suwidjana (1984) described the situation:

> the country's financial system was essentially made up of the following institutions:
>
> 1   Bank Negara Indonesia (BNI) with its five units: BNI Unit I – central bank functions; BNI Units II, III, and IV, all performing bank activities and Unit V – savings bank activities;
> 2   Bank Dagang Negara (a state commercial bank);
> 3   23 development banks: 1 state-owned (Bapindo) and 22 regional development banks (semigovernment);
> 4   2 private savings banks; and
> 5   87 private commercial banks.

The New Order quickly took steps to reduce the degree of centralization and government control. In 1967 the government permitted foreign banks to operate in Indonesia through branches, although their operations were heavily restricted.[2] In 1968 new banking laws separated the components of BNI. Unit I, became Bank Indonesia, the central bank. The other units became independent state-owned banks, each with its own area of specialization. The areas of specialization were arranged so that at least two of the state banks covered each major economic sector.

With the initiation of the second Five-Year Development plan in April 1974, Bank Indonesia introduced a program of direct credit control and allocation. Balino and Sundararajan (1986) describe the system as consisting of the following:

1   Credit ceilings for individual banks, with subceilings for various categories of loans
2   A complex rediscount mechanism, designed to reallocate credit and provide subsidies
3   Controls on interest rates of state banks, with private banks remaining free to set their own rates

Initially, the system of credit control appears to have been designed to control aggregate money and credit in order to limit expansionary pressures arising from the oil boom. But, increasingly, the new system came to be used as a mechanism for the allocation of credit, with detailed ceilings by type of credit for each bank together with subsidized interest rates (Woo and Nasution 1989). Although the ceilings were initially designed to control aggregate credit, allocation was influenced by increasingly detailed ceilings by credit type at each bank. Not all the criteria for credit allocation were economic and included

Table 9.1 *Share of state banks in Indonesian banking system*

Year	State Banks (% of total bank assets)	
1973	76.0(1)	
1974	77.1	
1975	77.2	
1976	79.5	
1977	82.9	
1978	82.3	
1979	80.5	
1980	80.2	79.0(2)
1981	83.0	79.8
1982	83.0	79.6
1983		77.0
1984		74.8
1985		73.4
1986		72.1
1987		71.3
1988		68.9
1989		59.4(3)
1990		52.9

Source: (1) S.G.V. Utomo, ed.*A Study in Commercial Banks in Indonesia*, cited in Suwidjana (1984, p.22).

(2) D. C. Cole and B. F. Slade, "Indonesian Financial Development: A Different Sequencing?" Bank Indonesia, *Annual Reports.*

(3) Bank Indonesia, *Annual Reports.*

the share going to pribumis (indigenous Indonesians) and to support rice production.

Both Woo and Nasution (1989) and Suwidjana (1984) suggest that the system of credit allocation determined the structure of the banking system because Bank Indonesia could set the shares assigned to any bank. They argue that the Bank actively favored the state banks, in part because their network of branches provided a suitable mechanism for distributing credit. Suwidjana also suggests that Bank Indonesia encouraged the development of private banks through the generous allocations of credit ceilings.

Table 9.1 shows that the share of both the state banks and the private banks expanded at the expense of the foreign banks from the introduction of the credit ceilings in 1974 through to their removal in 1983. Over this period the state banks increased their share of total assets of commercial banks from 77% to 83%. Over the same period, the private banks also increased their share from 7.5% to 10.0%. The gains of these banks came at the expense of joint ventures and foreign banks whose share fell from 15.5% to 7.0%.

9.3   The evolution of banking

The banking reform of 1983

On the eve of the reform of 1983, Indonesia had a tightly controlled credit system, with detailed central bank management of credit ceilings by sector and by bank. Bank Indonesia's control went beyond quantities alone; it also set lending rates for most types of credit while regulating and subsidizing the deposit rates of the state banks. Moreover, policies reserved certain areas of financial activity exclusively for the state banks. Despite the strong growth of the private banks during the period of credit controls, state banks still dominated the Indonesian banking system, holding more than 80% of total bank assets.

The financial reforms of 1983 were motivated as much by the general economic conditions in the Indonesian economy as by considerations in the financial sector itself. The decline in oil revenues produced a need for greater domestic savings to finance further development. Moreover, a more efficient and competitive financial sector could help attract the return of offshore deposits from Hong Kong and Singapore. Finally, it was hoped that the reduced reliance on direct allocation would improve the efficiency of credit use.

The 1983 reform represented a partial step toward restoring the market mechanism. It was intended to improve efficiency of the financial system by easing the restraints on the activities of existing banks, both private and state owned. More specifically, the reform had these principal elements:

1   Elimination of the system by which Bank Indonesia allocated bank credit by sector and by bank
2   Reduction of the number of categories of credit for which banks would be refinanced from Bank Indonesia on favorable terms
3   Removal of controls on most deposit rates paid by banks and on all loans except those refinanced by Bank Indonesia

4   Removal of the remaining subsidies on deposit rates paid by
state banks

Under the old system of credit ceilings together with liberal discount facilities at Bank Indonesia, banks had little incentive to compete for funds, because any funds collected in excess of a bank's
credit ceilings could not be loaned out domestically. Foreign exchange
banks could invest abroad, but smaller private banks without foreign
exchange powers could not. Prior to the reform, Bank Indonesia determined the volume of lending for the banks; after the reform the banks
themselves determined the allocation of credit through their ability to
attract deposits. The removal of the credit ceilings spurred commercial
banks to compete for funds.

The reform also restricted the system of liquidity credits by which
commercial banks could rediscount eligible loans with Bank Indonesia
at favorable rates. Balino and Sundararajan (1986) estimate that the
reclassification would have made 50% of the outstanding loans ineligi-
ble for priority status.[3]

The effects of the reforms on the banking system were felt immediately. Deposit rates at state banks responded quickly to the removal
of controls, closing much of the gap between these rates and those
paid by private banks. Despite this competitive effort, the state banks
were unable to overcome their reduced ability to refinance through
Bank Indonesia. For the first time in over a decade, they suffered a
decline in their share of total bank assets.

The PAKTO reforms of 1988

Despite the 1983 reform, competition in the Indonesian banking
still remained constrained in several ways. No new banks had been
permitted since 1968 and the expansion of existing banks was limited.
Although the extensive branch networks of the state banks had been
expanding slowly, the opening of new branches by private banks had
been at a virtual standstill because of restrictive regulatory requirements. In addition, only state banks were able to hold the deposits of
state enterprises, whereas only the state banks and the largest private
banks could carry on any foreign exchange business. Finally, other
burdensome regulation imposed costs on the banks, inhibiting competition further. Most notably, substantial cash reserve requirements,
high by international standards, artificially increased the cost of supplying banking services.

The Package of October (PAKTO) in 1988 removed most of the remaining impediments to competition. Its main elements included:

1 Removal of the moratorium on entry of new banks, thus permitting the establishment of new general banks by Indonesians and new joint venture banks with Indonesian and foreign bank ownership
2 Provision for new branches of general banks that met standards for soundness
3 Branching of foreign banks expanded to seven major cities, subject to meeting export finance requirements
4 Extension of foreign exchange powers to banks that met standards for soundness
5 Permission for state enterprises to hold up to 50% of their deposits with private banks
6 Extension to all banks of the power to issue certificates of deposit,
7 Reduction of reserve requirements from 15% for demand deposits and 10% for saving and time deposits to 2% of deposit liabilities

PAKTO also included measures to strengthen the soundness of the banking system. Legal lending limits on loans to single borrowers and groups of borrowers were introduced; capital requirements were raised for both general banks and rural banks; and banks were for the first time permitted to increase their capital by issuing new shares on the capital market. Finally, an anomaly was eliminated that gave a tax exemption to bank interest payments paid on time deposits.[4]

Post-PAKTO reforms

The PAKTO reforms have been followed by a succession of other packages that reflect a continuity of purpose. Most of the followup measures have been directed toward other parts of the financial sectors. Nevertheless, the packages have included some banking measures.

The Package of December (PAKDES II) in 1988 focused mainly on fostering the securities markets and specialized financial firms. The banking sector was affected by the introduction of licensing provisions for activities such as leasing, venture capital, securities trading, factoring, and consumer credit and credit cards. Banks were permitted to establish subsidiaries for leasing and venture capital and to engage in factoring, consumer finance, and credit cards as part of their normal business.

The Package of March (PAKMAR) in 1989, which affected the banks more directly, was directed entirely to strengthening prudential aspects of regulation. It clarified the lending limit provisions of PAKTO by defining the key concepts needed for implementation: the groups that are regarded as common borrowers and the measure of capital that sets the limits. It also modified the rules on foreign exchange commitments of banks by replacing a ceiling on offshore loans with a maximum net open position for foreign exchange of 25% of capital. In addition, PAKMAR limited the activities of commercial banks in equity markets. It restricted the equity holdings of banks in financial activities while requiring approval from the minister of finance for any other equity investment. It also prohibited general banks from underwriting securities. Finally, PAKMAR included one measure that further reduced Bank Indonesia's control over commercial bank lending by removing the requirement for approval of new medium and long-term loans.

In 1990 the Package of January (PAKJAN) continued the reduction of Bank Indonesia's role in the allocation of credit by abolishing the bulk of Bank Indonesia's liquidity credit arrangements for priority loans. Under these facilities, banks could lend to priority sectors at below-market interest rates and refinance a portion of the credit with Bank Indonesia at lower interest rates, the proportion and interest rate differing sector by sector. After PAKJAN, only a limited range of finance centered around the procurement and production of foodstocks qualified for liquidity credits. Moreover, the interest rates for further liquidity credits were moved closer to market levels.

Significantly, PAKJAN reversed the trend toward market allocation of credit in one respect by introducing a requirement that general banks allocate a minimum of 20% of their loans to small business (less than Rp. 600 million in assets ($315,000)). This measure was given force making a bank's performance with respect to this requirement a criterion for assessing its soundness.

In early 1991 the government moved to improve its prudential regulation by strengthening the bank capital requirements established in PAKTO 1988 through moving the definition of capital closer to the Basel standards and by setting a timetable for compliance. Banks were required to reach 5% by March 1992, 7% by March 1993, and the 8% international standard by December 1993. In addition, the loan to deposit ratio was introduced as an element in its soundness rating for banks.

Measures were also introduced to restrain the rapid growth of credit that had taken place over the past several years. The government required a number of large state enterprises to shift Rp. 8,000 billion out of bank deposits into SBIs. This measure alone reduced the monetary base by almost 40%. After a number of banks responded to this pressure by expanding their foreign borrowing, the government took further steps to limit this response. In October 1991 it restricted the private banks to $500 million and the state banks to $1 billion new foreign borrowing per year until 1996. Subsequently, in December 1992, this measure was strengthened by limiting offshore borrowing by individual banks to 30% of their equity and, at the same time, requiring that 80% of their foreign currency lending be made to exporting enterprises.

Many of the previous reforms became codified under the new Banking Law that gained assent in March 1992. This law significantly changed the status of the state banks by making them limited liability companies. It also provided for foreign ownership of Indonesian banks, a measure that was made effective later in the year. The Banking Law also included prudential measures such as limits to concentrated loans and loans to associated interests while strengthening the supervisory powers of the banking authorities by giving them power to issue directives and to close and liquidate unsound banks.

Reform in the rest of the financial sector

While much of the financial reform in Indonesia has been directed toward the banking system, parallel measures have been implemented in other financial sectors. These measures were intended to strengthen the stock market and other specialized financial institutions.

The stock market[5]

The Indonesian stock markets started in colonial times, but have had breaks in the continuity of their operations. The Jakarta Stock Exchange in its present form reopened in 1977. Woo and Nasution (1989) report that up to the time of the reforms trading had been virtually inactive with only 24 stock issues and 3 bond issues listed as of September 1986. Moreover, they argue that the 16 stock issues by foreign firms were not for the purpose of raising funds, but to comply with the need to have Indonesian participation in ownership. In their view, the underdevelopment of the stock market is attributable to the ease of gaining finance from domestic and foreign sources, the advantages of internal finance for tax evasion and the intrusive presence of Danareksa, a national investment trust. Danareksa not only was entitled to purchase 50% of all new issues, it also acted to stabilize stock prices.

PAKTO in October 1988, despite its emphasis on banking, started the reform of the stock market by removing two obstacles to its development. First, PAKTO eliminated a prohibition on share issues on the stock market by banks and nonbank financial institutions, permitting bank shares to be traded on the stock market for the first time. In addition, PAKTO removed the income tax exemption for time deposits held with Indonesian banks by introducing a final withholding tax of 15% on the interest of most time deposits.

PAKDES II in December 1988 introduced two further measures to strengthen the stock market. It established new licensing arrangements for securities firms, which specified capital requirements and licensing procedures and allowed both wholly owned Indonesian firms and joint ventures with up to 85% foreign ownership to operate as securities firms. The provision for joint ventures permitted an inflow of foreign expertise with respect to trading and underwriting and also increased access to foreign markets for Indonesian issuers. It also removed the requirement that gave Danareksa priority to purchase 50% of new issues, encouraging a broader distribution of securities both in Indonesia and abroad.

The stock market reforms had an immediate impact on the activity of the stock market.[6] From the end of 1987 through March 1990, the number of broker-dealers grew from 39 to 143 and, in addition, 12 integrated securities firms had been established. The number of share issues listed on the Jakarta Stock Exchange jumped from 24 in 1988 to 124 at the end of 1990 and the number of bond issues increased from 6 to 20 in the same period. Table 9.2 shows the rapid response of both the bond and the stock market to capital market reforms.

Banking reform in Indonesia: An overview

The effects of the 1983–90 banking reforms were cumulative. Each reform in general dealt with a different aspect of banking regulation. Table 9.3 summarizes the changes in the rules governing different aspects of banking that have taken place from the first deregulation package in 1983 through those in 1990. The top part of the table deals with the rules governing competition whereas the bottom part deals with prudential regulation.

As Table 9.3 shows, the degree of government and central bank involvement in the management of the banking sector has decreased

Table 9.2 *Capital market indicators*

A. The Bond Market: New Issues

Year	New Issues (billions of rupiah)
1990	1,385
1989	612
1988	320
1987	241
1986	13
1985	10
1984	11
1983	253

B. The stock market: Market capitalization

Year	Market capitalization (billions of rupiah)	Number of listed companies
1990	12,440	123
1989	4,359	57
1988	482	24
1987	112	24
1986	94	24
1985	89	24
1984	91	24

Source: Supervisory Body of the capital Market, Ministry
of Finance and Bapepam, computed by Institute for Economic
and Financial Research.

steadily throughout the 1980s. Where once the central bank determined all interest rates paid and charged by state banks, it now determined only the interest rates on government sponsored savings programs. Similarly, the central bank's role in determining the allocation of bank credit has declined substantially.

Even though the bank withdrew from administration of credit in the early stages of the reform, it still influenced the lending policies of banks through its liquidity credit programs. Here the extent of eligibility has been sharply curtailed first in the 1983 reform and subsequently in PAKJAN of 1989. Finally, many of the constraints on competitors of the state banks have been removed.

Several areas remain where market forces are limited. Foreign and joint venture banks must meet performance standards for export credit, whereas general banks are required to allocate 20% of their lending to small business. Both of these measures have been introduced during the period of reform and go against the trends of the rest of the reform.

Table 9.3 *Financial reform in Indonesia*

	Before Reform	After Reform	Date
I. COMPETITIVE MEASURES			
1.Entry of new banks			
a) private banks	moratorium since 1968	permitted	1988
b) foreign banks	moratorium since 1968	permitted to enter as joint venture	1988
2.Branching power			
a) private banks	restricted[1]	permitted for sound banks	1988
b) foreign banks	restricted to Jakarta	extended to seven cities	1988
3.Deposit rates			
a) state banks	controlled by Bank Indonesia	free to set	1983
4. Credit ceilings			
a) state banks	set by Bank Indonesia	eliminated	1983
b) private banks	set by Bank Indonesia	eliminated	1983
c) foreign banks	set by Bank Indonesia	eliminated	1983
5. Foreign exchange powers	moratorium to additional banks	permitted for sound banks	1988
6. Deposits of state enterprises	restricted to state banks	up to 50% with private banks	1988
7. Reserve requirements	15% of deposits	2% of deposits	1988
8. Entry into new activities			1988
a) Leasing		subsidiary	
b) Venture capital		subsidiary	
c) Securities trading		license required	
d) Factoring		directly	
e) Consumer finance		directly	
f) Credit cards		directly	
9. Export credit	subsidized	removed within 1 year	1989

Table 9.3 (Continued)

	Before Reform	After Reform	Date
10. Medium and long term loans	approval required from Bank Indonesia	no approval required	1989
11. Subsidy of Priority Credit		eligible categories reduced	1983
		eligible categories reduced	1990
II. PRUDENTIAL MEASURES			
1. Legal Lending limits	none	20% of capital to single borrower	1988
		50% to group	1988
2. Capital requirements			
a) General banks			
Indonesian owned		Rp. 10 billion	1988
Joint ventures		Rp. 50 billion	
		minimum 15% Indonesian ownership	
3. Foreign exchange exposure			
	Ceiling on off-shore loans	Net open position limit -25% of capital	1989
4. Underwriting		prohibited for banks	1989
5. Ownership of nonfinancial business		prohibited for banks	1989
III OTHER MEASURES			
1. Export Credits			
a) Joint venture banks		must be 50% of total credit	1988
2. Credit to small business			
a) National banks		must be 20% of total credit	1990

[1] Permitted in principle, but requirements made it prohibited in practice.

Source: Derived from Cole and Slade (1990b)

Table 9.3 also shows the progress that has been made toward strengthening prudential regulation. Over the period of the reforms, the government has introduced and strengthened loan ceilings to single borrowers, set limits to bank investments in equities of both financial and nonfinancial enterprises and introduced ceilings to banks' net open positions with respect to foreign exchange.

The effects of deregulation on the Indonesian banking system

As the preceding discussion shows, the framework of regulation governing Indonesian banks has been drastically changed from the early 1980s through to 1990. To what extent did these measures influence the structure and operations of the banking system?

Deposit rates

Many of the measures have been directed to increasing the role of market forces in the determination of interest rates paid and received by banks. The removal of controls on deposits rates that left the state banks free to compete should have a direct effect on the pattern of rates. Just as important may have been indirect influences such as the elimination of direct credit allocation by Bank Indonesia and the state bank monopoly on the holding of deposits of state enterprises.

Table 9.4, which shows the patterns of interest rates paid on deposits by state and private banks, indicates substantial differences between these rates prior to the first major deregulation package in 1983. Some rates such as those for time deposits at state banks of six months and more were set by regulation and held well below the rates paid on comparable deposits by private banks. Even the uncontrolled rates paid on shorter maturities by state banks remained substantially below those of the private banks.

The rates offered by state banks responded quickly to the removal of the credit ceilings and the interest rate controls in 1983. Six-month rates, for example, were controlled at 6% prior to the removal of the ceilings, roughly 11% below the rates paid on comparable deposits by the private banks. By the end of 1983, these rates had jumped to 13.1%, reducing the gap to just 5.7%. Similar adjustments occurred in the differences at other maturities that were decontrolled.[7]

A study by Chant and Pangestu (1987) provides a different perspective on the effects of the 1983 reforms by examining the banks' actual interest expense as a percentage of total assets. In 1982 the interest

Table 9.4 *Interest rates paid by state and private banks*

1. State Banks

	Less than 3 months	3 months	6 months	1 year	2 years
1980	7.2	8.2	6.0	9.0	12-15
1981	12.1	10.2	6.0	9.0	12-15
1982	7.7	8.6	6.0	9.0	12-15
1983	14.4	14.8	13.1	17.5	12.5
1984	15.1	17.1	17.2	18.7	17.2
1985	13.4	14.6	16.0	17.8	18.3
1986	13.3	14.2	14.7	15.2	16.0
1987	15.5	17.0	17.3	17.0	17.4
1988	15.8	18.1	18.4	18.7	18.8
1989	15.1	16.2	17.2	18.7	18.8
1990	20.5	20.7	20.7	20.5	20.0

2. Private Banks

	Less than 3 months	3 months	6 months	1 year	2 years
1980	14.2	16.1	17.8	20.1	19.3
1981	15.4	17.4	17.9	19.4	19.0
1982	16.9	17.1	18.5	19.3	18.8
1983	18.7	17.4	18.8	19.7	19.3
1984	19.8	20.7	20.7	20.4	21.0
1985	14.6	15.9	17.8	19.8	21.3
1986	14.8	15.5	16.2	17.3	20.1
1987	17.3	18.6	19.3	19.1	19.9
1988	20.2	20.1	20.3	20.2	20.9
1989	17.0	18.0	18.8	19.7	20.5
1990	20.9	21.3	21.3	21.2	21.0

Source: Bank Indonesia.

expense of the state banks averaged 4.0% compared to the 10.9% paid by the private banks, but by 1986, the third full year after the reforms, had increased by 2.8% to 6.8%. Although this rate was still below the 11.9% interest expense of the private banks, the gap in interest expense between the state and private banks closed by 1.8%.

The PAKTO reforms did not affect interest rates directly in the same way as the removal of interest-rate controls in 1983. Still, the measures generally encouraged competition by permitting easier entry

Table 9.5 *Average loan rates charged by
state and private banks (% per annum)*

I. State banks

	Working capital	Investment
1984	18.2	19.6
1985	19.9	18.4
1986	19.0	18.8
1987	18.4	18.3
1988	19.7	18.9
1989	20.5	19.6
1990	19.0	19.0

II. Large private banks

	Working capital	Investment
1984	24.4	18.6
1985	26.2	21.3
1986	23.8	23.1
1987	22.9	23.9
1988	23.5	23.3
1989	23.5	21.0
1990	20.7	20.0

III. Small private banks

	Working capital	Investment
1984	n.a	n.a
1985	30.1	27.3
1986	27.1	27.0
1987	25.4	22.6
1988	25.5	25.2
1989	25.8	25.2
1990	22.8	25.2

Source: Bank Indonesia.

and branching and allowing competition for deposits of state enterprises. Comparisons of the spreads between rates paid by state and
private banks suggests that the PAKTO reforms further enhanced
competition for deposits. The average spreads on the rates for deposits
of different maturities fell by 0.7% for six-month deposits and by 1.7%
for two-year deposits between the years 1984–7 to 1988–90.

Loan rates

Up to 1983, Bank Indonesia controlled the interest rates charged on
all loans made by the state banks. Table 9.5 shows that these rates
ranged from 6% to 13.5% per annum and varied by purpose and, in

some cases, the size of loan. The 1983 reform limited the scope of priority lending and also removed Bank Indonesia's controls over interest charged on nonpriority loans. Table 9.5 shows that interest-rate controls were removed from all but the smallest investment credits, from many areas of agriculture and agricultural processing and from all areas of manufacturing.

The patterns of loan rates since 1983 presented in Table 9.5 show that the rates charged by the state banks increased substantially immediately after the reforms, but still remained well below the rates of both private banks and foreign banks. For example, the margin between the average rate charged by state banks and large private banks for working capital loans fell from 6.3% to only 1.7%. On the whole, the narrowing of this gap took place through a decline in the rates charged by both the private and foreign banks.

The paper by Chant and Pangestu (1987) also provides a perspective on the interest rates charged by Indonesian banks. They examined the interest revenues earned by the banks as a percentage of their rupiah assets for the years 1982 and 1986. Their data show that in 1982 the state banks earned 7.3% and the private banks earned 18.5% on their domestic assets, a difference of 11.2 percentage points. By 1986 the return earned by the state banks had increased by almost 2 full percentage points to 9.2% while the return of the private banks remained the same at 18.5%, reducing the gap by almost 2.0%.

The change in rates on loans from the state banks after the reforms may overstate the actual change in the full costs to their borrowers by neglecting the costs of fulfilling application procedures, bargaining the terms of the loan and other similar costs that do not show up directly in the interest costs. Woo and Nasution (1989), for example, point out that "the state banks, unlike the private banks, seldom used up all their prescribed ceilings and had to lend out their excess reserves in the interbank market" (p. 91). They attribute this phenomenon to three possible factors:

> first, that the demand was actually high but bad bank practices by the state banks made them unable or reluctant to reach out to small customers. . . . Second, it could be the inability of the officers of the state banks to select projects which were acceptable both economically and politically. Third, the officers may have demanded too high side payments from prospective borrowers . . . It has been suggested that the graft could have been as high as 15 percent of the volume of the loan granted. . . . (p. 91)

To the extent that the latter interpretation is valid, the change to deregulated lending rates may have made some of the costs of borrowing explicit rather than implicit with a correspondingly smaller effect on the real cost of borrowing.

Spreads and the efficiency of intermediation

Financial reforms could be expected to improve the efficiency of the banking system. Measures that encourage entry and branching, that reduce the burden of reserve requirements and that make interest rates responsive to market forces should reduce the overall costs of intermediation by narrowing the spread between rates paid on deposits and rates charged on loans.

The efficiency of intermediation can be measured by both ex ante and ex post spreads. Ex ante spreads consist of the difference between the contractual rates charged on loans and the rates paid on deposits. Ex post spreads, in contrast, are based on the banks' interest revenues compared to their actual interest expenses.

The use of spreads to measure efficiency in banking is subject to the limitation that the banking services supplied must be the same for the points of comparison (Vittas 1991). Since the bearing of risk is an important dimension of banking services, any differences in the risks faced by bankers will tend to distort spread comparisons. The ex ante measures will be biased to the extent that differences in perceived risks are reflected in the ex ante yields. Ex post spreads would be biased if the differences in default were not reflected in the realized return. In the short run, such a realization would be unlikely because the risks of default taken on currently will only be realized some time in the future.

Ex ante spreads

The spreads between the deposit rates paid and the loan rates charged by various classes of banks are presented in Table 9.6. These data are from a variety of different sources and are not completely consistent.

Prior to the reforms, the measured spreads of the state banks were not very meaningful as indicators because Bank Indonesia determined the spreads on priority loans by setting both the rate that the banks could charge their customers and also the rate at which the banks could refinance the loans. In addition, Bank Indonesia set the interest rates that the state banks could pay on the majority of their deposits.

It is difficult to form any expectation with respect to the pattern of spreads for state banks after the reform measures of 1983. State banks had to contend with a new environment in which they decided on

Table 9.6 *Spread between loan and deposit rates of state and private banks*

I. State banks

Term of deposit:	Working capital		Investment loans	
	Less than 3 months	3 months	6 months	1 year
1983	3.8	n.a.	2.1	
1984	4.8	2.8	2.7	-.3
1985	5.6	5.3	3.0	1.0
1986	5.1(5.2)	4.2(4.3)	3.7	3.1(2.6)
1987	4.2(4.5)	2.7(3.0)	3.2	1.9(1.7)
1988	4.7(4.4)	2.2(2.1)	2.3	.9(1.8)
1989	3.9(4.6)	2.8(3.5)	1.8	.8(1.3)
1990	2.8(.0)	2.4(.5)	1.3	1.2(1.4)

II. Large private banks

Term of Deposit	Working capital		Investment loans	
	Less than 3 Months	3 Month	6 month	1 year
1983	5.7	7.0	-.2	-1.1
1984	6.4	5.5	.6	.9
1985	9.2	7.9	5.3	3.3
1986	8.1(8.2)	7.4(7.5)	7.7(8.7)	6.6
1987	6.2(6.3)	4.9(5.0)	4.0(4.4)	4.2
1988	3.3(3.6)	3.4(3.7)	-.5(.5)	-.4
1989	3.7(4.7)	2.7(3.7)	-2.3(-1.8)	-3.2
1990	8.6(4.2)	8.2(3.8)	1.3(-1.1)	.1(-2.0)

Note: Deposit rate – December; loan rate – March, year following. The numbers in parentheses denote deposit rates and loan rates, both in December.

Source: Bank Indonesia

credit allocation themselves and faced interest rates determined by market pressures. The PAKTO reforms could be expected to influence spreads more predictably because they more clearly fostered competition and reduced the direct costs of intermediation.

The spread between the one-month deposit rate and the loan rate for working capital for the state banks has varied from 1984 onward, but did not exhibit any clear trend at least to 1988. The observations for the two years since PAKTO, however, are consistent with its predicted effect of lowering spreads.

The effects on the spreads of the private banks are more predictable. Prior to 1983, private banks had little incentive to compete for funds beyond the limits of their ceiling allocations. The first reforms allowed the private banks to lend on the basis of their own profit considerations. Further pressure on their spreads of the private banks could be expected from PAKTO for the same reasons that affected the state banks. As Table 9.6 shows, the spreads of the private banks tend to be from 100 to 200 basis points higher than those of the state banks, reflecting the greater risks of lending to small and medium-sized business. Like the spreads for the state banks, there appears to have been no clear trend for the private banks up to 1988. The evidence seems stronger, however, that the spread for the private banks has declined in response to the pressures of PAKTO.

Ex post spreads

Chant and Pangestu (1987) have also measured the ex post spreads earned by the Indonesian banks for the years 1982 and 1986. The authors adopted the methodology of Hanson and Rocha (1986) who had compared the efficiency of the banking systems for a cross section of developed and developing countries. Because of limited data, the study focused on the gross interest margin for the banks' domestic business and on both the gross margin and net earning for the overall business of the banks.[8]

The Chant–Pangestu comparisons, because of the limited number of years, can only show the effects of first stage of the reform. The results of the various measures are quite consistent. Domestic margins declined from 1982 to 1986 for both state and private banks. The margin for the state banks fell from 3.3% to 2.3%, whereas the margin for the private banks fell from 7.6% to 6.6%. The weighted average of the interest margins of all the banks surveyed declined from 3.5% to 2.8%.

Much the same pattern can be found for the gross margin and the net earning for the overall business of the banks. Both measures declined for the state banks and the private banks over the period. For all banks, the gross margin declined from 6.0% to 4.9%, whereas the net earnings fell from 3.1% to 2.5%.

Real deposit rates

The experience of financial reform in other countries suggests that market pressures may push interest rates upward with the removal of direct controls. The resulting higher real rates have been judged a mixed blessing. Higher real rates may encourage financial savings. Moreover, in some circumstances, they may reflect a strong loan demand together with a decline in inflation. On the other hand,

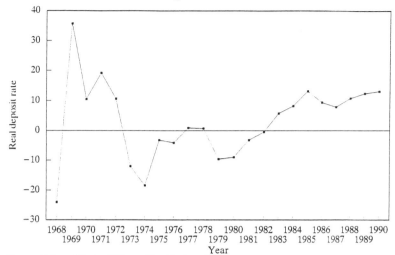

Source: Cole and Slade, 1990a and Bank Indonesia
Real deposit rate = one–year time deposit rate at State Banks – rate of inflation

Figure 9.1 Real deposit rates in Indonesia

excessively high real rates may cause problems because of financial distress among borrowers.

Figure 9.1 shows the development of real deposit rates in Indonesia from 1968 to 1990. Prior to the initial reforms in 1983, the real deposit rate had been negative in seven of the preceding nine years and marginally positive in the other two. Over the period 1979 to 1982, one-year deposits at state banks yielded a −5.2% real rate.

Real rates rose substantially from the first reform of 1983 onward. The first stage of reform produced an upward movement in real deposit rates that persisted for several years, leaving them strongly positive. This increase in real rates was caused by changes in both elements determining real rates: Nominal interest rates rose and inflation fell.

The substantial response in real rates in Indonesia seems somewhat surprising in light of the principle of interest arbitrage. Comparison of Indonesian real rates with the Libor rate adjusted for realized rates of inflation shows that Indonesian rates have remained consistently above those in international financial centers. However, the simple interest arbitrage condition abstracts from some important differences among financial markets such as the costs of managing bank credit, differences in taxation between countries and specific country risks.

Recent theories suggest that interest rates on bank loans will reflect the costs of monitoring and enforcing the credit risks involved in such lending (Chant 1987, 1992). Loan rates between countries should be expected to differ to the extent there are differences in the costs of assessing these risks. In the Indonesian case, there are several reasons for expecting these costs to be higher than in international markets. Lenders cannot depend on using the legal system for enforcing their claims to collateral. In addition, the program of directed credit that existed prior to reform may have left the banks without adequate procedures for assessing risks. If this were the case, the banks would have to charge higher loan rates to compensate for their expected costs of default.

Interest arbitrage comparisons must also be adjusted to take into account differences in tax treatment between jurisdictions and over time. In the case of Indonesia, the tax treatment of time deposits changed substantially as part of the financial reforms. Prior to PAKTO in 1988, all interest on time deposits was received tax-free by Indonesian residents. Afterward, interest on time deposits above minimal levels became subject to a 15% final tax. Though this change in tax treatment may account for a slight rise in real deposit rates from 1988 onward, it is neither sufficient nor suitably timed to account for the high postreform interest rates.

Specific country risk appears to be the main factor that could explain the persistent and high real interest rates in the Indonesian economy. Although the Indonesia rupiah depreciated slowly and relatively predictably against the U.S. dollar in the late 1980s, it had been devalued substantially against the dollar in 1978, 1983, and 1986. In addition, quite drastic monetary measures appear to have been required to avert another devaluation in 1987. While Indonesian policies have reduced inflationary pressures in the postreform period, the credibility of this commitment may take some time to be established. In face of this experience, investors may require a real interest rate premium in order to hold assets denominated in rupiah.

Bank lending

Commercial lending

The financial reforms of 1983 were designed to foster a greater role for market mechanisms in the allocation of credit. While market determined interest rates would be expected by many to allocate credit to its most productive uses by rationing out those uses unable to meet the higher interest costs, some economists suggest that a move to a market interest rate for bank loans may not have the desired effect (see Chapter 2 of this book). A general upward movement of interest

Table 9.7 *Lending by commercial banks,*
1981–90

Year	All banks	State banks	Private banks	Foreign banks
1970		232		13
1971		384		25
1972		471		48
1973		745		95
1974		1136		117
1975		1602		123
1976		2007		150
1977		2067		183
1978		2832		262
1979		3441		343
1980		4301		414
1981	7510	5881	834	548
1982	10251	8031	1197	666
1983	12843	9787	1884	861
1984	18003	13345	3042	1046
1985	21193	15374	4106	1010
1986	25258	17782	5506	1204
1987	31478	21676	7762	1379
1988	42454	28631	10714	1913
1989	62910	39579	18591	3115
1990	96978	53524	34975	7577

Growth rate (%)

Year	All banks	State banks	Private banks	Foreign banks
1971		65.5%		92.3%
1972		22.7%		92.0%
1973		58.2%		97.9%
1974		52.5%		23.2%
1975		41.0%		5.1%
1976		25.3%		22.0%
1977		3.0%		22.0%
1978		37.0%		43.2%
1979		21.5%		30.9%
1980		25.0%		20.7%
1981		36.7%		32.4%
1982	36.5%	36.6%	43.5%	21.5%
1983	25.3%	21.9%	57.4%	29.3%
1984	40.2%	36.4%	61.5%	21.5%
1985	17.7%	15.2%	35.0%	-3.4%
1986	19.2%	15.7%	34.1%	19.2%
1987	24.6%	21.9%	41.0%	14.5%
1988	34.9%	32.1%	38.0%	38.7%
1989	48.2%	38.2%	73.5%	62.8%
1990	54.2%	35.2%	88.1%	143.2%

Source: 1975–81 Suwidjana (1984, pp. 47–49). *1982–90 Bank Indonesia,*
Indonesian Financial Statistics.

rates in response to decontrol may jeopardize borrowers' ability to
repay. Lenders may, as a consequence, ration credit according to their
perceptions of creditworthiness and be unwilling to expand, or even
maintain, their volume of lending under the new conditions.

Table 9.8 *Liquidity credits and bank lending,*
1981–90

Year	Liquidity credits	Growth rate (percent per annum)	Total lending	Liquidity credit/ bank lending
1980	499			
1981	668	0.339	7510	0.089
1982	1078	0.614	10251	0.105
1983	1346	0.249	12843	0.105
1984	3377	1.509	18003	0.188
1985	7631	1.260	21193	0.360
1986	8672	0.136	25258	0.343
1987	10261	0.183	31478	0.326
1988	13472	0.313	42454	0.317
1989	16228	0.205	62910	0.258
1990	13668	-0.158	96978	0.141

Source : Bank Indonesia.

The experience after the reforms does not support the credit rationing view. Table 9.7 shows that total bank credit grew at over 40% in 1984, the first full year of the reforms, despite weakening economic conditions. At the same time, credit at the state banks grew by 36%, a higher rate than in all but two years in the previous decade.[9] Overall credit growth did decline in 1985 and 1986, but this slowdown of credit appears to have been caused more by the slump in economic conditions. Real per capita GNP had fallen in each year from 1982 onward and in 1986 was 20% below the peak level of 1982.

Despite the weak economic conditions, credit growth resumed its growth in each of the next two years. The increased competition fostered by the PAKTO reforms appears to have added momentum to credit growth. The growth of overall credit reached 48% in 1989 and increased further to 54% in 1990. The growth of state bank credit over these two years was higher than in any other two consecutive years since the period of rapid inflation in the early 1970s.

Table 9.8 shows that private banks expanded their credit more rapidly than the state banks throughout the entire postreform period, while credit from the foreign banks tended to grow slower than the other banks up to the time of PAKTO. The most striking result, however, is the difference in reactions to the reforms by the various types of banks. The limited evidence for the private banks shows a 50% increase from the year immediately preceding the first reform to 1984, the first full year after. The private banks also doubled the growth rate of their credit following the PAKTO reforms of 1988. The foreign banks, in contrast, appear not to have responded to the 1983 reforms because, as might be expected, these reforms did little to affect them. As expected, they did respond strongly to the PAKTO 1988 reforms which expanded their power to branch to additional cities. Finally, the state banks appear to have responded least to the reforms. While the growth of their lending increased during the years immediately following the reforms, it was much less than that of the private banks.

Liquidity credits

The terms of the extensive liquidity credit program were revised in two stages. Under this program,

> Domestic (state-owned and private) banks received "liquidity credits" from the central bank in the following manner: if the bank extended a loan under one of the government credit programs at the designated lending rate, then it could discount a certain proportion of the loan with the central at a rate that was set lower than the lending rate. (Woo 1991, p. 12)

The liquidity credit program benefited both borrowers and banks. The banks that originated loans could refinance part of them with Bank Indonesia at concessionary interest rates. The interest rates paid by the borrowers were also particularly favorable. Balino and Sundararajan (1986) report "Rediscount proportions varied widely, ranging from 100% in some cases, and averaged 43% as of December 1982, while the discount rate varied from 3 percent to 13 percent. The loan rate to priority-sector borrowers ranged from 5 percent to 13.5 percent."

The reform of 1983 removed the eligibility for categories of credit that accounted for almost 50% of the outstanding loans at that time. The PAKJAN reforms of early 1990 restricted further the categories of credit eligible under the program. The motive for reform differed in each case. In 1983 the scope of liquidity credits was reduced as part of an overall program of removing controls from suppressed credit markets. By 1990, in contrast, the problem differed because previous reforms had shifted the balance away from controls. The 1990 reform reflected concern that the liquidity credit program committed Bank Indonesia to supply base money to the banks regardless of the state of credit conditions.

Table 9.8 shows the amount of refinance of liquidity credits provided by Bank Indonesia for the period 1981 to 1990 together with total lending by the commercial banks. At the time of the initial reforms in 1983, the refinancing of liquidity credits from Bank Indonesia represented an amount equal to about 10% of the total lending of the commercial banks.[10] Despite the restrictions on eligibility, the growth of liquidity credits from Bank Indonesia accelerated sharply after the reforms of 1983, expanding by 151% in 1984 and a further 126% in 1986, significantly faster than the growth of bank credit overall, bringing total liquidity credits to 36% of commercial bank lending. Only from 1986 onward has the growth rate of liquidity credits slowed, falling to below 20% in three of the five years. This slowdown, together with the faster growth of ordinary bank credit, has decreased liquidity credit to banks from Bank Indonesia to an amount equal to 26% of bank lending by commercial banks at the end of 1989.

The surprising growth of the program following the substantial tightening of eligibility in 1983 has several explanations. Very soon after their introduction, the reforms to the liquidity credit program were effectively reversed. Balino and Sundararajan (1986) report that the repayment date for nonpriority liquidity credits was postponed by six months and that additional categories became eligible. Probably more important, however, were the stronger incentives created for both banks and their customers to qualify for the program. The decontrol of lending rates for ordinary loans offered by the state banks strengthened the incentives for their customers to qualify for liquidity credits. Many types of loans that previously had controlled rates of no more than 13.5% now were subject to market-determined loan rates that averaged 18–20%. Similar incentives were created for the banks by the removal of the controls on many of their deposit rates. The liquidity credit program became a means by which banks and their customers could avoid higher interest rates after the reform.

The second step to limit the liquidity credit program in January 1990 has had a much more substantial impact. Outstanding liquidity credits declined by over 15% in 1990. In face of the continued rapid growth of other bank credit in 1989 and 1990, the share of liquidity credits declined to an amount equivalent to 14% of overall bank credit by the end of 1990.

The different response of liquidity credits to the two attempts to cut back the program reflects their different concerns. The first attempt was part of a package directed at removing constraints on the loan rates and lending of the state banks. In the face of major changes elsewhere in financial markets, authorities may have been reluctant to restrict too closely the remaining source of credit on nonmarket terms. By 1990, the rapid growth of commercial bank lending had eliminated much of the concern about adequacy of credit. The need to assure control over base money was preeminent.

Table 9.9 *Number of bank offices in Indonesia*

Year	Commercial	Rural	Total	Population (millions)	Population per branch
1979	982	5870	6852	143	20,870
1980	994	5833	6829	147	21,526
1981	1015	5833	6848	151	22,050
1982	1030	5801	6831	155	22,691
1983	1064	5810	6878	158	22,972
1984	1111	5823	6934	162	23,363
1985	1130	5832	6962	165	23,700
1986	1216	5820	7036	168	23,877
1987	1265	5789	7074	172	24,314
1988	1331	5783	7114	175	24,599
1989	1483	5812	7295	179	24,537
1990	2392	6982	9374	182	19,415

Source: Bank Indonesia.

Entry

New banks

The moratorium on new banks in 1968 had effectively limited the number of banks until the PAKTO reform in 1988. New banks quickly entered in response to the removal of restrictions to bank entry. In 1989 and 1990, 43 new private banks were established, increasing the number of banks by 68%. The number of joint venture banks also rose from 11 at the end of 1988 to 28 at the end of 1990.

Branches

The number of bank branches provides one measure of the availability of banking services to the public. Table 9.9 shows the number of branch offices of different types of banks for the years 1980 to 1990. As can be seen, prior to PAKTO in 1988, banks added few new branches, with never more than 86 new branches opened in any year. Commercial banks opened 152 new branches in 1989, the first full year after the removal of the restraints, and a further 909 new branches the next year. The additions in these two years expanded the number of branches by 80%.

Table 9.9 also shows the trends in population per branch over the period 1979 to 1990. Up to PAKTO reforms in 1988, the growth in branches failed to keep pace with population. Only in 1989 and 1990 did the growth of branches surpass population growth. The expansion in these two years was sufficient that by the end of 1990, population per branch had fallen 10% below the 1980 levels.

Impact on the economy

It would be very difficult to trace the total effects of financial reform on the economy. Moreover, financial reform has been only one of many influences affecting the economy over the 1980s. For the present, the analysis will focus on a number of indicators of the performance of the financial system.

The size of the financial sector

The various stages of the Indonesian reform contained many elements to encourage the growth of the financial sector, as should by now be evident. Table 9.10 presents two measures of the development of the Indonesian banking system: the M1/GDP and the M2/GDP ratios. The latter, by including saving and time deposits in the numerator, emphasizes more the intermediation function and reflects the public's willingness to hold the claims of the banking system as an investment, permitting the banks, in turn, to finance the needs of borrowers.

M1/GDP

The Indonesian experience with deregulation shows a mixed pattern in the response of the M1/GDP ratio. The initial reform failed to raise the M1/GDP ratio with the ratio falling in both 1983, the year of the reform, and in the next year. In contrast, the PAKTO reforms of 1988 appears to have raised this ratio, though not all the increase should be attributed to the reform. Two coincident developments, the decline in inflation and the growth in per capita income, both would be expected to raise the M1/GDP ratio on their own.

Table 9.10 *Measures of financial development (% of GDP)*

Year	C/GDP (1)	DD/GDP (2)	M1/GDP (3)	M2/GDP (4)
1970	4.79	2.96	7.10	9.37
1971	4.56	2.77	8.24	12.07
1972	5.09	3.80	9.84	14.46
1973	4.99	3.91	9.42	13.95
1974	4.13	3.71	8.34	12.87
1975	4.48	4.48	9.55	15.15
1976	4.62	4.86	9.81	16.24
1977	4.78	5.02	9.99	15.60
1978	5.11	5.15	10.37	15.92
1979	4.45	5.26	9.66	15.02
1980	4.40	5.81	10.25	15.76
1981	4.40	6.76	11.08	16.61
1982	4.70	6.70	11.36	17.68
1983	4.29	5.45	9.76	18.90
1984	4.14	5.43	9.55	19.96
1985	4.58	5.85	10.44	23.89
1986	5.21	6.18	11.33	26.89
1987	4.68	5.54	10.18	27.16
1988	4.48	5.84	10.13	29.62
1989	4.63	7.22	12.36	35.20
1990	4.79	7.76	12.55	44.6

Sources: (1) and (2) Bank Indonesia and Cole and Slade (1990b). (3) and (4) Bank Indonesia and World Bank (1991).

Table 9.10 suggests that reform contributed to the jump in the M1/ GDP ratio. It shows that the increase in the M1/GDP ratio following PAKTO in 1988 consisted entirely of a shift toward holding more demand deposits relative to income. No such shift was evident following the 1983 reforms. This pattern of little response to the 1983 reforms and more visible response to the 1988 reforms appears consistent with the nature of the reforms: Earlier measures enabled the state banks to pay higher interest rates on saving and time deposits, a matter of little concern to holders of demand deposits. The 1988 reforms, in contrast, made banking services more readily available to the public through the entry of new banks and, probably more important, the expansion of branches by private banks.

M2/GDP

The additional element of M2, saving and time deposits, responds to different forces than the other components. Both stages of the Indonesian reforms had effects that would be expected to attract funds into saving and time deposits. The 1983 reforms freed interest rates on most saving and time deposits at state banks from Bank Indonesia's control and also freed the private banks to use their surplus funds for lending. The 1988 reforms also should have expanded the M2/GDP ratio by reducing the cost of reserve requirements to the banks, permitting private banks to compete for deposits of state enterprises and facilitating access to banking through entry of new banks and the opening on new branches. These expectations are borne out by the data. In the years up to the 1983 reform, M2/GDP had generally grown very slowly. This growth accelerated immediately after the 1983 reforms and continued at high levels thereafter.

Financial distress

Financial reform brings the danger that the changed conditions in financial markets will lead to the distress of either financial institutions themselves or other businesses that are dependent on external finance. Either form of distress can be costly to the economy. If the banking system suffers distress, it risks losing the confidence of domestic depositors who may transfer their funds offshore. In the extreme, such a loss of confidence could lead to the collapse of a large fraction of the banking system. In less extreme circumstances, it may just impair its functioning, disrupting the transfer of funds from ultimate lenders to ultimate borrowers. Similarly, if businesses suffer distress because of the initial effects of the reform, they may no longer be judged as adequate credit risks. To the extent the distress is widespread, firms may be unable to gain the credit required to finance their investment. In either case, the financial reform unintentionally impairs the ability of the economy to use credit productively.

Sources of distress

Financial reform could contribute to financial distress in several different ways. It may directly cause financial distress by changing conditions in financial markets in ways that harm banks or business firms. For example, any banks that loaned funds at fixed interest rates while they borrowed at variable rates would be harmed if financial reform raised the general level of interest rates. In the same way, a business that had borrowed to finance a project that would be profitable at the prereform interest rates would be harmed to the extent that the reform raised interest rates. As Gertler and Rose (Chapter 2) point out, higher interest rates will lower the net worth of the firm, reducing the security available to the lender. In this case, the difficulties of the business borrower will cause problems for the lending bank by raising the probability of default.

Reform may also precipitate financial distress by revealing existing insolvency. For example, a bank that holds bad loans made prior to the reform may have to face the insolvency more readily when market forces determine interest rates. With even mildly higher rates, the bank may be unable to compete for deposits and the transfer of deposits to other banks may expose its uneconomic loans.

De Juan (1987), has described both the symptoms and the causes of banking insolvency based on the experience of developing countries. While macroeconomic causes may often precipitate banking insolvency, the severity of the banking system's response to any shock will be determined by its current condition. De Juan identifies inadequate supervision, reserve requirements, political interference, and inadequate legal procedures for recovering loans as major causes of banking instability.[11]

The Indonesian banking system appears to have been somewhat vulnerable to financial distress at the time of the initial deregulation. Certainly bank supervision required strengthening in order to deal with the new environment.[12] To some degree, this may not have appeared as such a problem before the reforms because direct controls together with other elements of the system had served as a partial substitute for a well-designed regulatory system. In other dimensions, the Indonesian regulatory system scored low prior to deregulation in terms of the characteristics stressed by de Juan. The liquidity requirements – up to 15% of deposits – were high by international standards; political criteria had shaped the patterns of credit allocation; and the legal system did not provide adequate procedures for recovering loans. Most important, however, the removal of the direct control left the banks freer to determine their own policies, but in a limited regulatory framework. The Banking Law of 1968 lacked adequate prudential safeguards such as capital adequacy requirements, limits to large exposures and limits to loans to related parties.

While not an immediate response to deregulation, the strengthening of the regulatory framework has been an integral part of the reforms from PAKTO onward. In addition to new entry, PAKTO also required banks to meet substantial initial capital requirements and to establish a record of soundness before gaining branching or foreign exchange powers. PAKTO also established lending limits for single borrowers and groups relative to a bank's capital and reduced the burden of reserve requirements. The lending limit – a maximum ratio between loans to individual borrowers and bank capital – implicitly introduced the notion of capital adequacy into Indonesian regulation. Indeed, the only move in the other direction has been the small business lending requirement.

Evidence of distress

Banking distress may appear in different forms. Most apparent would be the widespread insolvency or threatened insolvency of a significant proportion of the banking system. The symptoms may also be less obvious. Banks may continue to operate even though on any realistic accounting, they may no longer have any equity.

Indeed in the case of the U.S. Savings and Loans, banks had incentive to cover up their losses in the hope that they could rectify the problems in their balance sheets. As is now well known, this postponement permitted a magnification of their losses.

From the early stages of the financial reform through to 1991, there was little evidence of financial distress in the Indonesian banking system. Despite much concern in some quarters, only two small banks had clearly shown themselves to be in severe difficulties up to 1992. In addition, Bank Indonesia had for a number of years held a stake in the ownership of a larger private bank in order to support it. This stake was reduced in 1991 with the sale of part of Bank Indonesia's share to private interests.

Until late 1992, the most visibly troubled bank in Indonesia has been Bank Duta, which ranked as one of larger private banks in the country. The much publicized problems of Bank Duta do not appear to be attributable to the financial reforms. Bank Duta's difficulties were caused by foreign exchange losses that were the result of unauthorized trading by an employee.

This absence of distress compared favorably with the experience of other countries that have undertaken programs of financial reform on a similar scale. Nevertheless, the World Bank (1989) cautions that often much financial distress remains hidden. When intermediaries have rolled over unpaid loans and have capitalized unpaid interest, their financial condition will not be apparent from their accounts. Accounting information may be kept confidential, and what is available is often unreliable. The absence of clear signs of financial distress, though of some comfort, did not mean that such distress was absent or that it would not create problems in the future.

Beginning in 1991, several signs of banking distress have become apparent. The government appears to have been aware of the problems and has introduced a number of measures intended to ameliorate the distress.

The troubled condition of Bank Summa, one of the larger private banks that was identified with a major industrial group, became increasing apparent over 1992. By the beginning of the year, few banks were willing to extend credit to it through the interbank market. In November Bank Indonesia suspended the bank from its check-clearing arrangements, forcing it to suspend its operations. At the time, Bank Indonesia disclosed that Bank Summa's bad debts totaled Rp. 1.6 trillion, or approximately 70% of its outstanding credit. The uncertainties about Summa Bank subsequently spread to other private banks, precipitating substantial deposit runs on three smaller banks.

Summa Bank reopened at the end of the November, allowing withdrawals by the 90% of its customers holding accounts with balances less than Rp. 10 million. These withdrawals were financed through a bridging loan from a consortium of 13 private banks. Despite this assistance and consistent with their long-announced policy of not rescuing failing banks, the Indonesian authorities revoked Bank Summa's license and announced its liquidation on December 14, 1992.

The Indonesian authorities have also recognized the troubled conditions of the state banks and have undertaken measures to correct them. For 1988 onward, the state banks faced increased competition from the private banks in the deposit market while holding many poor quality loans acquired prior the reforms. In addition, the private banks were competing strenuously for the state banks' better quality borrowers.

In September 1992 the Ministry of Finance accepted a $307 million loan from the World Bank for the purpose of recapitalizing the state banks. These funds were provided to the state banks subject to a number of conditions. The banks' managements were required to report monthly to the minister of finance on their progress in resolving their poor-quality loans. In addition, the minister has imposed controls on new lending by the state banks. Two of the five state banks have been prevented from expanding their loans recently, and the others have been placed under differing degrees of control.

The World Bank (1989) suggests that financial distress may also be manifested in the lending patterns of the banks. Several reactions may be found. If financial reform creates distress for the nonfinancial sector, the banking system, as argued by Gertler and Rose (Chapter 2), may find lending too risky and cut their supply of credit. On the other hand, banks may persist in lending to firms that are bad credit risks when any break in the flow of credit to these firms would make their inherent insolvency apparent. When a bank has many borrowers in the same condition, a failure by the bank to maintain credit flows to these customers may not only bring them, but also the bank itself, into insolvency.

The first reaction, the cessation of bank lending, has generally been absent in Indonesia through 1990. As already discussed, the Indonesian banks had increased their lending substantially through the period of the financial reforms through 1990. This pattern changed somewhat in 1991 and 1992. IMF data indicate that the growth of bank credit to the private sector slowed substantially from over 60% in 1990 to just 17.8% in 1991 and 7.9% in 1992. To an extent, this slowdown could be expected, given that past growth in credit was unsustainable in the long run.

The growth in credit during 1992 did fall below most expectations. Poor credit risks in the private sector together with the troubled condition of some banks undoubtedly contributed to the slowdown. Indeed, the government has explicitly encouraged slower growth in credit through its directives to the state banks to restrict their loans. Moreover, the need for banks to meet capital adequacy rules and to conform with the loan to deposit guidelines undoubtedly also contributed to the slower growth in bank credit.

The World Bank (1989) also identifies two other indicators of bank lending that is motivated to suppress financial distress. First, such lending, unlike normal bank lending to business, will be directed toward the payment of interest and will fail to produce any counterpart in terms of additional investment. Lending that covers up financial distress will also tend to be concentrated on the same sectors as previous lending and will not respond to changing economic conditions. Thus, bank lending patterns both before and after reform may give some indication of whether the postreform lending has been motivated by the necessity of supporting past borrowers.

Table 9.11 presents data on new credit extended by banks and on domestic fixed investment. As can be seen, the volume of investment far exceeds the volume of new credit throughout the whole period. More relevant, however, is the comparison between private fixed investment and new credit. Here also the volume of investment exceeds new credit extended. More interesting, however, is the changing pattern over the period. At the start of the period, domestic credit financed only a small portion of investment in the Indonesian economy. Throughout the period the share of investment, both total and private, financed by domestic bank credit increased substantially over the period. By the end of the period, the contribution of bank credit

Table 9.11 *Investment and new credit, 1981–90*

Year	Investment	Private share (%)	Private investment	Change in credit	Change in Credit/ Investment	Change in Credit/Private Investment	Credit
1990	39166			34068	0.87		96978
1989	34550	59.2	20454	20456	0.59	1.00	62910
1988	30980	54.2	16791	10976	0.35	0.65	42454
1987	29369	52.3	15360	6220	0.21	0.40	31478
1986	26893	52.2	14038	4065	0.15	0.29	25258
1985	25085	47.6	11940	3190	0.13	0.27	21193
1984	26690	54.2	14466	5160	0.19	0.36	18003
1983	25693	51.2	13155	2232	0.09	0.17	12843
1982	24210	52.5	12710	2741	0.11	0.22	10251

Source : Bank Indonesia; Pfeffermann and Madarassy (1991).

had increased eightfold for total investment and almost fivefold for private investment. This increasing reliance on bank credit in the years following reform together with the rapid growth of investment is consistent with the absence of distress: The nonfinancial sector became increasingly able to finance a continued high level of investment.

Again the pattern appears to have changed in 1991. As discussed earlier, the growth in banking system claims on the private sector slowed substantially in 1991. IMF data for claims on the private sector show growth falling from over 66% in 1990 to 17.8% in 1991. Their data also show a similar slowing in the growth of investment as measured by gross capital formation. The contribution of bank credit fell concurrently. Whereas growth in claims on the private sector equaled 53% of gross capital formation 1990, it had fallen to just 22% in 1991. As in the case of banking sector distress, the evidence from the role of bank credit in the finance of investment shows some financial distress becoming apparent in 1991. These data do not indicate whether the distress reflected weakness in the banking system or a lack of qualified borrowers.

With respect to the Bank's second indicator, alternative evidence presented in Table 9.12 shows that the banking system as a whole did change its patterns of lending after the initial financial reform of 1983. In particular, the banks decreased their lending to agriculture and manufacturing fairly consistently from 1983 onward.

This shifting of lending patterns for the banking system as a whole may be an artifact of the changing importance of different categories of banks rather than responses of banks to the reform. The bottom part of Table 9.12 shows the composition of the lending of state banks,

Table 9.12 *Sectoral distribution of lending by Indonesian banks (% of bank lending)*

	1981	1982	1983	1984	1985	1986	1987	1988	1989	1990
All banks										
Agriculture	0.11	0.10	0.10	0.07	0.08	0.08	0.08	0.09	0.10	0.07
Mining	0.01	0.01	0.01	0.01	0.01	0.02	0.01	0.01	0.01	0.01
Manufacturing	0.37	0.38	0.40	0.37	0.36	0.36	0.35	0.35	0.38	0.31
Trade	0.30	0.31	0.31	0.35	0.34	0.33	0.33	0.33	0.19	0.31
Service	0.17	0.17	0.17	0.17	0.19	0.16	0.16	0.16	0.18	0.18
Other	0.04	0.03	0.02	0.02	0.02	0.05	0.07	0.06	0.13	0.12
State banks										
Agriculture	0.13	0.12	0.12	0.09	0.10	0.11	0.12	0.12	0.12	0.11
Mining	0.01	0.01	0.01	0.02	0.02	0.02	0.02	0.01	0.01	0.01
Manufacturing	0.38	0.40	0.42	0.39	0.38	0.39	0.40	0.41	0.38	0.39
Trade	0.27	0.27	0.28	0.34	0.33	0.31	0.29	0.29	0.28	0.27
Service	0.18	0.17	0.15	0.14	0.15	0.13	0.13	0.13	0.12	0.14
Other	0.04	0.03	0.02	0.02	0.02	0.03	0.04	0.03	0.08	0.08
Private banks										
Agriculture	0.01	0.01	0.01	0.01	0.01	0.01	0.01	0.02	0.02	0.02
Mining	0.00	0.00	0.00	0.00	0.00	0.00	0.00	0.00	0.00	0.00
Manufacturing	0.22	0.24	0.29	0.29	0.29	0.27	0.22	0.22	0.20	0.20
Trade	0.55	0.51	0.46	0.44	0.39	0.41	0.42	0.44	0.43	0.39
Service	0.17	0.19	0.22	0.24	0.29	0.24	0.22	0.21	0.21	0.22
Other	0.04	0.05	0.02	0.02	0.02	0.07	0.13	0.11	0.14	0.16
Foreign banks										
Agriculture	0.00	0.00	0.00	0.00	0.00	0.00	0.00	0.00	0.01	0.02
Mining	0.00	0.00	0.00	0.00	0.00	0.00	0.00	0.00	0.01	0.19
Manufacturing	0.62	0.56	0.55	0.52	0.46	0.44	0.36	0.35	0.47	0.34
Trade	0.29	0.34	0.32	0.30	0.35	0.27	0.26	0.25	0.19	0.16
Service	0.06	0.07	0.12	0.14	0.13	0.14	0.19	0.17	0.17	0.18
Other	0.03	0.03	0.02	0.04	0.07	0.14	0.19	0.22	0.16	0.12

national private banks and foreign banks over the years 1981 to 1990. The different patterns for the types of banks suggest that, even though some of the changed aggregate pattern appears to have resulted from shifting shares of different types of banks, notable shifts in lending occurred within each category of bank. By 1990 both the state banks and the private banks had reduced lending to agriculture and manufacturing and increased their lending to the "other" sector. The relative increase was much larger, however, for the private banks than for the state banks, and most of the increase took place in the latter part of the period.

Overall, the evidence of possible financial distress resulting from the financial reforms is mixed. There was a remarkable absence of signs of distress from the beginnings of the reforms through 1990. The banks continued and expanded their lending. Moreover, the real sector continued and expanded its investment in fixed capital. In addition, the banks did not appear to be tied to any particular sectors as they might if some sectors were characterized by borrowers that were both distressed and heavily indebted to the banks. Banks as a whole, as well as the state banks and the private banks separately, shifted the composition both year by year and over the entire period. To the extent that this shift represents a shift toward real estate, it may be a warning signal, in view of the difficulties encountered by banks in other countries (including Malaysia, seen in Chapter 10).

Since 1990 some clear signs of distress have appeared. A major private bank has failed and the state banks have been shown to be weak and in need of recapitalization. The growth of bank credit and of investment have both slowed after 1990. Some factors other than distress, such as tighter prudential regulation, have undoubtedly contributed to the slowdown of bank credit but probably do not account for it entirely. Some distress in both the banking and the nonfinancial sector is present. The degree of distress will become more apparent from the experience of the next few years.

9.4   The real effects of the financial reform

Financial reform has clearly changed the structure and the working of the Indonesian financial system. Yet reform of the financial system is only a means to an end: the improved performance of the Indonesian economy. What then has been the influence of the financial reform on workings of the Indonesian economy?

Saving and investment

Saving

The impact of financial reform on saving will be difficult to isolate because of many other forces at work in the economy. The price of oil, Indonesia's primary export, which peaked at $35 a barrel in 1982, fell to $25 in 1985 and continued to fall further to $12 in 1986 (Woo and Nasution 1989). In addition, the worldwide currency alignment of 1986 aggravated the terms of trade because many Indonesian exports were priced in terms of the U.S. dollar. As a consequence, per capita

Table 9.13 *Savings and investment in Indonesia*

	Domestic/GDP Saving	Investment/GDP
1978	26.3	23.9
1979	33.6	26.6
1980	37.2	24.3
1981	33.7	29.6
1982	27.9	27.5
1983	29.0	28.7
1984	29.7	26.2
1985	29.8	28.1
1986	27.3	28.3
1987	32.9	31.4
1988	34.0	31.5
1989	37.2	34.7
1990	37.7	36.4

Source: World Bank.

income peaked in 1980 and 1981 and fell by over 20% by 1985. Finally, the rupiah was devalued by 44% in 1983 and a further 46% in 1986. Since then, the rupiah has depreciated at an annual rate between 3% and 5%.

It is difficult to find an immediate effect on the saving rate after the 1983 reform from the data in Table 9.13. The saving rates actually fell slightly below the average in the years immediately prior to the reform (30.8 to 31.7). In contrast, the saving rate appears to have responded strongly to the reform of 1988, increasing from 31.5% in 1988 to 37.2 in 1989 and 37.7 in 1990.

Investment

Investment would be enhanced by financial reform if either domestic saving increased, or if more domestic saving were channeled toward investment. As discussed earlier, both preconditions for an increase in the rate of investment were present.

The conditions at the time of the first reforms in 1983 were not propitious for an increase in investment due to the ending of the oil boom. Even though inflation had decreased, GDP fell steadily through the first four years of the period. Nevertheless, investment increased from an average of 26.4% of GDP in the five years prior to the reform to 29% of GDP in the first five years after the reform. Moreover, the share of investment increased in each year after the reform, and in

Table 9.14 *Share of private investment*

	Private I/GDI	Public I/GDI
1981	55.8	44.2
1982	52.5	47.5
1983	51.2	48.8
1984	54.2	45.8
1985	47.6	52.4
1986	52.2	47.8
1987	52.3	47.7
1988	54.2	45.8
1989	59.2	40.8

Source : Pfeffermann and Madarassy (1991).

1987 and 1988 reached a proportion of GDP that exceeded even the years of the oil boom.

Unlike the response of investment during the five years after the first reform, the response of investment after PAKTO took place in a strengthening economy. GDP had grown steadily since reaching its trough in 1987, reaching a level in 1990 30% higher than the 1987 level. In addition, despite the depressed oil prices, the general terms of trade had strengthened in favor of Indonesia as a result of the 1986 devaluation together with the relative success in containing inflationary pressures.

Still, the response of investment to PAKTO appears to have been stronger than can be explained by the combination of favorable factors. The investment/GDP ratio in the last four years studied exceeded the levels attained in any of the years prior to the reforms.

Further evidence supports the view that financial reform contributed to the strength of investment in the late 1980s in Indonesia. Pfeffermann and Madarassy (1991) present data on the share of private investment in total investment for developing countries. Their data, as presented in Table 9.14, show that the share of the private investment has fluctuated considerably since 1981. As might be expected, the share of private investment weakened with the decline of the oil boom, falling from 55.8% in 1981 to 47.6% in 1985. Despite the weaker economic conditions, private investment has grown relative to public investment since 1985, reaching a level in 1989 that exceeded its previous peak by 3.4%. Last, the evidence in Chapter 4 suggests gains in efficiency and in the extent to which small firms received credit by the late 1980s.

The effectiveness of monetary control

Loss of monetary control represents one of the possible costs of financial reform. The switch from a system of quantitative controls to the use of market instruments may create uncertainties about the central bank's control over money and credit in both the short and long run. In the short run, a transition problem can arise if the central bank either cannot predict the adjustments made by financial institutions and others, or is unable to respond quickly. In the longer run, financial reform may produce a system where the central bank is less able to control money and credit than before.

Transition effects

1983 reform: Developing the instruments of monetary control

The 1983 financial reforms affected Bank Indonesia's control over money and credit in two ways. First, the reforms removed Bank Indonesia's prime instrument of monetary control, the system of credit ceilings that gave it relatively precise control over money and credit. Second, they also reduced the scope of the liquidity credit program through which Bank Indonesia supplied base money to the banks.

Under the system of credit ceilings, Bank Indonesia could set the maximum credit that could be extended by individual banks, effectively controlling aggregate credit. As Woo (1991) notes, this system of credit ceilings also reduced both the likelihood and the impact of external disturbances from capital inflows. Disturbances were less likely because domestic banks would not have any reason to transfer funds from abroad when their credit ceilings were binding. The impact of disturbances was limited because, even though these capital flows would increase the monetary base, second round effects would be absent. Banks would gain excess reserves, but the credit ceilings would limit any expansion of the money supply based on these reserves.

The reforms effectively left Bank Indonesia without any direct instruments to control monetary and credit conditions because the absence of government debt ruled out any open market operations, a weakness recognized by the authorities. The financial reforms of June 1983 were followed by a succession of measures to strengthen monetary control. In February 1984, Bank Indonesia resumed issuing the Sertifikat Bank Indonesia (SBI), its own short-term debt instrument in which it could undertake open market operations.[13] On the other hand, it could increase base money only within set limits since it could purchase no more than the amount of outstanding SBIs.

Bank Indonesia developed the use of the SBI in gradual stages. Initially offered at fixed rates determined by Bank Indonesia, SBIs were auctioned for the first time in March 1984. By the end of June 1984, outstanding SBIs had reached a level of only Rp. 17 billion. The development of active monetary policy accelerated in reaction to unsettled conditions in the domestic interbank market in August 1984.[14] A speculative outflow of foreign exchange, an apparent response to a more rapid depreciation in the rupiah, together with a shortage of domestic liquidity had driven the interbank rate from an average of 22% in August to a peak of 90% in September. Bank Indonesia dealt with the foreign exchange outflow by reducing the ceiling on interbank borrowing for any bank from 15% to 7.5% of its total deposit liabilities, forcing some banks to repatriate funds from abroad. High interest rates, together with a reduced rate of depreciation, quickly produced a return flow of foreign exchange and restored the interbank rate to its original levels.

One aspect of this episode, noted by Cole and Slade (1990a), demonstrated the lack of a dependable mechanism for adding liquidity to the market on a permanent basis. The decreased ceiling on interbank lending put pressure on those banks that had depended on the interbank market for financing. To offset these pressures, Bank Indonesia was forced to provide emergency credit under its short-term discount facility, eventually extending the emergency credits for a maximum term of six months. To remedy this lack of a mechanism for adding permanent liquidity, Bank Indonesia introduced the Surat Beharga Pasar Uang (SBPU), an instrument that was "essentially a standardized banker's acceptance which Bank Indonesia was prepared to purchase at a discount from the banks" (Cole and Slade 1990a). The addition of this instrument gave Bank Indonesia a combination of instruments through which it could control the monetary base in either direction.

Within three years of the 1983 reforms, Bank Indonesia had managed the transition from a system of direct control of credit to one where it could control money and credit through the market mechanism using its management of SBIs and SBPUs. Despite the gradual start in using these instruments, by July 1986 – little more than two years after their introduction – SBIs outstanding had grown to Rp. 2,100 billion ($1.9 billion) while SBPUs had reached Rp. 368 billion ($323 million). With these amounts outstanding, Bank Indonesia had the potential to make full use of market instruments for monetary and credit control.

Two aspects of the transition after the 1983 reforms should be noted. The actual mechanics could have created doubts about the stability of the rupiah. Bank Indonesia had abandoned its main tool for managing credit conditions without gaining any apparent substitute. Nevertheless, the reforms did not precipitate any immediate reaction by either the banks or their customers. More attractive interest rates reinforced their incentives to keep holding rupiah deposits. In the event, when doubts did develop about the sustainability of the rupiah for other reasons, the self-adjusting mechanisms in response to the capital outflow tightened domestic credit conditions without the need for any active measures from the monetary authorities.

PAKTO: Managing excess liquidity

PAKTO 1988 created entirely different problems from those arising from the reforms of 1983. The SBI and the SBPU were well established and gave Bank Indonesia scope to influence the monetary base. The immediate problem resulting from PAKTO was dealing with the transition following the release of substantial excess liquidity through the reduction of reserve requirements from 15% to 2%.

In the first step of the transition, most of the base money released from the lower reserve requirements was absorbed by a forced purchase of three-month and six-month SBIs by the banks. For this component of reserves, the immediate effect of the reform was to reduce the cost of holding reserves by replacing non–interest-bearing reserves with securities bearing interest at rates of 16% for three months and 16.5% for six months.

As in any operation of this sort, it was difficult to judge the portion of the released liquidity that the banks would treat as excess. In the event, as Lane, Cole, and Slade (1991) observe, the combined effect of the lower reserve requirements and the compulsory acquisition of SBIs left the banks with lower reserves than they wished. Banks reduced their reserve holdings by only Rp. 1.2 billion while the special SBI issue absorbed Rp. 1.9 billion. The resulting pressure on liquidity raised interbank lending rates from the 14% to 15% range immediately prior to PAKTO to an average rate of 18% in the two months following.

The compulsory SBI purchase served only to delay the main problem for monetary policy: the orderly release of the excess reserves out of compulsory SBI holdings. The problem was reduced by a number of developments. Banks found themselves unable to reduce their actual reserves to levels below 5%. In addition, Bank Indonesia promoted the development of an active secondary market in SBIs so that banks would be willing to absorb the compulsory holdings of SBIs voluntarily when released. Finally, the government introduced a ceiling on net open foreign exchange positions equal to 25% of total bank capital, making domestic liquidity holding more attractive by limiting the use of foreign exchange holdings for liquidity management. By May 1989 when all the compulsory SBI holdings had been released, Indonesian banks had absorbed this liquidity by voluntarily holding excess reserves together with SBIs bought at the terms established by Bank Indonesia's auctions.

Long-run effects of reforms

It is difficult to find a single measure of the impact of financial reform on the central bank's ability to operate monetary policy effectively. The expansion or the volatility of money itself does not serve as an adequate indicator because, as discussed previously, improved efficiency of the banking system will induce the public to shift from other assets to bank deposits. Rapid growth, or even variable growth, in the money supply, rather than signaling lack of monetary control, may be required as an accommodation to the changing demand for deposits.

A reduced effectiveness of monetary policy could manifest itself in a number of ways in an open economy such as Indonesia. As in a closed economy, less effective control may show up in higher and more variable inflation. But in an open economy, these pressures will be quickly transmitted to the balance of payments. Thus, other indicators of impaired monetary control consist of signs of difficulty in maintaining exchange-rate objectives: at a discrete level, more frequent and larger devaluations and, less discretely, forced changes in the rate of depreciation of the crawling peg.

Inflation

Table 9.15 shows the rate of inflation for the Indonesian economy from 1970 through 1990. For the years before the 1983 reform, the rate of inflation averaged 16.1%, ranging from a high of 40.6% in 1974 to a low of 4.4% in 1971. From the first reform in 1983 onward, the average rate of inflation has decreased to an average of 7.5%, with a maximum of only 11.8% At the same time, the variability of inflation, as measured by the standard deviation, has fallen from 9.8 to 2.8. Thus, the

Table 9.15 *Economic indicators, 1970–90*

Year	Inflation (Percent per annum)	Rupiah/U.S. $
1970	12.4	378
1971	4.4	415
1972	6.5	415
1973	31.0	415
1974	40.6	415
1975	19.1	415
1976	19.9	415
1977	11.0	415
1978	8.1	625
1979	16.3	627
1980	18.0	627
1981	12.2	644
1982	9.5	693
1983	11.8	994
1984	10.5	1074
1985	4.7	1125
1986	5.9	1641
1987	9.2	1650
1988	8.0	1731
1989	6.4	1800
1990	7.5	
1970-82		
Average	16.1	
Standard deviation	9.8	
1984-90		
Average	7.5	
Standard deviation	2.2	

financial reform appears to have contributed neither to a higher nor a more variable rate of inflation.

Exchange rate

The exchange rate, also shown in Table 9.15, shows relative stability through the period, punctuated by three substantial devaluations, 50.6% in 1978, 43.5% in 1983 (immediately before the first reform), and 45.9% in 1986. In addition, after the 1978 devaluation, the exchange rate has been allowed to decline at a fairly steady, gradual rate.

These data by themselves provide little basis for determining whether the reforms affected Indonesia's ability to maintain a stable exchange rate. Both the period before and after financial reform experienced large devaluations of the rupiah. More relevant is the contribution of the financial sector to the devaluations.

The sole devaluation since the start of the financial reforms took place in September 1986. Woo and Nasution (1989, p. 110) show that the slowdown in the developed economies strongly affected Indonesia's trade position in oil and other commodities. The price of oil fell from $25 a barrel in 1985 to $13 a barrel in 1986. The nonoil terms of trade also deteriorated sharply. Despite a 10% increase in volume, the value of nonoil exports declined by 5% in terms of foreign purchasing power.

The continuing depreciation of the U.S. dollar against other currencies also aggravated Indonesia's balance of payments problems. The prices of most exports, especially oil were set in dollars, but over 70% of Indonesia's debt was denominated in other currencies. Woo and Nasution suggest that "the drastic drop of the dollar against the other currencies accounted for more than 70 percent of the $1.1 billion increase in debt service over the 1984–6 period" (p. 110) and conclude:

> With the worsening of the trade balance, the growing shadow of a debt crisis and the slowing down of economic activities, the September 1986 devaluation of 45% against the dollar was the single most effective step Indonesia could take to simultaneously improve its capacity to earn foreign exchange and stimulate its economy. (p. 111)

Thus, the evidence suggests that this devaluation was caused primarily by external factors rather than the financial reform.

9.5   Assessment of the reform

Cost and benefits of reform

Financial reform has substantially revamped the Indonesian financial system since 1983. From a system dominated by large state banks where key interest rates were determined and credit was allocated directly by Bank Indonesia, it has become one with competition between many private and state banks where flows of credit and interest rates depend mainly on market forces. Indonesia has not been alone in pursuing this type of financial reform. The experience of other countries have been wide and varied. What lessons can be derived from the Indonesian experience?

By most measures the Indonesian economy has benefited from the financial reforms through the greater effectiveness of the financial system. The price of banking services, as measured by the spreads between loan and deposit rates, has narrowed through the different phases of reform, though this is by no means conclusive evidence of efficiency gains in banking. The public has responded to the lower cost of intermediation by increasing its demand for financial services. The ratio of M2 to GDP, a measure of financial development, has increased 2.5-fold from 17.7 in 1982 to 44.6 at the end of 1990. With this greater financial development, the banking system in turn has increased its lending to the private sector.

These favorable developments in the financial sector appear to have strengthened the Indonesian economy overall. Despite external pressures from weak oil prices and rising external debt costs, investment has responded to the financial development and reached a higher share of GDP at the end of the period than ever before.

Experience elsewhere warns of the potential dangers of financial reform: financial distress, impaired monetary control, and instability of financial markets. None of these so far has turned out to be a problem. To date, there have been few clear signs of financial distress resulting from the Indonesian financial reforms: Bank lending has increased steadily since the reforms and has been reflected in higher levels of investment. Monetary control appears to have been convincingly maintained. The foreign exchange market also does not appear to be destabilized by the reform, despite one devaluation and one other crisis that provoked strong direct measures. Aside from these episodes, the authorities managed the depreciation of the rupiah against the dollar in an orderly manner.

Lessons from the Indonesian experience

What factors explain the relative success of Indonesia in avoiding the costs frequently associated with financial reform? Some of the credit must be given to the administration of the reforms. In particular, the phasing of the reforms appears to have reduced uncertainties about the outcome. In addition, some of the success can be attributed to two particular aspects of Indonesian economic policy: the absence of domestically held government debt and the lack of foreign exchange controls.

The phased reforms

As discussed, financial reform in Indonesia has been a continual process, beginning in 1983, continuing through PAKTO 1988 and its successors to present. This staging of the reform has avoided uncertainties and instabilities that would have been present had all the reforms occurred at once.

It might have been costly to have consolidated all the reforms into one package. As it was, the two measures that forced the greatest adjustment on the banks were placed in different packages. The 1983 measures changed the banks' environment by replacing credit ceilings and administered interest rates with market mechanisms, whereas the PAKTO reform introduced new entry through newly established banks and increased competition through easier branching.

The delay of entry measures until PAKTO in 1988 allowed existing banks a chance to adjust to the 1983 measures. These banks had operated in an environment where Bank Indonesia determined their lending opportunities and where much of their lending and deposit-taking had been subsidized. New entrants would have been unburdened by loan portfolios acquired under the former credit regime. The opportunity to adjust to the new rules before facing the competitive pressures from new entrants may have helped existing banks avoid or limit their degree of financial distress. Some aspects of the separation were, however, potentially costly, particularly the delay of prudential reforms to the later phases of the reform process. Raising capital requirements after reforms have been well underway led to a sharp slowdown in lending and a tightening up of lending standards. When prudential supervision cannot be upgraded rapidly, which is usually the case in developing and transitional economies, it may thus be advisable to raise capital requirements as early as possible. Also, losses in Indonesia's banking system might have turned out to be greater had not entry limits been maintained in the early years of reform.

Absence of domestic debt

The absence of domestically held government debt can be expected to reduce uncertainties about inflation. A government with domestic debt may be tempted to tolerate more inflation because it can appear to ease the burden of financing the debt. Thus, a government, like that of Indonesia, which does not have any outstanding domestic debt will be more credible in its determination to maintain price stability.

The credibility of a government's commitment to price stability can be critical to the success of financial reform. A financial reform will work if it induces the public to hold deposits and other claims of financial institutions. Uncertainty about inflation could create doubts, in turn, about the rate of return on financial assets and discourage the public from holding them.

In the case of the Indonesian financial reform, the credibility of the government's commitment to price stability was especially important. When the reforms began, the extreme inflation of the 1960s were no more than 15 years in the past. The reform would have had little chance of success unless the government had established an expectation of domestic stability.

Openness of foreign exchange markets

The openness of the foreign exchange market should also increase the chances for success of a financial reform. With strict foreign exchange controls, domestic financial assets may be held involuntarily as the best opportunity in absence of the opportunity to hold foreign exchange assets. In this circumstance, domestic financial markets and institutions will be in a state of imbalance.

It is difficult to predict how financial reform will affect this imbalance. If there is the possibility of removal or avoidance of exchange controls, domestic asset holders will make different choices than they would in the absence of controls. Some will avoid making choices that limit their flexibility in case controls are removed. All investors will be wary of, and protect themselves against, possible destabilizing effects, such as capital flight, that may be caused by the opening up of the foreign exchange market. Each of these reactions would be strengthened if the financial reform is viewed as part of a program that will eventually lead to liberalization of foreign exchange markets.

In the Indonesian case, the absence of foreign exchange controls may have actually eased the adjustment to the financial reforms. Investors with concerns about the stability of the financial system had already protected themselves by holding foreign currencies. In addition, the absence of foreign exchange controls would encourage Indonesians who held foreign currency assets abroad to repatriate them in response to the better domestic opportunities because if the better opportunities were not sustained, the investors could opt to return their funds abroad.

The openness of the Indonesian foreign exchange market at the time of the financial reform might be interpreted as evidence against the commonly prescribed ordering of financial reform before the opening of foreign exchange markets. Such an interpretation would be a misreading. The Indonesian reforms could succeed with less risk of jeopardizing the soundness of the banking system because the continued openness reduced the possibility of a vulnerable unbalanced system. To some extent, the flight had occurred gradually in the past as many Indonesians sought banking services abroad. The reaction to financial reform would have been very different in the absence of this safety valve.

To date, the Indonesian financial reforms have been reasonably successful by most measures. The scale of financial intermediation has expanded substantially and with it the capacity for domestic finance. The growth in intermediation has been accompanied by expanding investment, despite less than strong economic conditions. Still, some signs of financial distress have become apparent since 1990. A large private bank has failed and the weak condition of the state banks has become apparent. In response, the authorities have taken a number of measures to strengthen both prudential regulation and the banking system. Notably the reform has progressed without creating problems for monetary management. It is difficult to draw general lessons from the experience of one country. But the gradual, sustained pace of the reforms, coupled with the convincing commitment to low inflation, stand as cornerstones to the success of the effort.

NOTES

1 Much of the following discussion of the early development of Indonesian banking has been drawn from Suwidjana (1984).
2 Foreign banks could not offer savings deposits, were limited to two branches, and could not lend outside Jakarta.
3 The actual impact of the change on the volume of liquidity credits is discussed in Section 9.5.
4 The simultaneous removal of the tax exemption and the lowering of the cash reserve requirements appear to have almost offset each other in terms of the cost of funds for the banks.
5 The present treatment of the early development of the Jakarta Stock Exchange is based on Woo and Nasution (1989).
6 The following discussion is based on Cole and Slade (1990b).
7 The deregulation package of 1983 also appears to have influenced the patterns of short-term interest rates even though the rates paid by the state banks were not directly controlled. For example, the difference between the rates paid on three-month deposits fell on average from 8% in the years up to 1983 to 2.6% in 1983.
8 The gross interest margin measures the difference between domestic interest received and domestic interest paid as a percentage of domestic assets. The domestic comparisons were limited to this one measure, interest margin, because the banks did not break down their other income and operating costs between domestic and foreign income.
   The gross margin used for the overall business of the banks measures the difference between total income and total expenses excluding operating costs expressed as a percentage of total assets. Net earnings adjust the gross margin for operating costs.
9 The growth rate of credit at state banks is presented as an additional reference because of the longer data series.
10 The limited size of the program may appear surprising, given the appeal to both borrowers and their banks. The program, however, did not at that time offer Bank Indonesia any distinct advantage as an instrument in directing credit to different sectors. It was already able to direct credit through the system of credit ceilings.

11 De Juan's list of contributory causes extends well beyond those that are considered here. This paper discusses only those for which evidence is available. Internal control procedures of commercial banks, for example, may be just as important as any cause considered here. Nothing can be said about their degree of importance in Indonesia given the lack of available information.

12 With respect to weak supervision, de Juan observed: "Many developing countries show some major gaps in bank regulation. . . . [E]ntry requirements are very loose or, if very stringent, based on the wrong criteria. Capital adequacy requirements are set too low to cushion losses, allow for components of capital that hardly deserve the name, and are frequently measured as a proportion of deposits or assets irrespective of the risks involved. . . . Limits to large exposures or to loans to related parties do not exist or are very lax (one to three times the bank's equity in some cases)" (1991, pp. 5–6).

13 Woo and Nasution (1989, p. 93) note that SBIs were first issued in 1970, but were discontinued during the oil boom of the 1970s. Banks were encouraged to hold their funds in foreign assets so as to reduce the impact of oil revenues on the domestic money supply. Meek (1991) describes some of the operational issues in implementation.

14 For a more detailed description of this episode, see Balino and Sundararajan (1986) and Lane, Cole, and Slade (1991).

CHAPTER 10

Financial reform in Malaysia

Zainal Aznam Yusof, Awang Adek Hussin,
Ismail Alowi, Lim Chee Sing, and Sukhdave Singh

Liberalization of Malaysia's financial markets, tackled in earnest in the early 1980s, has been gradual and cautious. It has been a process of structural deregulation and prudential reregulation, with the authorities willing to change course when borrower net worth (and the banks) have come under pressure. The result appears to be a financial system that is more stable and competitive, with a wider public choice of financial instruments, as well as institutions, and more effective conduct of monetary policy by the Central Bank.

Malaysia began the reform process with a relatively deep financial sector, compared with the simple structure of the mid-1950s. It also had a relatively open economy, with little financial repression and negative real interest rates only at the time of the first oil shock in 1973. Yet there were many structural weaknesses in the economy and the financial system, which came to the fore only during the recession of the early 1980s. Malaysia's experience suggests that in financially repressed countries contemplating liberalization, governments should first administratively raise interest rates, sort out the health of banks, and at the same time build a strong central bank on both the regulatory and monetary side.

Malaysia's Central Bank was a key player in its financial reform. By keeping inflation down, the Bank helped the spread of long-term financial markets and facilitated the growth of money markets. The introduction of repos and swaps has broadened the range of monetary instruments, while the reforms in government securities' markets have made it easier for the Central Bank to conduct open-market operations, although these are still small. Moreover, new laws and regula-

The authors wish to acknowledge the comments of their colleagues at Bank Negara Malaysia and of Jerry Caprio. However, the views expressed here are those of the authors and may not represent the views of Bank Negara.

tions governing the conduct and accountability of banks and other financial institutions have allowed the Central Bank to act quickly to deal with delinquent firms and so give credibility and sustainability to Malaysia's financial reforms. The impact of these reforms on the Malaysian economy and their contribution to growth and development is the focus of this study.

Malaysia's macroeconomic background is covered in Section 10.1, followed by an overview of the financial system. Section 10.3 deals with the nature of liberalization and Section 10.4 with the effects of reform on the economy and financial system. The new regulatory and supervisory framework of reform is analyzed in Section 10.5 and, finally, the lessons of Malaysia's experience are drawn in Section 10.6.

10.1   The Malaysian economy: 1970–90

Malaysia generally has enjoyed rapid economic growth with rising per capita income and price stability. Real GDP growth accelerated from an average of 5.2% a year in 1961–70 to about 8% in the 1970s. However, it slowed down considerably in the early 1980s before bouncing back to 7% in 1986–90. The economic growth of the 1960s and 1970s was accompanied by rising per capita income and living standards, greater urbanization and access to health and education, and an improvement in the distribution of income. At the end of 1990, nominal GNP stood at U.S.$41 billion and per capita income at U.S.$2,300. In 1970–90 the government pursued a policy of diversification in agriculture and industry, and the role of public sector in the economy was reduced. Table 10.1 reviews GDP, prices, the balance of payments, and the government deficit.

The soaring seventies

Malaysia's growth performance in the 1970s was led by a rapid expansion of palm oil output, in the face of a modest expansion of rubber, a prior leading sector. Hence, the share of palm oil in agriculture value added increased from 9.6% in 1970 to 25% in 1980, while in rubber it decreased from 34.3% to 24.9%. With generous tax and other incentives, export-oriented and labor-intensive industries, such as electronics, textile, and wood products, also flourished. In 1970–80, the manufacturing sector grew by 12.5%, accounting for 20.5% of GDP in 1980. The expansion of crude oil production (by 31.6%) compensated for the decline in tin output. Much of the increase in Malaysian exports in the 1970s (7.6%) came from palm oil, crude oil, and manufactures.[1]

Table 10.1 *Malaysia: Key macroeconomic indicators*
(% change unless otherwise indicated)

		1971-79 Avg.	1980	1985	1989	1990
1.	Real GDP	8.4	7.4	-1.1	8.8	10.0
	Agriculture	5.2	1.3	2.0	5.8	1.7
	Mining	5.6	-2.2	-1.9	8.6	4.1
	Manufacturing	12.0	9.2	-3.8	12.0	17.8
	Construction	9.2	17.3	-8.4	11.6	16.0
	Services	8.7	10.7	1.7	8.6	10.6
2.	Real Aggregate Domestic Demand					
	Private Consumption	7.7	12.7	0.3	14.3	12.5
	Private Investment	17.3	17.9	-8.6	31.0	30.3
	Public Consumption	7.2	25.1	-0.9	7.6	5.0
	Public Investment	11.7	38.1	-10.4	33.5	14.0
3.	Domestic Prices	5.9	6.7	0.4	2.8	3.1
4.	Balance of Payments					
	Merchandise Exports ($b)	11.7	28.0	37.6	66.8	78.3
	Merchandise Imports ($b)	9.3	22.8	28.7	56.2	73.1
	Merchandise Account ($b)	2.4	5.2	8.9	10.6	5.2
	Current Account ($b)	0.2	-0.1	-1.5	-0.6	-4.5
5.	Federal Government Overall Deficit ($b)	2,013	7,104	5,707	5,260	5,516
	(Without transfer to Dev. Fund)	-1,635	-3,704	-4,407	-3,410	-3,437
	% of GNP	8.0	13.8	6.6	5.5	5.0
		-7.0	-7.2	-6.1	-3.5	-3.1

Redressing social and income distribution imbalances (in line with the New Economic Policy development plan for 1971–90) led to an expansion of the government's role in the economy in the 1970s. Total public investment increased from 5.7% of GNP in 1970 to 8.8% in 1980, while public consumption doubled to 20.2% of GNP. At the same time, private investment and consumption increased by 12% and 7.7%, respectively.

The external accounts were relatively favorable: in 1970–80, imports increased by 9.8%, mainly due to rising capital goods imports, in line with growth in private investment. However, imports of consumption and intermediate goods fell because of the import substitution policies of the government in the 1960s and early 1970s. In the 1970s Malaysia's overall balance of payments was consistently in surplus. Although the service account was persistently in deficit (due to investment income payments and freight and insurance outflows), the merchandise account surplus was in general somewhat larger. So, too, was the capital account, and substantially so, thanks to sustained inflows of corporate investment, as well as government borrowing abroad. As a result, external reserves of the Central Bank increased to $10.3 billion at the end of 1980, sufficient to finance about 5.5 months of retained imports.

Malaysia's gross national saving increased from 18% of GNP in 1970 to a peak of 34.8% by 1979, due to both a rapid increase in domestic income during the Third Malaysia Plan and attractive real interest rates on deposits, which were gradually deregulated during the decade (see below). Over the same period, investment increased from 17.8% to 30% of GNP. The savings–investment gap was always positive except for a few years in the early 1970s when a small gap of $3 million emerged.

Inflation, as measured by the consumer price index, was higher in the 1970s (5.8%, compared with less than 1% in the 1960s). It rose from 3.2% in 1972 to a peak of 17.5 in 1974, thanks mainly to the (first) oil shock of 1973. However, the CPI's increase moderated to only 4% per annum in 1976–9, due partly to government anti-inflation measures.

Adjustment in the 1980s

Malaysia's economic growth of the 1970s was halted in the early 1980s by a prolonged global recession, despite countercyclical policies adopted by the Government. The balance of payments and government budgetary positions also deteriorated. By 1982, the public sector deficit stood at 19% of GNP; the balance-of-payments current-account deficit was 14% of GNP, with an increase in external borrowing and foreign debt. After 1982, Malaysia's economic performance slackened further, revealing structural weaknesses embedded in the economy.

In mid-1982, the government embarked on a massive fiscal retrenchment exercise as part of a multiyear structural adjustment program. The government also took effective control over its activities and those of the nonfinancial public enterprises (NFPEs) to bring about an efficient management of the economy, while, at the same time, reducing the size and role of the public sector in the economy. The deficit was financed mainly by noninflationary domestic sources, while external borrowing was curtailed to reduce the debt/service ratio.

By the end of 1985, the budget and balance-of-payments deficit were reduced, respectively, to 6% and 2.1% of GNP. External debt increased by 14.2% in 1985, inflation was below 1%, and the Central Bank's international reserve amounted to $12.5 billion, enough to finance five months of retained imports. As noted below, the credibility gains from persevering with such a tough adjustment program appear to have been considerable.

Just as the economy was emerging from this adjustment process, it was hit again by the collapse of commodity prices at the end of 1985. International terms of trade fell by 4.5% in 1985 and by 14.9% in 1986. Thus, nominal national income declined by -5.8% in 1985-6, with lower aggregate domestic demand resulting in a 10.7% fall in real private sector expenditure.

In the mid-1980s, the government began promoting the private sector as the engine of economic growth. A new privatization policy, pursued partly to reduce the size of the public sector in the economy, saw nine projects privatized by 1986. The government also relaxed regulations on foreign equity participation in Malaysia, and parts of the Industrial Coordination Act 1975 were liberalized. Up to 100% foreign equity ownership of export-oriented companies was allowed; visa and work permit requirements for foreign employees of companies with foreign paid-up capital of U.S.$2 million or more were eased; approval of new investment projects made easier; foreign investment guidelines were loosened; and the Central Bank's scheme to promote exports and domestic linkages was revamped.

By the end of 1986, real GDP was rising by 1.2%. Notwithstanding this upward economic trend, unemployment increased from 8.5% in 1986 to 9.1% in 1987, leading to the adoption of measures to stimulate further growth and reduce unemployment. These included low-cost housing schemes, speedier approval of licenses for small business, easier transfer of land to the private sector for cultivation of commercial crops, new public infrastructure projects, and a crash program to retrain the unemployed. To reduce unemployment of university graduates, temporary employment schemes were adopted by some government agencies, private companies were encouraged to offer training and jobs, and the Ministry of Education's teacher-training scheme was intensified. The government also continued to keep a tight rein on public sector wage increases.

To encourage the private sector further, the 1988 budget saw (1) the reduction of corporation tax from 40% to 35% and the scaled abolition of the 5% development tax, beginning with 1% reduction in 1990; (2) the scrapping of the 3% excess profit tax on companies; (3) the extension of the reinvestment allowance period for another two years and increasing its rate from 25% to 40%; (4) the introduction of a $500 million soft loan scheme under the Enterprise Rehabilitation Fund to help Bumiputera industries (Bumiputera is the official term for Malays and other indigenous groups); (5) amendments to the Industrial Relation Act 1967, the Trade Union Act 1959, and the Employment Act 1955 to ensure greater flexibility in wage determination; (6) the launch of the ASEAN–Japan Development Fund (ASEAN is the Association of South East Asian Nations) to provide financing for small and medium industries (SMIs) for investment in manufacturing, agriculture, and tourism; and (7) the loan limit under a special loan scheme for small traders and hawkers increased from $2,000 to $3,000 ($5,000 in special cases), while the capital eligibility criterion was raised from $5,000 to $10,000.

To strengthen its budgetary position, particularly to overcome the deficit in the current account, the federal government (1) lowered wage levels for new recruits in the public sector; (2) introduced tighter controls of expenditures of statutory bodies; (3) privatized or closed unprofitable government enterprises; and (4) began prepaying and refinancing the government's more expensive external market loans. With better domestic macroeconomic policies and stronger world economic recovery since 1987, the Malaysian economy picked up again. Real GDP growth accelerated to over 9% a year on average over the last three years of the 1980s, while inflation averaged less than 2% per year.

10.2   The financial system

The Malaysian financial system can be divided into the banking system and the system of nonbank financial intermediaries. The Central Bank and the commercial banks constitute the monetary institutions, but the banking system also includes finance companies and merchant banks, which are regulated by the Central Bank, as well as the discount houses, money and foreign exchange brokers, and the Credit Guarantee Corporation, which provides guarantee cover for commercial banks on loans to small businesses.

Nonbank financial intermediaries, which are supervised by various government departments and agencies, can be divided into five groups – the development finance institutions, the savings institutions, provident and pension funds, insurance companies, and others, which include the building societies and unit trusts. The *capital market* comprises a primary securities market, in which issues of government and corporate securities are offered for sale, and a secondary market, in which such securities are traded. Funds raised by the private sector in the capital market were dwarfed by those raised by the federal government. However, in the secondary market (mainly the Kuala Lumpur Stock Exchange but also the Bumiputera Stock Exchange Division of the Komplek Kewangan Malaysia Berhad), the volume of business in corporate securities outweighed that in government securities, which are held mainly by the institutions (particularly provident and pension funds) and held mainly to maturity.

Total resources of the financial system, expressed in current prices, grew phenomenally to M$309.1 billion in 1990, compared with M$11.6 billion in 1970 and representing an average annual growth rate of 17.8% (see Table 10.2). Unlike Korea, which also saw rapid financial deepening over the same period, the banking system led the way in Malaysia, accounting for almost 75% of the 1990 total (and the Central Bank for 12.1%), significantly higher than the 64.1% in 1970. However, the share of the nonbank financial intermediaries declined from 35.9% to 25.5% over the same period. The *commercial banks,* which accounted for 44.2% of total assets in 1990 (38.4% in 1977), have seen strong deposit growth and branch-network expansion since 1970. By 1990 there were 38 commercial banks, of which 22 were domestic incorporated banks, and representative offices of foreign banks increased from 12 to 29. Bank branches doubled to 1,000, an average population-to-banking office ratio of 18,277.

Finance companies compete with commercial banks for savings and fixed deposits but, specializing in hire-purchase and housing loan finance, they complement the credit operations of banks. Between 1978 and 1990, finance companies increased their numbers from 33 to 45, and their branch network from 195 to 542. Their share of total assets also increased sharply – from 4.6% in 1970 to 12.8% in 1990. The first of Malaysia's 12 *merchant banks* was established only in 1970, and by 1990 their branches numbered 17. Accounting for about 3.6% of total assets in 1990 (2.4% in 1977), the merchant banks were mainly involved in wholesale banking, money market operations, and corporate finance. Malaysian *discount houses* are financial intermediaries that mobilize short-term funds from other financial institutions and companies that have excess liquid funds and want to temporarily "park" them as earning assets. They were required by the Central Bank to invest only in government securities. Since they enjoyed rediscounting and lender-of-last-resort facilities at the Central Bank, they were essential in making a secondary market for government

Table 10.2 *Assets of the financial system*

By Institutions	Outstanding ($ Million)				% Share			
	1970	1977	1985	1990	1970	1977	1985	1990
Banking System	7,455	26,098	118,509	230,243	64.1	69.6	71.4	74.5
Monetary Institutions	6,882	21,919	91,343	174,127	59.2	58.5	55.0	56.3
Central Bank	2,227	7,701	16,525	37,545	19.2	20.5	9.9	12.1
Currency Board	195	55	-	-	1.7	0.1	0.0	0.0
Commercial Banks	4,460	14,163	74,234	129,197	38.4	37.8	44.7	41.8
Islamic Banks	-	-	584	7,385	0.0	0.0	0.4	2.4
Non-monetary Institutions	573	4,179	27,166	56,116	4.9	11.1	16.4	18.2
Finance Companies	531	2,610	17,833	39,457	4.6	7.0	10.7	12.8
Merchant Banks	-	914	6,296	11,063	0.0	2.4	3.8	3.6
Discount Houses	42	649	2,830	4,871	0.4	1.7	1.7	1.6
Credit Guarantee Corp.	-	6	207	726	0.0	...	0.1	0.2
Non-Bank Financial Intermediaries	4,167	11,394	47,583	78,813	35.9	30.4	28.6	25.5
Provident, Pension and Insurance Funds	3,156	8,161	32,658	56,449	27.2	21.8	19.7	18.3
Employees Provident Fund	2,265	5,843	24,708	46,766	19.5	15.6	14.9	15.1
Other Statutory & Private Provident & Pension Funds	452	897	2,919	4,999	3.9	2.4	1.8	1.6
Life Insurance Funds	324	960	3,646	2,342	2.8	2.6	2.2	0.8
General Insurance Funds	115	461	1,385	2,342	1.0	1.2	0.8	0.8
Development Finance Institutions 1/	133	892	4,044	6,016	1.1	2.4	2.4	1.9
Savings Institutions 2/	645	1,759	8,096	10,001	5.5	4.7	4.9	3.2
Other Financial Intermediaries 3/	233	582	2,785	6,347	2.0	1.6	1.7	2.1
TOTAL	11,622	37,492	166,092	309,056	100.0	100.0	100.0	100.0

1/ Include Malaysian Industrial Development Finance Berhad (MIDF), Agricultural Bank of Malaysia, Borneo Development Corporation, Sabah Development Bank Berhad, Saban Credit Corporation, Development Bank of Malaysia, and Industrial Bank Berhad.

2/ Include National Savings Bank, Bank Kerjasama Rakyat and the co-operative societies.

3/ Include unit trusts, building societies, Pilgrims Management Fund Board, Credit Gurantee Corporation and Cagamas Berhad.

securities and providing liquidity for the financial system. The Employees Provident Fund (EPF), the largest of the *provident and pension funds,* is the largest mobilizer of private savings in the country. Accounting for 15.6% of the total assets of the financial system, it has been an important source of government financing.

Priority-sector lending and the financial system

The Central Bank did not issue guidelines on lending until the mid-1970s, when it began promoting a more development-oriented approach for banking in Malaysia. The 1975 guidelines required commercial banks and finance companies to extend a minimum of 50% of new net credit during that year to priority sectors. Almost immediately this fraction was lowered to 20%, and subsequently this was amended to a certain percent of the *outstanding* loans in a reference period. Limits were also placed on interest charged to some priority borrowers. Since the introduction of guidelines, the priority sectors have included (1) the Bumiputera community; (2) small-scale enterprises, including the Special Loans Scheme; (3) agricultural food production; (4) individual housing loans, including low-cost houses (of $25,000 and less); (5) manufacturing; and (6) the broad sector covering agriculture, fishing, and forestry; building, construction, and property development and manufacturing (Table 10.3).

Commercial banks and finance companies that did not meet the priority lending targets were required to place with the Central Bank deposits equal to their respective shortfalls for one year at a rate of interest to be determined by the Bank. Such funds were then on-lent to banks and finance companies that exceeded their targets. Sometimes the Central Bank would also on-lend to specialized agencies that lend to the private sector. But overall, the requirements were generally not binding on the financial system, especially regarding loans to Bumiputeras, since the actual amount of loans to this community tends to be higher than prescribed in the guidelines.

Since 1979 the Central Bank has issued annual priority-lending guidelines each March, suitably modified and adjusted in line with developments in the economy. Of key importance is that the guidelines were kept broad-based, with considerable discretion left to individual institutions in assessing and monitoring the credits. Most important, the system did not seriously distort interest rates since the fixed rate reflected the actual cost of funds to the banking institutions. In April 1987 interest rates on priority lending were pegged to the Base Lending Rate (BLR) but subject to a maximum level.

With banking deregulation, the Central Bank has reduced the number of priority sectors, as well as the proportion of loans covered by the guidelines. The latest (1991) set only two targets for banks – to the Bumiputera community and loans provided under the Principal Guarantee Scheme (PGS) of the Credit Guarantee Corporation for small businesses – and only one target for finance companies – just to

Table 10.3 Priority-sector guidelines and achievements of commercial banks (% and M$ million)

	Bumiputera Community		Manufacturing Sector		Agricultural Food Production		Small-scale Enterprises		Individual Housing Loans		Low Cost Housing	
	Target %	Achievement %	Target*	Achievement*	Target %	Achievement %	Target*	Achievement*	Target*	Achievement*	Target units	Achievement units
1975	50.0	56.8					10.0	12.1				
1976	20.0		25.0		10.0				10.0			
1977												
1978	20.0	21.7	20.0	19.0	10.0	8.3			10.0	13.3		
1979	17.0				6.0		20.0					
1980	17.0	29.8	$2573m	$3951m	6.0	9.5	20.0	28.9	$1417m	$2233m		19503
1981	17.0	25.0	$4018m	$5166m	8.0	11.1	12.0	13.7	10.0	13.4		21708
1982	18.0	27.5	$5166m	$5386m	10.0	12.4	12.0	12.6	10.0	13.7	20000	25738
1983	18.0	29.7	31.12.82		6.0	6.7	5.0	3.8	31.12.82		20000	26334
1984	20.0	31.7			6.0	6.2	5.0	3.2			20000	
1985	20.0	32.7			6.0	6.7	5.0	3.5			20000	
1986	20.0	31.9			6.0	5.4	$150m	$235m	80000	32658	48000	12458
1987	20.0	32.3			6.0	5.4	$150m	$217m	80000	68342	48000	29772
1988	20.0	31.8			6.0	5.2	$300m	$831m	75000	43156	45000	17903
1989	20.0	37.0					$600m	$1012m	75000	95069	45000	39525
1990	20.0	39.6					$200m	$132m				
1991	20.0						$150m					

*Initially in percent, then switches to $; "31.12.83" means that loans were to be maintained at the level of that date.

the Bumiputera community. Data indicate that commercial bank lending to the Bumiputera community accounted for 39.6% of all loans outstanding at the end of the base year (1988), well in excess of the minimum requirement of 20%. Finance companies had the same 20% but, in fact, their total lending to the Bumiputera accounted for 57.2% of all loans.

Priority lending and the government

To meet various social and economic objectives, the federal government has given loans to government agencies, as well as corporations partly owned by government. This practice has helped to avoid excessive implicit taxation of the financial system to carry out government priorities. Made from the federal budget, these loans carry interest rates that depend on the purpose for which the loans are given. In early years, loans for projects to relieve poverty were interest-free, while those for restructuring, infrastructure, strategic, and other related projects carried an interest rate of 2–5%. Commercial projects carried interest rates that reflected the full cost of government funds. The current practice is to charge one-half the cost of funds for loans to poverty-eradication programs run by financially strong government agencies, and as grants for other agencies. Loans for restructuring and other such projects have an interest rate between one-half and the full cost of funds. No government loans are given for commercial projects.

Many corporations have received such loans, as well as statutory bodies and cooperatives involved in extending credit to the private sector (Table 10.4). Bank Industri and Bank Pembangunan are development banks set up by the government to provide long-term financing for investment projects that have long gestation periods. Hicom, MSE, and Perwaja were set up to push the development of heavy industry in Malaysia. PNB and MARA respectively encourage equity ownership and the development of professional skills among the indigenous Bumiputera. The Agricultural Bank lends for agricultural projects, while FELDA, FELCRA, and RISDA are statutory bodies set up to develop land schemes and resettle the landless poor. ASEAN Bintulu Fertilizer is a joint venture with other members of ASEAN, formed partly to promote regional economic cooperation. Although these loans increased from $1.7 billion in 1975 to $9 billion in 1989, they declined from 22% to 9.8% of all outstanding loans of the banking system. Still, they can be viewed as an important "safety valve," reducing what otherwise could have been intense pressure for greater reliance on directing credit through the banks. Moreover, even with the low nomi-

Table 10.4 *Government loans to corporations and selected other agencies (M$ million)*

Corporations	1975	1980	1985	1989
		(M$ Million)		
1. MIDF	130.2	99.8	-	-
2. Food Industries of Malaysia Bhd	2.9	27.8	-	-
3. Chenderoh Electricity (M) Sdn Bhd	-	34.6	-	-
4. Syarikat Perumahan Pegawai Kerajaan	27.4	34.9	17.6	-
5. MISC	147.2	433.9	371.2	-
6. Permodalan National Berhad (PNB)	73.0	374.1	592.0	72.7
7. Bank Pembangunan Malaysia Bhd.	15.0	98.1	372.0	494.7
8. Malaysia Shipyard Engineering (MSE)	97.0	127.3	123.9	117.3
9. Malaysia Building Society Bhd (MBSB)	0.5	0.5	85.5	112.6
10. Malaysian Rubber Development Corp. Bhd	34.8	56.1	42.5	33.3
11. Syarikat Jengka Sdn Bhd	25.2	25.2	33.4	29.4
12. Pineapple Cannery of Malaysia Sdn Bhd	6.0	4.5	4.5	4.5
13. Malaysia Batek and Handicrafts Bhd	1.4	1.5	1.5	1.5
14. Syarikat Malaysia Explosives Sdn Bhd	-	14.0	13.3	12.0
15. Bank Industri Malaysia Bhd.	-	102.4	129.7	147.9
16. Syarikat Permodalan Kemajuan Perusahan	-	-	23.5	26.0
17. Syarikat Takaful Malaysia Bhd	-	-	1.0	1.0
18. Yayasan Pelaburan Bumiputra	-	-	600.0	525.0
19. ASEAN Bintulu Fertilizer Sdn Bhd	-	-	471.8	89.9
20. Komplek Kewangan Malaysia Bhd	-	-	27.0	22.4
21. Kumpulan Fima Bhd.	-	-	164.5	128.0
22. Perwaja	-	-	-	105.2
23. PETRONAS	-	-	-	385.8
24. PLUS	-	-	-	362.6
25. Sabah Forest Industries	-	-	-	266.7
26. Heavy Industry Corporation of Malaysia (HICOM)	-	-	-	626.7
Statutory Bodies (only those that extend credit to the private sector)				
1. Bank Pertanian Malaysia	20.0	125.8	262.5	410.1
2. Federal Land, Consolidation, and Rehabilitation Authority	51.4	165.3	403.3	634.3
3. Federal Land Development Authority	921.4	2012.4	3349.1	3906.4
4. MARA	151.1	326.0	325.1	219.8
5. RISDA	-	-	86.3	167.8
Co-operatives				
1. Bank Kerjasama Rakyat Malaysia	-	155.0	164.3	130.8
Total	1,704.5	4,219.2	7,665.5	9,034.4
(Relative size compared to total outstanding loans of the banking system to the private sector)	22.0%	16.0%	11.6%	9.8%

Table 10.5 *Finance sector's holdings of Malaysia government securities (outstanding) (M$ million)*

	1975	1978	1980	1981	1982	1983	1984	1985	1986	1987	1988	1989	1990
Banking System	1,225.7	1,991.5	2,812.7	4,149.3	4,256.8	4,499.3	5,063.6	4,902.9	4,966.0	7,801.5	7,863.4	10,004.3	10,039.5
Commercial Banks	1,131.6	1,806.5	2,445.9	3,818.1	3,942.8	4,027.5	4,554.3	4,248.7	4,093.2	6,661.6	6,055.5	7,819.7	7,845.7
Finance Companies	67.8	78.4	205.3	151.4	124.9	165.4	173.1	193.9	482.6	640.5	1,260.0	1,419.2	1,360.6
Merchant Banks	26.3	106.6	161.5	179.8	189.1	306.4	336.2	460.3	390.2	499.4	547.9	765.4	833.2
Other Financial Institutions	5,148.3	8,958.5	13,005.4	13,840.3	17,513.3	21,347.2	25,882.1	28,170.3	31,514.9	35,095.0	41,173.8	43,182.3	45,889.0
Central Bank	251.2	346.2	1,627.4	560.7	1,802.6	3,254.7	4,768.2	2,340.4	2,052.9	1,631.3	1,781.8	1,262.9	2,198.9
EPF	3,925.7	6,369.4	8,581.6	10,314.9	12,468.8	14,415.6	17,199.7	20,605.9	24,009.4	28,254.0	32,504.9	34,107.9	36,130.4
Insurance Companies	209.3	357.1	501.2	607.8	680.0	650.5	689.0	813.3	777.1	1,001.4	1,158.2	1,353.7	1,437.1

National Savings Bank	578.5	807.9	924.1	857.0	879.9	926.1	919.2	921.3	907.8	1,125.3	1,338.1	1,520.1	1,595.4
SOCSO	22.1	145.5	259.5	354.5	466.5	582.5	711.5	824.0	911.8	1,050.3	1,081.3	1,180.4	1,353.5
Discount Houses	151.0	748.2	889.7	976.3	1,148.4	1,208.8	1,361.6	2,134.7	1,996.3	1,461.9	953.0	1,670.4	1,190.9
Caganas Berhad										52.6	116.4	128.5	80.0
Others	10.5	184.2	221.9	169.1	67.1	309.0	232.9	530.7	859.6	518.2	2,240.1	1,958.4	1,902.8
Total	6,374.0	10,950.0	15,818.1	17,989.6	21,770.1	25,846.5	30,945.7	33,073.2	36,480.9	42,896.5	49,037.2	53,186.6	55,928.5
Total MGS Outstanding	7,354.5	11,931.9	16,795.5	20,586.4	26,170.4	30,037.3	33,090.2	36,681.1	41,300.8	48,794.0	55,830.2	58,213.4	62,106.1

nal interest rates charged, in real terms borrowers of direct credit lines paid mildly negative to slightly positive interest rates, compared with substantially negative real rates seen on some directed credit lines in developing countries.

Financing government

Malaysian government securities (MGS), the major instrument of financing for the government, constituted the largest share (89%) of domestic debt outstanding at the end of 1990. The financial sector accounted for 86.7%, 91.8%, and 90.1% of all MGS at the end of 1975, 1978, and 1990, respectively (Table 10.5), mainly because of statutory requirements imposed on institutions to hold MGS for prudential and liquidity reasons. For example, the Employees Provident Fund (EPF), the biggest provider of government finance, invested the bulk of its resources in MGS – 53.4%, 53.4%, and 58.2% of all MGS outstanding at the end of 1975, 1978, and 1990, respectively.

To meet liquidity requirements of the Central Bank, commercial banks, finance companies, and merchant banks also hold some in MGS. At end-1990, the banking system held 16.2% of all MGS outstanding, compared with 18.2% in 1978.

10.3   The nature of liberalization

Interest-rate reforms

In 1971 fixed deposits placed with commercial banks for more than four years were allowed to carry market-determined interest rates. From January 1972, interest rate ceilings were lifted for commercial bank deposits with maturity exceeding one year. From August 1, 1973, interest rates for deposits placed with finance companies were freed and from August 20, discount rates on Treasury bills were determined by open tender in the money market.

The major phase of reform came in October 1978. The Central Bank freed interest rates of the commercial banks, allowing them to determine rates to depositors and borrowers. Subsequently, rates tended to behave in an asymmetrical manner. When the cost of funds rose, the banks immediately passed it to their customers in higher lending rates. But when the cost of funds declined, lending rates moved downward only with a prolonged lag.[2] And, when the banks did lower lending rates, they were not evenly applied to all borrowers. As a result, the Central Bank introduced the base lending rate (BLR) on November 1, 1983. Every bank's or finance company's lending rates (except those charged to the priority sectors) were anchored to its declared BLR, which was based on the cost of funds, after providing for the cost of statutory reserves, liquid assets requirements and overheads. As the actual cost of credit to borrowers was determined by the BLR and an interest margin based on the borrower's credit standing, this was intended to remove much of a bank's discretion on which of its borrowers benefited or was penalized whenever interest rates changed.

Free market determination of interest rates was further interrupted during the tight liquidity period from October 1985 to January 1987, when controls on deposit interest rates were reinstituted. In the tight liquidity environment of 1985, interest rates rose sharply as the financial institutions bid for funds. The Central Bank got the commercial banks and finance companies to peg interest rates for deposits of up to 12-month maturities to the deposit rate of the two leading domestic banks with effect from October 21, 1985. The maximum differential vis-à-vis the lead banks was 0.5 percentage point for the commercial banks and 1.5 percentage points for the finance companies. This pegged interest rate arrangement was dismantled in February 1987.

However, the sluggish response of lending rates to the decline in deposit rates led to the Central Bank imposing new guidelines on September 1, 1987. These required the BLR of commercial banks to be no more than 0.5 percentage points above the BLR of the two lead banks. The margin by which lending rates can exceed the BLR was limited to not more than four percentage points, depending on the credit standing of borrowers. Penalties on delinquent loans were not to exceed 1% per annum. The finance companies were subject to similar guidelines. On February 1, 1991, the BLR was finally freed from the administrative control of the Central Bank. Except for some priority-sector lending, all interest rates are now determined by market forces.

Exchange-control liberalization and exchange-rate reform

On May 8, 1973, exchange-control regulations ceased to discriminate between countries in and outside of the Sterling Area and allowed for a freer flow of funds in and out of Malaysia. On January 1, 1987, new measures reduced the formalities with which businessmen have to comply when exporting their goods and provided investors with greater access to credit to expand productive capacity. In addition, the public was permitted to deal freely in gold. Existing exchange controls are meant mainly to ensure that export receipts are received promptly in Malaysia, to assist the Central Bank in monitoring the settlement of international payments and receipts and to encourage the use of financial resources for productive purposes.

In June 1972 Malaysia broke its historical link with sterling and adopted the U.S. dollar as the intervention currency. A year later, the ringgit was allowed to float upward. This implied that the Central Bank was no longer obliged to buy U.S. dollars with ringgit at the floor rate of M$2.4805 for U.S.$1. Moreover, the Association of Banks ceased to issue best-agreed merchant rates, and each bank was free to determine its own exchange rate for any foreign currency (including the Singapore dollar) for any amount. In September 1975 the value of the ringgit was determined by a basket of representative major currencies, weighted by the main currencies of settlement, as well as the trade shares of the major trading partners of Malaysia. This arrangement is still the basis for Malaysia's exchange-rate policy.

Prior to the mid-1980s, it was considered desirable to keep the ringgit relatively stable against the Singapore dollar. However, intervention through the U.S. dollar kept the ringgit relatively strong vis-à-vis the U.S. dollar. The unsustainability of an appreciating exchange rate in a weak economy, combined with speculative attacks on the ringgit, led to a shift in policy in late 1984: The ringgit was allowed to move freely against the U.S. and Singapore dollars. This led to a sharp depreciation of the ringgit exchange rate, which contributed to the gains in the level of international competitiveness since 1985.

From February 1987 the commercial banks, finance companies, and merchant banks were allowed to observe the *minimum liquidity requirement* (MLR) on a two-week average basis, with a maximum daily variation of 2 percentage points above or below the requirement. Previously the requirement had to be met daily. From January 1989 a similar ruling applied to the *statutory reserve ratio* (SRR), with a maximum daily variation of 0.5 percentage point and a common ratio for all banking institutions. The primary liquidity ratios of the finance companies and commercial banks were abolished in January 1989 and June 1990, respectively. Beginning July 1, 1990, the commercial banks, finance companies, and merchant banks were allowed to observe the SRR and MLR based on their average eligible liabilities (EL) over a fortnight, instead of a single day.

Different priorities

From April 1, 1987, the ceiling rates for priority-sector lending were pegged at 1.75 percentage points above the average BLR of the two lead banks or 9% a year, whichever is lower. In March 1989 these ceiling rates were removed from all priority-sector loans, save for those to individuals for owner-occupied houses (costing $100,000 or less) and for those to small-scale enterprises (SSEs) under the Principal Guarantee Scheme of the Credit Guarantee Corporation, although compulsory lending to the former borrower ceased in March 1990. Quantitative lending guidelines apply now only to the Bumiputera community and SSEs.

Developments in the capital market

A priority of the Bank in the 1980s was to develop the capital market in Malaysia, particularly a secondary market in government securities. One problem was that the yields on Malaysian government securities (MGS) were well below other financial assets. Moreover, the bulk of MGS were held by "captive" institutions, so limiting the amount available for trading on the secondary market and also reducing the Central Bank's ability to conduct open market operations and so, control money supply and credit.

Measures were taken to increase the role of the market in providing liquidity for MGS, reduce the scope of captive markets and move toward a market-based pricing of primary issues of MGS. These included adjustments of statutory and liquidity requirements, allowing well-capitalized finance companies to participate in the interbank money market and establishing the Interbank Funds Transfer System, the Scriptless Securities Trading System, the Kuala Lumpur Automated Clearing House, and the Day-One Settlement System. MGS with market-based coupons were first issued in 1987. In January 1989 there were other major reforms:

1   *Appointment of principal dealers.* Twenty-three financial institutions (9 commercial banks, 7 merchant banks, and all 7 discount houses) were appointed to underwrite new issues of MGS and to make a secondary market in them.
2   *Issue of MGS by auction.* MGS with maturities of up to 10 years are now auctioned through the principal dealers. Longer dated securities are still sold by subscription, although only to the Employees Provident Fund and the National Savings Bank.
3   *The Central Bank's open market operations* are now conducted through the principal dealers only. The Bank's role in the money market has now changed to one of maintaining liquidity in the system. Institutions with excess liquidity (or short of funds) have to square their positions in the market

and not with the Central Bank. Only principal dealers have
access to the Bank's discount window.

4 *Freeing of discount house operations.* Because discount
houses had become securities dealers, restrictions on their
investments were removed in June 1990. They are now free to
decide their portfolio structure, subject only to the adequacy
of capital on a risk-weighted basis. They can, also, invest in
securities with maturities of up to 10 years, previously limited
to 5 years or less.

The Central Bank also took steps to develop a market for corporate
bonds, when it issued guidelines on the issue of private debt securities.
A private credit-rating agency was also set up in November 1990.

Sequencing of reforms

Countries wishing to reform their financial systems must decide upon
the timing of measures to ensure a smooth transition with minimal
instability and disruptions to the economy. Should financial sector
reforms be undertaken prior to real sector reforms or vice versa? Or
should reforms in both be undertaken simultaneously? And should
liberalization of the capital account precede or follow liberalization in
the current account? Or both at the same time?

Although interest rates were liberalized in Malaysia in 1978, it is
not clear if there was a deliberate policy then of reforming the financial
sector. Liberalization became widely accepted only in the early 1980s,
following government policy to restructure the economy through a
multiyear structural adjustment program. It was targeted at the real
sector to overcome prolonged and deep recession, arising from a
sharp deterioration in the country's international terms of trade and to
address the large twin-deficits problem and widespread inefficiencies
in the economy. Liberalization of the real sector began with drastic
cutbacks in public sector expenditure; privatizations; reduction in
public sector employment; and promoting private sector investment
by relaxing investment guidelines.

Reform of the financial system was not pursued concurrently in the
early stages of real sector liberalization. Indeed, there was greater
control and supervision of the financial system because of difficulties
arising from mismanagement, overexposure to some sectors, and bad
debts during the recession. The government, worried about bank failures and the erosion of public confidence, brought in the system of
"lead banks." This was deemed necessary because interest rates were
escalating to excessively high levels due to fierce competition for

funds by the deposit-taking cooperatives (DTCs), speculation on the ringgit and the decline in the external sources of liquidity due to the collapse of commodity prices and deteriorating balance of payments.

So *real-sector reform preceded financial reform in Malaysia*. It was only in 1987, with economic recovery, that the government could take further guarded steps toward financial liberalization. Deposit rates were again allowed to be freely determined, but the base lending rate continued to be pegged to the two lead banks. It was only in February 1991, when the economy had recovered, that lending rates were determined freely by individual financial institutions. Lending guidelines on directed credit have also been relaxed progressively and, for all financial institutions, the uniform reserve requirements have been introduced and the scope of their activities and instruments dealt in have been broadened.

In Malaysia, *liberalization of the current account of the balance of payments came before the liberalization of the capital account*. Tariff rates were relatively high in the 1960s, a time of import-substitution strategy, but were reduced progressively in the past 20 years across the board, save for some products associated with the development of heavy industries.

Reform of the capital account has been more modest. This appears to reflect concerns that the opening up of the capital account should be carried out prudently to avoid massive capital outflows that could accompany a sudden dose of capital account liberalization. Even so, exchange control regulations have been increasingly dismantled. The few remaining controls are on the repatriation of export proceeds, foreign borrowing of above M$1 million by residents, and domestic borrowing of more than M$10 million by nonresident controlled companies. Although export proceeds must be repatriated within six months, controls on borrowing have been flexibly enforced where they are for productive purposes.

Financial deepening

Although the financial system in Malaysia has been transformed from the simple structure of mid-1950s, many changes have nothing to do with the liberalization of interest rates in 1978, but rather to the growing needs of the economy. Between 1978 and 1990 there was a big increase in the number of commercial banks and finance companies, both domestically and foreign owned. Of all insurance companies, 80% were domestically owned in 1990, compared with 50% in 1978. The number of companies listed on the Kuala Lumpur Stock Exchange (KLSE) increased from 254 in 1978 to 307 in 1989 but fell to

285 in 1990 following the split between the Malaysian and Singapore stock exchanges. The market capitalization of the KLSE increased from $18.3 billion to $131.7 billion and the funds raised by Malaysian companies increased from $53 million to $8.5 billion.

The deepening of the financial system has been a contributor to (and a consequence of) the increasing monetization of the economy. The ratio of M3 to gross national product (M3/GNP) rose from 0.46 in 1973 to 0.56 in 1978, and it peaked at 1.07 in 1986. By 1990 it had drifted down to 1.05, as the growth in savings was affected by the recession in 1985–6 and low interest rates which led to investment in nondeposit assets. Financial deepening in Malaysia can also be seen in the relationship between total assets of the financial system and GNP (FA/GNP). This ratio increased from 1.23 in 1975 to 2.91 in 1990 (Table 10.6), among the highest in the developing world. The dominance of banking in the Malaysian financial system is seen in the ratio of the banking system's assets to GNP – 1.69 in 1990, which represented about 58% of all assets of the financial system. Commercial banks alone accounted for 40% of the financial system's assets at the end of 1990. Part of this expansion likely reflects the rapid expansion of branching, leading to a sharp fall in the number of people per branch and a commensurately greater ability to deliver financial services.

10.4   Reform, the economy, and the financial system

Macroeconomic impact

Heavily and uneconomic regulation of financial systems, usually encompassing substantial intervention in the credit granting and pricing process, can adversely affect savings and, consequently, economic growth and development. Hence, financial liberalization can enhance economic growth and development. A major role of any financial system is to *mobilize savings* for investment. In Malaysia, financial savings increased by an average of 14% in the 1960s, 18% in the first half of the 1970s, and 23% in the second half of that decade. However, growth fell to 17% in the first half of the 1980s and 13% in the second half, but still exceeded GDP expansion and left the savings ratio at a peak. The proportion of financial savings to gross national saving (GNS) also increased rapidly – from 35% in the first half of the 1960s to 60% in the 1970s and 66–67% in the 1980s. Although income growth has played a big part in the rapid increase in savings, equally important has been the development of an efficient domestic financial system, both by maintaining attractive yields for savers and by fostering an increased variety of financial services.

Table 10.6 *Malaysia: Selected measures of monetization and financial deepening, 1975–90*

	1975	1980	1989	1990
M1/GNP	0.20	0.19	0.19	0.22
M2/GNP	0.46	0.54	0.70	0.76
M3/GNP	0.5	0.6	0.9	1.1
M3/M1	2.60	3.35	4.83	4.76
Currency/M1	0.51	0.49	0.46	0.41
M3 per capita	924	2,375	4,184	6,496
Per capita deposits	811	2,236	4,656	6,797
Persons per banking office ('000)	30	25	20	18
Total financial assets/GNP	1.23	1.44	2.35	2.91
Assets/GNP				
Central Bank	0.22	0.25	0.23	0.37
Commercial banks	0.50	0.63	1.03	1.17
Finance Companies	0.08	0.11	0.25	0.36
Merchant banks	0.02	0.04	0.09	0.10
Discount Houses	0.02	0.03	0.04	0.04
Bank Islam	-	-	0.01	0.01
Total banking system c/	0.62	0.80	1.41	1.69

	1971-75	1976-80	1981-85	1986-90
Net issues ratio a/ Financial System, of which	-1.7	1.5	0.9	1.7
-Central Bank	-0.3	0.3	0.0	0.2
-Commercial banks	-0.5	0.7	0.6	0.7
Income elasticity of net issues b/ Financial system, of which	-1.6	1.2	0.7	0.6
-Central Bank	-1.8	1.1	0.3	0.5
-Commercial banks	-1.0	1.3	1.1	0.6
-Total banking system c/	-1.3	1.3	1.0	0.7

a/ Ratio of change in assets to change in GNP.
b/ Ratio of rate of growth of assets to rate of growth of GNP.
c/ Banking System refer to CBs, FCs, MBs, DHs and BI.

Financial liberalization should *promote investment* growth through the availability of a larger pool of funds and investment efficiency should be enhanced as funds are allocated according to returns determined by the market. Gross investment grew on average by 21% in 1961–5 and by 31% in 1971–5, before falling to around 17% in the second half of the 1970s and, in line with the economic slowdown, to

11% in the 1980s. The ratio of bank credit to gross domestic product in Malaysia has been increasing over the past 30 years, reflecting the importance of bank credit for financing economic activities and coinciding with the rapid liberalization of the banking system, the development of a secondary market for government securities, and of private debt securities in Malaysia. The ratio of total credit outstanding to GDP and of the flow of credit to investment have also increased over the same period. Other sources, such as direct issues of shares, are still insignificant as a means of financing in Malaysia.

Interest rates

Patterns of behavior

The historical pattern of interest rates in Malaysia can be divided into prereform (up to 1978) and postreform (Figure 10.1). The three-month fixed-deposit rate (FD) of the commercial banks is taken to be representative of deposit rates and the seven-day interbank money-market rate (IB) is a proxy for money-market rates. Except for the spike in interbank rates during the tight liquidity and high inflation period of 1973–4, interest rates before reform appear to be more stable. The average level of the FD and IB rates increased respectively following reforms, from 5.45% to 6.8% and from 6.3% to 6.67% a year. More important, the variation in the interest rates increased significantly following reform. The statistical variance of the FD and IB rates prereform, was 0.3% and 3.3%, respectively, increasing to 5.7% and 5.5%, respectively, postreform.

Prior to 1979, FD rates diverged significantly from the interbank rates, mainly due to the fact that while the interbank rates were market determined, deposit rates were controlled by the Central Bank. After liberalization, with the financial institutions free to set deposit rates, these tended to follow the interbank rates more closely. The differential between the variance of the *average* FD and IB rates narrowed markedly, from 3% to 0.2% between the two periods; with the *average* levels of the two rates differing by only 0.1% after reform, compared to 0.8% before reform.

There was a sharp decline in the level and volatility of interest rates in 1987, due mainly to a sudden inflow of liquidity from strong export receipts and hesitant loan demand. Day-to-day fluctuations were dampened by the Central Bank, but high volatility in part reflected the daily reserve holding period. The new minimum liquidity requirement (on a two-week average basis, from February 1987) reduced the vola-

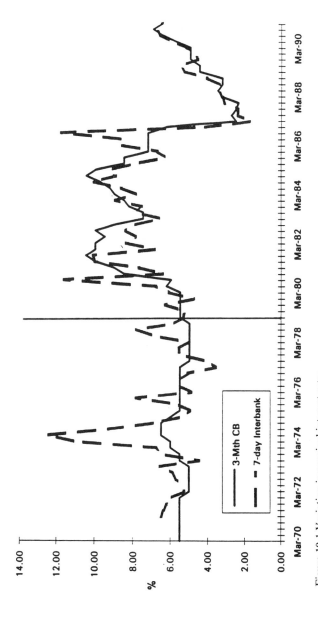

Figure 10.1 Variation in nominal interest rates

tility caused by banks seeking funds to fulfill daily requirements. Similarly, from January 1989 banks were allowed to observe an average statutory reserve ratio over a two-week period. The Day One Settlement System, introduced in 1986, helped interest rate stability by ensuring that, at the end of the check-clearing day, banks with a net surplus automatically lent those funds to those facing a deficit. This prevented scramble for funds by banks that were short, which would have pushed up interest rates.

Real interest rates

The sharp increase in inflation in 1973–4 led to negative real interest rates (Figure 10.2) as in many developing and industrialized countries. Immediately following reform, nominal interest rates remained higher than inflation, ensuring depositors a positive real rate of return and even when regulated, interest rates mostly offered positive returns to depositors. After liberalization, particularly in 1985–6, interest rates were high relative to Malaysian historical experience, but this was a natural market response to the tight liquidity conditions then prevailing.

The spreads between banks' and finance companies' average cost of funds and their lending rates (at times used as a measure of the institutions' efficiency) have widened during most of the 1980s.[3] One reason is the improved quality of services provided by the banks, for example, in electronic banking. However, spreads generally widen during (and after) periods of economic slowdown, for example, in 1981–2 and 1985–7 in the case of commercial banks. Banks become more risk averse in bad times and charge higher interest rates on loans. They also try to recover the costs of bad loans by passing these on to nondelinquent depositors and new borrowers. Conversely, interest margins have been narrowing over the late 1980s and early 1990s, as the improved economic environment led to a decline in bad debts.

Term structure

Following reform in the government securities market in 1987 and the introduction of the principal dealer auctioning system, there have been changes in the term structure of MGS yields. The yield curve has flattened and the difference in the yield between the shorter and longer maturities has narrowed. Only securities with maturities of less than 10 years are sold and so ensure market-determined yields. Those with

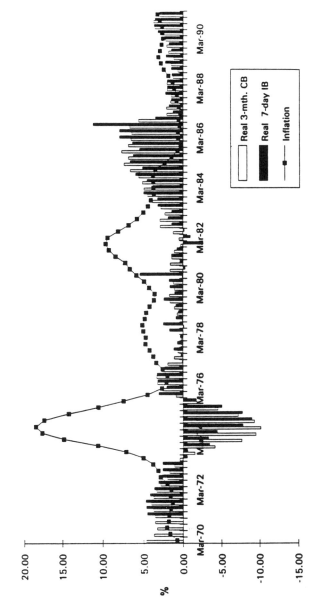

Figure 10.2 Real interest rates

longer maturities are sold by subscription to the National Savings Bank and the Employees Provident Fund, both being required by law to hold a fixed amount of securities. Thus, the government has no incentive to offer higher interest rates. The result is a flat yield structure that does not seem to reflect the "normal" liquidity and risk preference of investors.

A similar pattern is seen in the term structure of deposit interest rates. The kink between one-month and three-month rates prior to liberalization became smoother as the differential between the two rates narrowed. However, adjustments in domestic interest rates remained modest immediately after liberalization. But when the resource gap emerged in the early 1980s, the commercial banks not only adjusted deposit rates upward but also offered relatively higher deposit rates for shorter-term maturities. As a result, the yield curve became flatter in the early 1980s.

Between October 1985 and January 1987, when rates on deposits of up to 12 months' maturity were pegged to the rates of the two lead banks, the differential in interest rates between the one and 12-month rates was only 0.25 percentage point. However, there was a wide differential (3–4 percentage points) between deposit rates of 12- and 15-month maturities as commercial banks competed at the longer end by offering higher rates. (Rates on 15-month maturity and above were not subject to regulation.) The yield curve was therefore unusual, with a steep slope occurring at later maturities. With the unpegging of deposit rates on February 1, 1987, the yield curve showed a gradual upward slope. Then, uncertainty about future interest rates led to a further flattening of the yield curve, as the banks offered relatively attractive interest rates on the shorter maturity deposits in order to avoid taking in too much of the longer-term deposits.

Banks and finance company rates

Finance companies have always offered higher interest rates on deposits than commercial banks, and their lending rates have also been higher. Following liberalization, a narrowing of the interest differential between the two may have been expected, as the banks set interest rates at competitive levels. In fact, it did not happen because the scope for competition for loans is limited. Finance companies are involved mainly in hire-purchase finance, which allows them to charge higher interest rates, and so offer higher deposit rates for funds. The commercial banks, with interest-free demand deposits and corporate clients' deposits, have been under little pressure to compete.

Risky and riskless rates

The trend in the differential between the 12-month Treasury bills rate and the average lending rate of the commercial banks in 1975–90 has been on an upward trend at least until 1986 (Figure 10.3). Following reform, the differential widened mainly as a result of high lending rates. Since 1986 lending rates have declined due to recession (1985–6) and excess liquidity. More important, the decision by the Central Bank in 1987 to issue government securities with market-related coupon rates helped to push up the rates on TBs. Thus, the differential between the two rates has declined sharply since 1987.

The earlier liberalization of interest rates (in 1978) did not by itself promote competition among banks. It was only after the 1985–6 recession, when lending opportunities were scarce, that banks started to compete by offering prime customers loans with fine interest margins. Moreover, improvements in the health of banks' balance sheets in the late 1980s constituted another reason for increased competitive behavior. So, the benefits of financial reform may not manifest themselves immediately and, if there are macroeconomic shocks to the system, this may further delay adjustment.

Last, it should be noted that even when interest rates were controlled by Malaysia's Central Bank, they did not diverge too far from international rates. However, simple distributed lag analysis shows that liberalization had an impact on the *responsiveness* of domestic interest rates (commercial banks' three-month term deposit rate) to changes in international interest rates (Eurodollar 3-month rate). It seems that changes in international interest rates have more immediate effect on domestic interest rates following reform.

Banking system

Concentration

Before liberalization of interest rates, concentration in the commercial banking industry was high, with the 10 largest banks accounting for more than 80% of the industry's total deposits and loans and almost 80% of all assets. Following liberalization, concentration has been gradually reduced. Although no new banks have been allowed to enter the Malaysian financial system since the early 1980s, and foreign banks cannot expand their branch network, the share of deposits of the 10 largest banks had declined continuously from about 84% of the total in 1975 to 72% in 1986, before rebounding back to 77% in 1990. A

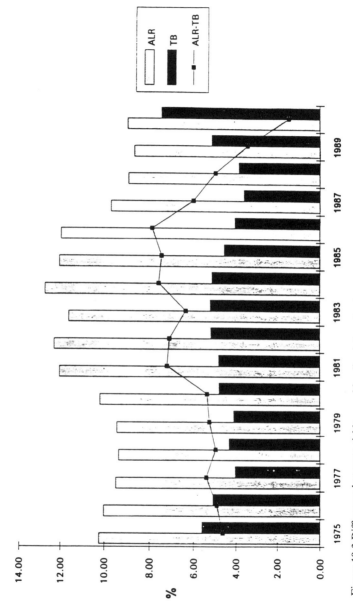

Figure 10.3 Difference between riskless and lending interest rates

similar trend can be seen for the top five and the top three banks (Table 10.7). The 10 largest banks' share of total assets also declined from 80% in 1975 to 72% in 1984–6, rose to 74% in 1989 and fell again to 72% in 1990.

The degree of concentration in commercial banking has remained high. At the end of June 1991, the industry continued to be dominated by two banks, accounting for 35.2% of all banking assets, their 343 offices representing more than one third of all bank branches. In addition, there are 10 medium-sized banks and 26 smaller ones, 16 of which are foreign bank branches or subsidiaries. Most foreign banks are small in terms of assets and operate only one office.

Composition of liabilities

Since liberalization, interest rates have become more volatile, competition among banks has increased, and customers have become more sophisticated. This has led to new delivery systems and product innovation – for example, banker's acceptances (BAs), repurchase agreements (Repos), and negotiable certificates of deposit (NCDs). Other new financial products include mortgage-backed bonds, private debt securities, gilt-edged securities (based on MGS), and property trust funds. Increasing competition also led to greater computerization, and the widespread use of automated teller machines (ATMs) and other electronic funds transfer services as well as credit cards galore.

New instruments, such as Repos, NCDs, and BAs, have more flexible maturity periods and negotiable rates of return, thereby allowing banks greater flexibility in managing assets and liabilities. And although traditional deposits (current, savings, and fixed) remained a principal source of funds, they had declined by 1990 to an average of 48% of total liabilities of all banks, compared to 75% in 1975–8.

There have also been big shifts between savings and fixed deposits and from currency and demand deposits to fixed and savings deposits. Demand deposits, for example, declined continuously after the 1978 liberalization of interest rates to account for less than 12% of all sources of funds at the end of 1990. The share of savings deposits also declined continuously until 1985, when automated teller machines, introduced in 1983, had become accepted by depositors. The share of fixed deposits, on the other hand, rose from an average of 41% (1975–8) to 43.4% at the end of 1984, before declining continuously to 26.2% at the end of 1990. New financial instruments (e.g., Repos, NCDs, and BAs) accounted for 17.2% (or $22.2 billion) of the total resources

Table 10.7 *Commercial banks' industry structure*

	1975	1978	1979	1980	1981	1982	1983	1984	1985	1986	1987	1988	1989	1990
Share in total deposits of:														
Top 3 banks	44.30	43.90	44.76	44.48	43.90	43.90	42.10	39.27	39.08	38.45	34.35	40.18	40.08	41.82
Top 5 banks	63.00	61.90	61.82	60.17	57.80	57.50	54.90	53.57	52.89	53.15	49.31	54.99	54.52	57.45
Top 10 banks	83.70	81.70	78.77	77.19	78.00	77.50	76.20	75.67	72.64	72.43	65.95	75.64	71.66	77.12
Smaller banks	16.30	18.30	21.23	22.81	22.00	22.50	23.80	24.33	27.36	27.57	34.05	24.36	28.34	22.88
Ratio of profit to total assets	1.33	1.48	1.37	0.92	1.42	1.48	1.38	0.65	0.47	-0.06	-1.20	-1.02	-0.17	0.21
Share of bad debts provision to total assets	0.36	0.52	0.61	0.45	0.76	0.76	0.77	1.09	1.44	2.14	3.98	4.00	4.02	3.55
Capital and reserves to total liabilities	3.12	3.21	2.84	3.00	3.92	4.08	4.98	5.38	5.58	5.59	6.31	6.14	5.47	5.35
Liquidity ratio of commercial banks	36.20	36.00	25.80	23.40	27.00	26.40	23.20	24.20	22.50	20.40	24.10	23.10	19.90	18.60
Share of long-term loans in total loans and advances	23.55	30.38	31.02	31.30	34.09	37.14	38.54	39.77	40.21	41.52	44.04	44.00	44.57	41.86
Share of long-term deposits in total fixed deposits	7.17	22.23	27.31	28.84	16.75	16.50	23.24	25.60	30.11	55.12	51.89	53.61	48.96	46.49
Percent share of total assets of commercial banks held by														
10 largest banks	79.82	76.80	75.05	74.64	75.14	74.93	73.13	72.14	71.45	72.32	73.58	74.00	73.11	71.57
5 largest banks	58.50	57.16	57.04	57.12	56.69	55.94	55.48	52.21	50.17	52.15	54.23	54.33	54.05	52.14
3 largest banks	41.72	40.70	41.12	41.98	43.09	42.78	43.75	39.53	38.22	39.26	40.73	42.08	42.26	41.16

mobilized by banks at the end of 1990. Repos and NCDs in particular grew rapidly – by average annual growth rates of 36.2% and 20.7% respectively in 1981–90.

As interest rates began moving up after 1980, depositors' preference also shifted toward shorter maturities. The share of total long-term deposits to total fixed deposits of commercial banks fell from 28.8% in 1980 to 16.5% in 1982; subsequently, it rose to 55.1% (at the end of 1986) due partly to adjustments in the term structure of interest rates and partly to the tax exemption of interest earned on fixed deposits of more than 12-month maturities. However, when the exemption was removed in 1988, the share of long-term deposits fell again – to 46.5% at the end of 1990. Notwithstanding this high ratio, the decline of fixed deposits relative to total liabilities suggests that the deregulation of interest rates, in general, has led to a shortening of the maturity structure of the commercial banks' deposit liabilities and has increased the variability of their cost of funds.

Composition of assets

Most resources of commercial banks have been used to finance loans and advances to sectors of the economy. The share of loans and advances to total assets rose from an average of 59% in 1975–7 to 60–66% in 1978–90. In terms of the direction of credit, the change over time in the share of credit to sectors of the economy to total loans and advances have generally followed changes in the share of each sector in total GDP and the changes in the capital productivity of sectors. However, following the liberalization of interest rates, which coincided with a property boom, the share of credit to the property sector (real estate development, construction and housing) rose from 21% at the end of 1978 to a peak of 36.6% at the end of 1987. This sharp increase in property loans was in contrast to the low increase in the relative importance of the building and construction sector in total GDP and reflected the improved profitability of the sector, through capital appreciation. The liberalization of interest rates allowed banks to charge higher interest rates for property loans, yet the real interest rates were low relative to gains from capital appreciation and perhaps included some speculative element as well (Figure 10.4). This has made property projects profitable, at least ex ante, and hence bankable.

By loan type, there was a progressive decline in the use of over-drafts for short-term financing – from 37.2% of total loans and advances at the end of 1978 to 29.7% by the end of 1990 – mainly

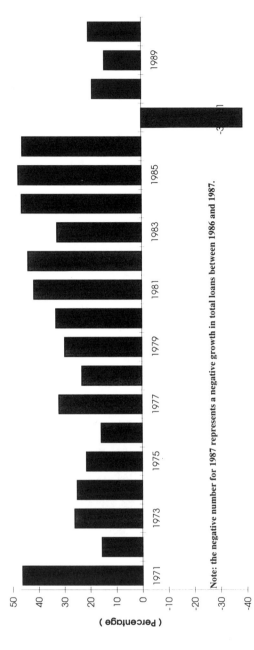

Note: the negative number for 1987 represents a negative growth in total loans between 1986 and 1987.

Figure 10.4 Malaysian commercial banks: The share of lending to the property sector in total new loans

Table 10.8 *Nonperforming loans of the commercial banks (%)*

	Interest in Suspense / Total Loans & Advances %	Provisions for Bad Debts / Total Loans & Advances %	Non-Performing Loans / Total Loans & Advances %
1980	0.5	1.7	-
1981	0.6	1.7	-
1982	1.4	1.6	-
1983	1.1	1.7	-
1984	1.2	2.5	-
1985	2.2	3.8	10.3
1986	4.4	6.2	20.8
1987	6.0	7.3	26.8
1988	7.9	7.7	32.6
1989	7.9	7.3	24.5
1990	7.5	6.2	20.8

reflecting rising interest rates after deregulation and growing sophistication of the Malaysian corporate sector, both in liability and cash management. A 1% commitment fee on unused overdrafts facilities from February 1982 also contributed to the decline. So, too, did the Central Bank's urging of commercial banks to place more emphasis on term lending because of the large overhang of unutilized overdraft facilities and its impact on liquidity management.

Asset quality

The share of bad-debt provisions of banks to total assets is shown in Table 10.8. The sudden jump in the mid-1980s was due partly to the introduction of Central Bank guidelines provisioning against previously unprovisioned loans, but it mainly reflects the severe recession of 1985–6 and the souring of property loans. Despite warnings from the Central Bank, banks continued to lend to the broad property sector, which in 1986 accounted for 55% of the total flow of new loans, compared with 32% in 1980. When the property market collapsed in the mid-1980s, many banks and finance companies were left with a large percentage of their property loans that were nonperforming.

As is often the case, the decline in the quality of bank loans resulted from insufficient diversification, in this case overconcentration of loans to one sector or a small group of large customers. The ratio of total provision for bad and doubtful debts (plus interest in suspense) to total loans and advances rose from an average ratio of 2.8% in 1980–4 to 6% at the end of 1985 (Table 10.8). This worsened to a peak of 15.5% at the end of 1988, before falling to 13.7% at the end of 1990.

Despite the problems of the 1980s, the banking system ended the decade with a substantial improvement in profitability and financial strength. The speedy pick-up in the property market, the bullish stock market in 1989, the expansion of manufacturing, which contributed to recovery, as well as the resolution of many nonperforming loans, helped boost the industry's earnings.

Finance companies

Mobilizing resources

Total resources of the finance companies had expanded rapidly, to M$39.5 billion by the end of 1990, 101 times those at the end of 1969. Growth averaged 24.6% annually, compared with 17.9% per annum for commercial banks over the same period. Much of the growth of finance companies since 1969 stemmed from increased deposits, particularly fixed deposits, which at the end of 1990 accounted for over 90% of all deposits placed with them; the balance was savings deposits. Fixed deposits grew at an average of 25% annually, against 16% for banks over the same period. The rapid growth of finance company deposits reflected not only high income growth but especially the higher interest rates that finance companies could offer, especially prior to October 1978, when banks were facing a ceiling on interest paid on deposits.

With increasing competition for funds after the liberalization of interest rates, finance companies' growth slowed somewhat in 1979–90, with total financial resources increasing by 23.1% a year, against 26.7% annually in 1970–8. Total resources of $39.5 billion mobilized by the finance companies were less than one quarter of resources mobilized by the banking system at the end of 1990. Similarly, growth in finance companies' deposits (excluding NCDs and Repos) eased to 21.2% per annum in 1979–90 (29.6% per annum in 1970–8), while loan operations grew at an average 24.4% a year between 1979 and 1990 (27.7% in 1970–8). Fixed deposits accounted for 93.1% of new deposits mobilized by the finance companies in 1979–90 and their market share had risen to 29.8% of total deposits of $95.3 billion mobilized by the banking system at the end of 1990 (15.4% in 1978).

Table 10.9 *Gross interest margins (% per annum)*

	Finance Companies			Commercial Banks		
	Average Lending Rate	Average Cost of Deposits	Interest Margin	Average Lending Rate	Average Cost of Deposits	Interest Margin
1980	12.32	9.10	3.22	10.22	6.20	4.02
1981	15.58	11.23	4.35	12.07	7.77	4.30
1982	15.88	10.64	5.24	12.34	7.17	5.17
1983	15.87	9.40	6.47	11.64	6.61	5.03
1984	15.22	10.64	4.58	12.80	7.98	4.82
1985	14.66	9.72	4.94	12.10	6.81	5.29
1986	13.96	9.13	4.83	12.02	6.45	5.57
1987	12.62	5.75	6.87	9.73	3.63	6.10
1988	12.47	4.69	7.78	8.95	3.27	5.68
1989	11.95	5.47	6.48	8.70	3.79	4.91
1990	11.87	6.92	4.95	8.99	4.50	4.49

After reform in 1978, there was a change in the structure of the finance companies' deposits. With depositors' shifting toward shorter maturities in the latter half of 1980s, the share of deposits of more than one-year maturity to total deposits fell from a peak of 66% in 1986 to 40.9% in 1990. Since March 1990, selected finance companies have been allowed to issue NCDs; by the end of 1990, these NCDs accounted for $1.6 billion (or 4.2%) of all resources mobilized by finance companies.

Although finance companies' total resources grew at a faster rate than the banks' in both the pre- and post-1978 periods, the differential between their rate of growth and banks' narrowed from 8 percentage points in 1970–8 to 5.8 percentage points in 1979–90.

Interest margins and profitability

Despite stiff competition after the 1978 reforms, the gross interest margins of the commercial banks and the finance companies widened in 1980–90 (Table 10.9). For example, despite the lower interest rates in 1982 and 1983, lending rates remained "sticky" downward and the gross interest margin of finance companies widened dramatically from 3.2 percentage points in 1980 to 6.5 percentage points in 1983.

With the new system of interest rates for the finance companies in October 1984, lending rates moved in line with changes in the cost of

Table 10.10 *Pretax profit/loss*

	Finance companies	Commercial banks	Finance companies	Commercial banks
	M$ million		as percent of assets	
1980	133	461	2.4	1.4
1981	119	539	1.6	1.3
1982	171	583	1.9	1.2
1983	229	(232)	2.0	(0.4)
1984	227	642	1.5	1.0
1985	112	(261)	0.6	(0.4)
1986	(75)	(332)	(0.4)	(0.4)
1987	(245)	310	(1.2)	0.4
1988	(160)	661	(0.6)	0.7
1989	241	895*	0.8	1.0*
1990	428	1278*	1.1	1.2*

* Excluding one commercial bank,

funds but at a slower rate. For example, although the cost of deposits of the finance companies had declined from 10.6% in 1984 to 4.7% per annum in 1988, the average lending rate was slower in responding – falling only by 2.8 percentage points to 12.5% a year. This reflected mainly high-cost property and commercial loans booked in earlier years, a significant proportion of which was nonperforming. The result was a widening of the interest rate margins from 4.6 percentage points in 1984 to 7.8 percentage points in 1988, a peak for the 1980s. However, the interest margins had narrowed to under 5 percentage points by 1990, reflecting greater competition among banking institutions.

Higher interest margins in 1986–8 did not always mean higher profits for finance companies (Table 10.10). For example, although finance companies had an interest margin of 7.8 percentage points in 1988, they had, on average, overheads (including staff cost) of 2.4% a year and bad-debt provisions and interest-in-suspense of 7.5%, leaving a net loan margin loss of 2.1 percentage points and a negative return on assets. Although finance companies generally remained profitable after 1978, their return on assets has not exceeded that of commercial banks since 1985.

Deposit-taking cooperatives

Like commercial banks and finance companies, the cooperative movement has come a long way since it was introduced in 1922. Growth has been remarkable, especially among Deposit-Taking Cooperatives (DTCs). The number of DTCs has increased from three at the end of 1975 to 39 at the end of 1985 and total membership expanded from 54,988 to 1.03 million. Despite the formation of new DTCs during 1986, the collapse of another 24 in that year severely affected the industry's performance; their numbers fell to 17 and membership to 554,678 by the end of 1990. Total assets, which had touched M$2.2 billion at the end of 1986 had fallen to M$1.1 billion at end-1990.

Total resources mobilized by the DTCs rose from $247 million at the end of 1975 to $1.1 billion at the end of 1980 and increased at an average annual rate of 28.3% in 1981–5, reflecting the relatively high deposit rates offered, the government's 1983 decision to allow a large DTC (Cooperative Central Bank) to accept deposits from statutory authorities and insurance companies, and the nationwide mush-rooming of branch offices. Moreover, DTCs were less regulated (by the Cooperatives Development Department) than was the banking system, and so confronted fewer impediments to their expansion.

Nonfinancial corporate sector

Evaluating the relationship between investment decisions of the NFCC (which refers mainly to companies engaged in manufacturing) and their financing is difficult due to data constraints and for compara-tive reasons. In Malaysia there have been several studies relating to the link but three which complement each other are those of the Central Information Collection Unit (CICU) of PNB database, Bank Negara Malaysia's private investment surveys and the IMF study on interest rates in Malaysia. Generally these show that company size is an important determinant to accessibility to credit, that companies resorted mainly to internally generated funds to finance investments, and that the level of interest rates influenced investment decisions.

A study by the CICU showed that larger companies had easier access to external sources of financing than small and medium-sized companies, as expected. Bigger companies have better track records and reputation, and financial institutions impose on them less stringent requirements. The data used for the analysis was for 1983–90 and the companies in the database were listed companies. In terms of the average cost of credit (the ratio F/BT), the larger companies benefitted more than the small and medium-sized (Table 10.11). This could be due to the higher levels of investment (I/K) and lower rate of return on assets $(S/K$ and $P/TA)$ by the small and medium-sized companies. This "discrimination" was more pronounced during the recessionary years of 1985–6, when the average cost of credit for the large companies

Table 10.11 *Summary: Statistics of real and financial performance*

By Size	Period	I/K	S/K	P/K	P/TA	BT/K	BL/BT	F/BT	Yi/Y	Ii/I	dBTi/dBT
Small & Medium	83-84	0.259	0.318	0.044	0.004	1.767	0.996	0.142	0.02	0.021	0.055
	85-86	0.18	0.033	(0.382)	(0.03)	2.043	0.963	0.216	0.022	0.017	0.015
	87-90	0.049	(0.552)	(1.089)	(0.148)	4.118	0.991	0.153	0.005	0.001	0.005
Large	83-84	0.123	0.186	0.109	0.044	0.338	0.964	0.112	0.98	0.979	0.945
	85-86	0.084	0.11	0.05	0.021	0.411	0.973	0.108	1.978	0.983	0.985
	87-90	0.145	0.14	0.085	0.038	0.436	0.662	0.088	0.995	0.999	0.995

Note:

I = Purchase of fixed assets (gross investment)
K = Total fixed assets
S = Operating profit
P = Profit after tax and interest payments, net of depreciation
TA = Total assets
F = Interest payments
BT = Total debt
BL = Loans from financial institutions
Yi/Y = Share of sales of group i to total sales
Ii/I = Share of investment of group i to total investment
dBTi/dBT = Share of new debt of group i total investment

Size: Small & medium = Shareholders' funds < M$2.5 million.
Large = Shareholders' funds ≥ M$2.5 million.

was 10.8%, compared with 21.6% for the small and medium-sized enterprises (SMEs). In terms of the level of indebtedness of the companies (the ratio of total debt to total fixed assets, or *BT/K*), the small and medium-sized companies were more highly indebted compared with the large. During the 1983–6 period, this ratio ranged between 177% to 204% for SMEs, compared with 34% to 41% for the large companies. Even during the 1987–90 postrecessionary period, the levels of indebtedness of SMEs were far in excess of the large companies, despite the former's lower levels of investment. Loans from domestic financial institutions dominated the total debt outstanding of the SMEs during the 1980s, while large firms had access to loans from government and especially foreign institutions.

Large firms also appear to have been more profitable, as measured by rates of return *(P/K or P/TA)*. Indeed, SMEs had negative rates of return during the recessionary period and the smaller firms did not share in the profit turnaround during the recovery period. In this environment it is not surprising that SMEs only had access to bank debt and not to any significant direct financing.

Overall, a Bank Negara survey for 1986–90 revealed that internally generated funds accounted for between 45–64% of total financing. In 1988 the figure reached 84%, in part thanks to a lower level of capital expenditure. Bank loans were viewed negatively by companies, no doubt because of high interest rates. For the manufacturing sector, even despite a sharp increase in its growth in the mid-1970s, there was a reduction in the share of credit it received from banks, as this was the period when property and construction lending was becoming popular. Central Bank guidelines issued in 1978 attempted to correct this imbalance, even as interest rates were being initially freed. However, the rising net worth of the manufacturing sector led it to rely increasingly on internally generated funds, and their debt ratios subsequently declined.

10.5   The regulatory and supervisory framework of reform

While encouraging financial institutions to diversify and innovate, the Central Bank has, at the same time, beefed up the regulatory mechanism. Although liberalization has been considered a desirable goal, it has been tempered by the stronger concern for a stable financial system. For this reason, the approach to liberalization in the Malaysian financial system has been one of cautious and gradual structural deregulation and prudential reregulation.

Bank Negara Malaysia was established under the Central Bank of

Malaysia Ordinance 1958 as the Central Bank of the nation. Among its main objectives is the promotion of monetary stability and a sound financial structure. Its powers were extended and strengthened by the *Banking and Financial Institutions Act 1989* (BAFIA), now the major legislation governing the financial system. For the Bank, the Act provides the framework to supervise three broad groups of financial institutions:

1   *Licensed institutions.* The major deposit-taking institutions – commercial banks, merchant banks, discount houses, finance companies, discount houses, and money brokers.

2   *Scheduled institutions.* Major nonbank sources of credit and finance, which include issuers of charge cards and credit cards and travelers' checks, operators of cash-dispensing machines, development finance institutions, building societies and housing credit institutions, factoring companies, and leasing companies. Also included are *representative offices* of foreign banks or institutions, which conduct business of finance companies or scheduled institutions.

3   *Nonscheduled institutions.* Statutory bodies (financial institutions set up by statute and supervised in most cases by authorities other than the Ministry of Finance) and any person or corporation, which are neither liable to be licensed under the BAFIA nor subject to the provision governing scheduled businesses and representative offices but are engaged in the provision of finance.

Apart from the Central Bank, which regulates the formal banking system, there are many other bodies that regulate various bits of the securities and equity market. Under the Securities Industry Act 1983 and the Companies Act 1965, the Kuala Lumpur Stock Exchange (KLSE) is responsible for ensuring that companies listed on the KLSE are of sound financial standing. The Capital Issues Committee (CIC) supervises the issue of shares and other corporate securities, including disclosure requirements of all pertinent financial information. The Registrar of Companies (ROC) administers the SIA 1983, ensures that stockbrokers comply with their statutory obligations and, under the Companies Act 1965, has both administrative and regulatory powers governing companies and their officers. The Foreign Investment Committee (FIC) implements government's guidelines (e.g., of the New Economic Policy) on acquisition or takeovers and is responsible for major issues of foreign investment. Finally, the Panel on Take-overs and Mergers (TOP) scrutinizes all takeovers and mergers, and the interests of minority shareholders are protected.

The Central Bank monitors the financial institutions (FCs), requiring them to submit regular financial returns so as to ensure that they are operating within prudential limits and observing legal requirements. The Bank also issues guidelines to regulate FCs. It can, too, conduct more thorough examinations of financial institutions, including (1) appraisal of asset quality; (2) verification of the types and size of various liabilities; (3) appraisal of management; (4) asset or liabilities management; (5) compliance with legal and regulatory requirements and broad national policies; and (6) evaluation of records, systems, and internal control. The major operations reviewed are credit operations including trade financing and loan portfolio; deposit operations; remittance operations; investments, money and foreign exchange market operations; and off-balance-sheet businesses.

Troubled financial institutions

Most institutions that have run into trouble did so following the 1985–6 recession. In the banking system, there was a big overhang of nonperforming property loans and imprudent share-based lending, which resulted in substantial provisions for interest-in-suspense and bad debts. On top of that, there were some cases of weak and fraudulent management. Some of these institutions suffered such large losses that their capital was eroded to the edge of bankruptcy.

Because of legal constraints, the Central Bank's initial approach to troubled institutions was limited to directing a change in management, entrusting them with stemming losses while detailed rescue plans were formulated. Later, legislation was introduced to allow the Central Bank, with the approval of the minister of finance, to grant secured loans to, or purchase any shares of, a licensed bank or finance company. Such measures were essentially short-term; to eliminate any conflict of interest between its role as a supervisor of the banking system and as a shareholder of banks, there was a phased withdrawal by the Central Bank from its equity holdings as the delinquent institutions were rehabilitated and put on a sound financial standing.

There was a moral hazard in allowing errant shareholders, responsible for the predicament of the ailing institutions, to benefit from the retention of their equity stake after rescue by the Bank. So, under new legislation, the Bank could apply to the High Court to reduce the institution's capital to the extent that it was lost or was unrepresented by available assets. In effect, shareholders had to bear responsibility for imprudent banking and mismanagement.

10.6   Lessons from Malaysian financial reform

Although the reasons for liberalization were mixed, the financial reforms introduced in the 1970s (including allowing commercial banks to determine interest rates for depositors and borrowers) were a deliberate move to promote a more free and competitive financial system. Encouraging the growth of a more market-oriented financial system can also be seen with the introduction of two new money-market instruments – banker's acceptances (BAs) and negotiable certificates of deposits. Other financial reforms were also undertaken to increase the responsiveness of bank loan and deposit rates to market forces. In 1983 (November), all banks' and finance companies' lending rates (except the priority sectors) were anchored to their base lending rate, because lending rates tended to behave in an asymmetrical fashion and due to a concern about borrower net worth in the face of severe macro shocks. Indirect controls over interest rates in 1985–7 (when interest rates for deposits up to 12-month maturities were pegged to the deposit rate of the two lending banks) were removed when the economy recovered and when liquidity – and borrower net worth – increased in the system. There was further deregulation in early 1991 (February), when the base lending rate was freed from the Central Bank control and commercial banks and finance companies were allowed to set base lending rates on the basis of costs of funds. This was done to encourage market-oriented yield curves that will benefit the capital market, especially the development of secondary markets for public and private securities.

Liberalization cannot be seen as a uniformly linear process (i.e., once set in motion, its course cannot be redirected or qualified). This study has revealed that liberalization can have a stop-and-go approach. Interest rate reforms, for example, were initially implemented in 1971, when fixed deposits with commercial banks for maturities exceeding four years carried market-determined interest rates and (from January 1972) rate ceilings were lifted for all commercial bank deposits with maturity exceeding one year. In August 1972 the interest rates for deposits placed with finance companies were freed and, in the same month, the discount rates on Treasury bills were determined by open tender. In the early and mid-1980s, however, indirect controls on interest rates were reintroduced because it was believed that high interest rates were inconsistent with recession. Thus macroeconomic considerations, unsurprisingly, can exercise a decisive influence on the course and pace of reform.

The sequencing and speed of Malaysian liberalization supports the view that the complete opening of the capital account should follow the opening of the trade account, that a gradualist approach is more appropriate, and that the timing should take into account the state of the economy.[4] The Malaysian economy can be characterized as one that has enjoyed long periods of economic stability and strong supervision of banking. Between 1970 and 1990 the economy went through only two economic downturns, in 1975 and 1985. With the exception of 1973–4 and 1980–1, price stability was maintained; in the 1970s, prices increased at 5.9% a year, and by 3.3% per annum in the 1980s. This allowed financial liberalization in "phases." Villanueva and Mira-khor's (1990) conclusion that the stability enjoyed by the Malaysian economy has enabled the government to liberalize interest rates fully in less than three years without the adverse consequence of an immediate increase in interest rates, however, needs to be qualified. Liberalization of interest rates began as early as 1971 and further measures were taken in 1973, 1975, with important changes made in 1978, 1981, and, more recently, in 1991. It would, therefore, be difficult to sustain the conclusion that the Malaysian experience is one of a strategy of complete interest rate liberalization implemented in a very short period similar to that of Chile, Argentina, Uruguay, and the Philippines.

Another lesson of the Malaysian experience is that economic policy changes cannot succeed if conditions are not right to allow reforms to take root. Without the shock of the recession in the early 1980s and without government commitment to introduce policy changes in response to the recession, reforms would not have seen the light of day. What appeared to be a retreat from reform during the early 1980s was only a strategic one, and institutional development, led by an independent and capable Central Bank, continued. And political stability was an invaluable ingredient: despite internal disputes in the National Front, the ruling coalition party and, especially, within United Malays National Organization (UMNO), there was political stability and continuity in Malaysia, and a clear sense of direction – and marked consistency – in the policy package, which has helped a great deal in providing credibility to economic and financial reforms. The banking system responded to clear, credible, and consistent policy signals, helping to make the reforms sustainable in the long run.

NOTES

1 In the 1970s, the share of palm oil in total exports increased from 9.8% to 25.3% and of manufactured goods from 11.1% to 20.6%, while minerals' share, largely crude oil, rose from 22.8% in 1970 to 34.5% in 1980.

2 During 1981, when the average cost of deposits (ACD) of the banks *increased* by 1.57 percentage points, the average lending rate (ALR) immediately rose by 1.85 percentage points. However, in 1982, when the ACD *fell* by 0.6 percentage points, the ALR *increased* another 0.27 percentage point.

3 As John Chant recognized (Chapter 9), wide spreads also can reflect portfolio problems, the type of clientele of the banks, etc.

4 Villanueva and Mirakhor (1990) have provided a typology of the initial macroeconomic environment: taking into account whether the macroeconomic environment is stable (SM) or unstable (UM) and has adequate bank supervision (AS) or inadequate bank supervision (IS). They also classify economies into four types: (a) UM/IS strategy, where macroeconomic instability interacts with weak bank supervision; (b) UM/ AS, where the potential interaction between economic instability and moral hazard is largely offset by bank supervision; (c) SM/IS strategy, where the economy is stable but moral hazard in banks presents a potential problem because of inadequate supervision; and (d) SM/AS strategy, where the economy is stable and the banking system is adequately supervised. They typify Malaysia as following the SM/AS sequencing strategy.

PART III

LIBERALIZING THE CAPITAL ACCOUNT AND
DOMESTIC FINANCIAL REFORM

CHAPTER 11

An open capital account: A brief survey of the issues and the results

James A. Hanson

11.1 Introduction

The increase in trade, the increasing internationalization of production, and improvements in communications, together with the legalization of foreign currency instruments in a growing number of countries, have led to a de facto liberalization of the capital account. In line with the greater reliance on open goods markets and a de facto opening of the capital account, governments of developing countries naturally are raising questions about fully opening the capital account. As a background to answering such questions, this chapter surveys the existing literature on opening up domestic capital markets, much of which was written prior to the debt crisis, as it applies to the current situation.

A liberalized or open capital market here is defined as one in which individuals and firms can access international financial markets freely, not just one in which the government intermediates international capital flows to balance differences in private saving and investment. In fact, private agents in many developing countries currently have greater access to international capital markets than their governments, particularly given the possibilities that private agents have for collateralizing their debt. This situation is a dramatic reversal of the situation of the late 1970s, when governments of developing countries intermediated large volumes of foreign funds at low real interest rates while private agents lacked comparable access to international capital.

This survey begins with a brief summary of the costs and benefits of liberalization of capital accounts paying particular attention to the issue of the loss of policy effectiveness and noting the new theories of capital flows based on international portfolio diversification of risky assets, which raise the possibility of benefits from capital-account liberalization that are not linked solely to higher investment rates. The survey then reviews quite briefly the evidence on the results of open capital account. Next, the survey reexamines the question of sequencing the liberalization of the current and capital accounts, to provide a background for programs to liberalize the capital account. Conclusions are presented in Section 11.5. Unfortunately, an assessment of the evidence on capital-account opening is beyond the scope of this chapter, but interested readers can turn to the earlier version (Hanson 1992) for a full discussion, and to the conclusions below, for a summary of those results.

11.2   The costs and benefits of capital-account liberalization

The traditional analysis

The traditional welfare analysis of capital-account liberalization in a developing country focuses on the benefits of allowing foreigners to own more domestic capital (MacDougall 1968). This analysis begins from a situation of autarchy, in which the rate of return in the domestic market is assumed to exceed the rate in the rest of the world. Once the capital account is opened up, this differential generates a capital inflow and a larger capital stock in the home country. In the final equilibrium, GDP is higher because of the larger capital stock. Domestic laborers gain at the expense of both domestic and foreign owners of capital, so GNP also is higher. A similar analysis applies in the context of growth theory: Foreigners will support a higher level of capital in country at lower cost, in terms of forgone consumption, than domestic saving alone. (See Appendix 11.1.)

The traditional analysis seems more appropriate to liberalizing the rules governing direct foreign investment than to liberalizing the rules on financial flows or the capital account as a whole. In effect, foreign investors are assumed to bring in capital goods and take away part of the additional production, thereby resolving the transfer problem and leaving the country better off because of higher demand for its labor. According to this analysis, financial flows would raise welfare only to the extent that they lead to a higher capital stock. Analogously to the optimum tax on trade, welfare may be increased by taxation of foreign capital inflows, if their supply to the country is not perfectly elastic or depends on the total volume of the country's borrowing as well as the returns to individual projects (Kemp 1964; Hanson 1974).

This analysis indicates only that more foreign saving is desirable. Since foreign saving could be intermediated by the government's borrowing externally, the analysis has no implication for opening the capital account to all participants.

In addition, by effectively beginning from autarchy, this analysis ignores the substitutability that exists between an open current account and an open capital account. As Samuelson (1948) points out (and Mundell 1968a reiterates):

> Commodity movement is almost certainly a substitute for factor movements, in this sense: if trade does not originally equalize factor prices and this causes factors to migrate so as to wipe out the difference, nonetheless before migration has proceeded far enough to equalize factor proportions, factor migration will come to a stop as commodity trade either will have equalized factor returns or will have so reduced the differential as to make the cost of transporting another unit of the factor greater than the present discounted value of the higher earnings it can hope to secure abroad.
>
> (Samuelson 1948, p. 11)

Thus, within the standard Hecksher–Ohlin world, opening the current account lowers the rental rate on capital – and the interest rate (see Samuelson 1965) – in the country with more abundant capital while raising it in the other. Capital-account liberalization and current-account liberalization thus are substitutes in the standard trade models. These models imply that the capital account need not be opened to equalize rates of return if the trade account is fully open. Of course this process will take time. Even in the United States, where internal capital flows were free, there were significant and persistent per capita income differentials (Borts and Stein 1964), probably associated with differential returns on real capital. Moreover, this argument does not contradict the desirability of opening the capital account in order to obtain direct foreign investment that would bring with it technology that cannot be transferred effectively through licenses or trade.[1]

Intertemporally based trade and capital flows

The standard Hecksher–Ohlin model determines the pattern of trade based on the relative abundance of factors, ignoring differences in demand patterns. Intertemporal considerations enter only to the extent that differences in time preference explain differences in saving and, ultimately, in factor proportions.[2] In contrast, intertemporal differences in production are the traditional starting point for models of forward markets (Stein 1962). Intertemporally, seasonality can be smoothed to some degree within an economy through forward contracts and storage. However, if two countries have seasonally opposite patterns of production, then, in theory, international trade in goods and financial claims could smooth consumption at less cost (Stockman 1988 and works cited there).

For example, Southern Hemisphere producers could export temperate zone products produced during their summer to the Northern Hemisphere during its winter. Rather than contemporaneously importing goods with the export proceeds – a continuously balanced current account matched by a balanced-at-zero capital account – Southern Hemisphere producers might build up financial claims on the Northern Hemisphere producers. These claims could be exercised later, during the harvest season in the Northern Hemisphere. Over a year, the trade and the capital account each would be balanced, but in each semester the current and capital account would show equal but opposite imbalances. Provided the relevant transport costs were less than the storage costs, real resources would be saved by allowing international trading in financial claims.

While interesting theoretically, this model does not yet seem to have much empirical applicability. For example, although Chilean temperate zone fruits and vegetables are abundant in winter markets in the Northern Hemisphere, the reverse trade does not seem to have developed. Whether this is because differences in market size or seasonal variations in transport costs make exporting the Northern Hemisphere's summer production to Chile unprofitable, or because of residual Chilean protection, is hard to say.

In addition, on a theoretical plane, the argument simply suggests that international borrowing and lending could reduce the costs of intertemporal differences between production and consumption, which does not necessarily mean a fully open capital account. One theoretical alternative would be for the government to build up and run down international reserves during the year – individual preferences could be indulged by allowing forward trading against the country's reserves. Of course an open capital account would be the most straightforward solution to obtaining the benefits of trade based on intertemporal considerations.

Risk

Recent analysis emphasizes the role of risk bearing and risk sharing in financial markets and, by extension, international financial markets. If the prices for bearing or sharing certain risks differ between countries, then there would be gains from trade in international financial assets embodying these risks that are analogous to the gains from international trade in commodities (Svensson 1988; Persson and Svensson 1985). "All of the arguments against restricting international trade in goods also apply to restricting international trade in financial assets, whether these restrictions occur in the forms of direct controls, taxes or regulation of financial intermediaries" (Stockman 1988, p. 536). Similarly, all the caveats regarding the benefits of free trade in goods also would apply to the benefits of free trade in risky assets.

Bringing in the element of risk is thus a major shift from the traditional analysis of capital flows, because it uncouples the welfare implications of an open capital account from its effect on investment. *Even if saving and investment are unaffected by allowing capital flows – that is, even if the private capital account were exactly balanced by inflows and outflows of capital – the individual agents of the economy would benefit from trade in risky assets.*[3] Moreover, the argument that individuals should be allowed to trade assets internationally, based on differences in preferences, production and evaluation of risk, is, analogously to the trading of commodities, perhaps the strongest argument for open capital markets in the sense defined in the introduction.

Taxation and the risk of taxation

Analysts of developing countries when asked to rationalize a closed capital account, often answer with some variant of "otherwise we would lose all our savings." In terms of the traditional analysis, this view suggests that capital in the country would fall if the capital account were opened. If this view were true, it would suggest that the rate of return in the economy is *less* than the rate of return in the rest of the world. However, developing countries generally are thought to have lower levels of capital per worker than developed countries, which should imply higher rates of return in developing countries in the absence of capital movements.

Underlying country risk, unrelated to country policy, is one possible explanation for outflows of capital from developing countries, despite domestic rates of return that exceed world rates. For example, borrowers from a monoexporter would face a risk premium in international markets related to the price risk on the monoexport; residents would try to diversify their assets into instruments that have a different risk. However, an open capital account might also attract investors interested in diversifying their portfolios by purchasing assets with a different risk–return trade-off than prevails in their own countries. Gross capital outflows would certainly occur, but the effect on the capital account would depend on the balance of the inflows and the outflows, and the degree to which the monoexporter allowed the development of attractive instruments for foreign investors.

Taxation and the risk of taxation probably are a more important explanation for the apparent paradox of capital outflow from what should be high return countries than underlying country risk. To investors, high taxes and potential taxes on capital in developing countries, including the possibility of expropriation, easily could offset higher-than-international rates of return to capital and financial assets.

The tax issue is compounded by the tax preferences offered foreigners in many industrial countries and banking centers. Offshore banking centers, and many industrial countries, do not tax interest earned on savings accounts or, at least, interest earned by foreign holders of savings accounts. For example, the United States has not taxed interest income on savings accounts belonging to foreigners since the 1970s. Moreover, competition for deposits among financial centers has meant that data on foreign owners of deposits are not available to income tax authorities in the country of origin – if one center were to provide the information, then tax considerations would cause capital to shift to other centers. The differential tax treatment of foreign and domestically owned deposits could, in theory, give rise to two-way capital flows based on tax avoidance, so called round-tripping (Tanzi and Blejer 1982).

Taxation of financial instruments takes many forms besides simple income taxation. For example, inflation represents a tax on all financial instruments that have zero or fixed interest rates. Reserve requirements that are unremunerated or carry fixed remunerations are another way of imposing the inflation tax. However, the incidence of the implicit tax arising from reserve requirements may fall on depositors or borrowers. This means that, with an open capital account, an increase in the inflation tax on reserve requirements may motivate capital inflows as well as outflows. For example, with an open capital account, depositors in banks would be able to demand deposit rates equivalent to international rates. This would mean that the impact of higher-than-international costs of reserve requirements would be felt solely in lending rates, where differences in information reduce competition between foreign and domestic banks more than in deposit taking. The higher lending rates, in turn, would induce foreign banks to increase their direct lending from home offices, thereby generating a capital inflow. Firms that could borrow internationally would do so, another source of capital inflows.

The risks of potential taxation, as well as actual differences in taxes, represent a rationale for "capital flight." The potential for higher future taxation means that domestic financial assets must carry a risk premium to be equivalent, in the minds of potential asset holders, to assets in the rest of the world.[4] There also exists a risk that a country may default on its international obligations, over and above the risk associated with individual projects (Dooley and Isard 1980; Hanson 1974). Thus there may be a number of risk premiums, in addition to the risk premiums associated with the various forms of taxation, and differences in the variability in inflation, the exchange rate, and domestic interest rates. These risk premiums, and changes in them, are one explanation of the imperfect substitutability between financial assets of different countries. They also explain why interest rates may be higher than international rates in countries that are presumed to have low capital/labor ratios. Such risk premiums have a real cost, in terms of reducing the domestic capital/labor ratio and domestic consumption below what it otherwise would be (Appendix 11.1). Hence, any policies that can reduce this risk premium would tend to raise GNP.

To summarize, "country risk" explains why an open capital account might lead to capital outflows from what are potentially high-return countries. Capital-account controls are needed in order to tax domestic capital at higher-than-international rates. To the extent that the capital account can be kept closed, preventing capital outflow that otherwise would occur because of higher rates of actual and potential taxation, and to the extent that legal arrangements can be made to offset the potential negative impact of these capital controls on capital inflows, then the negative effects of capital account controls can be partially offset. In these circumstance, there may, indeed, be costs of opening the capital account. This is particularly true taking into account the distributional implications of being able to tax capital more heavily than would be possible with an open capital account.

A critical question is whether the de facto internationalization of capital already makes it difficult to tax capital. In answering this question, it is important to note capital controls and high taxation are likely to motivate attempts to internationalize domestic capital, by establishing channels through which capital can be transferred internationally. The longer capital controls have been imposed, the more porous they are likely to be. To the extent that capital can be moved fairly freely internationally – for example by overinvoicing imports and underinvoicing exports – then laws to keep the capital account closed simply represent a hindrance to domestic capitalists, which encourages corruption. Maintenance of such ineffective laws is not a valid reason for not opening the capital account.[5]

Moreover, since capital controls are only partially effective, they change the incidence of capital taxation. Some types of capital can be moved less easily internationally than others, some savers and investors have less access to international markets than others. These types of capital and these agents thus are more subject to capital taxation than those that are de facto internationally mobile. If capital that is de facto internationally mobile also is owned largely by large capitalists, then any favorable distributional implications of capital taxation cum capital controls may be reduced or even reversed. Indeed, one argument for allowing an open capital account is that it allows all citizens, not just those with easy access to foreign exchange, to reduce the burden of taxes on savings, such as the inflation tax.

Open capital markets as limitations on the effectiveness of policies

The possibility of avoiding taxes when the capital account is open is one example of the general point that an open capital account limits the impact of government policies. An open capital account limits governments' ability to tax capital or financial assets, to the extent that economic agents can easily switch their portfolios internationally to escape taxes. Although in a closed economy the impact of various taxes also can be reduced, by substitution in production and consumption into goods with lower rates of taxation, in an open economy even more options are available.

Another widely known example of how an open capital account may reduce policy effectiveness is Mundell's (1968c) analysis, showing that monetary policy is ineffective in a small economy with a fixed exchange rate, open capital markets, and perfect substitutability between domestic and foreign assets.[6] In Mundell's model, the domestic interest rate is fixed by international flows of capital and cannot be affected by variations in the growth of domestic credit. Thus monetary policy becomes ineffective. These and other examples of policy ineffectiveness often are cited as costs of opening the capital account. However, the importance or even the correctness of this argument is far from clear.

In general, an open capital account does not eliminate the effectiveness of policy instruments, it only reduces it. In variants of the Mundell model, price stickiness and wealth effects mean money does have a role in determining output, even if interest rates are determined by free international capital flows (Dornbusch 1976). In addition, imperfect substitutability between assets means monetary policy can affect the differential between foreign and domestic interest rates (the risk premium) and thus change the domestic interest rate, even in a completely open capital market.

Targeting the interest rate, rather than the money stock, is another way to take advantage of the imperfect substitutability between domestic and foreign assets, although it is likely to lead to a loss of international reserves. To lower domestic interest rates, a government may offer to lend below international interest rates or roll over government bonds at less than world rates. This will lead to capital flight and loss of international reserves. Thus, whether this policy increases investment, or only capital flight, depends on the elasticity of capital outflow. Raising the interest rate, by offering interest rates above international rates, may be more successful in affecting (reducing) investment. Surprisingly, however, this policy also is likely to lead to a decline in *net* international assets. For example, the Central Bank or the Treasury could maintain domestic interest rates above international rates by selling high-interest-rate bonds. This policy will attract net capital inflows and raise the interest rate to domestic borrowers. However, it also will generate *net* obligations for the country, since the inflows of capital can only be invested at the lower, international rate. The country's net external obligations will grow, and eventually raise the risk premium in world markets. Thus, the eventual result of trying to target the interest rate below *or* above the world rate is a loss in net reserves. Since declining net reserves often are viewed as an indicator of country risk, either policy is likely to lead to a rise in the interest-rate premium facing the country in international markets and, eventually, to higher domestic interest rates.[7]

Finally, if only the degree of effectiveness of a policy variable – the impact multiplier in the language of econometrics – is changed when capital markets are opened up, then the ability to make policy is not affected. A larger dose of the same instrument will achieve the desired effect. If the application of a policy instrument has no cost, then changes in the impact multiplier are not important. However, if the cost of using a policy instrument does rise with the size of the intervention, then there may be some costs of capital-account liberalization, in terms of policy effectiveness, but these must be set against the benefits of opening the capital account.

One option to overcome any loss of policy effectiveness would be to use an alternative instrument to achieve or to enhance the effectiveness of a policy instrument. For example, again referring to the Mundell model, the use of a floating exchange rate, as opposed to a fixed exchange rate, restores the effectiveness of domestic monetary policy despite an open capital account.[8] Thus, monetary independence can be restored at the cost of the government's giving up control over the nominal exchange rate and allowing it to float freely. The free float clearly would entail an increase in the variability of the exchange rate and correspondingly greater risks for exporters and importers than a fixed rate system.

Viewed in this light, capital-account controls, to the degree to which they can be made effective, are simply an alternative to flexible exchange rates in making monetary policy effective. Countries often have tried to use a different exchange rate or a free float only for capital-account transactions – in effect trying to create another policy instrument – in order to obtain monetary independence or maintain control over the nominal exchange rate applicable to trade. However, the difference between the multiple exchange rates, and thus the degree of monetary independence, clearly is limited by the ease of arbitrage between the markets.[9]

It also should be noted that the effectiveness of some policies may be enhanced by an open capital account. For example, in Mundell's analysis, fiscal policy becomes more effective with an open capital account because there is less crowding-out.[10] Fiscal policy thus represents not only an alternative instrument to monetary policy for the control of short-run fluctuations in aggregate demand, but one that is enhanced by an open capital account. Any cost of a decreased effectiveness of monetary policy thus must be weighed against the benefit of an increased effectiveness of fiscal policy.

A more fundamental question is whether the changes in the effectiveness of policy instruments represent a cost to society. If an open capital account permits residents to escape the inflation tax, or other distortionary taxes, at low cost, then an open capital account does not a priori represent a cost to society defined as the sum of individuals; it may even be a benefit.

Some authors have extended this argument: An open capital account, by placing a limitation on the effectiveness of certain government policies, reduces the incentive for their enactment. Thus a country's credibility improves and the risk premium may decline. However, this argument should not be overstated. Even the most credulous investors recognize that "a government intent on extracting an inflation tax from its own residents . . . has substantial incentives to deviate from a regime of flexible exchange rates and capital mobility" (Sargent 1983, p. 113). An open capital market can easily be closed if the government wishes to engage in distortionary policies. Perhaps the argument is better stated by noting that once a capital account is opened, and maintained open for some time, then the incentives to close it again are reduced, because many savers and investors will have diversified their portfolios internationally in the interim, and this will reduce the effectiveness of policy and thus the incentive to engage in such policies.

In sum, it is difficult to conclude whether the impact of opening the capital account on the effectiveness of policy instruments represents a cost or a benefit to society.

Instability

Another common, related argument against open capital accounts is that they can lead to greater instability. Flows of "hot money" not only can offset monetary policy, as discussed in the previous section, they can cause substantial variations in the nominal and real exchange rate, interest rates, and output. An open capital account also can exaggerate or offset terms of trade shocks, depending on how international creditors react to such shocks.

Economic theory suggests that capital inflows are likely to move sympathetically to a terms of trade shock and thus magnify its effect (see Appendix 11.1). Moreover, the experience of a number of countries during the debt crisis suggests that the problem of importing world fluctuations through the capital account is only partly a matter of hot money. The debt problems of the severely indebted, middle-income countries reflect a period in which private medium- and long-term inflows, as well as short-term inflows, first grew to unsustainable levels, and then were cut off at the same time as the terms of trade collapsed and real interest rates were high. The initial inflows reflected unsustainable and contradictory macroeconomic policies in the borrowing countries, but also rapid monetary growth in the industrialized countries and, in the case of oil exporters, favorable terms of trade.[11] For the foreseeable future, such lending excesses are unlikely to recur. Nonetheless, the experience of this period suggests that the flows of external capital may well magnify shocks.

An open capital account could, in theory, cushion temporary fluctuations in tradeables and their prices. To some extent that may even have happened in the mid-1970s and at the beginning of the 1980s in some petroleum-importing countries. Among the various types of capital flows, direct foreign investment may be the best shock absorber, since it acts like equity rather than debt. For example, Reynolds shows that in Chile, the flow of resources from the copper companies to the country were more stable than the terms of trade. However, theoretically and empirically, capital inflows tend to move sympathetically to permanent changes in the terms of trade. This means that at best capital flows can ease adjustment, not substitute permanently for it.

The validity of the instability argument is not, however, solely a question of whether capital flows move pro- or contracyclically to variations in international prices. Rather, it also depends on whether the main source of domestic fluctuations is external or internal, much like the classic arguments for and against the flexible exchange rates. If the main source of fluctuations is variations in saving and investment rates in the rest of the world or variations in the rest of the world's evaluation of country risk, and if the economy is operating under a fixed-exchange-rate regime, then an open capital account might increase fluctuations (leaving aside the shock absorber argument) because these shocks would enter through the capital as well as the current account. However, if the main source of fluctuations is variations in the balance between domestic saving and investment, such as those that arise from unstable domestic policies, then international capital flows could reduce fluctuations in output. Also, an open capital account makes it difficult to apply the inflation tax or conduct an independent monetary policy, as noted in the preceding subsection. Moreover, if a government had a tendency toward the erratic use of the inflation tax, but could be convinced to keep an open capital account, then that capital account policy would induce a more stable policy framework by reducing the incentives to use the inflation tax. Thus, the key issue is whether domestic fiscal and monetary policies tend to offset fluctuations in the domestic economy or cause them.

11.3   Results of open capital accounts[12]

The foregoing theoretical analysis of capital account liberalization suggests three ways of judging or measuring the empirical outcome of an open capital account: the degree of linkage of domestic and international interest rates, the degree of linkage between domestic and world saving and investment, and the extent of trade in risky assets. There is, however, no empirical analysis of the extent of or benefits from trade in risky assets, other than to follow Bryant and observe that an enormous two-way trade in financial assets has developed over the past 30 years[13] and that this trade is probably linked to trade in risky assets.

Most of the evidence on the impact of opening the capital account relates to industrialized countries and concentrates on two issues: the degree to which foreign capital inflows finance domestic investment and the degree to which uncovered interest rate parity typically is achieved. In general, the results for industrial countries suggest:

1 Foreign capital flows (net) finance, on average, only 10–15% of investment in industrialized countries. Various authors have argued that this result reflects similarities in savings and investment functions in these countries, similarities in the business cycle across developed countries, policy-related shifts within domestic saving and investment that do not affect external finance, country size–risk premium effects as well as imperfect capital mobility.

2 Uncovered interest-rate parity typically is not achieved even between industrial countries. It is not clear if this reflects a market failure, econometric difficulties with the model (the estimates typically are a joint test of the hypothesized pattern of expectations and market equilibrium), or variations in the risk premium.

Regarding studies on the developing countries, there are no specific studies of the financing of investment. Some of the studies of foreign capital inflows in developing countries include industrial countries; this inclusion (and studies including more smaller industrial economies) suggests that foreign saving represents a larger fraction of investment than in the larger industrial countries. (However, the developing country results may reflect large aid flows to countries with low incomes or statistical difficulties, rather than larger private flows.) Data on the gross *stock* of external debt suggest a high ratio of external debt to domestic capital stock in many developing countries, which is also indicative of large flows.

Regarding interest rates, many of the studies in developing countries also analyze the extent of uncovered interest parity, usually allowing for a constant risk premium. A number of these studies are of Latin American countries during periods when they followed a policy of using the exchange rate (and in some cases the interest rate) to slow inflation. This suggests the possibility of a "peso" problem in the estimates – that expectations of devaluation may well have been high and even increasing over time but standard, distributed lag approaches to estimating expectations suggest a long period in which uncovered interest parity, even allowing for a constant risk premium, does not hold. In recent periods the risk premium in these countries may have risen because of their external debt overhang – this reflects not only risks of higher taxes (including inflation) to service debt, but also the alternative of investing in external debt, an option that is increasingly feasible given the growing breadth and sophistication of that market. Recent studies of a more diversified sample of countries with more stable macroeconomic environments suggest that the domestic interest rates tend to follow international interest rates to a fair degree, after appropriate allowance for a risk premium. These analyses suggest that capital mobility, although imperfect, may have reduced domestic interest rates by as much as 5 percentage points compared to the autarchic situation.

11.4   The sequencing and speed of capital- and current-account liberalization

The preconditions for capital-account liberalization

A stable macroeconomy is a precondition to international financial liberalization. Opening the capital account increases the opportunity for currency substitution, which increases the rate of inflation (in domestic currency) needed to mobilize a given volume of resources through the inflation tax. However, it is important to realize, as noted earlier, that under conditions of high and variable inflation the capital account may, de facto, be substantially open. Leaving the capital market legally closed increases the incidence of the inflation tax on those without easy access to foreign exchange.

Allowing easier access to international capital markets during conditions of high inflation also can increase the variability of the economy substantially. In high inflation, the domestic currency money base falls as a percentage of GDP. Every nominal and real shock, and every shift in expectations, then has a proportionately greater impact on domestic financial variables. The resulting variability will be further magnified if shifts into foreign-exchange-denominated assets are made less costly by capital-account liberalization – the money base will become even smaller and the shifts in response to a given shock will become even greater. A sustainable fiscal deficit, which requires only a minimal inflation tax, thus is a particularly important precondition to international, as well as domestic, financial liberalization.

External borrowing, directly or indirectly, could, of course, be used to reduce the need for the inflation tax and reduce public sector "crowding out" of domestic investment.[14] (Notice that such increased external public sector borrowing does not mean international financial liberalization as defined in the introduction to this chapter.) However, this policy option is fraught with dangers, as McKinnon (1982) and McKinnon and Mathieson pointed out, and as recent experience suggests. In the late 1970s and early 1980s, many developing countries used substantial external borrowing to avoid reductions in public sector deficits and to sustain overvalued real exchange rates that were inconsistent with aggregate demand policy. When the initial inflow of funds slowed, real interest rates increased, and commodity prices fell, the debt crisis occurred, which depressed growth rates for many years in the more severely indebted countries. Of course external borrowing has become difficult for many developing countries with the onset of the debt crisis.

It is sometimes argued that opening the capital account will force the government to reduce its reliance on the inflation tax, by lowering the base of the tax significantly. This argument is sometimes extended by saying that opening the capital account will endow anti-inflation programs with greater credibility. To some degree, these arguments are based on the idea that the inflation tax results from the government's rational reflection on the optimal combination of taxes. However, analysis of episodes of hyperinflation suggests that these episodes often reflect a desperate attempt to continue spending rather than a rational portfolio decision about the optimum combination of taxes. Moreover, as noted earlier, governments that intend to use the inflation tax typically close the capital account first. This can be done fairly easily, although, once individuals have built up some assets denominated in foreign exchange during the period of an open capital account, it is difficult to reclose the capital account. Overall, it would seem that merely opening the capital account will not increase the credibility of a stabilization program very much.

Domestic financial liberalization, to a significant degree, is the second precondition to international financial liberalization. If domestic citizens are to be given easy access to international financial markets, through foreign banks, then the domestic banking system must face essentially the same regulations and controls on interest rates and portfolio composition as foreign banks in their home markets to remain competitive. Moreover, the domestic banks must have sound portfolios. Unless these two conditions are met, liberalizing the capital account is likely to lead to disintermediation that will put pressure on the domestic banking system, force closures of domestic banks, and increase claims on the government in its role as explicit or implicit insurer of deposits.

In a financially closed economy, the domestic banking system often suffers from severe regulation, which benefits the government and other preferred borrowers at a cost to domestic savers and nonpreferred borrowers. Perhaps the most important form of such regulation is the control of interest rates and portfolio composition, which manifests itself in high, unremunerated reserves requirements and below-market directed credit. Such regulations lead to large spreads between rates on deposits and rates on nonpreferential loans (Hanson and Rocha 1986). Once depositors and nonpreferred borrowers obtain access to international financial markets, these spreads make domestic financial intermediaries uncompetitive – because of the regulations they are unable to set interest rates that will prevent the loss of deposits and their nonpreferential loan customers. Such regulations can be applied to foreign banks operating in the domestic market, but they are likely to be less effective than on domestic banks because: (1) foreign banks and associated nonbank intermediaries can often facilitate transactions with home offices that avoid such regulations or (2) they can avoid such regulations within the country using modern technology.[15] Hence, such regulations reduce the competitiveness of the domestic banking industry and are likely to lead to a loss of business that may imperil some domestic banks.

The domestic banking sector may be charging high spreads because of high costs and the need to provision against poor loan performance. High costs may reflect a number of factors in addition to poor technology and management, such as the sharing of monopolistic profits with members of bank unions and extensive branch networks that were useful for capturing low-cost deposits in a period when interest rates could not be set competitively. Poor portfolio quality may reflect not only poor loan decisions and unexpected shifts in relative prices but high-risk, directed credits and favorable terms to non–arm's length borrowers. Competition from foreign banks and an open capital market is useful in reducing high spreads that result from poor technology and management, and extensive branch networks. Competition also may force better portfolio selection. However, it probably is desirable for the government to take action to reduce costs associated with the stock of outstanding bad loans (by fully recognizing such loans) and with high labor costs before allowing foreign banks to compete fully with domestic banks. Otherwise the playing field will not be fully level for domestic banks and some of them could be imperiled, for example by the burden of poor portfolio quality, leading to the government's being forced to assume responsibility for their deposits.

The sequence of liberalization: Capital or current account

An extensive body of literature focuses on the question of sequencing external liberalization, whether the capital or current account should be opened first. Interest in this question was particularly aroused by the different paths of liberalization in the Southern Cone of South America in the latter half of the 1970s. Chile is generally characterized as liberalizing the current account first, Uruguay and Argentina the capital account first, and, in an influential paper, McKinnon (1982) argues that much of Chile's success, relative to Argentina, is due to the different sequencing of their reforms (and to Chile's fiscal surplus as opposed to Argentina's stubborn fiscal deficit). It should be noted, that there is a substantial debate in Chile on the timing of the capital-account liberalization and its role in the crisis of the early 1980s, as noted in Chapter 12. Of course, a number of other factors were at work and, eventually, all three countries' attempts at liberalization suffered reverses in the debt crisis. (See, for example, the works contained in the 1985 *World Development* issue edited by Corbo and de Melo; Corbo, De Melo, and Tybout 1986; Edwards and Cox-Edwards 1987; Hanson 1986; and Harberger 1982.)

The initial view on sequencing (McKinnon 1973) was that capital-account restrictions should be relaxed only after trade reform, and policymakers should "deliberately avoid an unusual or extraordinary injection of foreign capital" (McKinnon 1973, p. 161). The rationale for this view is as follows: Current-account liberalization typically requires a real depreciation of the exchange rate, to offset the negative effect on the balance of payments of cuts in the average level of protection. In contrast, capital-account liberalization tends to produce a real appreciation of the exchange rate. If capital-account liberalization were to produce a stable net transfer (capital inflow, less interest payments),[16] then opening both accounts simultaneously might yield something like the final real exchange rate, and resources could then be reallocated in accordance with that objective. However, capital inflows must be paid for, so the initial net transfer following the opening of the capital account is likely to be larger than the final net transfer (see Appendix 11.1). Moreover, the responsiveness of capital to the pent-up demand for local assets is likely to be much faster than the responsiveness of trade flows to the opening of the current account, leading to an unsustainable appreciation of the real exchange rate (Frenkel 1982). Hence, opening the capital account before the current account produces incentives for resource allocation that will have to be reversed in the final equilibrium (Krueger 1986), and could retard the adjustment to the reduction in protection.[17] To avoid "unnecessary" resource shifts, a number of authors (for example, Edwards 1984; Frenkel 1982; Khan and Zahler 1983; McKinnon 1973, 1982) have concluded that it is preferable to open the current account before the capital account.

There are, however, some difficulties with this sequence. First, the volume of capital resources over time is not necessarily the same under the two different sequences of liberalization. Whenever the capital-account liberalization occurs, it tends to cause an appreciation; the point is that once protection is reduced in a capital-scarce country, the rate of return is reduced, as discussed in Section 11.2, decreasing the incentive for capital inflows. Thus, there are fewer "unnecessary" resource shifts in the current account–capital account sequence in part because there is a smaller stock of capital – the costs of this lower capital stock have to be evaluated relative to the benefits of lower costs of adjustment.

This type of argument has led some authors (Little, Scitovsky, and Scott 1970; Michaely 1986; Krueger 1981, 1984) to argue for simultaneous liberalization of the current and capital accounts. In their view, short-run adjustment costs and the opposition to reforms that they generate are an important problem in liberalization. Foreign funds can be used to reduce or offset the costs of these frictions. Thus, these authors generally argue that the capital account should be liberalized at the same time as or even prior to the current account. Of course, this argument is for larger capital inflows; these need not be provided through greater individual access to foreign capital (capital-account liberalization) but could come through government intermediation of foreign capital.

These points are examples of a more general questioning of much of the sequencing literature. A strict economic analysis of sequencing requires an intertemporal analysis, allowing for different volumes of capital inflow as well as different degrees of misallocation. Moreover, the analysis should not be limited only to distortions between domestic and foreign prices, but should allow for domestic distortions as well. Some attempts to carry out this type of analysis have already begun (see, for example, Khan and Zahler 1983; Rodrik 1987; Edwards 1989; and Edwards and van Wijnbergen 1986); not surprisingly, the argument for the current account–capital account sequence seems to depend on the type and degree of the initial distortions. Moreover, the whole sequencing argument understates the benefits of capital-account liberalization because of its neglect of risk.

The speed of liberalization

Capital-account liberalization often is treated as instantaneous in the foregoing sequencing literature. (See, for example, Edwards 1984 and Frenkel 1982), in contrast to the well-known debate on gradual versus rapid trade reform. (See, for example, Krueger 1986; Michaely 1986; and Little, Scitovsky, and Scott 1970; Edwards and van Wijnbergen 1986.) In fact, the capital account may be opened gradually in a variety of ways, analogously to the methods used in opening the current account gradually. For example, taxes on capital inflow (including differential reserve requirements on banks' use of foreign capital) can be varied, or limitations on banks' and other financial intermediaries' use of foreign capital can be varied as was done to some extent in Chile at the end of the 1970s (see Edwards and Cox-Edwards 1987) and again at the end of the 1980s. Another approach would be dual foreign exchange markets – in contrast to the usual situation the rate applicable to capital-account transactions would *appreciate* initially relative to the current account rate, which could be unified once the first burst of capital inflow slowed.[18] In principle such policies would mean that capital-account liberalization could proceed at a pace linked to current-account liberalization, thereby avoiding the overshooting of the real exchange rate. One corollary of this argument is that the problem with the capital-account liberalization in Chile in the latter half of the 1970s was not opening of the capital account, but the abrupt switch from a closed account, which created pent-up demand for Chilean assets, to a completely open account.

The speed of current-account liberalization also is an issue because of positive relation that exists between expectations of devaluation and the domestic interest rate, even in economies with relatively closed capital accounts. As noted earlier, reduction of trade barriers typically needs to be compensated by a pari passu depreciation of the real exchange rate to avoid an increase in the current-account deficit. Generally it is thought that this real depreciation can be achieved with lower costs of adjustment by depreciating the nominal exchange rate, rather than through a reduction in domestic wages and prices. However, depreciation in the nominal exchange rate tends to raise the *real* interest rate in the economy, because of the increased gains to be made from holding financial assets denominated in foreign exchange. The higher real interest rate tends to depress the rate of investment.

This argument suggests that the *pace* of trade liberalization and the rate of compensatory depreciation could be important determinants of the rate of investment and growth, even in a fully credible process of liberalization. The relationship is not linear – very slow trade liberalization requires very little compensatory real depreciation and hence has only minimal effect on the real interest rate and investment; very rapid trade liberalization means a high real interest rate only for a short period; thereafter no real devaluation is needed and the expected rate of devaluation and, correspondingly, the real interest rate decrease. It is only gradual trade liberalization, spread over say three to five years, that is likely to have an important effect on the real interest rate and investment. Even in such programs, the effect could be limited, by initially overshooting the exchange rate necessary to maintain a constant trade balance.

An example may clarify these points. Consider a program of trade liberalization intended to reduce the average rate of protection of imports by 50%. If done over five years at a steady rate, this might require a real depreciation of 3–5% per annum to match the growth of imports to the higher growth of exports. However, this depreciation would require an increase of 3–5 percentage points in the real interest rate in order to maintain the attractiveness of financial assets denominated in domestic currency, relative to those denominated in foreign currency. This higher real interest rate would have a negative effect on investment. If the trade liberalization were spread over 10 years, the required real depreciation and corresponding increase in the domestic real interest rate would be small; if the full trade liberalization were done at once, or if the exchange rate were devalued sharply early in the program of protection reduction, then there would be a much smaller effect on the real interest rate. Clearly the importance of this effect varies from country to country, depending on the degree to which the rate of depreciation affects the domestic interest rate and the effect of the domestic interest rate on investment. However, this argument suggests that it should not be surprising that programs of gradual trade liberalization show little impact on the rate of growth: Such programs tend to depress investment through their impact on the real interest rate and thus reduce the rate of adjustment to the new incentive framework.

11.5   Summary and conclusions

The question of the costs and benefits of opening the capital account has become moot to some degree. De facto, capital has become internationalized by the growing integration of the world economy. Compared to, say, the 1960s, economic agents have much greater access to foreign currency assets. This reflects the freer international mobility

of goods, people, and information, as well as the greater legal availability of such assets in the domestic financial system of many countries. In many cases, for individuals and nonfinancial firms, it is not
access but the menu of assets that is limited. This limitation largely
reflects the remaining restrictions on financial firms. It nonetheless
seems useful to examine the costs and benefits of opening the capital
account, the empirical results of opening the capital account (from
Hanson 1992), and the timing and sequencing of opening the capital
account, in order to assist countries in the process of capital-account
liberalization.

Theoretically, perhaps the main benefit in opening the capital account – in the sense of allowing individuals and firms full access to
international capital markets – seems to come from the greater scope
for exercising individual choice in diversifying risk. If domestic and
international prices of risky assets differ, then there are benefits from
allowing individuals to trade assets or goods and assets. These benefits
are analogous to the benefits of free trade in goods, and, correspondingly, are subject to many of the same caveats as the arguments for
free trade.

The traditional argument for opening the capital account in developing countries is somewhat different – that capital inflows will finance increased investment more cheaply, in terms of forgone consumption, than domestic saving. This argument is perhaps less forceful
in theoretical terms than the risk-diversification argument. First, under
this argument, the benefit of capital-account liberalization is much
smaller, as it is based only on the difference between capital inflows
and outflows. Ignoring the benefit from trading in risk is roughly
analogous to saying that the benefit from free trade is based on the
difference between exports and imports. Second, focusing on this
argument raises a problem of evaluating the benefits, to the extent that
the reduction in the rate of return, as a result of increased capital
flows, reduces the domestic saving rate.

Third, if the only rationale for capital flows were an excess of
riskless investment opportunities over domestic saving at the world
interest rate, then, in theory, a credible, maximizing government could
borrow funds internationally and either reduce domestic "crowding
out" or intermediate these funds through the domestic financial system. There would be no need for individual economic agents to access
international capital markets. The traditional argument also does not
imply a need to open both sides of the capital account. From the
standpoint of attracting foreign investors, who are interested only in
transferring their earnings, the question is one of the current account,

not the capital account. Guarantees of convertibility for debt service and profits, in theory, could be given. In practice, of course, many governments have found it difficult to carry out such intermediation effectively, or to offer credible guarantees, often have overborrowed, and have been lax in recovering on-lending when international funds have been intermediated through the domestic financial system. Governments also have suspended guarantees of profit remittances during foreign exchange crises. Experience thus suggests that, in practice, opening the capital account may be a more effective way to mobilize and allocate international funds. This argument for opening the capital account is particularly true for foreign direct investment, which is often motivated less by considerations of financing investment and more by considerations of technology transfer, management improvement, risk diversification, and so on.

The standard argument against an open capital account in a developing country is that it would cost the country much of its saving. To some extent, such capital outflow may represent diversification of underlying country risk, not related to economic policy. Inflows also may occur as foreigners attempt to diversify country risk; the net flow resulting from the diversification of underlying country risk will depend on the country's underlying characteristics and the degree to which it develops instruments to allow the diversification of risk.

To a greater degree the loss-of-saving argument probably reflects the diversification of risk arising from economic policy and is a reflection of the limitations that an open capital account places on the taxation of income from capital and financial assets. To the extent the capital account is closed de facto, developing countries are able to tax financial assets and, to a lesser extent, capital. If the capital account were open, then capital flight would occur unless such taxation were reduced. This is particularly true given the tax shelters for external funds in many industrial countries, as well as in the tax havens, which in fact are being used by many citizens of developing countries.

Countries using the inflation tax, or in which there is a future risk of the inflation tax, are particularly vulnerable to the potential loss of saving. Inflation, or the threat of inflation, leads to growing use of foreign exchange in transactions and a reduction in the yield of the inflation tax, the more so as the capital account is opened. This limitation on the use of the inflation tax should not, however, be considered a cost, since this tax is one that does not require public approval; falls heaviest on the poor, who have a large share of their portfolio in local currency assets with zero or fixed interest rates; and has very distortionary effects, particularly in the financial system. Indeed, opening the capital account might even be considered to improve the income distribution, because it equalizes access to international assets at the same time as it reduces the base of the inflation tax.

Since opening the capital account reduces the incentive for reliance on the inflation tax, it sometimes is argued that an open capital account represents a signal that the government will refrain from using the inflation tax. Interestingly, the signal is certainly a weak one, since the first act of a government intending to use the inflation tax is to close the capital market.

An open capital account also limits a country's ability to conduct monetary or exchange-rate policy and increases exposure to international monetary shocks. With an open capital account, attempts at targeting the monetary stock through open market operations tend to be offset by economic agents undertaking capital flows (at the government-set exchange rate) in order to obtain their desired stocks of financial assets at the prevailing international interest rate. The loss of monetary independence implied by open capital markets also is felt in the greater exposure to international monetary shocks, through the capital as well as the current account.

In an open economy, interest-rate targeting may temporarily enjoy greater success than attempts to target the money stock, but carries with it some problems. A government may offer bonds above or lend below international interest rates and thereby affect the domestic interest rate, but only so long as it is willing to run down its *net* international asset position. Offers of loans or rollovers of bonds at less than world rates will lead to capital flight and loss of international reserves. However, offers of interest rates above international rates also lead to a decline in *net* international assets, because the influx of foreign funds takes place at a negative spread on the bonds that are sold. In either case the ultimate result will be a rise in the interest rate premium facing the country in international markets.

Monetary independence can be restored at the cost of the government's giving up control over the nominal exchange rate and allowing it to float freely. However, a free float clearly entails an increase in the variability of the exchange rate and correspondingly greater risks for exporters and importers than a fixed-rate system. Countries occasionally have tried to obtain monetary independence and maintain control over the exchange rate for trade by applying a free float to capital account transactions – in effect trying to create another policy instrument. However, the difference between exchange rates in the two markets, and thus the degree of monetary independence, clearly is limited by arbitrage possibilities.

Empirical analyses suggest that developing countries would obtain some benefits from opening up the capital account, even leaving aside the benefits from trading in risky assets. The financing of even 10–15% of investment, suggested by studies of the developed countries, would be welcome in many developing countries, especially if accompanied by improved technology and management. The potential reduction in the interest rate also seems fairly sizable, as noted by Hanson (1992).

The sequencing and speed of capital-account liberalization remain important issues. The preconditions for capital account liberalization are a sound fiscal and monetary situation and a reasonably sound and liberalized domestic financial system. The need for fiscal control is perhaps best illustrated by the experience of some countries in Latin America. Large public sector deficits were financed increasingly with external funds. When exchange-rate policy became clearly inconsistent with the fiscal deficit and external borrowing became clearly unsustainable, capital flight ensued and additional borrowing was done to sustain the exchange rate. Given the magnitude of the policy errors, capital flight would have developed in any case. However, the degree of openness of the capital account certainly contributed to the capital flight and excess borrowing.

The rationale for a reasonably liberalized and sound financial system has no corresponding illustration. However, it is important to adjust financial regulations such as reserve requirements, capital requirements, portfolio composition (including limits on offshore investments), and interest-rate limitations, as well as labor restrictions, so that domestic institutions do not face unfair competition from foreign institutions. If the regulatory framework favors external institutions significantly, then it eventually may lead to bankruptcy of domestic institutions and require costly government support for depositors. Similarly, unless the domestic institutions are reasonably sound, then allowing foreign institutions into the domestic market is likely to put excessive pressure on domestic institutions. Either the government must clean up the portfolios of domestic institutions, or the institutions must be allowed to earn high enough profits to recuperate themselves, before liberalization. The sequencing of capital-account and current-account liberalization has been analyzed at length. Conventional wisdom seems to be that the current account should be liberalized before the capital account. The argument is that the responsiveness of financial flows to capital-account liberalization typically would lead to an unwarranted real appreciation of the real exchange rate and an incorrect allocation of investment between tradeables and nontradeables. However, this argument neglects the points that (1) whenever the capital-account liberalization occurs, it would tend to cause a real appreciation, and (2) the amounts of resources available to an economy would be greater if the capital account were liberalized earlier. The positive impact of capital-account liberalization on resource availability has led some authors to argue for simultaneous current and capital-account liberalization. Other authors have pointed out that the optimum sequencing of liberalization depends on the type and size of distortions prior to liberalization.

The traditional literature on sequencing current- and capital-account liberalization seems to consider capital-account liberalization as occurring all at once, while current-account liberalization can take place at various rates – witness the whole argument regarding the appropriate pace of cutting protection. In fact, capital-account liberalization also can take place over time – various instruments and institutions can be legalized at different times and the size of operations can be limited to varying degrees, although such limitations are probably less effective than similar trade limitations.

The recognition that current-account liberalization can take place at varying speeds also suggests some undesired interactions can occur between the current and capital account. In particular, a slow current-account liberalization may require a compensating real devaluation over a number of years. The implied upward pressure on the real interest rate via the capital account may discourage domestic investment, particularly in nontraded goods. This suggests that the economic response to slow trade liberalizations may be less than to rapid trade liberalizations and that exchange-rate policy during the period of trade liberalization should take into account the capital as well as the current account.

Appendix 11.1:   The neoclassical growth model and capital inflows

This appendix analyzes the role of capital flows within the context of the standard, one sector, constant returns to scale, neoclassical growth model. The analysis of capital flows based on the Harrod–Domar model suggests that capital inflows will tend to raise the growth rate, compared to a closed economy. However, the solution is very much a knife edge, in keeping with the strong assumptions of the model (Domar 1950; Johnson 1961). A number of later studies analyze growth in open economies with neoclassical, as opposed to fixed-proportion production functions (see, for example, Borts and Stein 1964; Hanson 1974; Hanson and Neher 1967; Fischer and Frenkel

1974; Frenkel 1976). This appendix draws together some of the results of these studies.

The following analysis of capital inflows uses a variant of the diagram of marginal productivity of capital (Hanson and Neher 1967) that also has been used in the traditional analysis of the welfare implications of foreign investment (MacDougall 1968). The horizontal axis of Figure 11.1 measures the capital/labor ratio, k, the capital intensity. The vertical axis measures flows per year in percentage terms such as the average product of capital or the marginal product of capital, which in this simple, one-good model can be identified with the rate of profit or the rate of interest. In Figure 11.1, the lines AA' and AM' represent the average product of capital, O/K, and the marginal product of capital, respectively, drawn as straight lines for simplicity of graphical analysis. The average and marginal productivity fall as capital intensity increases because of the law of diminishing returns to a variable factor.[19] Also shown is the constant growth rate of labor, g, as the horizontal line GG'.

Growth in the closed economy

The analysis begins by analyzing neoclassical growth in a closed economy. For simplicity assume a constant, Keynesian-type saving ratio out of income, s. With saving equal to investment, the growth rate of capital is simply sO/K, shown graphically as KA', proportionate to AA'.[20]

With the addition of the growth rate of capital line KA', Figure 11.1 becomes a phase diagram of the growth rate of the capital labor ratio. The long-run equilibrium capital/labor ratio is determined by the intersection of the downward-sloping growth rate of capital, KA', and the constant growth rate of labor, GG'.[21] If the capital/labor ratio initially is less than K^1/L^1, then capital grows faster than labor, increasing the capital/labor ratio. However, the increase in capital intensity reduces the average product of capital because of the law of diminishing returns. Hence the growth rate of capital declines. This reduces the difference between the growth rate of capital and the growth rate of labor.

Eventually, the capital/labor ratio converges to K^1/L^1. Since capital and labor are both growing at the rate g, then income also grows at the rate g.[22] The analysis can easily be reversed for the case when the initial capital/labor ratio is less than K^1/L^1.

In this simplest of neoclassical growth models, output per unit of

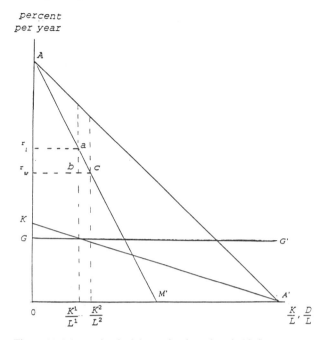

Figure 11.1 A neoclassical determination of capital inflows

labor is constant in the growth equilibrium. This result clearly is unrealistic. However, the model can be modified easily to generate a constant increase in output per unit of labor by adding Harrod-neutral technical progress (pure labor augmentation). With such technical progress, each laborer's productivity increases each year by p percent. The labor force can now be redefined in terms of efficiency units, equivalent to the productivity of a laborer in some base year, with a corresponding redefinition of the capital–labor ratio. In these efficiency units, the (efficiency) labor force grows at $(g+p)$ percent per year (ignoring the cross-product term, which is small). In the long-run equilibrium, capital and output grow at the same rate as efficiency of labor, following the arguments discussed previously. The capital per efficiency laborer and the output per efficiency laborer are constant in this long-run equilibrium analogously to the simplest model. However, since the number of efficiency laborers per laborer increases by p percent annually, the output per laborer also increases by p percent per year.

Growth in the open economy with capital inflow

The simplest way to analyze the impact of capital inflows on neoclassical growth is to consider a small open economy that, analogously to the small open economy of international trade theory, faces a horizontal supply of capital at a constant interest rate, r_w. The constant world rate is assumed to be below the domestic interest rate, r_1, that would prevail in the absence of capital movements.[23]

The implication of the horizontal supply curve of capital is that foreign capitalists send capital into the economy to whatever extent that domestic investment opportunities, created at the world interest rate, exceed saving by nationals. This flow of capital ensures, by assumption and ignoring the time needed to adjust portfolios, that the domestic rate of interest equals the world rate. The corresponding capital stock thus is maintained at all times. Hence, rises or falls in saving by nationals have no effect on the productivity of capital; they only raise or lower the proportion of the capital stock owned domestically. This is in contrast to the closed economy model, where increases in the saving rate increase the long-run capital–labor ratio and reduce the marginal productivity of capital.

The welfare analysis of capital flows in this context is most easily carried out holding fixed the initial capital–labor ratio, that is, assuming a constant *amount* of saving per worker, as is done in the traditional analysis (MacDougall 1968) rather than a constant saving rate. Analogously to the welfare analysis of trade, the small open economy is assumed to be at long run, closed equilibrium with an initial capital–labor ratio K^1/L^1 and interest rate r_1. Once the economy is opened up to capital flows, the capital–labor ratio increases to K^2/L^2, and the interest rate falls to r_w.[24] Foreigners now hold part of the capital stock – $K^2/L^2 - K^1/L^1 = D/L$ – they receive $r_w D/L$ (the rectangle bc K^2/L^2 K^1/L^1 in the Figure 11.1) in factor payments.[25] In the new, long-run equilibrium, output, labor, capital, and capital inflows all grow at the same rate, g, as in the closed economy.

Factor payments to foreign capitalists make it important to distinguish between domestic income and national income in evaluating welfare. Graphically, domestic income is the area (integral) under the marginal productivity curve, while national income is domestic income less payments to borrowers, $r_w D/L$. Thus, national income increases by the triangle *abc*, provided the saving of nationals continues to maintain their ownership of K^1/L^1 units of capital.[26]

The increase in national income can be explained heuristically as follows: The rise in capital, because of the capital inflow, lowers the rate of return to capital and raises the wage rate. Within national income this simply represents a shift in the distribution of income from capitalists to laborers. However, the nonmarginal increase in foreign-owned capital also means that foreign capitalists suffer from the reduction in the rate of return – in effect, the "late" arrivals, in their competition for labor to work with their capital, bid up wages and reduce the rate of return on capital. The increase in wages, at the expense of foreign capitalists, raises national income above its autarchic level.

It also is important to note that this increase in national income occurs even if more is paid out in interest to foreign capitalists than is received in new direct foreign investment, that is, even if net transfers are negative. As noted, annual payments of interest to foreigners are $r_w D/L$. New foreign capital is gD/L in the long-run equilibrium, when capital, labor, and income are growing at the rate g. Hence, net transfers are negative or positive as r_w is greater or less than g. However, following the argument in the previous paragraph, *welfare improves the relative magnitudes of r_w and g*. Foreigners will maintain capital above the autarchic level at a lower cost than domestic citizens would be willing to do so $(r_w < r_1)$, benefiting domestic wages at the expense of foreign capital.

Comparative statics

A rise in the world interest rate, r_w, because of a rise in the risk premium, for example, tends to lower the desired amount of external capital in the small, open economy, and reduce the capital/labor ratio. Graphically, a rise in r_w shifts upward the horizontal supply schedule of external capital. Given the domestic marginal productivity of capital schedule, the desired amount of foreign capital in the economy falls. Unless the domestic saving rate rises to offset the decline in foreign investment – that is, the economy becomes an exporter of capital as a result of the rise in the world interest rate – the capital–labor ratio in the economy also would fall.

A change in the terms of trade is not easily modeled in the one-commodity world. However, some heuristic results can be derived by assuming that capital goods are wholly imported at a fixed price and are not the same as the good produced in the economy. A shift in the terms of trade is then effectively a similar proportionate shift in the marginal and average productivity schedules of capital. Thus, a decline in the terms of trade of the domestically produced good against the capital good would be shown as a proportionate downward shift of the marginal and average productivity schedules. With a fixed world interest rate and constant domestically owned capital, foreign capital would decline.

Simple welfare aspects of capital movements

As noted, the gains from capital inflows reflect the decline in the rate of return paid to the "first" foreign capitalists to invest in the economy. The same result can be shown in differential terms, rather than discrete changes. National income (GNP) is

(A.1)

$$GNP = f'\,(k+W) - f'D/L.$$

where f = Marginal productivity of capital
W = Ratio of wages to rental on capital.

Differentiating with respect to D/L, holding the domestically owned capital stock constant, yields

$$d\text{GNP}/dD = -f''' > 0. \tag{A.2}$$

A critical point in evaluating welfare is that it is done holding the volume of domestically owned capital stock constant. In some sense, this is the initial situation when moving from autarchy in capital movements to free capital movements – at that point the domestically owned capital stock is fixed. The analysis shows that with the domestically owned capital stock held fixed, potentially there is a rise in GNP – it would be possible for the gainers from capital inflows to compensate the losers from capital flows and still have something left over. Thus, welfare is increased by free capital movements in the same sense that welfare is increased by free trade.

The actual outcome, particularly in terms of GNP, may, however, be somewhat different because of changes in the saving rate. The decline in the rate of return when the economy is opened up to capital movements may decrease the rate of saving. This will tend to decrease the national ownership of the capital stock and national income. On balance, the capital stock and the national income will rise or fall, depending on whether the negative effect of the lower interest rate on national saving is greater or less than the tendency for national income to rise because of the lower returns earned by the "initial" foreign investors.

Thus far the analysis of welfare has been conducted in terms of GNP. However, it also is worth examining the implications of capital inflows for national consumption. The willingness of foreign capitalists to support the domestic capital stock at a fixed interest rate offers the possibility of raising consumption per head, even if GNP falls.

The gain in consumption from a given change in the equilibrium of nationally owned capital stock ($E/L = e$), brought about by a change in the saving rate, is equal to the change in national income minus the change in national saving. The change in national income is simply f', the marginal productivity of capital – under the assumptions of the model, foreigners will replace the reduction in domestically owned capital stock at a cost of $r_w = f'$. The change in national saving can be derived by differentiating the equilibrium condition for national saving:

$$sf'\,(e + W) = ge \qquad\qquad\qquad (A3)$$

with respect to e. Thus the change in national saving implied by a unit change in national capital is g. National consumption will rise or fall, in the long run with a rise in e, as r_w exceeds or is less than g. These results are nothing more than the standard golden rule analysis, extended to an open economy (Hanson and Neher 1967). However, as with golden rule analysis in the closed economy, there is a transition problem.

Consider, first, the situation where r_w is less than the equilibrium rate of domestic growth, g. Foreigners will support the domestic capital stock at r_w, a lower cost, in terms of forgone consumption than domestic saving, g. Hence, it pays to reduce saving in order to raise consumption in the present as well as the future. The degree to which this saving policy can be pursued may, however, be limited by a rising risk premium as foreigners begin to own more and more of the domestic capital stock (Hanson 1974).

The intertemporal welfare analysis is more complicated in the case in which r_w exceeds g. The comparison across dynamic equilibria suggests that higher saving rates would pay off through reduction of "expensive" foreign capital, in terms of more consumption in the new, growth equilibrium. However, in the short run until domestically owned capital increases, higher saving implies lower consumption. The fact that r_w and r_d initially exceed g implies that individuals value consumption fairly highly. After all, any individual by reducing consumption today and saving enough to raise his capital one unit, could raise future consumption by $(1 + r_w)$. That this is not done in the aggregate, and that foreign capital is required to bring the rate of return down to r_w, suggests that individuals value current consumption fairly highly and would be made worse off by a forced rise in saving, despite the eventual rise in long-run consumption per capita.

NOTES

1 See Moran (1974) for a discussion of a theory of direct foreign investment along these lines.

2 See Deardorff and Hanson (1978) for a two-country model that links saving rates and factor proportions and the pattern of trade over time.

3 Of course, this assumes differences in the autarchic prices of comparable risky assets across countries. Svensson (1988) develops a model in which trades in assets may occur because of differences in the autarchic pricing of similar risks and because of differences in the autarchic pricing of payments over a given time span.

4 See for example Dooley (1988). The existence of such risk premiums and the possibility that foreigners will be treated more favorably than domestic assets holders can lead to simultaneous borrowing abroad and capital outflows (Dooley 1988; Dornbusch 1984; Khan and Haque 1985).

5 This is even more so to the extent that governments must make special legal arrangements to encourage certain capital inflows by eliminating the capital controls in particular cases. Since these arrangements typically would require government controls over the inflows, they also might encourage misallocation of resources and corruption. This is another cost of capital controls that must be borne in mind.

6 Still another example is the possibility that direct foreign investment can offset protection intended to stimulate domestic, import-substituting industry.

7 While a government undoubtedly can lower interest rates to certain preferred borrowers and to savers without access to international markets, the resulting reduction in the availability of savings will *raise* interest rates to the marginal borrower.

8 In Mundell's (1968a) model of a small open economy with a floating exchange rate, a one-time increase in domestic credit depreciates the exchange rate, changing either national output or prices, but not necessarily the interest rate. In other versions of the model, with more complicated policy changes, the domestic interest rate may also change.

9 See, for example, Fleming (1971), Lanyi (1975), Gros (1988), and Dornbusch (1986). As Lanyi and Gros each point out, if there is a permanent condition (shock) that leads to a difference between the two exchange markets, then arbitrage will develop that eventually will eliminate the gap between the two markets or will require intervention in both markets – in effect a tax-subsidy arrangement – to maintain the gap.

10 Of course, a fully open capital account, as defined in this chapter, is not necessary to achieve this result – the government could simply borrow or lend internationally as needed to carry out the desired fiscal policy.

11 The historic record suggests that there was not much difference between private and public borrowing from the standpoint of the risk to the borrowing country. The governments of many developing countries, including Chile, that had emphasized private–private lending without government guarantees, found themselves forced, by a combination of domestic and external pressure, to take responsibility for private external debts that originally had not been guaranteed by the government. These "nationalized" debts continue to complicate macroeconomic policy in many countries even today.

12 This section is a brief summary of Hanson (1992).

13 Moreover, this trade is severely underestimated in the balance-of-payments accounts, because of the use of differences in stocks at two points in time, rather than actual transactions, to measure short-term international capital flows.

14 The public sector can borrow abroad directly, or the government can allow domestic banks and firms to borrow externally (perhaps with a government guarantee), either way reducing the pressure on the domestic financial system from a given volume of public sector borrowing.

15 For example, reserve requirements must be computed on some deposit base. Computer programming can be used to "sweep" large depositors just before the deposit base is calculated and place the funds in accounts with lower reserve requirements or higher interest rates.

16 This case is analyzed in Edwards (1985).

17 This argument, of course, resembles the discussion of the impact of direct foreign investment on the highly protected Latin American economies during the 1960s (for example, Diaz-Alejandro 1970). A number of theoretical studies suggest that in the presence of distortions, direct foreign investment can reduce welfare.

18 The difficulty with dual foreign exchange markets is, of course, the problem of separating the two markets and the incentives set up to avoid the separation. In the usual case, there is some desire to maintain an overvalued rate for goods transactions to avoid the inflationary consequences of a devaluation. Capital flight occurs depreciating the rate applicable to capital-account transactions and creating incentives to undervalue exports and overvalue imports, in order to bring back foreign exchange through the capital account. In contrast, the problem with liberalizing the capital account discussed in the text is that the initial burst of capital inflow accompanying the opening of the capital account temporarily *appreciates* a unified exchange rate. The incentives would be to *overvalue* exports and *undervalue* imports to escape the effective tax on capital inflows, in much the same way as export incentives in Colombia and Turkey led to "fictional" exports at various times. Since any separation of the markets for foreign exchange would be short lived, there probably would not be time to evolve sophisticated mechanisms to escape the separation of markets. The chief difficulty is likely to be the government's unwillingness to unify the markets when the capital account rate begins to drop below the current account rate.

19 The assumption of a constant returns to scale, neoclassical production function means that the average product of capital is a function of the capital–labor ratio, i.e., a doubling of the inputs results in a doubling of the outputs, leaving the average productivity of either factor the same.

20 Depreciation is ignored.

21 The existence condition for the long-run equilibrium is that the average product of capital is a continuous function that approaches infinity (or at least is larger than g/s) as the capital–labor ratio becomes small and is less than the growth rate of labor (specifically, less than g/s) as the capital–labor ratio becomes large. (See, for example, Inada 1964.)

22 Income growth could be represented in the graph as a downward-sloping line (not shown) between the growth rate of capital and the growth rate of labor, since income growth can be shown, by Euler's Rule, to be a weighted average of the growth rates of capital and labor, with the weights equal to the elasticities of output with respect to the two factors.

23 The interest rate r_w can include a constant risk premium. To the extent that external lenders consider the probability of default or expropriation to be positively related to the volume of foreign capital, even a small economy may face an upward sloping supply schedule of capital and may find it beneficial to limit foreign borrowing to some extent because of the difference between the marginal and average cost of

external capital (Kemp 1964; Hanson 1974). However, this complication is ignored in the following analysis for the sake of simplicity.

24 This analysis assumes capital inflows instantaneously reduce the domestic interest rate to "world" levels. The world level can include a constant risk premium.

25 This analysis ignores the transfer problem.

26 Notice that if saving is a proportionate fraction of national income, then the domestically owned capital stock increases. On the other hand, the fall in the rate of return to saving may lower the rate of saving. The domestic capital stock rises or falls depending on the net of these two offsetting movements. See the section on the Simple Welfare Aspects of Capital Movements, below, for a further discussion of nationals' saving.

CHAPTER 12

Financial liberalization and the capital account: Chile, 1974–84

Salvador Valdés-Prieto

12.1   Introduction and overview

Many countries, developed and developing, are liberalizing their domestic financial markets. Often such liberalization is accompanied by a reduction in regulatory and other barriers to international capital mobility. In the aftermath of several liberalization experiences, however, the compatibility of these reform measures – liberalization of domestic financial markets and opening of the capital account – has been questioned. One of the main reasons is the unfortunate (some would argue anomalous) Chilean experience. Between 1975 and 1977 Chile liberalized its domestic financial market. In 1980 the capital account was liberalized for domestic banks, a policy that some authors regard as one of the main causes of the excessive buildup of foreign debt and the subsequent steep recession that ensued in 1982. For example, analyzing this episode from a macroeconomic point of view, Harberger (1985) argues, "The process of relaxation of capital controls should have been slower and more cautious, with the end in view of not letting the inflow of capital get more than, say, a couple of percentage points above the sustainable level."

This study discusses whether the 1980 opening of the capital account for domestic banks was indeed an important causal factor in the dismal macroeconomic performance of the subsequent period. In order to sharpen the analysis, the study also examines a number of counterfactual policies, such as liberalizing earlier and maintaining capital controls for banks in 1980, given the other distortions that were present.

This paper also examines developments outside the period 1977–82. The preceding period, 1974–6, shows that foreign capital suppliers' confidence is as important as the legal restrictions on capital account

357

transactions. The analysis of the following period, 1983–4, demonstrates that the domestic government can provoke a large rise in the premium for international finance and a steep reduction in the volume of available international credit without introducing restrictions on capital account transactions. These analyses contain lessons for avoiding fluctuations in foreign capital suppliers' confidence, which may be useful for other countries.

The chapter has six main points: The first is that Chile's capital account actually had been opened to a large extent after 1975; the main limitation was a prohibition on banks' borrowing abroad, which remained until 1980. Although the additional capital inflows intermediated by the domestic banking sector after the April 1980 liberalization were large, nonbank inflows continued to be important. Hence, the notion that the policy of international financial liberalization for banks was the primary cause of excessive capital inflows is not supported by the evidence.

Second, several factors that are not related to international financial liberalization can be identified as promoting excessive capital inflows in Chile in 1980–1: (1) an imprudent supply of funds by international banks; (2) imprudent regulations on domestic banking; (3) excessive consumer spending; (4) the stabilization measures of 1979–82, particularly the use of the exchange rate as a policy instrument to reduce inflation. The regulatory failure involved banks abusing the government's deposit insurance but also bank debtors taking advantage of banks. The risk-loving behavior of domestic banks contributed to higher domestic interest rates and helped to attract more foreign funds. The presence of these other factors implies that the Chilean opening of the capital account to domestic banks cannot be blamed for the dismal macroeconomic performance of the period. However, an examination of the design and timing of the 1980 international financial liberalization yields some additional insights.

Third, the April 1980 international financial liberalization made an independent contribution to increasing the already excessive capital inflows in Chile in 1980–1. When domestic banks were allowed to borrow abroad, they added their quotas of access to foreign credit and attracted more funds to the country. The inclusion of the banking sector along with nonbanks thus prompted a one-time infusion of capital, equivalent to a transitory increase in the rate of capital inflow, and reduced domestic real interest rates on a sustained basis. This is the standard effect of eliminating a quota on capital inflows, and cannot be avoided unless a compensating policy is used simultaneously.

However, the additional and significant capital inflows by nonbanks after the April 1980 international financial liberalization suggest that the liberalization with respect to banks is only a partial explanation for the macroeconomic instability that ensued. This conclusion is reinforced by the fact that the April 1980 international financial liberalization was not really as complete as it has been represented by some authors. In particular, domestic banks continued to be legally prohibited from bringing in capital through some of the legal mechanisms available to nonbanks.

Fourth, the Central Bank's requirement of a minimum term for new foreign loans was counterproductive, as it provided an implicit real exchange-rate guarantee. When the Central Bank intervenes by regulating the terms for loans among domestic and foreign parties, it in effect supports the view that it is somehow guaranteeing foreign liquidity. This is because the Central Bank can regulate the terms of cross-border loans only if takes responsibility for foreign liquidity risks. In this respect, firms trusted that the Central Bank guaranteed the availability of foreign funds for repayment at a reasonable real price for the length of the loan contracts that were being signed, that is, over six years. This implicit guarantee implied a subsidy to international intermediation, and also induced excessive capital inflows. The fiscal cost of this guarantee turned out to be high.

The Central Bank's requirement of a minimum term for new foreign loans also led domestic banks to overexpand. In normal circumstances, the large arbitrage profits available in international intermediation would had been perceived as transitory. Hot money would have flowed to Chile as a result of these potential profits, but it would not have led to branch expansion or hiring new personnel in domestic banks. However, the Central Bank regulations required international intermediation to be long-term (minimum 2 years to avoid a 100% reserve requirement and at least 5.5 years to avoid a 10% reserve requirement), and even assured banks that if no domestic borrowers were found in future, it would retake the funds. This led Chilean banks to increase their scale of operations, investing in quasi-fixed factors of production, a costly choice given that in the longer term the domestic financial system would still be too inefficient to compete with direct cross-border lending by international banks to the larger Chilean borrowers. In this way, the term requirement on foreign loans compromised the future solvency of the Chilean banking system.

Fifth, this study's analysis suggests that an earlier international financial liberalization, possibly in 1977, might have improved the outcome in Chile, as it did in Uruguay in 1974–8 (Hanson and de

Melo 1985). Apart from the standard gains from such a policy, this conclusion reflects the existence of the other distortions that existed at the time. Also, a later liberalization would have prevented the extra capital inflow of 1980 and 1981 that was stimulated when domestic banks were allowed to borrow abroad. In other words, the precise timing was exactly the wrong one.

Last, the Chilean experience is also valuable for other developing countries by illustrating how unstable foreign finance can be frightened away by ill-considered official declarations regarding the insolvency of domestic banks. Insolvency of domestic firms involving foreign creditors should be treated on a strictly legal basis, with no interference by the domestic government other than the enforcement of the laws. In this regard, a clear insolvency procedure for local intermediaries is necessary before the capital account is opened and those intermediaries are allowed to issue debt to foreigners – especially if existing procedures are subject to government discretion or are extremely costly to apply.

Apart from the bank-takeover episode, the experience of Chilean capital account policy in the 1982–4 period is instructive, as it shows how liberally inclined authorities can be forced by the necessity of maintaining positive international reserves to introduce more restrictions. The lesson in this respect is that a government that wants to liberalize the capital account has to avoid all perceived and announced exchange-rate guarantees, and must be willing to use fiscal and monetary policy to avoid wide fluctuations in international reserves. In addition, it must be prepared to inform the private sector realistically about future prospects, helping it to achieve an efficient spending path. The failings in these respects of Chilean macroeconomic policy in 1979–82 account for the need to reregulate the capital account in 1982–4.

12.2   A brief summary of international finance in Chile before 1974

Chile became completely open to international finance in 1820, after independence. In company with many countries controls over capital movements were imposed in the 1930s. In 1932 the first Exchange Control Law was imposed in an attempt to cope with a dramatic 80% reduction in export revenue. As Chile recovered from the Great Depression, controls proved unable to curb international capital mobility, as indicated by the ineffectiveness of the devaluation of the official exchange rate in 1935 (Valdés-Prieto 1987). Exchange controls were not scrapped however; they were used to tax foreign-owned export industries as well as to subsidize favored sectors.

The free foreign exchange market stopped floating freely in 1935, when the government fixed the rate. An illegal foreign exchange market evolved in response; although initially small, in times of foreign exchange shortages the volume of transactions became substantial. The tightness of official regulations and penalties fluctuated predictably in response to the availability of foreign exchange. Capital flight became important after 1939, with increased financial repression and higher inflation. This rise in inflation made binding the bank-deposit interest-rate controls that had been introduced in 1929, and eventually led to the destruction of domestic banking institutions and the domestic bond market. Quantitative credit controls were authorized in 1953 and were implemented in 1956.

The secular trend in 1940–73 was toward more financial repression and tighter exchange controls. Around this trend exchange controls were tightened and relaxed several times, and domestic financial repression mirrored this cycle. Notable in these changes was Conservative President Alessandri's exchange control law of 1963, which made it an offense punishable by incarceration to own any foreign currency without previous authorization.

Allende's attempt to move Chile toward central planning (Larraín and Meller 1990) intensified these trends. In 1971 Chile's Congress unanimously approved expropriation of the copper companies without compensation. After three months in power, Allende had nationalized more than 50% of the existing private commercial banks. This was in addition to the volume already intermediated by State banks (Banco del Estado, CORFO). By September 1973, 73% of lending by independent banks was funded by the Central Bank, subject to strict relending rules. The domestic financial market was in disarray, with inflation reaching 606% in 1973. State control over official foreign exchange transactions, especially the capital account, was almost complete. At the same time, capital flight was widespread and the premium in the illegal parallel exchange rate market was enormous.

12.3   The disappearance of foreign finance, 1974–6

By 1973 Chile had lost its credibility in international financial markets. The high social cost of the associated increase in the premium for international finance for Chile became apparent in 1974–6, as the subsequent government tried to grapple with the economic legacy of the Allende years.[1]

The attempt to restore credibility

The restoration process began in 1974, when many firms illegally nationalized by the Allende government were returned to their original owners – on the important condition that they renounce compensation for losses. GDP stopped its downward spiral and annual inflation was cut by over half to a still high 300%. The domestic financial market began to be liberalized in March 1974, when new, unregulated intermediaries called *financieras* were permitted to operate. Commercial banks were privatized and freed from interest-rate controls in early 1976 (de la Cuadra and Valdés-Prieto 1990).

However, Chilean international trade lacked easy access to short-term finance through foreign banks. By 1974 several American copper companies expropriated by Allende had obtained court orders in several countries to seize Chilean-owned goods as compensation, creating uncertainty. In addition, the new regime's policy of repression against Allende's followers persuaded several foreign governments to suspend bilateral aid and loans to Chile. Multilateral credit also dried up so that Chile was forced to begin amortizing its outstanding official foreign debt.

The authorities tried several approaches to mitigate these problems. First, they sought an amicable solution with the American copper companies that had been expropriated in 1971; however, it took negotiators until 1976 to reach an accord. Second, an amnesty on tax and exchange-control violations was decreed in early 1974. The funds registered at the Central Bank under this amnesty would be considered legitimate sources of funds by the tax authority. However, only U.S.$100 million was garnered, since the domestic private sector continued to fear the political system after Allende's levies on capital. Later the 1975 recession and the losses on some types of deposits made it plain that returning funds to Chile could be extremely risky. In 1975 the amnesty regulation was replaced by "window purchases": Any person selling foreign currency to a commercial bank would remain anonymous. The commercial bank was required to turn over those funds to the Central Bank. The documentation originated in these operations was not considered by tax authorities as a legitimate source of funds for purchasing assets.

Third, the government reformed the Foreign Exchange Control Law (FECL), allowing the Central Bank to elect not to restrict repatriations of foreign loans and foreign direct investment. Article 14 of the new FECL allowed the Central Bank to set up a system for registering incoming funds: Such funds could be exchanged in one common foreign exchange market (instead of on a case-by-case basis with the Central Bank), while the repatriation of capital and interest or profit could also be exchanged in (a potentially different) common foreign exchange market. In addition, the draconian penalties for violations of the FECL were reduced. Domestic banks were discriminated against, in that they were not authorized to be a domestic counterpart for capital inflows arranged by a nonresident. In other words, only domestic banks were prohibited from using Article 14 to bring foreign-debt funds to Chile.

Fourth, the authorities attempted to reduce other risks incurred by long-term foreign direct investment by nonresidents. Decree Law 600 allowed foreign investors to sign a contract with the same standing as a law (subject only to constitutional reform), whereby the government fixed the tax regime that applied to the investment and assured the investor of nondiscrimination relative to local investors as well as access to the official foreign exchange market for dividend and capital remittances. The requirements stipulated that incoming funds would be exchanged in the official market; the government would sign the said contract; and that repatriation of capital – not profits – was subject to a minimum residency requirement of three years. Law 600 extended similar guarantees to credit inflows associated with the same investment project. These inflows were negotiated case by case, so no short-term arbitrage was possible.

This law, strikingly modern in concept as it addressed directly the credibility problem caused by previous exploitive behavior, did not induce an immediate surge in foreign investment, suggesting that credibility can only be restored gradually. With its approval the government gave up its membership in the protectionist Andean Pact, and allowed the installation of subsidiaries and branches of foreign banks, plus foreign direct investment in commercial banking. This permitted Citibank (in Chile since 1912) to resume operations in peso deposits and loans. However, it took the first foreign commercial banks until 1977 to renew operations in Chile. A month before abandoning the Pact, Chile had invoked an exception and allowed up to 49% foreign direct investment in "development" banks. This authorization allowed the first private development bank to appear in 1975, owned by a consortium of three foreign banks; the 49% restriction on foreign ownership of development banks was lifted in 1978. Unlike commercial banks, these banks were allowed to lend at terms greater than three years.

In the wake of DL 600, Article 14 of the FECL, and window purchases, by 1975 the capital account was almost completely open to nonresidents, including both for investment and repatriation. In particular, between 1975 and 1979, short-term portfolio investment by nonresidents was welcome under Article 14 of the FECL, which provided clear legal status. Article 14 also permitted nonbank residents to borrow abroad; thus the capital account for inflows also was open to them, although they could not lend or invest abroad legally.

Thus it appears that the lack of capital inflows in the period prior to 1980 that has been noted by Edwards (1985) and most other commentators probably was *not* due to legal restrictions. Rather, the huge premium for international finance that prevailed between 1975 and 1977 was due to other factors, in particular perceptions of risk, which would disappear gradually over the following years. This point is critical for analysis of the 1977–82 period; it implies that on the inflow side only domestic banks were affected by the lifting of regulations in 1980; nonresidents' inflows (and remittances) largely were unconstrained by regulations throughout 1977–82, as such regulations had been eliminated in 1975.

The cost of lack of access to international finance

The government's efforts to obtain access to capital inflows became even more urgent in early 1975. The international price of copper, which at the time comprised 75% of Chile's exports and provided a substantial part of fiscal revenue, had fallen by half. This compounded the terms-of-trade shock that had occurred in 1973–4 when oil prices had multiplied sixfold. Initially it was thought that the fall in copper prices was temporary, reflecting the recession in industrialized countries. The appropriate response was to smooth spending: Financing this spending implied contracting foreign debts and allowing more capital inflows. The authorities soon found, however, that nobody would lend Chile the amounts required.

Confronted by this austere climate, the government imposed harsh spending reductions, cutting its own expenditures by 20% in real terms across the board. The plan to reduce inflation was abandoned given that the inflation tax revenue was considered vital to avoid further reductions in government spending. The plan to liberalize interest rates in the banking sector was shelved as well, since that would have reduced the tax revenue generated by financial repression measures and reduced the base for the inflation tax as well.

Lack of access to international finance thus contributed to the need for strong adjustment, which in turn contributed to the 12.9% drop in GDP for 1975; the rise of unemployment to 25%; the rise of short-term real annualized interest rates from -19.6% in the last quarter of 1974 to $+47.6\%$ in the last quarter of 1975; and the bankruptcy of the entire savings and loan system. It is unlikely that the government would have been able to borrow enough to fully offset the terms of trade shock. However, if more financing had been available, then the adjustment could have been less severe, and it is quite possible that the drop in GDP would have been less. Thus the cost of loss of access was quite high.

In sum, the effective premium for international finance had become exceedingly high based on nonregulatory factors. In the case of Chile, these causes included the uncompensated expropriations that took place during the Allende administration and the subsequent repression of political opposition by Pinochet. In addition, the recession induced many residents to engage in capital flight. In such a volatile environment, it is not surprising that opening capital inflows to nonbanks was ineffective; moreover, permitting unrestricted capital outflows would have induced even larger capital outflows and a deeper recession. This explains why the liberalization was not extended to capital outflows by nonbank residents.

12.4   The boom−bust episode of 1977−82 and capital mobility

Background

To analyze whether this policy of international financial liberalization precipitated Chile's subsequent economic woes, two areas will be reviewed: (1) the large buildup of foreign debt by the private sector and (2) the deep 1982−3 recession. The large foreign debt buildup was a problem in its own right, in the sense that it supported a transitory real appreciation and increased vulnerability to external shocks − both rises in international interest rates and declines in the terms of trade (because of exhaustion of the country's external borrowing capacity). As for the deep 1982−3 recession, the external debt buildup was not the only cause. Any account of this recession must consider the effects of the several additional factors to be mentioned in the next section. The steep reduction in aggregate demand appears as the primary cause of the 1982 recession − although the excessive foreign debt certainly contributed.

The magnitude of the effect of opening the capital account to banks is difficult to gauge without a fully specified model. However, four main topics warrant a detailed review: (1) description of the regulatory barriers to international capital mobility; (2) the impact of the April

1980 international financial liberalization on the macroeconomy, with emphasis on the interaction with the stabilization policy followed by the Central Bank, which pegged the exchange rate to the dollar between July 1979 and June 1982. (3) the effect of regulatory problems in the domestic banking sector on the outcome of the April 1980 international financial liberalization; and (4) the implication of the April 1980 international financial liberalization for implicit real exchange-rate guarantees. A counterfactual scenario is presented in which the 1980 opening of the capital account banks is undertaken earlier (1977) to examine what an earlier international financial liberalization might have achieved.

Overview of the 1977–82 period

Domestic versus foreign causes

The foreign debt buildup of the Chilean economy can be compared with that in other middle-income developing countries under a typical foreign debt policy. Valdés-Prieto (1989) shows that only in 1981 did Chile deviate from the pattern of the average for middle-income developing countries. This, plus the substantial rise in domestic real interest rates in 1981, suggests that a division of the analysis in two subperiods, 1977–80 and 1981–2, is useful.

The comparison also suggests that the share of foreign debt buildup that can be credited to specific Chilean policies or foreigners' specific perceptions about Chile, including capital-account policy, can account for about half the total debt buildup. The other half, including all foreign debt up to 1980, should be assigned to a positive supply shock in international bank credit and the rise in international real interest rates, also experienced by many other middle-income developing countries.

A brief review of macroeconomic events of 1977–80

The 1977–80 period was characterized by strong GDP growth, averaging 8.5% per year. With this growth GDP more than rebounded from the contraction of 1975. Investment grew faster than consumption between 1977 and 1980. The fiscal balance exhibited a surplus in 1980 of 0.6% of GDP. Open unemployment fell over time to 10.4% in 1980, and domestic real interest rates declined substantially, averaging 7% for deposits and 13% for loans in the last three quarters of 1980. The real exchange rate remained at an historically very high level from

1976 to 1979, but appreciated by 17.5% in 1980. Domestic inflation fell until 1978, but then continued at a stable level – around 30% or 20 percentage points above foreign inflation rates. The Santiago Stock Exchange price index boomed in real terms until late 1980.

The continuing inflation was particularly troublesome because the nominal exchange rate had been fixed to the dollar in July 1979, and the authorities announced they would keep it fixed permanently at that level. This stabilization policy was a continuation of similar preannounced devaluations followed since 1977. Over 1980 domestic inflation was 31.2%, even though the nominal exchange rate had been pegged for the last 18 months. Part of the explanation lies in the fact that the dollar had depreciated steeply against the deutsche mark, and yen in 1979. Since Chile was pegged to the dollar, effective international inflation for Chile was unusually high that year. Nevertheless, Chilean inflation was higher than U.S. inflation, suggesting a substantial part of the inflation differential has to be explained within the stabilization process, including the ineffectiveness of the exchange rate based stabilization in bringing down inflation quickly within the context of Chilean institutions.

Meanwhile, a large foreign debt was being contracted by the domestic private sector. Initially, only nonbanks had borrowed abroad, but after the April 1980 authorization for domestic banks to participate, they became the heaviest individual borrowers. Moreover, those banks and nonbanks affiliated with the two large business groups were the heaviest foreign borrowers of all. At the same time, the government decided to reduce its foreign debt. The Central Bank lowered domestic credit while buying a huge volume of international reserves, so it sterilized in part the effects of capital inflows on the money supply.

A brief review of macroeconomic events in 1981–2

Domestic inflation fell steeply in the first half of 1981, and Chile began to enjoy inflation below international levels. The fall in Chile's inflation can be partly attributed to the rise of the U.S. dollar against the deutsche mark and yen, but the underlying factor probably was that the deflationary phase of the stabilization program had arrived. The contraction phase of the stabilization coincided with the rise in international real interest rates. During late 1981 the prospects for domestic growth darkened considerably, in part due to a fall in the international price of some exports. Expectations of devaluation developed among a substantial segment of economic agents. The ominous rise in domestic real deposit rates, to 34.5% for 1981, had begun early in the year, showing that something was not working well in the economy.

These factors led to a reduction in expenditure, first noticeable in some types of investment and then rapidly spreading to consumption, as the expected growth rate of income and perceived wealth fell dramatically. In 1982 the recession showed up in an explosion of unemployment, which climbed quickly to 17% in March and 25% in September. GDP entered a free fall, while real interest rates in deposits rose to 47.7% in the first half of 1982.

The recession combined with the worldwide slowdown in international bank lending to produce a reduction in capital inflows. The surplus in Chile's capital account declined from an average of U.S.$1.2 billion for the first three quarters of 1981, to U.S.$0.3 billion in the second quarter of 1982. Nonetheless, the capital-account balance continued to be slightly positive up to mid-1982, so no massive run occurred. In 1981 the Central Bank lost reserves because the current account was in substantial deficit, but the 1982 recession sharply reduced that deficit also.

These developments suggests that most agents adjusted their expenditures over this period until June 1982. However, other indicators showed that the stabilization program was in trouble. First, high unemployment, the fall in GDP, and high real interest rates created strong political pressure to find scapegoats, increase spending, and deflate debts. Second, the huge real interest rates and the fall in expenditures made insolvent many entrepreneurs who had followed conservative debt policies, let alone the ones who had followed high-debt strategies. Many hid their assets from creditors while renewing loans – regardless of the interest rate charged. This large demand for credit pushed real interest rates ever higher in late 1981 and 1982, deepening the recession. Third, changes in the external outlook recommended a depreciation of the real exchange rate, but the pace of deflation was too slow to provide it rapidly. Hence in mid-1982 the government changed the exchange-rate policy and made a maxidevaluation.

The stabilization debate

A lingering question is to what extent the exchange-rate policy was responsible for the foreign debt buildup and the recession of 1981–3. The debate centers around the wisdom of using the nominal exchange rate to stop domestic inflation when there is no fiscal deficit and its implication for debt buildup.

The method of fixing the exchange rate proved successful to reduce inflation in several countries in the European Monetary System (Giavazzi and Giovannini 1988). However, it has been argued forcefully that this stabilization policy was ill-conceived in the Chilean context for several reasons (Edwards 1985; Corbo et al. 1986; and Edwards and Cox-Edwards 1987). First, the initial inflation differential was high; hence, if convergence took two years, which was optimistic, a substantial real appreciation would result. This would in turn require a future real depreciation, which would likely require *deflation*. Second, convergence could not be rapid because government-mandated wage indexation prevailed.

These arguments certainly are relevant to Chile. Eliminating inflation by fixing the exchange rate certainly entails costs. However, the alternative methods of reducing inflation also are costly. Each method places the burden of adjustment on a different sector, and it has not been shown that the one applied in Chile is generally the most costly. It is not altogether clear why this method of disinflation by itself could lead to a such a severe recession as Chile experienced after 1982, nor such a large external debt buildup, which itself was a factor in the severity of the recession.

Regarding the link between the exchange-rate policy and the debt buildup, if future deflation is not credible, then speculation against the fixed exchange rate raises domestic real interest rates (as occurred) but it would tend to *reduce* the foreign debt buildup in the real appreciation phase. An alternative approach is taken by some economists who assign the blame for the debt buildup and the high costs of the stabilization effort on the April 1980 international financial liberalization, which extended the nonbanks' access to international capital to the banking sector. Other economists blame the lack of supervision in the domestic banking sector. The approach taken below analyzes these views, beginning with a description of the barriers to international capital mobility that prevailed over the period 1977–82.

Barriers to international capital mobility for banks and nonbanks between 1977 and June 1982

This section provides a description of the administrative prohibitions, taxes, quotas, and other barriers to international capital mobility for banks and nonbanks between 1977 and June 1982.

The nonfinancial private sector in 1977–80

The authorities effectively allowed free international capital flows for nonbanks in 1975–9 via three channels, from which domestic intermediaries were excluded until April 1980. The three channels were (1) international trade credit; (2) Article 14; and (3) window purchases and sales.

International trade credit

The volume of international trade credit in Chile between 1977 and 1980 was heavily influenced by the substantial trade liberalization over those years, involving an average nominal tariff declining from 84% to 10% between 1975 and 1979, with all tariff rates fixed at the lower figure. The consequence was a rapid increase in the volume of international trade (and trade credit) and the diversification of exports among many firms.

A feature of international trade reform was that it allowed the trading firms to earn additional profits from international interest-rate arbitrage. Importers were usually able to bargain with their foreign suppliers for longer-term credit, up to the level where the marginal interest rate on further loans equaled the lending rate they could obtain in the domestic market. An analogous situation applied to exporters, who routinely asked for prepayment from their customers or their bankers. The liberalization of international trade automatically implied a higher degree of capital mobility because it increased the supply of international finance to nonbanks. Domestic banks participated in the intermediation of part of this new credit but were subject to strict pressure by their clients, who could resort directly to international banks whenever they wanted. The Central Bank improved the bargaining power of nonbanks by authorizing operations that formalized Chilean traders' ability to obtain trade credit directly from foreign banks.

International capital mobility for trading firms is a partial substitute for complete international financial liberalization, since it reduces the premium for international trade finance compared to the premium for other international finance. The same applies to domestic suppliers' credit, which for many small firms provides external finance at a lower premium than other external finance.

Article 14 for nonbanks

Between 1977 and 1980 a proliferation of international loans was registered by nonfinancial firms and individuals, under Article 14 of the Exchange Control Law – available since 1974. However, no public information is available that allows a differentiation of the returned capital-flight funds from actual borrowing by large domestic firms in international banking centers. In any case, direct credit operations with foreign financial institutions became exempt from local laws pertaining to credit operations following Decree Law 2,349 of 1978 (Errázuriz 1982).

In April 1979 the Central Bank imposed regulations requiring Article 14 inflows by nonbanks to meet a minimum average amortization period of 5.5 years (66 months) to avoid a reserve requirement (on which no interest would be paid). This was 15% for average maturities over 36 months and 25% for average maturities between 24 and 36 months, with shorter periods prohibited. The imposition of this tax on shorter maturities reduced the value of the nondiscrimination guarantee for repatriation afforded by Article 14. Nonbanks only retained the option of moving the funds out of the country on short notice through limited window sales, and the parallel (illegal) foreign exchange market.

Window purchases and sales for nonbanks

After 1975 the Central Bank maintained an additional channel to facilitate capital inflows, known as window purchases. This channel allowed any person to sell foreign currency to a commercial bank, which would later turn it over to the Central Bank, with the seller remaining anonymous. Since these operations provided no documentation to justify purchases of assets to the tax authorities, and provided no guaranteed access to a wide foreign exchange market for repatriation, the large volume of operations registered by this mechanism must be explained by the transaction costs of Article 14. Domestic banks were not allowed to intermediate through this channel.

In the second quarter of 1979, when the nominal exchange rate became fixed, the Central Bank also allowed any person to *buy* foreign currency up to U.S.$10,000 per month in any bank with no conditions. This was called window sales. The volume of these operations was small up to 1980 (Lagos and Coloma 1987). One result of the opening of both windows was the nearly complete elimination of the illegal foreign exchange market after mid-1979. The following table (12.1) shows that these inflows were substantially larger than bank-intermediated inflows between in 1976 and 1980, even though banks began to intermediate in September 1977.

Capital inflows intermediated by individuals and nonfinancial firms dominated the international financial arena in Chile until April 1980. Thus substantial amounts of funds were supplied to the domestic capital market before international intermediation by domestic banks

Table 12.1 *Capital inflows received by the private sector (U.S.$ million)*

| Period | Non-Financial Private Sector | | | Financial Intermediaries | | |
| | Article 14 | | Window Purchases by Chilean Banks | Total Non-Banks | Article 14 | |
	Amount Disbursed	Average Term months			Amount Disbursed	Average Term months
1976a	262	17	not av.	not av.	-	-
1977a	330	28	not av.	not av.	-	-
1978	446	30	not av.	not av.	304	37
1979	688	44	756	1444	511	67
1980	796	61b	1038	1834	1605	66

Source: For Article 14 figures, *Boletin Mensual*, Central Bank of Chile. For Window Purchases, Hachette (1989).

Note a: The sectoral decomposition of Article 14 is not available for 1976/77. However, we know that Financial Intermediaries were not allowed to do Article 14 operations until September 1977, while the Public Sector had very few operations. The numbers shown are total operations for 1976 and 1977.

was allowed. This was further augmented by adding the funds from international trade credit. Both Article 14 and window purchases legislation had been in effect since the foreign exchange crisis of 1975. Moreover, the trade-liberalization was a policy decided independently of its effects on the trade credit market. Therefore, there was no explicit policy of opening the capital account to nonbanks, although the April 1979 regulation governing Article 14 loans restricted its use by nonbanks.

In reality, foreigners and residents alike reduced the premium they required on international finance to Chile over 1978–1980. This was undoubtedly a response to the free-market reforms (later called "structural") initiated in 1974 as well as the large GDP growth rates between 1977 and 1980. However, the indirect evidence that will be presented later shows that these channels always had natural limits. The supply curve of foreign funds from these sources still sloped steeply upward, at some level, which was itself increasing over time.

Capital controls on domestic financial firms, 1977–80

Before April 1980 Chile was far from international financial liberalization, although there was reluctant progress toward it. The most strik-

Table 12.2 *Highlights of the Chilean international financial liberalization, 1977–80*

> September 1977: Commercial banks were first authorized to
> obtain foreign loans using the Article 14 mechanism, which
> offered more guarantees to foreign creditors. However, tight
> limits were placed on the stock of Article 14 loans,
> including trade credit (150% of capital and reserves) and on
> Article 14 monthly inflows (5% of capital and reserves).
>
> April 1978: Banks are granted an increase in the quotas; to
> assure the increase would be used in the form of longer term
> credit only, new quotas are imposed specifying maximum
> stocks of foreign debts if the average amortization term is
> below three years.
>
> April 1979: In addition to the quotas, reserve requirements
> (with no interest paid) are imposed on foreign loans (to
> banks as well as non-banks) through Article 14 that have an
> average amortization period of less than 66 months. The
> rates were 25% for average terms between 24 and 36 months,
> 15% for terms between 36 and 48 months, and 10% for terms
> between 48 and 66 months. Terms below 24 months but above
> the quota already filled by trade credit, were subject to a
> 100% reserve requirement.
>
> June 1979: The so-called "overall" quotas on the stock of
> foreign debt plus Article 14 foreign debt are eliminated.
> However, the quota on Article 14 monthly inflows is
> *tightened*, while the reserve requirements and the quota for
> short-term loans remain. This latter quota was fully used
> with trade credit intermediated through domestic banks. The
> monthly quota was the larger of US$ 2 million or 5% of
> capital and reserves.
>
> April 1980: The previous restrictive policy is reversed. The
> quota on Article 14 monthly inflows is eliminated; however,
> the reserve requirements and the quota for short-term loans
> remain.

ing feature of the capital controls affecting financial institutions is their extreme complexity, with dozens of regulations affecting each institution. These regulations included quotas and reserve requirements. Few people actually understood the overall effect of each of these regulations, and many of them became redundant over time. The main highlights are seen in Table 12.2.

Prior to 1980 these regulations effectively prevented domestic banks from engaging in international financial intermediation (the quotas were so low that at most they could finance trade). Therefore, this intermediation business accrued to nonbanks. The authorities were undisturbed by this outcome and even took occasional steps to encourage it; for example, they created window-sales for nonbanks in mid-1979. It was recognized that reserve requirements were a constraint to capital flows; however, it was argued that they were similar to tariffs, which are superior to the previously existing quotas (Bardón and Bacigalupo 1980). One argument for putting term-related reserve requirements on banks was that the "supply of foreign capital to the country has proven in the past to be unstable." In other words, the authorities were trying to smooth the fluctuations in the capital account, since they had little faith in the foreign private sector's savings and investment decisions. It is notable that the authorities had not worried when nonbanks did the same intermediation.

In April 1980 the Central Bank effectively ended the discrimination against domestic financial intermediaries by eliminating the monthly quota on capital inflows of individual banks. However, reserve requirements were retained. The result of this international financial liberalization was a striking increase in the volume of capital inflows intermediated by private banks, with no reduction in inflows by nonbanks. Although the April 1980 liberalization allowed a substantial increase in capital inflows to domestic banks, this does not mean that international interest rate arbitrage operated at minimum cost. In addition to the term-related reserve requirements, Sjaastad (1982) pointed out that banks were prohibited by other regulations from taking a net position in foreign exchange – that is, borrowing in dollars and lending those funds in pesos. They were allowed to lend their dollar funds only as dollar-indexed peso loans, effectively transferring the exchange-rate risk to the final borrowers. This risk was not eliminated; instead it resurfaced as a new source of credit risk, since some borrowers became more likely to default. However, Sjaastad failed to note that nothing prevented nonfinancial firms from taking positions in foreign exchange; so they could have done the required arbitrage.[2]

The large impact on total capital inflows of the April 1980 international financial liberalization (IFL) for banks warrants commentary. It should be underscored that international banks were never barred from creating a nonfinancial subsidiary in Chile that, under Article 14, could be considered a nonbank and bring funds to relend subsequently to the local branch of the bank. Even so, these banks had been unwilling to attempt such an arbitrage operation. The owners of domestic banks, on the other hand, had not been barred from convincing foreign lenders to lend directly to their holding companies, against a lien on equivalent dollar-denominated deposits in the affiliated bank, and then replicate the strategy available to international banks. Similarly, nothing barred them from giving a nonbank a guarantee and have it bring the funds, under the condition that those funds be deposited in the bank at an agreed interest rate. In fact, there is evidence that suggests domestic banks were doing this; however, the large response to the April 1980 international financial liberalization suggests that it was not a dominant phenomenon.

The limited volume of such operations may be explained by unwillingness to use such conspicuous methods to evade the laws of the country. However, we must also ask whether international banks were waiting for the implicit guarantee the government had given domestic banks since 1977 to lend more to Chile. This will be investigated in Section 12.4.

Further international financial liberalization, 1980–1

Chilean banks were never allowed to lend abroad, except for some reserve keeping, even after the April 1980 international financial liberalization. However, the Central Bank reformed thoroughly its international financial policy and allowed the domestic banking sector to compete both internationally and in Chile (with local branches of foreign banks) on an even regulatory basis.

For this purpose, Decree Law 3,345 allowed Chilean commercial banks to invest more in bank equity abroad, raising the limit on all such investments from 10% to 100% of capital and reserves. Development banks and *financieras* had similar limits raised from zero to 100% of capital and reserves. These investments continued to need previous approval from the Central Bank, and a new approval from the Superintendency of Banks was introduced. Direct branches were still banned.[3]

Law 18,010 of June 1981 modified the commercial code to allow documentation of bills in foreign currency. In addition, for the first time variable-rate long-term loans were considered, and were subsequently exempted from the limit on interest rates after the first period of issue. The law also widened the usury limit on interest rates expressed in foreign currency to take into account foreign inflation. In addition, this law clarified the legal situation of those obligations denominated in foreign currency and of those expressed in foreign currency but payable in domestic currency. This situation was previously obscure due to the superposition of the Foreign Exchange Law and the laws on credit operations. Where the credit operation was in foreign currency, the new law recognized explicitly the right of the creditor to access the foreign currency markets and acquire such currency, if paid in domestic currency. Finally, the judicial steps required to demand payment of credit denominated in foreign currency or expressed in foreign currency were simplified (Errázuriz 1982).

Table 12.3 *Chile: Foreign bank subsidiaries, 1978–83*

Dec 31st of	No. of Foreign Banks (50% own. or +)	Share in Fin. Syst. Loans	Share in Fin. Syst. Deposits	Share in Fin. Syst. Capital	Main Foreign Banks (Share of For. Bk. Loans
1978	5	2.4%	0.5%	3.7%	BUF: 72%; Citi: 12%
1979	12	4.2%	2.2%	6.2%	BUF: 47%; Republic: 18%
1980	14	4.9%	2.7%	7.8%	BUF: 39%; Citi: 18%
1981	20	8.7%	7.0%	13.0%	BUF: 28%; Citi: 14%
1982	21	12.6%	14.8%	16.6%[a]	(b) See Note b
1983	19	9.2%	13.8%	16.2%[a]	(b) See Note c

Source: Compiled by the author from *Informacion Financiera.* The financial system includes commercial banks, Banco del Estado, *Financieras,* and IFICOOP.

a.   This is the share of capital after considering the infusions of capital to domestic banks by the Central Bank, occurred in 1982 and 1983.

b.   In 1982 four foreign banks had 60% of all foreign bank loans: BUF: 17%; Espanol Chile; Citibank: 15%; Morgan-Finansa: 12%.

c.   The four largest foreign banks had 64% of all loans by foreign banks. In December 1983 the four largest were Espanol-Chile: 22%; Citibank: 15%; Morgan-Finansa: 14%; Centrobanco: 13%.

Law 18,022 of August 19, 1981 authorized domestic banks to open branches in foreign countries. Branches, unlike subsidiaries, enjoy the guarantee of the parent bank. This was an important event for three domestic banks, who used it to open two small subsidiaries and one branch, respectively, in Panama, Uruguay, and New York.

From the point of view of efficiency, it was important to equalize regulatory conditions with those granted to international banks with branches in Chile. For this purpose, standard reserve requirements on domestic banks were reduced drastically in 1980, from 42% to 10% on demand deposits and from 8% to 4% on all other deposits (Bardón and Bacigalupo 1980). A side effect was a large impulse to expansion of domestic intermediation.

International banks had been opening separately capitalized branches in Chile since 1974, when Citibank was authorized to partici-pate in the peso markets. Later it opened a formal branch. In 1975 bank BUF was founded by a consortium of foreign banks. In 1978 a Spanish bank and another Brazilian bank opened small branches in Santiago. In 1979 seven newcomers started a tide, to be followed by two more in 1980, six more in 1981, and one that came late in 1982. Their participation in the domestic market is shown in Table 12.3.[4]

The majority of these branches concentrated on serving multina-tionals and speculating in local bonds and other instruments. Most were little more than "representation" offices plus an investment man-

Table 12.4 *Capital inflows received by the private sector / nonfinancial private sector (U.S.$ million)*

Period		Non-Financial Private Sector			Total	Domestic Banks	
		Article 14		Window		Article 14	
		Amount Disbursed US$ m.	Average Term months	Purchases by Chilean Bank	Non-Fin. Priv. S. US$ m.	Amount Disbursed US$ m.	Average Term months
1980	1	150.9	58	284.9	435.8	132.8	62
	2	115.9	59	219.1	335.0	513.2	68
	3	208.0	63	232.7	440.7	421.8	65
1981	4	322.0	61	300.8	622.8	537.0	66
	1	279.7	65	478.1	757.8	435.0	66
	2	289.0	61	487.6	776.6	995.2	59
	3	333.2	63	518.5	851.7	879.6	57
1982	4	232.3	61	549.8	782.1	968.6	58
	1	165.1	53	523.0	688.1	264.9	59
	2	147.0	49	517.4	664.4	352.9	60

Source : For Article 14 figures, *Boletin Mensual* , Central Bank of Chile. Window Purchases from Hachette (1989), Table 11.

ager who invested the bank's capital. A few, like BUF and Citibank, attempted to penetrate local credit markets and trained substantial numbers of local managers, putting considerable competitive pressure on locally owned banks. Others decided to grow by acquiring failed local banks. Banco de Santander bought Español-Chile and Centrobanco bought Banco de Talca, after their intervention in November 1981. Morgan started a joint venture with a *financiera* called Finansa. All of them except Citibank suffered huge losses in the 1982–3 crisis. BUF was liquidated in January 1983, while Morgan pulled out of Morgan-Finansa. Santander and Centrobanco absorbed huge losses in the loan portfolio they purchased. These banks' capital performed the useful role of helping to cushion the fiscal costs of the 1981–3 banking crisis.

Capital-account performance in 1980–2

Starting in mid-1979, the Central Bank allowed any individual to buy up to U.S.$10,000 per month from commercial banks with no questions asked. These window sales represented the only opening to outward capital mobility of the period. Its main purpose was to enhance the credibility of the new fixed-exchange-rate policy.

When the recession struck in 1981, and as the expectation of devaluation became widespread, window sales (of dollars) became the favorite route for capital flight by individuals, rising from $450 million in

1980 to over $950 million and $1.2 billion in the subsequent two years, suggesting that expectations of devaluation had begun to develop since mid-1981. The sales ended in October 1982, when Finance Minister Lüders reinstated exchange controls and closed this window to individuals. Simultaneously with window sales outflows, inflows through window purchases and Article 14 remained strong. Although window sales outflows increased, window purchases and Article 14 inflows were growing also, so two-way capital movements are important feature of 1981 (see Table 12.4).

Capital inflows by nonbanks continued very strong until mid-1982, even after the April 1980 international financial liberalization. These data cast serious doubts on the notion that only banks were responsible for the steep foreign debt accumulation of 1981. The comparison with other data suggest that expectations of devaluation were diverging widely in late 1981 and 1982 among economic agents; thus, the nonbanks that borrowed heavily nor the individuals that used the window sales channel can be considered representative.

These findings deflate the expected importance of the April 1980 international financial liberalization. This result is weakly confirmed by Corbo and Solimano (1991), who estimate a time-varying coefficient of openness to international mobility without reference to institutional data. This coefficient fluctuates around 0.70 for the entire period (1978 to June 1982), and the numbers suggest that the April 1980 international financial liberalization, if anything, reduced the degree of capital mobility. This suggests that the capital account was quite open both before and after the April 1980 international financial liberalization.[5]

Macroeconomics and the credit markets

Was the April 1980 international financial liberalization a cause or an aggravating factor in the high costs of the stabilization program? And was the international financial liberalization a causal factor in the foreign debt buildup or the subsequent recession? These questions require investigation of two further puzzles: namely, the apparent failure of international interest arbitrage and the exceedingly high level of domestic real interest rates in 1981 and 1982.

The puzzle of international interest arbitrage

Commentators who have analyzed capital-account policy in Chile always allude to the puzzle implicit in the large differential between domestic and foreign interest rates that persisted – even in the face of large capital inflows and the reduction of administrative restrictions on capital mobility in 1980–2. Of course, one problem is to identify the expectations of devaluation in the absence of a forward market for foreign exchange, given the absence of formal surveys of exchange-rate expectations. If the expected devaluation is assumed to be sufficiently high, then the interest arbitrage puzzle disappears.

Heterogenous marginal expectations among individuals suggest that models with one representative agent will never answer the issue. On the one hand, the large capital inflows by the nonfinancial private sector in 1980–2 suggest that expectations of devaluations were not dominant until the June 1982 devaluation. On the other hand, the growing volume of window sales shows that devaluation was around the corner for many agents.

We offer a comparison of the interest rates that a nonbank (with country risk only) would have had to pay when borrowing at home versus borrowing abroad. Three series for expected devaluation are used. We define the following concepts:

Cost of Domestic Borrowing = SIR = Santiago Interbank Rate[6]
Cost of Foreign Borrowing = $[(1 + i^* + p)^{1/12}(1 + d\ln E/dt)] - 1$.

where

i^* = 180-day LIBOR in U.S. dollars, in the last day of each month, in annual terms

p = average spread over LIBOR, in annual terms, paid by Article 14 loans to the nonfinancial private sector in each month.

$d\ln E/dt$ = the expected monthly devaluation rate of the Chilean peso vis-à-vis the U.S. dollar.

Three alternatives are given for the cost of foreign borrowing that differ in the way expectations are treated. The series called "Ex-Post Cost of Foreign Borrowing" assumes that expected devaluation was equal to the actual devaluation before July 1979, and that the fixed exchange rate was fully credible up to June 1982. Figure 12.1 shows that the monthly differential between average interest rates was substantial both before and after the July 1979 devaluation and fixing of the exchange rate. After the April 1980 international financial liberalization, the differential fell but did not disappear. The remaining spread was substantial, 1% to 2% per month, and exhibited no tendency to decline over time.

Replacing actual devaluation for LeFort and Ross's (1985) one-month-ahead expected devaluation, the monthly differential disap-

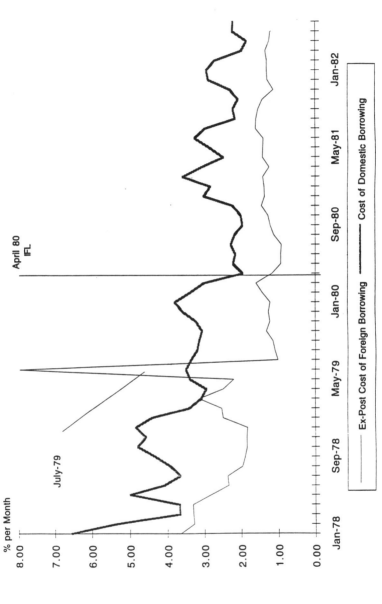

Figure 12.1 Interest arbitrage in Chile with perfect foresight

peared by January 1981 (see Figure 12.2). This expected devaluation series is based on a Bayesian technique that calculates the probability of devaluation based on reserve changes only. It excludes reserve levels, which were very high in 1981, and the information about agents' beliefs contained in capital flows to the nonfinancial sector, which were growing in 1981. Figure 12.2 implies that agents took nine months, April '80 to January '81, to achieve interest parity after the international financial liberalization. However, interest parity is also violated by this series given that a large spread is predicted against foreign borrowing after January 1981.

Hernández's (1991) one-month-ahead expected devaluation between May 1980 and May 1982 assumes interest parity held after the April 1980 international financial liberalization, but that there existed a "peso problem" or a credibility gap. Hernández obtained his expected devaluation series as follows: First, a reaction function for the Central Bank's exchange-rate policy is estimated for the period March 1974 to June 1979. This is used to generate an expected devaluation series, given that the Central Bank abandons the fixed exchange rate and returns to its traditional policy. On the other hand, the probability of abandonment of the fixed-exchange-rate regime is modeled as a function of the following exogenous and predetermined variables: a time trend, the lagged rate of change of industrial production, the lagged rate of change of domestic credit, and the price of copper. The coefficients are estimated assuming that interest parity holds and using the previously obtained series on the expected devaluation given abandonment. Finally, expected devaluation during the fixed-exchange-rate regime is considered the product of the probability of abandonment and the expected devaluation when abandonment occurs. The results can be seen in Figure 12.3. Hernández's series assumes perfect arbitrage to estimate the lack of credibility of exchange-rate policy. Therefore, it assumes away alternative explanations of the spreadlike positive premium for international finance.

Valdés-Prieto (1992) follows this approach, and sets up a model where the premium for international finance is positive and endogenous; he then examines the effects of the 1980 international financial liberalization. He shows the existence of limits on international finance means that international interest-rate arbitrage can be ineffective in reducing real interest rates. An inexplicable interest-rate spread emerges when the premium for international finance is not considered in the analysis. The result is that interest parity does not hold for average data. Conversely, the premium for international finance can be presumed by assessing the size of the failure of interest-rate arbi-

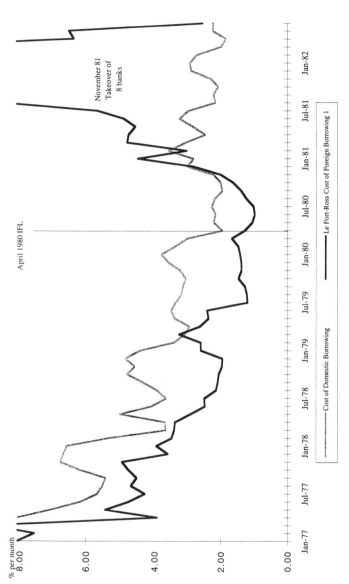

Figure 12.2 Interest arbitrage with LeFort and Ross's expected devaluation series

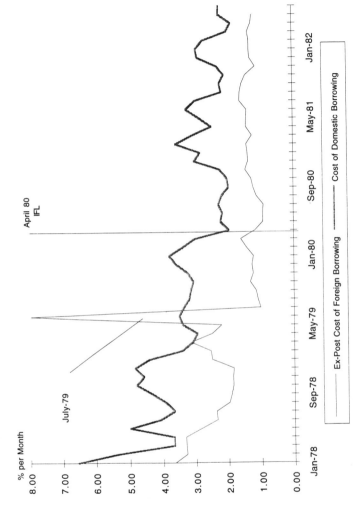

% per Month

8.00
7.00
6.00
5.00
4.00
3.00
2.00
1.00
0.00

Jan-78   Sep-78   May-79   Jan-80   Sep-80   May-81   Jan-82

July-79

April 80
IFL

Ex-Post Cost of Foreign Borrowing   Cost of Domestic Borrowing

Figure 12.3 Interest arbitrage with Hernández's expected devaluation

Table 12.5 *Real-expost loan rates in pesos (% per annum)*

Quarter	Interest Rate	Quarter	Interest Rate
1979: 1	40.9	1981: 1	21.0
2	14.0	2	28.3
3	6.2	3	47.6
4	18.2	4	42.6
1980: 1	29.8	1982: 1	49.4
2	8.7	2	45.9
3	12.7		
4	-2.4		

Note: Annualized commercial bank lending rate on 30 to 89 day loans, deflated by actual CPI.

Source: Boletin Banco Central.

trage. Using this approach to examine the July 1979 fixing of the exchange rate, he finds that the level of domestic real interest rates is not affected and the premium for international finance increases one for one with the reduction in expected devaluation, which is consistent with the evidence in Figure 12.1.[7]

The puzzle of high interest rates between 1981 and June 1982

The real interest rate followed a puzzling path in Chile (see Table 12.5). The high real interest rate in peso loans observed in Chile in 1981 and 1982 can be explained in several ways. First, there is a distinction between actual inflation and expected inflation. In this explanation, the peso interest rate was high because expected inflation was high; however, expected inflation did not materialize for several consecutive months. In turn, expected inflation was higher than actual inflation for two reasons: First, expected devaluation was positive because of limited credibility while actual devaluation was nil; and second, the dollar was expected to remain constant relative to the deutsche mark, though in fact it depreciated in 1979 and appreciated in 1981.

The overall credibility of exchange rate policy cannot be an important explanation, as the evidence shows that some groups were increasing their net foreign indebtedness while others were reducing it. Regarding the dollar–mark exchange rate, the problem is that the share of Chilean trade in dollars relative to all trade was nearly 50%; so those tradeables represent at most 25% of the Chilean CPI. As the magnitude of the gyrations in these exchange rates did not exceed 20%, this effect can explain at most a 5% cumulative inflation surprise.

The second explanation is the rise in international real interest rates. In the United States, for example, real interest rates on safe short-term debt rose from nearly 0% in 1978 to 10% by 1982. On the other hand, real interest rates did not rise as much in Europe or Japan because of the continuing appreciation of their currencies. This reduces the importance of the rise of real interest rates in the United States probably by half. Additionally, domestic interest rates began to rise before foreign real interest rates did.

A third explanation is that the margin of intermediation of banks had to rise in late 1981 in response to a substantial increase in lending risk. In fact, de la Cuadra and Valdés-Prieto (1990) report that this spread grew from an average of 5.2% per year in 1980 to an average of 10.5% per year in the first half of 1982. This increase is too small to explain the rise in domestic real interest rates by itself. However, adding it with the other explanations, they account for almost 15.3 of the 34.9 point rise of the average for 1980 and the average for the last four quarters in Table 12.6.

The fourth explanation, emphasizing distress borrowing and moral hazard in the financial sector for 1981 and 1982, will be analyzed separately in section 12.4. The fifth explanation emphasizes an abrupt reduction in the supply of domestic saving. It argues that myopic behavior of ordinary consumers, engaged in a spending binge financed with credit, reduced private savings to historical lows. This effect would be strengthened by the backward indexation rule that affected wages, because consumers used the extra income to finance down payments to purchase additional durable goods. The mindset of wage earners was probably influenced by the flow of optimistic government pronouncements in 1981. This fifth explanation has been documented by Schmidt-Hebbel (1988) and supported by much incidental evidence.

More important for our analysis, Valdés-Prieto (1992) shows that real interest rates and the premiums would have been substantially higher in 1981–2 if the April international financial liberalization had not occurred in April 1980. That is, the April 1980 liberalization helped to alleviate the financial distress associated with these high real interest rates, and not to worsen it. The flip side of this coin is that the liberalization made an independent contribution to the foreign debt buildup.

Problems in domestic banking and the April 1980
international financial liberalization

This section provides an overview of prudential supervision and moral hazard in domestic banking to determine if the April 1980 international financial liberalization worsened or improved matters in this regard.

Table 12.6 Interest-rate spreads in domestic U.S.$ deposits and loans (% per annum)

Quarter		US$-denominated Deposits			US$-indexed Loans		
		Spread paid by Chilean Bank	Volume of Deposits (US$ m.)	Local Rate on US$ Loan	LIBOR plus Non-Bank Spread	Spread earned by Chilean Bank	US$-index loans as % of all loans
1981	3	5.66	358	22.83	19.69	3.14	
	4	7.57	361	21.58	17.70	3.88	40.7%
1982	1	5.66	345	20.17	16.69	3.48	
	2	6.30	350	20.46	16.24	4.22	
	3	6.42	372	18.67	15.71	2.96	41.8%
	4	5.79	413	15.12	12.83	2.29	

Source: The first and second columns, from Lagos and Coloma (1987), who average the monthly difference between the interest rates earned by U.S. $ deposits in Chilean banks and the commercial paper interest rate in the United States. The third column, from *Informacion Financiera* (simple average of the monthly *Interes Corriente en Prestamos en U.S. $*, a series that started in July 1981). The fourth column, from *Central Bank Bulletin* (one-month lagged simple average of LIBOR and "spread" paid by the nonfinancial private sector in Article 14 loans). The last column, from *Informacion Financiera*, Colocaciones con Recursos Propios.

The regulatory framework and the business groups

Beginning in 1977, the government's banking policy was to take over failed intermediaries – unless they were small savings and loan cooperatives. The takeover of Banco Osorno in January 1977 and others during 1977 led to a widespread belief that bank depositors – not shareholders – enjoyed a bona fide guarantee issued free by the government (de la Cuadra and Valdés-Prieto 1990).

The government shied away from imposing state prudential supervision in 1977–80, since it did not want to dictate to private banks its own risk assessment of debtors. Instead it strengthened the legal rights of creditors. In January 1978 the government introduced new financial and banking offenses subject to criminal penalties so that depositors and other creditors would be encouraged to seek legal remedies in case of fraud, typically associated with bank failure. In 1978 banks were forced to hire external auditors to assess whether their accounts reflected their true financial position, in the hope that this process would provide a safeguard for the public and foster accountability among banks.

The 1977–80 period was also one of domestic bank expansion, given their new freedom from interest-rate and credit controls, obtained in 1976. However, this growth occurred under an inconsistent prudential regulatory framework: Very few state prudential regulations applied to banks, while the government was implicitly guaranteeing all bank deposits and debts. The only defenses against moral hazard were external auditor reputations, the bankers' reputations (although free entry allowed self-selection in favor of fraud-tolerant groups), and quasi-rents.

This weak approach to bank supervision caused no problems in 1977–80, except for fraud at Banco Español. The reason was that expected future quasi-rents provided by the high growth of the banking industry created a large nontangible asset that kept most bankers reasonably prudent. The evidence shows that before 1980 almost all bank profits were ploughed back to increase bank capital; hence, the notion of moral hazard or willful abuse of deposit guarantees is not supported by the data up to 1980. In fact, capital/asset ratios were kept more or less constant in the face of substantial growth. On the other hand, analysis suggests that bad loans from the 1975 recession fell dramatically in relative importance up to 1980 (de la Cuadra and Valdés-Prieto 1990). The 1977–80 period cannot be characterized as an time of rampant abuse and moral hazard, although fraud at Banco Español and other intermediaries certainly existed.

Of course, this favorable environment could not last since free entry permitted fraud-prone individuals and groups to increase their share in the banking industry. In addition, the approaching end of the high growth period assured that competition would increase among banks, reducing quasi-rents and encouraging moral hazard. The same can be said of borrowers, for whom a good payment record was valuable in a boom but not in a bust. Even more troubling, the fast expansion of banking implied inadequate time to accumulate experience in risk assessment, foreclosure, and more generally asset protection. In this sense, the loans contracted between 1977 and 1980 were not solid, although the projects they financed were mostly sound investments, with few agents actively engaging in moral hazard before 1980.

The government's bank regulation policy began to change in mid-1980, after fraud in Banco Español gave leverage to officials who worried about the fiscal cost of the deposit guarantee. Further investigation by the Superintendency of Banks concluded that a substantial portion of bank loans had gone to affiliated groups, that is, firms related to the bank's controllers, referred to here as "self-loans."

In August 1981 the military government reformed the banking law and defined self-loans to be unacceptably risky. The Superintendency asked the banks to submit plans to reduce the level of self-loans substantially in the subsequent five semesters. This created havoc in the two large business conglomerates, which had grown rapidly between 1976 and 1981 through acquisitions mainly financed by self-loans by their captive banks.[8]

The tremendous rise in real interest rates in 1981 and the bleak prospects for the coming years meant these groups were moving rapidly toward insolvency. When in 1982 GDP slumped to 14.1% and unemployment rose to 25% the net worth of the two business groups became negative. Their creditors clearly had a right to exercise their option to seize their assets. However, the control these two groups exercised over big banks meant they were able to delay declaring bankruptcy for a substantial time in expectation of a bailout. This delay inflicted losses on many small debtors and other business groups that were solvent, forcing unneeded layoffs and bankruptcies. As in most countries, there are no special provisions in Chilean law to manage the bankruptcy of large business groups who own banks.

During 1981 and 1982 the two largest business groups attempted to evade the new restrictions on self-loans, which led to an escalation of hostility with the authorities. The government was unwilling to bail out these groups, even though an agreement would have allowed a reduction in the social costs of reorganization and bankruptcy. By this time the government had become convinced this was not a liquidity crisis, but rather both groups were insolvent. Still, the government adopted some policies to smooth reorganization associated with the recession.

The 1981 rise in domestic real interest rates and the 1982 recession led the business groups into distress borrowing to delay impending insolvency. Given their relative size, they clearly raised further domestic interest rates, which explains part of the rise in real rates in 1981 and 1982. However, they were not alone in their distress, since many other medium-sized and small business groups also had pursued a high-debt growth strategy and became insolvent. The difference was that the latter did not control banks, so they were unable to delay their insolvency. Even firms that had pursued an average leverage policy were caught in the trap of 45% ex post real interest rates on loans in 1981. The final result was that almost all banks became insolvent in 1982, and not only those that belonged to the main business groups. In June 1982 the Central Bank offered to all domestic banks a long-term repurchase agreement of bad loan portfolios. Two expansions of this programs had to be offered in 1983, and one more in 1986.

The evolution of bank supervision, 1981–2

When the recession began in mid-1981, moral hazard had become widespread. The advent of recession wiped out future quasi-rents that had kept bankers and bank debtors prudent. The data for 1981 show that banks did not reinvest any of the previous year's profits, suggesting that bankers realized the previously expected stream of future quasi-rents had disappeared. Despite valiant efforts, the government was unable to implement rapidly an effective method of bank solvency evaluation and risk control. It was only in mid-1980 that authorities reluctantly decided to nationalize the bank supervision function rather than continue to wait for the private sector to take the initiative (de la Cuadra and Valdés-Prieto 1990). This policy decision occurred too late, since prudential supervision could not be implemented quickly. The earliest date in which banks were required to make reserves in proportion to individual loan risk was March 1982, 15 months too late.

This does not mean the quality of state bank supervision did not increase rapidly. The November 1981 intervention of four banks and four *financieras* was a response to the problems detected by bank supervision. These banks had issued about 8% of the system's deposits, with the main reason for intervention being fraud. This was due to the extremely liberal implementation of entry restrictions into banking. During 1981 adverse selection in favor of fraud-prone bankers was rampant, as shown by later interventions of bankers who entered the industry at this time.

A worrying feature of the Chilean domestic financial liberalization was that moral hazard by bankers against the government who insured its deposits may have been surpassed by massive moral hazard from bank debtors against banks. There is evidence that bank borrowers of all sizes – especially the large business groups with captive banks – embarked on distress borrowing at any cost hoping the government would save them or that international interest rates would suddenly fall. This was possible because the fledgling Chilean banking sector had not yet developed experience in managing insolvencies and foreclosing assets in a timely way. The same happened with risk assessment. Just a few bankers did their homework and attempted an assessment of the overall solvency of their large debtors; it is noteworthy that the ones that did so escaped the crisis in much better condition. *This means that a substantial part of the fiscal cost of moral hazard was due to the inexperience of domestic banks that had expanded rapidly in the previous years.*

International financial liberalization and prudential issues

The April 1980 international financial liberalization may have been imprudent in the sense that prudential preconditions needed to ensure success were not met. This could be due to the concept of introducing an international financial liberalization in a country with an immature domestic financial liberalization, or to faults in the design of the international financial liberalization itself.

For example, the inducement for long-term loans contained in the schedule of reserve requirements for Article 14 loans was not prudent relative to the solvency of the domestic banking sector. Given that the cost of intermediation was higher in Chile than abroad, the domestic financial system would be too inefficient to compete after the stabilization with international banks for borrowers and depositors with access to international finance. However, the international financial liberalization was authorized in the transition period of the stabilization, when the inflation differential was much larger than the expected devaluation. The timing of the international financial liberalization in the middle of the stabilization stimulated overintermediation by domestic banks.

If this overintermediation were perceived as transitory, then the large arbitrage profits would not have attracted excess investment in the banking sector. Hot money will flow through, but there will be no branch expansion or hiring of new personnel. This is good for bank solvency. Most factors of production in banking are sunk costs in the medium term, so a sudden and large reduction in long-term intermediation volume can bring about insolvency. However, if Central Bank regulations require international intermediation to be long-term, banks know they must increase the scale of their operations. In this case, the large arbitrage profits were sunk in quasi-fixed factors of production. This was risky, because as soon as the stabilization ends, domestic intermediation must necessarily be reduced in scale, and bank solvency will be jeopardized. In this sense, the long-term requirement imposed by the Central Bank on Article 14 loans contributed to impair the solvency of the Chilean banking system. The criticism is not against the international financial liberalization, but rather that the international financial liberalization was not bold enough to eliminate term-related reserve requirements.

There is evidence of heavy loan marketing efforts by domestic banks during 1981, especially loans with terms linked to the peso–dollar exchange rate. The average spread over LIBOR charged by domestic banks on dollar-index loans, was just 2% to 4%, smaller than what could be earned by lending to an affiliated firm who would take the foreign exchange risk and then relend in pesos. This was much less than the cost of funds when the funding source was dollar deposits in Chile. Unfortunately, it is impossible to estimate whether the cost of the lax evaluations of credit risk in these loans made the difference regarding the ultimate insolvency of many banks.

A different argument is that some of the further measures toward international financial liberalization taken in 1981 were imprudent. Most notable was the authorization for domestic banks to open branches and invest in subsidiaries abroad. These authorizations to domestic banks were criticized afterward because some banks used them to escape the rules against self-loans to affiliated companies issued in late 1981. This criticism should not be levied against these authorizations per se, but rather that the state's prudential supervision policy adopted in mid-1980 was still under implementation, and thus had limited capacity to control foreign subsidiaries or coordinate with foreign supervisors. This could explain why these authorizations have not been removed from Chile's banking law since that time.[9]

Related to this is whether international banks when lending to domestic banks took into account the implicit guarantee the Chilean government had given domestic banks since 1977. The potential fiscal cost of living up to these implicit – but expected – guarantees was ignored by the authorities, who opted for liberalization. However, by the end of 1980, the Superintendency of Banks was beginning to reverse its laissez-faire policy and put into place an efficient prudential supervision system. By late 1980 the banking system was still basically healthy, the protection against moral hazard being the large quasi-rents expected from the rapidly growing industry. Given that growth was expected to continue some time into the future, the expected value of the deposit guarantees involved was not substantial at that time. Therefore, these guarantees were not very valuable in April 1980; thus it is unlikely they had much influence on lending decisions by international banks.

In 1981 and 1982, however, such guarantees became more and more valuable, as Chilean banks slipped into insolvency. This means that international banks were influenced by these guarantees in 1981 and early 1982, a period when they doubled their exposure to Chilean banks. In those years the problem was confronted directly – but with delay – by introducing strong domestic supervision. Given these efforts, limits on international capital movements were an inferior tool to deal with this problem in the long run. However, this important effect would have been absent if the April 1980 international financial liberalization had been delayed to 1983. Although this was not the result of the international financial liberalization per se, but of the failure of domestic supervision, this is a convincing reason for delaying international financial liberalization in the short run as explained below.

A similar point can be made regarding the authorization of entry to many branches of international banks. These branches increased the degree of competition in the Chilean banking sector, accelerating the end of the transitory quasi-rents that kept moral hazard and the risk of fraud at bay. Although the same argument applies to entry by domestic banks, this suggests that a policy of restricting entry of international banks is a second-best transition policy when prudential supervision is not yet in place. On the other hand, if foreign banks bring fresh capital and are willing to buy bank assets, as they did in Chile, they help to reduce the risk ultimately suffered by the Chilean Treasury by guaranteeing deposits. The evidence suggests that this was an important contribution of foreign banks in Chile up to 1985.

Real exchange guarantees and the April 1980
international financial liberalization

Since 1978 the Chilean authorities had argued that because the premiums for international finance vary substantially over time, (1) it is not wise to finance too much investment with foreign saving, and (2) it is even less wise to anticipate consumption of the fruits of such growth. The changing sentiment of foreign creditors and the fact that most of the investment projects were long-term combined to create a recurrent liquidity crisis in foreign financing. The proposed solution was to tax short-term capital inflows, assuring that foreign savings could come into Chile only if it were long-term – that is, not subject to changes in creditor sentiment.

The Chilean experience showed this remedy to be ineffective. In fact, the long-term nature of the debt contracted in 1979–81 did not prevent a liquidity crisis arising from changes in creditor sentiment in late 1982 and 1983. The reason is that in a country that draws heavily on foreign saving, both residents and nonresidents allocate their portfolio among domestic and foreign investments, and these portfolio movements are always large enough to cause a liquidity shortage if confidence falters, that is, the premium for international finance rises and the exchange rate depreciates.

How does a market economy manage this situation? The risks of fluctuation of the premium for international finance are incurred by each firm that borrows abroad on a revolving basis, because it can have its credit cut and be forced to pay on short notice. Therefore, each firm borrowing abroad must protect against this risk by seeking favorable contract terms with his lender. There is no externality in this problem, so government intervention cannot help in its solution. This occurs all the time in domestic credit markets, where it would be unthinkable for a government to intervene by requiring a minimum term on loans to a certain group just to protect it from a possible liquidity crisis.

On the other hand, the intervention of the Central Bank as a regulator of the term of loans among private parties might suggest that it is in some way guaranteeing the conditions of the contract. The parties may come to believe that the Central Bank guarantees the availability of foreign funds for repayment at a reasonable price for the length of the contract. This belief materialized ex post in the Chilean case, with the preferential dollar subsidy of 1982–5 with long-term credit contracts. With long-term contracts, plus such a perceived real exchange-rate guarantee of the Central Bank, the private sector borrower is spared the risk of a change in perception of foreign creditors as well as any eventual credit cutoff.

This implicit guarantee acts as a subsidy to international intermediation, inducing excessive capital inflows. In this regard, the minimum-term requirement adopted in Chile passed to the Treasury the risk of foreign credit cutoff, charging a zero price to the private sector beneficiaries of the liquidity guarantee, which implies a real exchange-rate guarantee. As with any subsidy, the minimum-term requirement stimulated exposure the same risk the government sought to avoid. Therefore, the design of the April 1980 international financial liberalization must be criticized because it did not liberalize as fully as needed for the undistorted operation of the international capital movements.

Another implicit foreign exchange-rate guarantee was created by the interaction of the stabilization policy and the weaknesses brought by the nationalization of the prudential supervision function. The State prudential supervision system, imported from the United States during 1981, showed in Chile a vulnerability to conflicts of interest with other areas of the government. In many countries the Ministry of Finance or the Central Bank governor controls a substantial part of the financial risks of the economy and serves also as the chief of the Superintendency of Banks. In Chile it was naive to expect bank supervisors, who are a dependency of the Ministry of Finance, to require special provisions on loans to borrowers exposed to currency depreciation risk, since the minister of finance publicly reiterated there would never be a devaluation in Chile.

Of course, one should expect the minister of finance of any country that has pegged its currency to deny all rumors of devaluation. However, this creates trouble for the operation of a prudential supervision system run by dependents of the minister of finance. In Chile this conflict was known by bank managers, who could safely pretend that they did not believe a devaluation risk was important when assessing their own loans portfolio. This led bankers to assess the foreign exchange risk of their self-loans as very low.

In fact, the risk of devaluation was substantial and increased as negative external shocks accumulated. The recession that began in mid-1981 led to a 25% unemployment rate in 1982, and deflation became the rule. The reaction of the large number of heavily indebted firms and individuals was to gamble that the government would keep the exchange rate fixed, as promised. They were willing to change their peso debt into dollar-denominated debt, betting that the recession would end shortly and that there would be no devaluation. If the opposite happened, they relied on state help. Many remembered the 1960–2 attempt to fix the exchange rate that had to be abandoned in a balance-of-payments crisis, where the government rose to bail out most dollar debtors.

Counterfactual analysis of a different timing for the Chilean international financial liberalization

What would have happened if the international financial liberalization policy had been adopted much earlier, say in 1977? If adopted earlier, should it have been designed differently?

An early international financial liberalization, say in 1977, will be analyzed first. This option was chosen by Uruguay in 1974, with substantial success until 1978, when other problems became dominant (Hanson and de Melo 1985). For Chile it is useful to discuss the interaction of an early international financial liberalization with the three deep causes of the dismal macroeconomic performance discussed in the previous sections.

Regarding the stabilization attempt that started in 1979, a substantial advantage of an early international financial liberalization would have been that their effects on the real exchange rate would not have reinforced each other. In addition, the participation of banks in the extra opportunities for international interest-rate arbitrage afforded by the stabilization program in 1979 and up to April of 1980 would have increased their profits and equity, with the positive side effects of delaying the onset of the moral hazard problem.

From a macroeconomic point of view, an earlier international financial liberalization means that more capital inflows would have come in 1977–8, domestic real interest rates would have fallen earlier, and investment would have been higher. The small real appreciation caused by the international financial liberalization alone – smaller than the one actually experienced – would have happened earlier, and producers of tradeable goods would have suffered earlier. The same is true of the imprudent supply of funds by international banks. An early international financial liberalization would have avoided the simultaneity with the period of excessive lending by these banks, but some inflows were probably unavoidable.

Regarding the excessive spending by myopic consumers, an early international financial liberalization would have merely reduced somewhat the interest rates at which they would have borrowed anyway. The response of these consumers was feasible because of the domestic financial liberalization, with little effect coming from the international component. Probably that outcome was inevitable, as consumer credit became available with the domestic financial liberalization for the first time in many years.

The richest lessons come from analyzing the interactions between the timing of an international financial liberalization and the problem of moral hazard in domestic banking due to an immature domestic financial liberalization.

First, an early international financial liberalization would have allowed international banks to lend to domestic banks much earlier, suggesting a faster expansion of domestic banks. However, the Chilean banking sector expanded at breakneck pace in 1976–80, due to the domestic financial liberalization. Therefore, it is hard to believe it could go much faster, given the limited supply of the required human resources. The same happens with the suggestion that earlier foreign contact with Chile would have brought an earlier wave of branches of international banks, which would have increased competition earlier. The speed with which the international banks set branches in Chile seems hard to emulate, so this factor is probably secondary.

Second, an early international financial liberalization includes a factor that delays substantially the onset of moral hazard, giving more time for prudential supervision to establish itself. This is that banks would have had access to the large profits afforded by international interest arbitrage in 1977–9. It must be remembered that rampant abuse appears only as quasi-rents are exhausted, which in Chile happened in 1981. These profits were large enough to form the basis of the wealth of the big business groups that flowered in that period (de la Cuadra and Valdés-Prieto 1990). If a share of those profits had gone to the banking sector instead of flowing exclusively to big nonbanks as they did, the capital base of domestic banks would have been much stronger, pushing the onset of moral hazard years into the future. If a delay of two years had been achieved, then the prudential supervision machinery installed in 1981 could have become operative in time to reduce substantially the size of abuses.

Third, with an early international financial liberalization international banks may have lent massively to Chilean banks earlier, taking more advantage of the implicit government guarantee for domestic bank liabilities. However, the record of foreign lending to nonbanks and the experience of Uruguay in 1974–8 suggest otherwise. The existence of premiums for international finance, and the fact that lending quotas to Chilean residents grew steadily starting from very low levels, suggests that the aggregate volume of lending was not influenced very much by legal changes in Chile. Chilean nonbanks could barely obtain a few hundred million dollars in 1978, even though a large share of those loans were guaranteed by Chilean banks. On the other hand, nonbanks were able to obtain huge amounts of foreign credit in 1981, even though only a small share was guaranteed by Chilean banks.

Fourth, consider the effect of imposing the minimum term requirement earlier, together with an early international financial liberalization. If this had been imposed in 1977 to banks and nonbanks, probably no funds would have come to Chile initially. With this result, it is possible that policy would have changed to reduce this requirement. Even if it had been maintained, and the real exchange-rate guarantee had been present, an early international financial liberalization would have reduced the interest arbitrage profits for nonbanks; so nonbanks that followed a high-debt policy would have failed earlier, with no chance to gamble on the implicit real exchange-rate guarantee that subsidized capital inflows. In addition, an early international financial liberalization would have spread over time the expansion of the banking sector, reducing its maximum degree of overexpansion.

Fifth, consider the possibilities for moral hazard that an early international financial liberalization would have opened to Chilean banks regarding freedom to lend abroad since 1977. It would appear that an international financial liberalization always increases the magnitude of the moral hazard problem, since it allows the scope of moral hazard in the banking sector to be international, not just national. However, in the Chilean case the April 1980 international financial liberalization did not include authorization to lend abroad. The establishment of subsidiaries and branches was allowed only in 1980 and 1981, and that was still subject to case by case authorization. Therefore, it is hard to believe that much abuse could have taken place through this channel in the event of an early international financial liberalization.

Assuming that the timing of prudential supervision policy remained the same, in this case a delay in implementation until mid-1981, the relative magnitude of these conflicting effects suggests that an earlier international financial liberalization would have had a beneficial effect on the date at which the problem of moral hazard appeared in Chilean banking. In this regard, Harberger's (1985) conclusion that the April 1980 international financial liberalization should have been delayed indefinitely seems unwarranted.

On the other hand, if an early international financial liberalization had accelerated the onset of moral hazard, in the Chilean setting it also might have hastened the adoption of prudential regulation, since state prudential supervision was adopted in response to moral hazard problems (see de la Cuadra and Valdés-Prieto 1990). Experience shows that Chilean authorities abandoned their previous position regarding bank supervision only after the abuse at Banco Español became transparent in 1980. It is not unlikely that earlier abuses, associated with quicker liberalization and an earlier international financial liberalization, would have tilted earlier the balance of power within the government toward the "supervision school."

Now we turn to the alternative timing policy of delaying the April 1980 international financial liberalization. For this analysis, it is assumed that the opportunity for an early international financial liberalization was lost already, and that the other distortions identified in the Chilean economy are present. A late and an early international financial liberalization share the advantage of avoiding the reinforcement of the effects of the stabilization program and the international financial liberalization in appreciating the real exchange rate.

Still, the analysis is not a mirror image of the previous one. A later opening would have prevented the extra capital inflow that became feasible when domestic banks borrowed abroad in a period of extraordinary willingness to lend by foreigners. As a premium for international finance existed, nonbanks would not have taken more than a fraction of the supply of foreign credit to domestic banks. Regarding moral hazard in domestic banking, a delay in international financial liberalization would have weakened the capital base of domestic banks, because the profits from international arbitrage would not have reached domestic banks during 1980 and 1981. Finally, two advantages of a delayed international financial liberalization are that domestic banks would not have undertaken special expansion programs, and that the real exchange-rate guarantee would not have induced more foreign borrowing. The overall assessment is that a delayed international financial liberalization would have been better, in a second-best sense, than the actual timing in April 1980. However, an early international financial liberalization would have been even better.

The previous discussion is rather narrow because it restricts the range of admissible policies to a change in the timing of the international financial liberalization. We discuss now additional policies, with the restriction that the opportunity for an early international financial liberalization was lost already.

Obviously, a better emergency policy was to confront directly the deeper causes of Chile's dismal macroeconomic performance. From a macroeconomic standpoint, it would have been much better to complement a substantial delay in the international financial liberalization with strong quantitative limits on capital inflows intermediated by nonbanks. This second-best policy would have curbed capital inflows, so external debt could have grown less. In addition, it would have been desirable to dispense with the minimum term on capital inflows intermediated by non-banks, avoiding the implicit real exchange-rate guarantee.

From the point of view of the need to limit moral hazard by domestic banks, it would have been much better to replace a delay in the international financial liberalization with a quantitative ceiling on domestic bank credit. This would have limited the scope of moral hazard directly, regardless of the source of funds of banks, while prudential supervision became effective. A quantitative ceiling that covers external funds only is certainly inefficient in comparison. It should be noted that the proposed second-best regulations are strictly transitory, and more important, are tightly designed to confront specific distortions and problems.

In conclusion, the timing of the Chilean international financial liberalization in April 1980 and its accompanying policy could have been much better. Another point is that in Chile, the second-best restrictions did not fall in international financial operations by banks per se. That is, international financial repression was not part of the second-best policy, but only of third or fourth-best policies.

12.5 After devaluation: Depression and restrictions on capital mobility

This section provides an analysis of the period from June 1982 until mid-1985, which corresponds to the depression in Chile. The emphasis is on the closing of the international financial market for Chilean residents, and on the regulations that affected capital mobility and interest arbitrage.

Overview of major events

In June 14, 1982, the authorities decided to abandon the fixed exchange rate in view of massive unemployment and the abundant signs of deflation. Although domestic inflation had been below the international level since late 1981, the speed with which relative prices adjusted had proved to be extremely slow. The 18% maxidevaluation accompanied two other policy changes. First, the exchange rate would be pegged to a basket of foreign currencies, and not to the U.S. dollar alone. A constant devaluation rate of 10.2% with respect to the basket was announced for the next 12 months. Second, backward indexation by law of all wages was abandoned. Beginning June 14, both unions and firms were left free to bargain over the terms of any cost-of-living adjustment. The backward-looking aspect of the previous rule had contributed to increase the real wage substantially in September 1981 – just when the economy was sliding into recession, creating excessive unemployment.

The evolution of inflation showed that the authorities had been right in diagnosing a deflation. The 18% devaluation yielded a 1.8% rise in the CPI by July. Over a longer period, the nominal devaluation led to a large real devaluation (Corbo and Solimano 1991).

One of the arguments against devaluation, that it would provoke a run on the peso, also proved correct. The quarterly reserve loss experienced by the Central Bank increased from U.S.$258.6 million in the second quarter of 1982 to U.S.$643.6 million in the third. The devaluation triggered capital flight, as expectations of future devaluation came to cloud the financial horizon.

This induced exchange-rate policy to change again in August 5, 1982, when the authorities announced a move to a floating exchange rate. Chile had not had a freely floating exchange rate since the early 1920s. The announcement contained the costly promise of a Central Bank credit line to help those that had foreign currency debts outstanding. Perhaps this explains the 22.8% rise of the IPSA share price index in August 1982. This promise materialized in August 23, when the Central Bank announced the "preferential dollar," a foreign exchange guarantee arrangement. The implicit real exchange rate guarantee had become explicit at last. The Central Bank committed to pay the difference between the exchange rate that corresponded to August 6 according to the previous intervention rule, plus CPI variation, and the actual exchange rate in the official market. The subsidy benefited all debtors that had registered foreign debts, and debtors of domestic banks in U.S.$ index or U.S. dollars. It was badly targeted, as it helped all these debtors regardless of whether the real depreciation hurt or helped them in the long run. The authorities agreed to this subsidy because they had to face their responsibility, derived from their previous announcements that borrowing abroad didn't involve additional risks.

The peso depreciated drastically when it was left to float, due to rising uncertainty. Another factor was the Mexican default of August 1982, which darkened the prospects of attracting foreign funds to Chile. The rising price of foreign exchange brought about insolvency of a large number of debtors that had accepted the dollar-indexed funds lent by banks. This raised commercial risk generally – since it was not known who held how much foreign debt – and justified a prediction of deepening domestic recession, as many firms had to be reorganized. The risk of insolvency also threatened many domestic banks, who depended on highly leveraged borrowers that were unable to sell their output. In this setting, many banks decided not to attempt foreclosure, instead waiting for a general rescue package financed by the government.

This inaction, which continued up to late 1983, was a factor behind the −14.2% GDP decline in 1982. In any case GDP had started falling in the first half of 1982, when domestic demand plummeted. The preferential dollar guarantee proved insufficient to remedy the insolvency problem, as many projects and plans were ceasing to be viable given the fall in domestic demand, the very high real interest rate abroad, and the world recession, which effectively reduced many export prices.

The experiment with floating exchange rates lasted for only 54 days, as the peso depreciated 43% in that period, from $46 to $66 per dollar. The subsidy through the preferential foreign exchange rate had risen to 14 pesos per dollar, as the preferential exchange rate was pegged at $52 per dollar. In September 29, after a change of authorities, the Central Bank announced a new intervention rule that fixed the official exchange rate for the next six months. A fee of 2% was introduced for both sales and purchases of foreign currency to commercial banks, which enabled the exchange rate to fluctuate up to 4% within a band around the fixed value.

By the end of 1982, Finance Minister Lüders had established contact with the International Monetary Fund to seek a balance of payments loan. Although conversations were well advanced, the events after the intervention of the large domestic banks in January 1983 forced a redesign of the program.

The Central Bank lost U.S.$1 billion of reserves during the first quarter of 1983. The magnitude of this reserve loss, and the associated cut of international finance to Chilean borrowers, shows that inadequate management of the January 1983 intervention was a major factor in delaying recovery for a full year (which is analyzed below). GDP fell 0.3% in 1983. There was a larger fall in GDP in the first two quarters, balanced by a rise of 0.8% in the third quarter and 5.6% in the fourth quarter. The trade balance began to show a surplus, as imports fell 22% while exports grew by 4%.

When Finance Minister Cáceres replaced Lüders in February 1983, he started to put together a new debt-rescheduling package. The goal was to obtain a rescheduling agreement with the international banks.

The IMF was asked to lend first as a guarantee of proper macroeconomic management. The rescheduling was completed in July 1983. The total reserve loss for the year was U.S.$600 million, even after the inflow of U.S.$1.3 billion in IMF lending and U.S.$1.3 billion of "new money" agreed in the rescheduling.

The domestic real interest rate fell dramatically in 1983, after the January intervention. In part, this was the direct result of the recession, because it induced the scrapping of investment plans. On the other hand, the end of distress borrowing by some large debtors, especially the two largest business groups, also helped reduce the demand for credit. In this setting of high commercial risk, government debt became very attractive for investors. As the government came to be the main borrower, and as it controlled most of the banking sector after the January 1983 intervention, it acquired monopsony power over domestic interest rates. The government used this market power to reduce real interest rates. Several domestic debt rescheduling programs were used to distribute credit to special sectors, and also helped to reduce average interest rates.

As the rescheduling with the IMF and the banks turned out to be an insufficient arrangement, Minister Cáceres obtained a second rescheduling agreement in February 1984. This agreement provided a substantial amount of new money, and was instrumental in financing the 6.4% GDP recovery of 1984. Government officials confirm that at no time did the Chilean government try to devise an optimal strategy of direct default, since any gain in reduced debt service was believed to be offset by a resulting loss of confidence of the domestic private sector – which was the only sector that could embark on an efficient investment program for recovery. One of the conditions imposed by IMF before going ahead with the 1984 rescheduling was to begin scrapping the preferential dollar subsidy, which had created a serious budget problem. Another IMF condition was a special limit on the net external debt of public enterprises.

By early 1984 the domestic political consequences of the prolonged recession were taking their toll, with unemployment at 30%. Protests in the streets and increasing uneasiness among the middle class prompted President Pinochet to replace the minister of finance, Cáceres, with Escobar, who had campaigned for domestic expansion, and was able to use the funds obtained by Cáceres in the rescheduling. However, he pressed on with additional expansion of domestic credit, and by September 1984 he had induced a balance-of-payments crisis. Apparently he had financed part of the extra spending by going beyond the limits on public enterprise foreign borrowing agreed with the IMF.

This forced a maxidevaluation, at which time he raised the uniform tariff from 20% to 35%. Since the preferential exchange rate was not devalued simultaneously, the fiscal cost of that subsidy soared. In early 1985, Pinochet replaced Escobar with Büchi.

The January 1983 intervention

In January 1983 the authorities decided to take over five private banks and liquidate three others. The five banks included the two largest, controlled by the two largest business groups, which had expanded rapidly between 1975 and 1981. The intervention was triggered by the default of one of the major enterprises of the Cruzat–Larraín group. This default clearly showed this group had become illiquid and signaled creditors they could exercise the option of taking over the assets of the group.

Implementation was not easy, however, since the main creditor was Banco de Santiago, an affiliate of the same business group. Bankruptcy proceedings could be protracted, with preferential treatment among different types of lenders, since some affiliated companies would support their subsidiaries and others would not. Because the group was structured as a complicated network of holding companies, the opportunities for delay were innumerable. In this context, the government decided to take over Banco de Santiago and Banco de Chile, stopped renewing short-term credit, and cut credit lines to all affiliated companies, forcing them to confront their creditors simultaneously. Negotiations dragged on for two years. The Vial group (the second largest) was liquidated over several years.

After the Mexican crisis of August 1982, the willingness of foreign creditors to maintain their exposure to Chilean banks – several now intervened – had become questionable. That is why, just after the intervention, the government told foreign creditors of the intervened banks they would have to share the losses. This was an important policy error. The banking industry does not have clear-cut rules about how to manage an insolvency and subsequent loss distribution among creditors. This means governments usually guarantee all creditors, as U.S. experience demonstrated in the late 1980s. The government decided to guarantee local deposits in the intervened banks but did not want to do the same with foreign creditors. Many of the foreign creditors were international banks, so they could save part of their funds by not renewing short-term credit to the intervened banks. To avoid Chilean government retaliation against them, and to increase their leverage against the government, they also stopped renewing loans to solvent banks and companies resident in Chile. This "contagion" effect caused the largest quarterly reserve loss in Chilean history.

The policy error was to announce the placement of a part of the loss on creditors who could leave without either:

(a) offering a clear and well-defined loss allocation procedure that gave assurances of fair treatment, or

(b) following a well-coordinated default strategy. This implied freezing the repayment of *all* Chilean debt to the creditors of these banks to force them to accept some loss. This would have included short-term debt for international trade finance.

Even though the government had never planned to follow alternative (b), the reserve loss forced the Central Bank to decree a 90-day freeze on payment of foreign debts, effective February 1, 1983. The run out of Chile also led to the formation of a foreign bank cartel. The bigger money-center banks recognized that a substantial part of the loans were long-term and could not be recalled, so coordinated measures were needed. On the other hand, their dominant position in world markets gave them the clout to influence Chile's smaller creditors. At the cost of paying an excessive margin, Chile benefited from these coordination efforts, which in the end stopped the run.

The bank cartel was able to obtain better treatment than domestic creditors: In the case of the three liquidated banks, domestic creditors lost 20%, while foreign creditors lost nothing. In any case, this was not the result of a fair procedure that evaluated and distributed losses. The 20% loss was an arbitrary figure chosen by the government, who ordered the state bank to purchase deposits in those banks at 80% of par.

The cost to Chile of this huge rise in the premium for international finance should not be measured by reserve losses. First, there was a massive increase in the level of uncertainty within the country. Second, many export and import firms lost access to international credit that financed working capital, and were forced to paralyze operations until alternative credit arrangements could be put in place. The international liquidity crisis shown by Table 12.7 helps to explain the continuing fall in GDP during the first half of 1983.

This experience shows how fluctuations in the premium for international finance can be triggered by careless behavior of the authorities. The insolvency of local banks with foreign creditors seems to be a particularly sensitive area that merits continual attention.

Net capital flows to Chile probably would have become negative,

Table 12.7 *Voluntary capital inflows through the official market from June 1982 to 1984 (U.S.$ million)*

Period		Nonfinancial Private Sector				Domestic Banks	
		Article 14		Window		Article 14	
		Amount Disbursed US$ m.	Average Term months	Purchases by Chilean Bank	Total NFPL	Amount Disbursed US$ m.	Average Term months
1982	3	119.2	30	471.0	590.2	129.1	59
	4	109.0	32	571.4	680.4	40.5	56
1983	1	44.5	21	0.0	44.5	22.4	59
	2	3.4	51	0.0	3.4	34.3	26
	3	44.5	50	0.0	44.5	11.8	14
	4	59.0	43	0.0	59.0	24.8	32
1984	1	39.0	53	0.0	39.0	59.5	14
	2	17.1	52	0.0	17.1	37.7	18
	3	4.7	38	0.0	4.7	11.5	28
	4	56.1	42	0.0	56.1	1.8	56

Source : For Article 14 figures, *Boletin Mensual* , Central Bank of Chile. Window Purchases from Hachette (1989, table 1).

even without the January 1983 attempt to share losses with foreign creditors. The negative publicity of the Mexican and other Latin American country defaults, and the fact that Chile was highly indebted, with a 25% unemployment rate and a 14.1% fall in GDP for 1982, would have assured a large rise in the premium for international finance.

Lessons of the 1982–5 period

During the 1982–5 recession, a number of capital controls were adopted, as the government devalued, moved to floating exchange rates and then a formal crawling peg.[10] This period was characterized by explicit foreign exchange guarantees (swaps) and the development of a large black market premium for foreign exchange following the takeover of the main banks in 1983. By the end of 1983, the liberal approach to capital-account policy, which in July 1982 had guided the elimination of the minimum term to repay imports, was abandoned.

In early 1984 the preferential dollar arrangement was eliminated for exporters and public enterprises. This was long overdue; however, as import substituting industries continued to have access to the subsidy, exporters appealed to the Supreme Court on the grounds of arbitrary discrimination. The Central Bank was able to win a favorable outcome on a legal technicality. The total elimination of the tremendously expensive preferential dollar subsidy occurred only in 1985, when

Finance Minister Büchi took over and initiated a new approach to recovery from the debt crisis.

The experience of Chilean capital-account policy in the 1982–4 period is instructive, apart from the bank takeover episode, as it shows how liberally inclined authorities can be forced by the necessity of maintaining positive reserves to introduce more restrictions. Of course, capital-account policy during the Escobar period was not liberal but simply was used as a means to support further expansion of domestic demand. The main message of this period is that a government that wants to liberalize the capital account has to avoid all perceived and announced exchange-rate guarantees, and must be willing to use fiscal and monetary policy to avoid wide fluctuations in international reserves. In addition, it must be prepared to inform the private sector realistically about future prospects, helping it to achieve an efficient spending path. The failings in these respects of Chilean macroeconomic policy in 1979–82 account for the need to reregulate the capital account in 1982–4.

12.6   Concluding thoughts

This study has explored the complex nature of opening the capital account to domestic financial intermediaries when the latter have been undergoing a domestic financial liberalization. The rationale for a domestic financial liberalization appears at first blush to be the same as that for an international financial liberalization, so the pressures on the authorities to go ahead in the international side of financial reform are commonplace. However, the higher complexities increase the possibility of policy errors, as apparently simple measures may have unexpected side effects of telling macroeconomic importance.

The large social cost of some of the policies evaluated here is not surprising. Such is the case with the simplistic policy of expropriating foreign companies in 1971–3, and later the disregard of political relations with the governments of the main lending countries – which in 1975 left Chile without access to international finance just when the price of its chief export, copper, fell by half. This also occurred with the naive 1983 attempt to push an unspecified part of domestic bank losses onto foreign creditors.

The worrying episode for policymakers is the 1977–82 period. The complexity of dynamic interactions during the maturation process of the domestic financial liberalization, the lags in adopting a standard banking supervision policy, the stabilization attempt through fixing the exchange rate, and the response to the external shocks of excess risk taking by international banks and sharp rises in real interest rates, look truly daunting for any policymaker. The second-best analysis of counterfactuals suggests that an optimal policy is often elusive and depends on a fine reading of a dynamic situation. *That is why the overall 1974–84 Chilean experience at first glance may appear to support the view that the wisest policy is to delay financial liberalization in general, while avoiding opening the capital account to financial intermediaries in particular.*

The correct reading is different. Chile was very unlucky to undertake international financial liberalization in a period when unusual foreign shocks affected the economy. In addition, the dynamics induced by both the macroeconomic and banking policies were not understood as they are now. This may explain why a suboptimal timing for the international financial liberalization was chosen.

The knowledge that has been gleaned from the Chilean experience is that many policy measures were available that would have provided genuine relief. Most notable are a priority to improvements in domestic supervision, a moratorium in authorization of new banks and branches of foreign banks, the avoidance of an overlap with a period of disinflation, and in case of emergency, imposition of quantitative ceilings on assets and loans to domestic banks that do not exhibit spotless solvency. On the other hand, we find that a simplistic delay of the international financial liberalization would have helped little. Continuing repression of international intermediation per se was never second-best, at most fourth- or third-best. The Chilean experience after the period under study confirms this conclusion. Beginning in 1985, the domestic banking sector was devolved to private ownership, and most important, exhibited a remarkable recovery. Undoubtedly, part of that recovery was simple growth from depressed levels, and bank solvency was bound to recover with the associated increase in the financial health of domestic debtors. However, GDP growth did not stop after recovery, and the banking sector continued to develop its supply of financial services. Moreover, these services have increased in sophistication and coverage, while risk-assessment procedures have continued to improve steadily. The 1989–92 spurt in investment would not be feasible if Chile did not have a smoothly running and reasonably sophisticated capital market – which in turn assures risk-adjusted project evaluation and allows imaginative risk-sharing.

The recovery itself allowed an unusually large growth in GDP because of the high level of investment in 1977–81 – an important part of which was due to financial liberalization, which extended credit access to thousands of investors at all levels. In 1991 the Chilean banking sector began to take advantage of the first reductions in capital-account regulations after the crisis to start new business lines in international markets.

A more balanced view is that the current Chilean success is partially due to the previous failures in the financial industry, due to both domestic and international causes. A review of the history of banking in OECD countries shows an amazing sequence of collapses and financial scandals, many with macroeconomic consequences, of which Chile suffered a concentrated dose. Many authors have argued that it is the experience of previous financial collapses that prevents more frequent collapses. The Chilean experience confirms that incentives and institutional development matter. In private interviews with Chilean financial executives, most suggested they were able to handle the 1990 minirecession prudently mainly because of their vivid personal experience during the 1974–84 period. Financial contract design is critically dependent on the ways in which distress borrowing, rescheduling, and foreclosure are handled in the existing institutional setting. The implication for policymakers is that some degree of risk must be accepted when liberalizing financial markets, but that this risk can be minimized by paying attention to the incentives facing financial intermediaries.

Another facet of the current Chilean success is the decisive restructuring of financial sector linkages with large business groups. As explained earlier, part of the Chilean problems of 1977–82 was due to the purchase of the main banks by speculative business groups, which thereby grew to unprecedented size financed by self-loans from their domestic banks.

When the government took control of the failed banks and found itself confronted by the prospect of paying the financial cost of saving domestic bank creditors, it confronted a fundamental dilemma of development strategy: Should it use the newly gained control of the financial sector to influence resource allocation and force investment and growth, as South Korea did in 1950–85 (Chapter 8), or should it merely place domestic banks up for bid, as Chile did in 1975, and possibly encourage the growth of new large business groups? Finance Minister Büchi took a third route, namely to abide by the 1981 decision of the military to ban bank loans to affiliated firms, but also to promote a competitive, atomistic, and privately owned financial sector.

NOTES

1 Several types of barriers always exist to international trade in risk bearing and in specialized information on asset values, in addition to regulations, and thereby create a "premium" for *international* finance relative to the cost of domestic transactions. One source of this premium is the reduced ability to enforce cross-border contracts, in comparison to within-country contracts. The government of either country might restrict the actions of the local party and force it to renege on its contractual obligations. This is related to the "premium for external finance" discussed in Chapter 2. In that case the funds are "external" to the firms' managers; the premium arises because of limitations on contract enforcement (e.g., an independent court of justice is either not available or ineffective). It is usually assumed that in domestic transactions the government will not intrude into contractual disputes to favor one of the parties. The premium for international finance, on the other hand, reflects this type of risk because of its current importance among developing countries, and until the 1940s, in European countries; this risk should be distinguished from sovereign risk, which is the risk involved in lending to somebody not subject to, or in a position to escape from, court-enforced contracts. Note that some premium for international finance would undoubtedly remain given international differences and substantially weaker law enforcement for cross-border contractual agreements.

2 Sjaastad also suggests that as most of the foreign funds obtained by banks were long term (average of 61 months for 1980 disbursements), while their domestic loans were short term, this regulation artificially raised the cost of international arbitrage. This argument seems invalid for several reasons. First, interest-rate risk was not large, since over 90% of the debts were contracted at floating interest rates (LIBOR plus a spread). Interest rate losses could occur from a permanent reduction of the spread between LIBOR and Chilean domestic dollar-indexed loan rates – which was unlikely. Second, the Central Bank guaranteed it would take idle Article 14 funds from commercial banks if no borrower wanted dollar-indexed funds. This guarantee solved simultaneously the risks of a fall in the spread and the risk of excess liquidity (inability to place the funds). However, the minimum term regulation was damaging for other reasons.

3 This decree law also attempted to reduce the exceptional benefits afforded to firms engaging in international trade. The diversification rules on bank credit prohibited loans to each individual debtor above 5% of bank capital and reserves, but this limit was 25% if suitable guarantees were offered for the difference, and an extraordinary 50% in the case of international trade credit denominated in foreign currency. This reform reduced the 50% limit to 40% and eliminated the power of the Superintendent of Banks to raise it to 75% in individual cases of export financing. However, no prudential regulatory machinery to assess risk on cross-border loans was yet in place.

4 The Chilean authorities favored branches over subsidiaries to ensure assistance by the parent banks. That is why only three authorizations for subsidiaries were granted by the Superintendency in this period.

5 This confirmation is weak since the methodology used requires a hypothetical scenario to predict what the domestic interest rate would have been if all private capital flows were banned. Corbo and Solimano depart from Edwards and Khan (1985) by assuming that the money supply in the hypothetical scenario at the end of period t would have been the actual money at the end of period t minus the private capital

account balance during t. This assumes there is no sterilization of capital inflows, which is precisely what Central Banks like to do – and Chile's did – when the capital account is partially open.

A reduced emphasis on the importance of the April 1980 international financial liberalization is confirmed by the recent work of McNelis and Schmidt-Hebbel (1991). A drawback of most macro models is their assumption of instantaneous interest-rate arbitrage, such that the volume of capital inflows and external debt buildup are determined only by the financing needs of the current account. McNelis and Schmidt-Hebbel address this point by assuming slow adjustment in the money and credit markets. Using a Kalman-filter, varying-coefficient technique to account for international financial liberalization, they find that the coefficient of the foreign interest rate on the domestic interest rate rose only slightly, from 0.54 during the period with international financial repression (1977–9) to 0.56 during the liberalized period (1980–2).

6 The SIR is the average of monthly rates on very short-term interbank credit in Santiago. Using interbank rates excludes the varying risk premium charged to the average bank debtor. This is a desirable feature, because the risk premium charged to many large companies controlled by the failing business groups rose dramatically in late 1982. However, using the SIR as a basis for comparison imposes the cost of assuming a zero risk premium charged to Article 14 borrowers by foreigners over and above country risk. The benefits outweigh the costs in this case. It is natural to use dollar interest rates for foreign rates because the Chilean capital market historically has been far better integrated with that currency than with any other since the 1920s. The existence of future markets among major currencies assures us that this choice will not influence our results. The use of nominal interest rates permits escape from the biases inherent to the construction of appropriate price indices. In the case of foreign inflation, the problems caused by fluctuating exchange rates among major trading partners are substantial.

7 Of course, this will not be a long-run equilibrium, since the exchange rate will not remain fixed in the face of a 20% per year inflation differential, which existed in Chile in 1979 and 1980.

8 One reason for this policy change was that the military began to fear the power of the two largest business groups. The other reason was that by mid-1981 the authorities had completed a secret estimation of the consolidated balance sheet of these groups, and concluded they were solvent but highly leveraged by late 1980.

9 The supervisory problems associated with international expansion of domestic banks were confronted later through a legal reform. This reform allowed the Superintendency of Banks to presume that a loan to a foreign-owned corporation in Chile, or to a foreign corporation, was a loan to an affiliated party, unless the bank were able to prove otherwise. This was not an effective solution compared to international coordination of supervisory bodies. However, it seems a better short-run approach than delaying an international financial liberalization indefinitely.

10 See Valdés-Prieto (1992) for a detailed history of the restrictions on the capital account in 1982–5.

PART IV
SUMMARY

CHAPTER 13

Policy issues in reforming finance: Lessons and strategies

Gerard Caprio, Jr., Izak Atiyas, and James A. Hanson

Financial reforms – and doubts about them – are documented at least as far back as the Scottish free banking era of the eighteenth and nineteenth century, and it is likely that, in the wake of the banking crisis of 33 A.D., Romans debated putting a hitherto liberal banking system under government control.[1] Financial reform in the modern era is unusual at least in its frequency: Most industrialized countries have embarked on measures to liberalize finance in some manner in the last two decades, and a growing number of developing countries are moving along that course more recently. Even if university courses in development traditionally have attributed little role to finance in the development process, practitioners in the field as well as increasing numbers of academics seem to be convinced both that finance matters and that "market-oriented" financial systems can exert a positive influence on the economy, albeit with significant differences as to the proper or optimal role for market forces.

This study has considered the impact of financial reforms on both the real and financial sectors of selected countries. The cases examined here differ markedly in their economic, political, and institutional development, which, along with their meager number, raises problems in drawing lessons. Moreover, it is difficult to describe any of these efforts as complete. Reforming the financial system should be thought of as a process, not an event, both because most governments enact reforms in stages, and, in particular, because institutions take substantial time to adjust. Even in the case of New Zealand, where many liberalizing changes were introduced abruptly and virtually simultane-

It should be emphasized that the conclusions represent those of the authors of this chapter and are not necessarily shared by all of our colleagues who participated in the two research projects that are summarized in this volume.

413

ously in late 1984, it would be premature to consider reform as complete.

The study's conclusions about financial reforms also should be viewed with caution because these experiments – even in Malaysia and Chile, where reforms began in the early 1970s – are relatively recent. *New regulatory structures require at least a full business cycle, and preferably several, to permit a balanced assessment of the resiliency of the financial system in good times and bad.* Thus, the popular culprit in U.S. banking problems – moral hazard problems associated with deposit insurance – was present in the 1950s and 1960s, but serious problems, and a reconsideration of deposit insurance, did not develop until the 1980s. An important factor likely was the gradual erosion of the franchise value of bank licenses – reflecting regulatory and technical change as well as increased competition – which in turn led to greater voluntary and involuntary risk taking by banks.[2] The changes associated with low franchise value, which contributed to the problems in the United States and, as seen in Chile, in developing countries, take time to become evident because they involve alterations of bank incentive systems ("bank culture"). Thus, a degree of circumspection is called for in making claims of success for policy changes in this area.

In addition to these caveats, there are serious challenges to measuring the success of financial reform. The main tasks of finance are to mobilize resources and allocate them efficiently; as part of this process, intermediaries provide instruments that allow for the diversification and hedging of various risks, thereby permitting economic agents to concentrate on other productive activities and utilize financial resources efficiently. Regarding mobilization, as noted in Chapter 4, the present consensus is that the relationship between interest rates and aggregate saving may be only mildly positive, though higher rates tend to increase the share of saving intermediated by the financial system. Other aspects of reform – more branches, better service, more diversified savings vehicles – may contribute to a deepening of the financial system and thus might raise aggregate saving as well. However, without much more and better data covering several business cycles for a number of countries, it will be difficult to provide convincing evidence for this effect. Still, it is at least interesting that of the six countries covered in Part III, all but New Zealand have experienced their highest sustained rate of savings since the early 1970s (Figure 5.4), and in New Zealand there is at least a hint (Chapter 7) that savings in the postreform era is higher than it might otherwise be.

Savings in the financial sector increased in all the countries. The standard financial depth ratios (some measure of money relative to GDP) rose, in some cases considerably, and quasi-liquid liabilities, which can be thought of as a nontransactions component of broad money, expanded rapidly following reforms (Figure 5.2), except in New Zealand, where the innovation of electronic funds transfer directly to the point of sale led to a temporary shift toward narrow money within an overall financial deepening. Deepening typically coincided with a broadening of the menu of assets available to firms and individuals, as appears for example in Korea (Chapter 8), and is at least suggestive of a greater use of finance to hedge risks.

Assessing improvements in the efficiency of resource allocation also is problematic: The presumption is that an effective financial system will maximize efficiency by allocating credit to industries and firms where it can be best used. However, total factor productivity is subject to a myriad of influences, is difficult to measure economywide, and ideally a number of years – pre- and postreform – would be desirable to sort out its determinants. Moreover, in most countries financial reform has been carried out simultaneously with significant policy changes in other areas, in particular in foreign trade, which also are likely to increase aggregate efficiency; hence the impact of changes in financial policy are often difficult to isolate. As noted in Chapter 4, the standard measure of efficiency, the incremental output/capital ratio (IOCR), only gives a good indication of efficiency under the assumption that factors of production are used in fixed proportions. For those who accept these simplifications, gains in this measure of efficiency were seen in five of the seven cases examined in Chapter 4 from the prereform period to 1988–9. And in Malaysia, which, along with New Zealand did not experience efficiency gains over this period, the comparison is biased by including pre-1973 data; more recently there has been a recovery of the IOCR there.[3]

More tellingly, firm-level data in a few countries (Chapter 4) show an association between financial reforms and significant increases in the allocation of credit to efficient firms, even when the firms' efficiency is judged solely on the basis of prereform data.[4] In Ecuador, not only does average efficiency rise, but the dispersion of efficiency among firms declines by the end of the period. Whereas large firms there saw a relaxing of the extent to which investment decisions are constrained by financing, in Indonesia small and large firms enjoyed this benefit of reform, because these firms were more efficient than their medium-sized counterparts. Small firms are precisely those that might be expected to be discriminated against in formal directed-credit programs, even in programs designed to direct credit to this group.[5]

Although these results do not prove that financial reform improves allocational efficiency – after all, they are only for a few countries and cover a short period – they do represent the first microeconomic evidence of the positive real effects of financial reform, effects that have been assumed but never substantiated. In sum, these results, along with the cross-country studies of Gelb (1989) and King and Levine (1993), are the most promising evidence to date of efficiency gains from financial reform. Together, the findings should influence the way in which development economists think about finance.

The next section presents a summary of the lessons from the studies presented in this volume. The key points are as follows:

- The performance of the financial sector is inextricably linked to that of the real sector, in particular through the evolution of borrower net worth. Reform programs should be designed and modified to take account of these linkages.
- Initial conditions in finance – the portfolios of banks, their "information capital," their human capital, and their internal incentive systems – play a key role in determining the success of reform efforts, and implicitly offer a blueprint for the design of reform programs.
- These two points create a bias in favor of moving promptly on various aspects of institution building in finance and more gradually (but still steadily) on interest-rate deregulation and the removal of portfolio restrictions. Early bank recapitalization and restructuring, without paying attention to human capital and incentive systems, is dangerous.
- A variety of sequences of financial reforms have been tried; several countries even opened their capital accounts prior to or simultaneously with domestic financial reforms, with no obvious difference in success. Policy credibility may have been enhanced in economies with an open capital account, and attempts to bottle up capital flows may increase the riskiness of the domestic banking system. However, the sustainability of unconventional sequences in part results from special factors, including in Indonesia the absence of government debt and in Malaysia and New Zealand a high degree of central bank independence.

After these key lessons and others are elaborated in Section 13.1, the subsequent, strategy section then tries to apply these points to the reform process, offering a guide as to how to proceed and what sequences should be avoided, followed by some concluding thoughts on the reform process.

13.1 Some lessons

Real and financial sector linkages

The essence of finance is information and its imperfections. Mark Gertler and Andrew Rose (Chapter 2) emphasize the problems posed by limited information (or information asymmetries) and enforcement capabilities, relative to the case of a world of perfect information, where borrowers' and lenders' incentives can be easily aligned through contracts envisaging every possible contingency. In fact, in the absence of information and enforcement problems, financial intermediation would not be profitable, as borrowers and lenders could costlessly come together and sign – and enforce – contracts for any outcome. Given these imperfections, intermediaries focus on borrower net worth, with higher levels aligning borrower and lender incentives more closely. Borrowers have to pay a premium for external finance (that is, financing from sources outside the firm), one that rises as their net worth is lower. Gertler and Rose thus illustrate the close relationship between the real and financial sectors: simply put, finance is not likely to thrive when the real economy is performing poorly. Consequently the evolution of borrower net worth will play an important role in postreform developments. Shocks, such as adverse terms of trade shifts or higher real interest rates, that reduce borrower net worth will drive up the premium for external funds, reduce investment, and impact negatively on financial intermediaries. This linkage suggests that governments that attempt reforms during times of positive or neutral macroeconomic shocks will encounter greater success. However, it is not a prescription for inaction. *In order to benefit from good timing, the authors suggest that authorities move more aggressively on financial reform in good times and more slowly when borrower net worth is being reduced by negative shocks such as recessions* or *losses due to terms of trade.*

To the extent that financial reform entails an end to subsidized or negative real interest rates, reform itself induces a drop in the net worth of existing borrowers and the value of bank loans to them. This will reduce banks' willingness to lend to the existing clients. However, it should be noted that while ending interest-rate subsidies reduces the net worth of subsidized borrowers, it may improve that of other borrowers, who likely were paying high premiums to obtain unsubsidized credit in informal credit markets.[6] Thus an important additional issue, discussed in the next subsection, is the extent to which intermediaries can locate and finance these potential new clients in the short run. If the banks are unable to do this, then the net result of reform could be lower investment and more finance for government, as appears to have occurred in the early 1980s in Turkey (Chapter 6) and in Uruguay in its financial reform of the mid-1970s. The results of financial reform are likely to be much better when other shocks are at least expected to be neutral, or when the government has taken steps to offset negative shocks.

In the economies studied, financial reforms appear to have progressed most smoothly when attention was paid to borrower net worth (and bank portfolios) and shocks were positive. Zainal Aznam Yusof et al. discuss how financial liberalization in Malaysia, which began in the early 1970s and accelerated in 1978 with the freeing of interest rates, was halted and even reversed in 1983, as the economy was adjusting to the elimination of a large fiscal deficit (19% of GDP) brought on by an attempt to smooth out the effects of the global recession and higher oil prices. Highly visible reforms remained largely on hold through the 1985–6 collapse of commodity prices, giving the banking system time to deal with a large nonperforming loan problem. In particular, the recontrol of interest rates prevented banks in difficulties from bidding away funds from sounder banks, as occurred to some extent in Chile and the United States. Liberalization efforts were resumed in earnest in 1987 as the economy improved, with full deregulation of lending rates only in early 1991.

Korean authorities also appear to have paid great attention to borrower net worth and to the initial conditions of bank portfolios. As described by Sang-Woo Nam (Chapter 8), Korean authorities waited until well after the economy's adjustment to the 1979 oil price shock, a large devaluation in 1980, a beginning of trade liberalization, and a significant deceleration of inflation before attempting to eliminate preferential interest rates and to allow banks some discretion in setting interest rates on loans. By starting late and going slowly, Korean authorities were able to allow for the work out of preexisting nonperforming loans and to benefit from both a realistic set of relative prices and healthier corporate balance sheets. This process also involved direct government injections of funds into banks to cover losses.

Indonesia (Chapter 9) also undertook reforms in less favorable circumstances but with good results, according to John Chant and Mari Pangestu. The first phase of reforms, in 1983, came with oil prices near historic highs but clearly declining, budget and current account deficits growing, and protection actually increasing (up to 1985). However, initial financial reforms followed on the heels of a 46% devaluation, with more significant financial sector reforms coming in the late 1980s (after a second large devaluation). Importantly, banks had five years to adjust to the significant retreat of the government's role in allocating credit before new entry into banking was allowed, thus providing time for the banks to work out their bad portfolios before strong competition was introduced. Moreover, Indonesia for quite some time had an open capital account, and financial repression in the decade prior to reform was not severe. Thus it was unlikely that there would have been an information capital problem, as described in Chapter 3, and indeed the quite rapid rate of credit expansion there has been the antithesis of a credit crunch. So the lesson here is that macroeconomic conditions need not be ideal in order for financial sector reform to pay large dividends.

Turkey's experience with two interest-rate liberalization episodes also supports the Gertler–Rose hypothesis. During the first episode, Izak Atiyas and Hasan Ersel (Chapter 6) note that in the early 1980s, removal of controls on interest rates and an opening of entry was carried out in an environment of disinflation, and was accompanied by a significant deterioration of operating earnings in the corporate sector. The ensuing period of distress borrowing further weakened companies' balance-sheet positions and generated a fierce competition between weak banks to attract deposits to finance nonperforming loans, endangering the stability of the banking system and leading to a recontrol of interest rates and entry. By contrast, the rapid increase in interest rates following deregulation in 1988 did little damage to corporations, which, thanks to comfortable operating earnings, could rely on internally generated funds to reduce their demand for short-term borrowing.

In sum, macroeconomic circumstances may never be ideal; the role of borrower net worth is important in highlighting how real sector developments can impinge on the evolution of finance. When political factors permit, authorities should attempt to liberalize finance more aggressively in times of favorable macro conditions and *pay attention to other policies that can strengthen borrower net worth.*

Initial conditions in the financial sector

Gerard Caprio, Jr. (Chapter 3) complements the Gertler–Rose analysis, arguing that various aspects of the initial condition of the banking system are an important determinant of the impact of reform. Not only the net worth of banks, but their initial composition of assets and liabilities, their information set, or information capital, their endowment of human capital, and their internal incentive systems, all reflect the preexisting set of controls and will determine the banks' response to reforms. *Reforms that take account of these facets of banks are expected to fare better.* For example, financial reforms when banks have negative net worth – as arguably was the case with the U.S. S&Ls – are likely to lead to unwise risk-taking activities. Thus banks' net worth matters as well as the real sector's net worth. When banking skills are in short supply and bank incentive systems are geared for following government instructions on credit allocation, a sudden move to a laissez-faire system would most likely result in large losses. Similarly, when there are severe information asymmetries, banks' main source of information will arise from long-standing relationships with their clients. Destruction of this information capital, through devaluation, reduction in protection, or cutbacks in public investment spending, can lead the banking sector to retreat from lending and can thereby deter investment. This consideration does not imply that such changes should not be made, only that their impact on banks' willingness to lend should be taken into account.

The argument that postreform developments likely will depend greatly on initial conditions highlights the key role played by banks' portfolios and the stock of information capital. Not just aggregates of assets and liabilities, but the division between different categories of each can have an impact on the response of individual institutions and the entire financial system to reform. For example, in many countries – both among those covered in this volume and more widely, including the industrialized economies – problems with nonperforming loans in the real estate sector followed on the heels of attempts to deregulate finance. In addition to the possibility of interest rate mismatching, in some markets it has been argued that there was an inflation of property prices spurred by bank lending.[7] In certain cases it appears that, prior to the onset of financial reforms, real estate loans had been "crowded out" of banks' portfolios by other priority sectors, so that as intervention was lessened, banks began to adjust their portfolios in favor of this sector. However, a widespread portfolio reallocation by a sizable part of the financial sector always entails some dangers: It can lead to higher asset prices in the favored sector, and persuade bankers that their initial portfolio reshuffling was so profitable that they should invest even more in the growing sector, thereby contributing to real resource shifts that later may well be reversed.[8]

Malaysia appears to fit this case, with a dramatic rise in the real estate exposure of banks (from 12% to 36% of bank assets), and Indonesian data are suggestive as well. More generally, the point is that financial reform usually entails a portfolio shift, away from forced holding of government securities and directed credit. Allowing the shift to occur suddenly both can move in asset prices and may place great demands on banks not accustomed to new portfolio decisions. And banks rarely have the staff and management skilled in understanding and monitoring the risks associated with portfolio and credit decisions. The less the prereform control by banks over their assets, the greater will be the expected learning problems and the wider the likely swings in asset prices.[9]

Abrupt portfolio shifts might be prevented by some speed limits on portfolio diversification – that is, a gradual relaxing of forced lending and other portfolio controls – along with prudential oversight of the total portfolio. The great difficulty is in deciding on appropriate limits. Total lending *in real terms* by Indonesian banks rose at an average annual rate of 24% over the 1983–90 period, that is, doubling in real terms approximately every three years, a speed that would defy many supervisors' estimate of a safe rate for loan growth. Yet real investment has grown rapidly, and inflation has decelerated and remained in the single-digit range during the second half of the 1980s. However, some warning signs apparently led the authorities to raise capital requirements in 1991–3 in order to slow lending, and subsequently portfolio problems and the failure of a major bank have come to light. And in Malaysia, the rise of property loans in bank portfolios occurred steadily over the 1971–87 period, making it difficult to determine an excessive pace of diversification.[10] Outright regulatory limits on exposures to various sectors are both difficult to defend and can resemble in practice the highly interventionist approaches that many governments are abandoning because of their negative effects.

A less recognized and perhaps more crucial initial condition is the banks' stock of human and managerial capital at the time of reform. Reform programs should take account of the absence, in countries with prolonged financial repression, of incentives for banks to invest in credit assessment, monitoring skills, and risk analysis. Long-standing pay restraints in the financial sector will also contribute to a weakening of the skill base in this area. A history of severely repressed interest rates means that the market – in most cases, the banking system – has not been allocating credit; consequently, it is not surprising that the stock of human resources and internal controls in such a banking system will be far less than in one charged with the credit allocation task. In Malaysia banks were left in control of a large portion of their portfolios during the decade prior to reforms. However, Korean, Indonesian, New Zealand, and Turkish banks faced far greater intervention by government authorities in the prereform period. In Korea a well-developed nonbank financial sector helped mobilize and allocate resources, but part of the reason for the Korean government's direct involvement in the restructuring of private companies was the financial system's perceived deficiency of workout specialists (see Leipziger 1988). In Indonesia and New Zealand, banks were given time to improve their skill base before new entrants were allowed, and the reform process began with an already significant foreign presence. Malaysian banking remained relatively concentrated, with the 10 largest banks accounting for about three-fourths of bank assets over the last 20 years. In Turkey foreign banks remained insignificant in terms of market share after the reform. However, they played an important role in training a new generation of middle-level bank managers, who were subsequently employed in domestic banks.

More flexible attempts to deal with exposure questions through the supervisory process may be preferred, but it will be difficult for supervisors to halt a boom in individual sectors. In theory supervisors could even take the lead in requiring risk management systems in banks. However, supervision alone does not appear capable of preventing sizable losses in banking, judging from the experience of industrial countries.

Higher capital requirements – or risk-based capital requirements, which could be geared to rise with the exposure to individual sectors – are one effective mechanism for limiting exposure: the 8% risk-adjusted Basel ratio is just coming into force in most industrial and a few developing countries, but it is difficult to believe that this ratio is high enough, especially in less diversified economies, and there are some calling for higher ratios in the industrial world.[11] Some highly regarded international banks have operated with 10% to 12% capital ratios. These banks also consistently rank among the highest in terms of profit rates, suggesting that restoring some franchise value to bank licenses may be important, and indeed may be the quickest way to ensure that banks invest in upgrading their skills and management systems.[12] Bank supervisors, of course, can assist bank management in planning for various scenarios, such as reversals in commodity prices and swings in real estate prices; this focusing on the impact on bank portfolios of various shocks may prove sufficient to avoid unbalanced expansions. Finally, it must be realized that when more than one sector is booming, the policy problem is more in the domain of monetary and fiscal authorities.[13] The best supervisory authorities – and perhaps even the best bank managers – will have little success reining in risk-taking behavior if aggressively expansionary policies remain in effect for very long.

The supervisory system itself is another (often recognized) initial condition likely to be of great importance. In determining how much countries should invest in supervision, however, one is confronted immediately by the difficulty in measuring supervision, and even if measurement were possible, judgmental assessments of supervisory capacity suggest that countries with deep financial systems usually have better developed supervision *and* better developed bank management systems. Most observers agree that supervision is important: when bank losses are large enough, governments inevitably are held accountable and few are able to resist the pressure to bail out at least some deposits. Some supervision therefore accompanies this fiscal responsibility. Financial intermediary activities frequently have been subject to fraud, embezzlement, and mismanagement, and supervisors have an important role to play as allies of bank managers in strengthening internal controls and risk-assessment systems. The activities of financial intermediaries also are subject to significant externalities. In particular, financial distress in a small number of intermediaries is likely to be propagated to the rest of the financial system through, for example, increased competition for financial resources.

Improving bank supervision – importantly, shifting it from a passive check on compliance with government lending guidelines to a prudential review of banks' risk-management systems – should be thought of as part of "getting out of the dark."[14] *But bank supervision alone cannot be the first line of defense against unsafe and unsound practices; better regulation – creating or restoring a high franchise value for bank licenses, requiring high levels of bank capital, and encouraging liberal loan loss provisions – along with improved supervision, would help ensure that bank management had ample incentive to police itself.*[15] Bank supervisors then would be a backup or ally for bank management. Clearly, authorities have to be wary of excessive limitations to competition; the point is that as long as implicit or explicit deposit insurance is being provided, the basis for wide-open entry into banking will encourage risk taking with public funds, a dangerous combination. And if supervisory skills are in scarce supply, either raising capital requirements or creating a high franchise value will be especially important. Either action would limit competition, and the two actions differ only by the means of distributing bank licenses: the first by charging a high admission fee, hence favoring those already quite rich, and the second by giving licenses away with the promise of future profits. While the latter is more easily subject to abuse, at least ensuring that proposed owners have a substantial portion of the net worth at risk, in addition to banking skills and an impeccable reputation for honesty, should in principle be possible.

Liberalizing the capital account

This study throws into doubt the presumption, based on the experience of Latin American countries, that opening the capital account should necessarily be the last step in the liberalization process. James Hanson argues, in Chapter 11, that if capital liberalization will lead to currency appreciation, then it will produce this appreciation whenever the capital account is opened. Moreover, the same forces producing an appreciation will lead to greater availability of resources and may provide some credibility for government policies, so early opening cannot so easily be ruled out. Governments often argue that capital controls are needed in order to tax capital and financial assets (including the inflation tax). Put differently, an open capital account may force authorities to rely more on taxing income or consumption than on savings. Hanson notes that the de facto internationalization of capital may greatly circumscribe the ability to tax capital – such taxes mainly fall on those with less access to international markets. Viewed in that light, an important reason for an open capital account is to allow all citizens to reduce the burden of taxes on savings. Finally, Hanson's argument strongly emphasizes the need to put both the domestic fiscal accounts and the financial system in order before opening the capital account and allowing foreign financial intermediation. Otherwise, large capital outflows may develop and the government could then end up bailing out the weakened domestic financial system at a cost to the taxpayer, as discussed previously.

Salvador Valdés-Prieto notes, in Chapter 12, that opening the capital account itself cannot be blamed for the macroeconomic difficulties encountered by Chile in 1977–82, but that the culprit was a combination of several factors, some related to macroeconomic policies. A key factor appears to have been an implicit exchange guarantee, a notion to which the Chilean authorities at the time contributed by public statements. Recalling the aforementioned argument on realistic capital requirements, Valdés notes that banks with a foreign exchange mismatch were not required to hold higher capital or to add to provisions. Moreover, Valdés argues that an earlier opening up could have proved beneficial, both because it would have reduced the later shock to the system and because it would have increased bank profits. Thus authorities in other countries should not abstain from opening the capital account merely on the basis of the Chilean experience, which reflected a number of country-specific factors including a long prior history of prior repression, a peculiar exchange-rate–based stabilization program, and an ill-timed approach (rife with moral hazard) to opening the capital account.

Empirical evidence, cited by Hanson, suggests that de facto liberalization of capital accounts is growing, a move that will place pressure on authorities to liberalize their domestic financial systems. Governments in small economies in particular should be inclined to welcome such changes, as without them their domestic banking systems will be forced to hold an undiversified basket of domestic assets, and will as a consequence tend to be much more fragile than banking systems either in large economies or in those where the banks are permitted to invest abroad.

Liberalization fears

Popular perceptions of the impact of financial reform are heavily colored by the Southern Cone experience. As noted, however, the causes of difficulties there went beyond the financial sector, and experience outside this area is quite different. Dimitri Margaritis et al. (Chapter 7) recount that New Zealand authorities also suddenly reformed a highly protected economy all within a matter of months, removing tariffs, floating the exchange rate, and embarking on rapid financial sector reforms. When similarly rapid reform, albeit with a different exchange-rate policy, was attempted in Chile, unsustainable capital inflows and a real exchange rate appreciation, according to conventional wisdom, were argued to have unravelled the reform program. In particular, false signals were thought to have been sent by disequilibrium relative prices. However, part of the sharp (166%) rise in Chile's terms of trade over the 1973–82 period occurred in the wake of widespread political and economic change; over a shorter period (1977–82) the terms of trade rose by 26%, comparable to the 30% rise following reforms in New Zealand. While these shifts are large, huge swings are not a foregone conclusion; actual or incipient exchange-rate movements will depend on the efficacy of prereform controls (the greater their effectiveness, the more the expected diversification out of domestic assets following reforms, ceteris paribus) and on the combination of monetary and fiscal policies pursued at home and abroad. Officials in reforming economies should only respond by not putting policy, including that toward the capital account, on automatic pilot. The real appreciation of Chile's currency likely could have been limited by not providing an exchange guarantee, in effect a free option for investors. And New Zealand's terms-of-trade gain certainly was in part attributable to the shift in monetary policy toward fighting inflation since the mid to late 1980s. Tighter fiscal and easier monetary policy would have reduced the upward pressure on interest rates, thereby reducing capital inflows.

Another popular reason for avoiding financial reforms is fear of high real interest rates, again based on the Southern Cone experience. Yet elsewhere real interest rates were generally well behaved, as summarized in Chapter 5. The exception was Turkey, where real deposit rates were quite volatile and reached 20% in the early 1980s, subsequently fluctuating from slightly negative to modestly positive levels (up to 9%); lending rates are harder to determine but appear to have been quite high and variable across different types of borrowers, in part because of a large degree of macroeconomic uncertainty. Wide spreads between borrowing and lending rates can reflect a lack of competition and a large nonperforming-loan problem, but also follow directly from high reserve and portfolio requirements when required holdings earn little or no interest. These requirements were lowered significantly in Indonesia and Malaysia, whereas in Turkey the weak budget situation led to continued reliance on financial sector taxation. Especially in Malaysia, where bank competition was not very intense, the reduction of financial sector taxation likely helped banks to earn higher spreads, and for part of the period lending rates were restrained by the government's cost-plus guidelines.

Fears of a loss of monetary control also often inhibit developing country authorities from reforming financial markets. However, the evidence for New Zealand, Indonesia, and Malaysia is that monetary control was maintained, as is attested to by the favorable inflation performance of these countries. *It is important to note that all three countries at the commencement of reforms had highly capable central banks, suggesting that building up the research and implementation sides of central banks is a critical precondition for successful reform.* Indonesia also had a relatively favorable fiscal position, while central banks in Malaysia and New Zealand enjoyed an especially high degree of autonomy, and all three countries appear to have had a consensus for achieving and maintaining low inflation. With high but still imperfect substitutability among currencies, monetary control and capital account openness demands a reasonably agile response on the part of policymakers, and it is unlikely that control could have been maintained in a less disciplined fiscal environment. In Turkey, even though the Central Bank was institutionally capable, efforts to gain independence were often unsuccessful due to the government's authority to raise limits on Central Bank advances to the Treasury. In 1991, with increasing budget deficits and inflation, the Central Bank had to abandon the practice of designing annual monetary programs, which was initiated only a year earlier. Indeed, Turkey's progress in many aspects of financial reform has been less marked than in the other cases examined here, as highlighted by its limited progress in financial deepening, in part as a result of continued demands placed on financial institutions to absorb government paper. Reserve and liquidity requirements are back to 35% of deposits, a higher proportion than in any of the other countries in the sample.

Central banks also are in a position to help the reform process by stimulating the growth of markets and instruments, as elaborated by Meek (1991). This contribution to financial deepening is most noticeable in the cases of Indonesia and Malaysia, where money market development was vigorously pursued by the monetary authorities. Indonesian authorities developed Central Bank certificates and banker's acceptances in order to permit the withdrawal and injection of liquidity, and oversaw the deepening of money markets. With Malaysian money markets already relatively well established, the authorities in the 1980s concentrated on the development of a viable secondary market for government securities and mortgage paper, by changing operating procedures, and limiting the scope of "captive" markets for government debt, thereby moving to market pricing. Similarly, in Turkey the Central Bank played a major role in the establishment of interbank money and foreign exchange markets.

13.2 Toward a strategy for financial sector reform

Authorities interested in reforming finance first should think of what types of interventions in the financial sector are desirable for their societies, and then consider how to get from the current set of arrangements to the desired one. Perhaps the primary issue is the amount of subsidized, targeted credit. Arguments in favor of intervention never are in short supply. Various constituencies seek support for farmers, small and medium enterprises, exporters, and students, not to mentions specific commodities or activities, such as oil or coffee. For a policymaker, targeted credit is often the most convenient intervention and has a low political visibility since it usually does not require approval of the legislature. At the same time the evidence suggests that targeted credit has a number of costs. In the real economy, targeted credit usually worsens income distribution since it usually ends up going to the better-off; it is unlikely to increase output much, as it often substitutes for investors' own funds or leads to the recipient's intermediating the funds rather than investing them; and to the extent output increases this reflects an undesirable increase in the capital intensity of targeted activities.

Targeted credit also tends to weaken the financial sector. To the extent the subsidy comes from the financial sector through forced lending at below-market rates, rather than the treasury, depositors receive lower rates and nonfavored borrowers pay higher rates, reducing the financial sector's ability to mobilize and allocate resources. Moreover, targeted credit tends to weaken banks' incentives to assess credits, monitor them, and even to collect on debts (and for borrowers to repay them). The resultant weakening of the financial health of banks can lead to eventual large fiscal outlays when the losses have to be covered.

These problems argue for keeping targeted-credit schemes small, leaving them broad based, so that responsibility for credits remains with individual banks, and limiting as much as possible the subsidy element, not only to reduce the distortion of the cost of capital but also to remove any notion that directed credit is a grant. Establishing a sunset provision for the ending of the scheme would ensure that credit today is not being directed at old priorities, in effect forcing authorities to revisit the debate over which activities should be favored. And where subsidies are desired, they should be done directly from the budget. Malaysia comes closest to this type of intervention, of all the countries studied here, while among other countries postwar Japanese authorities also adhered to these guidelines (Japan Development Bank 1992). Korea most deviated from them, being saved, as Nam notes, by a large and lightly regulated nonbank financial sector.

If authorities are determined to reduce government intervention, the importance of information in finance (Chapters 2 and 3) has major implications for both goals and strategies, implying that correcting information and enforcement problems is highly important to financial and real sector development. *This means that vigorous attempts are needed to develop the accounting, auditing, and banking professions, as well as pursuing judicial and legal reforms that will facilitate the prompt enforcement of contracts and punish fraudulent activities.*

Because of the significant externalities, it is in precisely these areas that government intervention is "first-best" policy: Only governments can do this.

Sequencing of efforts in all of these areas is straightforward: They all take a considerable amount of time, and should be commenced upon as soon as possible in the reform process. Although some aspects of financial reform must await the achievement of macroeconomic stability and, where price controls are widespread, moves to market-determined prices, that is not the case with financial infrastructure. Institution building lacks the glamor of more visible aspects of reform, such as an immediate deregulation of interest rates, but there is a good deal of evidence – both from countries considered here and from others at various stages of development – that progress in these areas is essential for successful implementation of other reforms in the financial sector. Attempts to correct perceived shortcomings in financial markets, without developing these building blocks and without addressing their likely causes – high inflation, uncertain government policies, and severe information asymmetries – likely will prove self-defeating.

Institutional assessments

The need for and emphasis on institution building will depend to a great extent on the history of financial repression. If interest rates have been severely repressed, say below negative 5%, for a significant time, then experience indicates that banks will have underinvested in credit assessment and risk monitoring skills. But even without significant financial repression, governments should first "get out of the dark" about the condition of their financial sector, especially of their banks. *Simple financial audits often reveal little about banks.* Instead, as argued in Chapter 3, risk–asset reviews (RARs) are needed to assess borrowers' financial condition, collateral values, portfolio risks under various scenarios, and the adequacy of provisions, complemented by an inventory of the human capital in the banking system.[16] RARs help form an assessment of banks' ability to plan and to evaluate the risks they face, and can assist in changing their internal incentive systems; in effect, these reviews can be a form of technical assistance in training bank managers to think about and evaluate their business. In the limited cases in which RARs have been attempted, a typical finding is that internal systems are (often grossly) inadequate for an evaluation of the risk confronting banks, and the reviews have been instrumental in establishing such systems. Highly and even mildly repressed banking systems, also typified by low levels of bank capital, will sorely need precisely this type of assistance.

These measures should not be interpreted as merely technical; they require substantial political will. In most cases they will uncover significant problems with the financial health of major borrowers, and are likely to call into question the existing interventions in the financial system. These measures also are likely to indicate problems in the intermediaries, including possible decapitalization of the system, leading to calls for government action to remedy the state of the financial institutions.

Restore and recapitalize?

Ordinarily, at this stage in the reform process the government must decide either to restore the financial health of banks with negative net worth, place strict limits on their growth and permitted activities, or close them down. *In general,* restoration efforts are not likely to pay off and the banks should be closed or downsized unless there are well-run banks as merger candidates or other sources of managerial expertise, or unless the needed institution building, as mentioned, is well under way. This point must be modified where doing so would involve essentially closing down the entire financial system (see Box 13.1). Restoration – either through replacing bad loans with government bonds, merger with another institution, or a combination of the two – and recapitalization are recommended *only* when the resulting institution(s) will be less likely to make bad (nonperforming) loans than the predecessor(s).

Recapitalization will have to be paid for by the public (through higher taxes or lower government spending), if the government provides the capital; or by borrowers and depositors (through higher spreads), if banks are allowed to work out their own problems and new entry is limited (an approach followed in Turkey, Indonesia, and Malaysia). Fiscal arguments often are made that cleaning up banks is expensive, and will enlarge the budget deficit. But the replacement of bad loans with government bonds has no macroeconomic effect *given that the authorities have effective control over monetary policy.* The proper measure of the government's current deficit used to gauge the impact of fiscal policy on the economy does not change at all from the stock effect of the operation, although the cost of the interest payments will, indeed, have to be financed, and may be substantial.

Allowing banks to work their way out of a serious problem of nonperforming loans is politically attractive, since it requires no government resources and appears to be a more market-based solution. However, this approach also has some dangers. New investment and depositors have to pay a "tax" to cover existing losses, which may reduce growth. Moreover, decapitalized banks, especially if privately owned and not otherwise controlled by government, may well bid up deposit rates and invest in overly risky assets. This can create distress in some initially sound borrowers and lead to higher losses in the system eventually. Moreover, banks may conceal their problems by rolling over bad loans, leaving a time bomb that can go off in the future. Many of these problems occurred in Chile and in the U.S. S&L industry.

If banks are allowed to work out their problems, then, at a minimum, bankers should be separated from their bad loans so as to avoid the tendency to evergreen problem loans; well-managed banks perform this function themselves, creating separate units or subsidiaries to handle problem loans.[17] To establish incentives that will minimize future problems, bank managers and owners responsible for poor internal controls should face some consequences, at the very least, loss of jobs and capital. Wherever bad loans are placed, it is important for fiscal and incentive reasons that every effort be made to collect; collections are likely to be maximized when private agents – including if applicable the originating bank – are paid (handsomely) on a commission basis. *Given the dangers, strong, early intervention is probably the least risky – and lowest cost – solution to a nonperforming loan problem.*

Among the countries studied, Korea enjoyed a rapid growth of investment against the backdrop of banks saddled with large nonperforming loans in part because it had an exceptionally deep – and much less regulated – nonbank financial sector that was able to help finance investment, as well as booming macro conditions and an already high savings rate that facilitated an increasing degree of self- and equity-finance.[18] In addition, the government funded substantial restructuring of some of the indebted enterprises and, as noted earlier, injected funds directly into the banking system.

Malaysian, Indonesian, Turkish, and Chilean authorities permitted banks to work out their own problems, though often with strong guidance or limitations imposed by the authorities. Only a mild increase in bank spreads was required in Malaysia to cover a smaller nonperforming-loan problem, in conjunction with some interventions for problem banks. Indonesia controlled entry, which might have allowed banks to build up capital positions, but banks there until last year have focused more on loan growth, and there are signs that a nonperforming-loan problem is emerging. In Turkey, freeing of rates and a large fiscal deficit in the early 1980s led to a bidding up of real interest rates and some financial distress. Eventually, deposit rates were recontrolled and entry restricted.

The Chilean case was the least successful, at least in the early 1980s. Interest rates were freed in the mid-1970s and remained very high for most of the decade in real terms, in part reflecting risk of devaluation. When the debt crisis began in 1982, it became clear that banks had a substantial volume of nonperforming loans, in many cases to borrowers closely related to the bank's management, which had been hidden by rolling over the debt service. Confronted with this large nonperforming portfolio and massive private international borrowings, the authorities took over the banks, transferred bad loans to the central bank and then recapitalized the banks using Central Bank debt. The treasury and the new owners of the reprivatized banks were obligated to service the resulting debts with the Central Bank. In effect, this spread out the financing of the losses over time. However, the Central Bank remains with a quasi-fiscal deficit of some 3% of GDP as a result of these operations, which hinders its ability to make monetary policy.[19] Also, the Chilean financial system by the late 1980s showed many signs of health, including a well-developed funded pension system that has added depth to long-term markets.

Restructuring of the real sector

Restoration of banks' financial health unavoidably requires decisions about what to do with nonperforming loans. Whether these remain on banks' balance sheets or are transferred to a government agency, such as the Central Bank, serious efforts to collect the loans are desirable. Collection reduces costs of the financial sector restructuring and indicates to future borrowers that they should expect to repay their loans. This often implies that borrower companies will be liquidated, for example, through bankruptcy courts. Efficient cleaning of banks' balance sheets often also entails substantial reorganization of banks' claims over the corporate sector, provided that borrowers may regain profitability once they are restructured. In such cases, restructuring in the financial sector becomes the mirror image of that in the real sector. If extensive intervention by government to bail out of enterprises, or widespread and economically unjustified liquidations are to be avoided, the major claim holders of companies in the real sector, or their agents, the banks, will need to play an important role in the restructuring of the assets and liabilities of borrowers.[20]

Financing restructuring is a complicated and risky activity. It presents a case where informational and contractual problems of the type described in Chapters 2 and 3 are severe and requires banks to assume sufficient control rights to ensure that resources they advance are used to maximize their claims (or the value of the debtor company) rather than being unproductively consumed by managers or owners. Banks may be unwilling to assume such a role, either because of regulations that limit their ownership of nonfinancial institutions, or because they lack the managerial and technical expertise that would be necessary to monitor restructuring efforts in the real sector. Whenever restructuring needs in the real sector are widespread, reform of bankruptcy legislation (to introduce a reorganization procedure that provides banks with adequate control rights) or introduction of time-bound special legislation may be useful in allowing the banking sector to play a constructive role in real restructuring. Promotion of private institutions that provide turnaround skills also may help overcome a critical institutional barrier and speed up bank restructuring. These institutions provide specialized skills in financial engineering and have a deep understanding of problems in industry; hence, they are in a good position to design and obtain agreement on restructuring programs that are acceptable to both banks and the borrowers.[21] *As difficult as this process is, success in financial reform critically depends on and can be enhanced through appropriate policies that encourage and facilitate restructuring in the real sector.*

Next steps

Beyond the initial institution-building phase, and assuming that the banking system has positive net worth, attention should be switched to the institutional capacity to adapt to reforms and the expected near term evolution of borrower net worth. With respect to the former, where banks already appear to be able to allocate prudently the fraction of their assets over which they have had control, and where capital levels are high, more rapid rates of decline of requirements on portfolio composition and directed credit can be considered. But where banks have faced substantial reserve and liquidity requirements, it would be unwise, even where budget situations permit, to shrink abruptly or end these requirements until banks are prepared to deal with the ensuing portfolio decisions. The dangers of simultaneous portfolio adjustment (noted previously) can be minimized by a gradual reduction of the control of assets. Moves toward market financing of government debt may be constrained by budget realities. *However, even where these constraints are severe, it is important to begin the transition to market funding in order to maintain pressure to shift taxes away from the financial sector.*[22] Waiting instead for "free" budget resources may well delay reforms indefinitely.

Regarding borrower net worth, its influence on the behavior of financial institutions implies that the financial system's response to reforms as well as its future evolution is closely linked to the performance and credit worthiness of the real sector. As noted in Chapter 3, financial sector reforms usually occur concomitantly with real sector reforms, including prominently changes in trade and exchange rate regimes. Adjustment can be eased by direct interventions in support of borrower net worth, including the use of investment tax credits, or by amending other policies, such as the taxation of inflation-linked capital gains, which unwisely limit retained earnings. As noted, rather than use concerns about borrower net worth as an excuse to delay indefinitely financial reforms, authorities should examine measures that can help reduce the likelihood that firms' net worth will be suffering as reforms are instituted.

Other, more indirect measures that affect performance of the real sector also may improve borrower net worth and the outcome of financial sector reform. For example, fixed costs in acquiring information can justify subsidy of its collection and dissemination, such as by fostering the development of rating agencies and accounting standards. Such policies will benefit both the financial sector and the economy as a whole. Also, policies that help firms adjust – for example, to switch their sales from domestic to foreign markets – will minimize the destruction of firm-specific information capital and therefore can help avoid a postadjustment learning period for banks.

What to avoid

Interest-rate deregulation in general should proceed in stages, with complete deregulation awaiting later stages of reform. Both the cases examined here and experience in other countries suggest that the following criteria be satisfied before *complete* deregulation[23]:

- Macroeconomic conditions are reasonably stable.
- The financial condition of banks and their borrowers is sound.
- At least a minimal base of financial skills has been attained.
- Some checks are in place to limit collusive behavior among banks in the determination of interest rates.

When these conditions are not satisfied, interest rates may rise to exorbitant heights in real terms, threatening the net worth of borrowers and ultimately the soundness of the financial system, as was seen in Chile and, to a lesser extent, in Turkey in the early 1980s. Malaysia and Korea adhered most closely to these criteria, in fact both waiting until 1991 to achieve complete interest-rate deregulation (albeit in Malaysia's case this was the second time around). This recommendation is not without some cost: Continued government intervention in setting interest rates can easily be biased toward significantly negative real rates. Nonetheless, when these criteria are not satisfied, going to free market determination of interest rates has proven to be quite risky given an explicit or implicit government guarantee of deposits. Short of full deregulation, interest rates at least can be raised to within the neighborhood of inflation rates, a gradual and sustained easing of portfolio requirements and directed-credit programs can start, and the vital steps of institution building can commence.

Other steps and sequences also can be ruled out. For example, deregulating interest rates completely in a country just entering a recession, or with a large percentage of shaky banks can never be advocated. Nor would an open entry policy for banking ever be recommended, but especially not for a country with little or no bank supervisory capacity.[24] New entry can be dangerous if banks need to build up their capital; it may be especially dangerous if domestic banks have positive but low net worth, in particular if the new entrants are foreign banks who may be able to take some of the highly profitable banking business.[25] Nor is *suddenly* raising capital requirements desirable. Although it is an effective way in the long term to increase the safety of the banking system, in the short term it may lead to a cutback in credit growth, as has been intentionally accomplished recently in Indonesia. Therefore governments might ascertain that the schedule for attaining a target capital ratio is consistent with the macroeconomic environment: Too steep an increase can produce a recession, while an excessively slow increase can lead to a prolonged continuation of unsafe banking practices.

Last, governments should avoid regulations that serve to concentrate the risk in their financial sector institutions. Limiting banks to financing a single sector can easily produce problems when that sector turns down. Similarly, in small economies with specialization in a few commodities, banks limited to solely domestic investments surely will run into difficulties when commodity prices move unfavorably. Extremely high capital requirements – on the order of 50% to 100% – an end to restrictions on banks' global diversification, or reliance on foreign banks are the few options when a market is too small to support well-diversified institutions.[26]

13.3   Conclusions

Financial reform, in all of its diverse forms, is timely in many developing countries because of the widespread distress in the financial sector and because with funds scarce, authorities are rightly concerned about the mobilization and efficient allocation of resources. This study provides the first concrete microeconomic evidence, albeit from only a few countries, of efficiency gains following financial sector reforms, and illustrates how authorities in selected countries have gone about the reform process. The results of the study suggest a gradual – but sustained – process is preferred. Of course, political factors can present unique opportunities to point an economy rapidly and permanently toward a more market-based system, and these opportunities should be seized. Thus even though the approach in New Zealand may not have been ideal, many there argue that the economy is better off having instituted its "big bang" reforms. The lessons presented here, to paraphrase Vaclav Havel, are meant to give a sense of strategy for countries in which reform is not an all-or-none choice, and not to present a rigid or unique sequence for financial reform.

The case for gradual reforms is not one for inaction. Indeed, the conclusions of this study suggest that financial reform is worth the effort and that, with due attention to institutional environments, the lessons can be applied elsewhere. Authorities can do much to increase the market orientation of their financial system, with all its benefits, even without a big bang, and as it becomes increasingly easy to move funds across borders, they may have a more difficult time in stalling financial reforms. They can scale back interventions into the credit decisions of banks. As rapidly as the budget permits, they can rationalize interest rates – that is, eliminate the grossest interest subsidies and raise deposit rates at least to only slightly negative or modestly positive levels. In several countries examined here, authorities ended mild financial repression early in their reform efforts, while still retaining some controls. Of those that moved fastest to deregulate interest rates, New Zealand and Indonesia met most of the aforementioned conditions, with some uncertainty about the health of their banks at the point of deregulation. However, in both cases banks had a window of a few years before new entry was permitted, thus allowing them some time to adjust before competition intensified. In the language of the Foreword, caution regarding entry helped to limit the reduction in the franchise value of bank licenses, especially given the limitations on supervisory skills. Moreover, in both cases deregulation coincided with falling world interest rates.

In contrast, the reforms in the Southern Cone during the 1974–82 period, which are usually cited as reasons to avoid reform, took place in the context of a lengthy history of severe financial repression, numerous weak banks, macroeconomic instability resulting from exchange-rate–based stabilization programs, and a massive increase in the supply of external debt (compounded in Argentina by a large fiscal deficit), limited attention to improving bank regulation and supervision or to maintaining the franchise value of intermediaries and, toward the end of the period, sharply higher world interest rates. Unless one can count on good fortune, it seems wisest to move gradually and improve the fundamentals until the above conditions are met, particularly given most governments' explicit or implicit commitment to deposit insurance. Although this eclectic approach to financial reform may appear to be more difficult to manage than immediate and complete deregulation, it appears born out by the experience of the country cases presented here and the theoretical approaches of Part I. Financial reform, as judged from these experiences, calls for more nuance than simply "letting the market work." But in many countries the direction of change is clear, in favor of greater, rather than lesser, reliance on the market to allocate credit. This study suggests that focusing on this goal, and on concentrating on developing the enabling environment for finance, will offer a far higher return than has been experienced with more direct forms of intervention in financial markets.

Box 13.1 Financial reform in transitional socialist economies

Some of the lessons and the strategy advocated here seem irrelevant for transitional socialist economies (TSEs), which have in effect no financial sector – at least by Western standards – nor many skilled in various aspects of central or commercial banking, insurance, securities issuance, and other financial sector activities. And it certainly is true that building a financial system from scratch is different than reforming an existing one once a certain level of development has been attained. But the focus on institution building as the heart of financial reform is quite relevant. TSEs, endowed with a relatively well-educated labor force, require technical assistance on an unprecedented scale in all aspects of finance, including in most cases the establishment of a payments system. Immediate deregulation of interest rates, however, is fraught with danger.

With no supervisory capacity, which will take years to develop, and with former financial wealth in many instances reduced by inflation, TSE authorities will need to create pools of capital and ensure that banks are conservatively managed, so as to minimize the future cost of a bank bailout. Both goals likely can be met by licensing only a few banks, thereby creating a high franchise value for bank licenses. The cost of this policy is that it will necessitate high spreads for banks. This is actually a benefit, however, because although greater competition might limit spreads, in a high-risk environment, which surely will characterize most TSEs for years to come, banks need large spreads to balance the possibility of large future losses. As supervisory capacity grows and the economic environment stabilizes, greater competition can be allowed, but it would be wise to keep capital requirements high, thus encouraging more self- and equity-finance, both inherently better tools for aligning incentives.

One point that deserves some modification concerns foreign banks. Their entry might be destabilizing in countries where the banks are fragile. However, with so little expertise in banking, and in many cases with banks already confronting substantially negative net worth, TSEs have little to lose and much to gain from foreign banks. To the extent that authorities want to encourage the development of domestic banks and other financial intermediaries, they should not give away licenses to just any foreign bank but instead grant licenses to institutions willing to commit resources for the training of local staff, including those working at domestic institutions. As noted earlier in this volume, Turkish and Indonesian banks in particular have benefited from the presence of foreign financial institutions.

Another point that needs modification concerns the recommendation in the text to shut down "bust banks" when there are no merger candidates or other sources of managerial expertise. Even though other institutions would eventually emerge, it would be unwise to shut down an entire banking system. Old state enterprises need restructuring or closing and new private firms will need financing. Instead, an attempt could be made to carve out the few clearly good assets and staff trained in Western banking methods and to privatize the resulting institution. Other new private banks could be licensed, using local residents alone where there is sufficient experience, or as a joint venture bank with foreign institutions. And foreign branches or subsidiaries should be encouraged. But the great danger in reforming TSEs is that the demands for credit from all quarters will overwhelm the monetary authorities and lead to pressures to license many new banks and to allow banks to leverage themselves highly. In addition to the short-run monetary-control issue, there is a longer-term risk that new institutions growing at an excessive pace will produce substantial loan losses, creating a future fiscal problem. Limiting bank licenses and requiring banks to hold high levels of capital are the main hopes of preventing this scenario from becoming reality.

NOTES

1 See Calomiris (1989) for a description of this "classic" example of a banking panic.
2 See Caprio and Summers (1993) for an elaboration.
3 In New Zealand the slight decline of the IOCR may reflect in part the lower output path associated with disinflationary macroeconomic policy and may therefore be temporary. At the same time, all of these comparisons are over relatively short time horizons, and therefore at least in part may represent cyclical forces. And as noted in Chapter 4, there are significant problems in estimates of the real capital stock, so for example the different data series for Ecuador show different swings of the IOCR.
4 This methodology thus allows for the possibility that firms could become more efficient by greater access to credit. Note that efficiency gains following reform are expected to be larger the greater the government's prereform involvement in credit-allocation decisions – especially, the greater the government's role in allocating credit at the firm level, as this activity is (wide) open to rent seeking.
5 In Korea investment by small and medium-sized firms became less constrained, and that by large firms more constrained, following the reforms of the 1980s. However, although reliance on directed credit decreased, and real interest rates became modestly positive, this change also reflects a shift in directed credit away from large firms.
6 A real interest-rate increase from slightly to very high levels likely means that funds

are flowing to exceptionally high-risk borrowers alone – that is, it effectively reduces the net worth of all creditworthy borrowers.

7 By interest-rate mismatch is meant the phenomenon whereby banks fund long-term fixed rate loans with shorter-term deposits.

8 This story applies to the diversification of U.S. banks into developing country debt, to the rise in oil lending by Texas banks and S&Ls, and to the boom in property lending in the United States, Japan, the United Kingdom, Scandinavia, and other industrialized nations. While the role of regulation and interferences with credit allocation was different, in each of these cases the simultaneous shift of bank portfolios appears to have contributed to a temporary move in asset prices, the reversal of which led to an impairment of bank portfolios.

9 True, reform may be more urgent in a more controlled environment. The point is that highly controlled banks will likely have portfolios and staff poorly suited to a completely deregulated setting. Section 13.3 elaborates more specifically on strategy for financial reform.

10 However, in some years property-related lending reached 50% of the flow of new credit, a proportion that most bankers and supervisors would deem excessive (see Chapter 10).

11 Note that in the United States and Germany in the nineteenth century, capital/asset ratios of 25% or higher were common. Governments were more likely to let depositors lose their funds, and so the banks reacted by holding more capital.

12 A few international banks have in effect created their own franchise value by establishing their reputations, to the point that firms are identified as top performers by an association with these banks. Reforming and economies can artificially create franchise value by not licensing an excessive number of banks.

13 In this regard, Indonesia's achievement of low inflation despite rapid credit growth, and the evidence of increased efficiency (Chapter 4), should give pause to any critics of their expansion.

14 Villanueva and Mirakhor (1990) argue that an adequate supervisory system is a requirement for successful financial reform, but they do not provide a description or measurement of such a system.

15 Sheng (1993) and Caprio and Summers (1993) both argue that while bank supervision in developing and industrialized countries has performed an important function, more attention needs to be devoted to the incentive environment in which banks function. Caprio and Summers also cast doubt on the ability of depositors to monitor banks effectively, citing studies showing that the stock market generally does not anticipate bank failures, and that even insiders – that is, bank managers themselves – apparently fail to anticipate them, as evidenced by their stock purchases immediately prior to the downgrading of their bank. If the market and even insiders cannot clearly anticipate bank failure, depositors – and perhaps even supervisors – will have difficulties in performing this role.

16 See McNaughton (1993) for a description of risk–asset reviews. Although courses on banking, accounting, and finance can help, courses alone are not as likely to capture the attention of senior bank managers as well as the glaring inadequacy of their own internal controls. In effect, a banker's own institution offers the best case study possible.

17 Evergreening consists of granting new loans to facilitate the repayment of past debts. Note that if banks are actively working with their clients in restructuring or rehabilitating firms, some new lending may be necessary. In many cases, however,

new loans are made only to disguise bank losses and do not include any significant attempt to improve the viability of enterprises. Japanese banks are cited (Hoshi, Kashyap, and Scharfstein, 1989) for continuing to lend to distressed firms but at the same time taking an active ownership role in restructuring. Banks in systems that prevent equity links may not be able to assume such a role, in effect facing a greater agency problem, and thus must choose between recognizing losses abruptly or lending more and hoping that the client performs.

18 The proportion of investment in Korean industries funded by self- and equity-finance rose fairly steadily from 28% during the 1980–2 period to about 60% in 1988–9.

19 It should be noted that once the losses reached a large size – about 60% of GDP – then even a slow rate of growth of the losses (say 5%) would have matched the interest cost associated with the transferral of bad loans. In other words, had the authorities not intervened, the eventual "bill" in all likelihood would have been much larger. So the only criticism of the Chilean effort was that the authorities waited until the losses were so large.

20 Main banks in Japan often play such a role. See Aoki (1990).

21 On the role of turnaround entities in financial and industrial restructuring, see Atiyas, Dutz, and Frischtak with Hadjimichael (1992).

22 Occasionally it is mentioned that in much of the postwar period up to the late 1970s, Japanese authorities relied on captive financing of government debt, implying that the same reliance should be possible for developing countries. However, this argument overlooks the point that Japan ran budget surpluses until 1965, and that deficits remained tiny until after the 1973–4 oil shock. When the tax imposed on the banks by forced holdings of government paper grew large, the banks' rebellion in 1979 was an important factor in beginning the financial reform process.

23 See Caprio and Levine (1994) and Caprio and Honohan (1991) for an elaboration on these criteria for, respectively, transitional socialist economies and developing economies.

24 Entry into banking should require adequate capital, evidence of some banking expertise, and a sound reputation, as noted earlier. Open entry is meant to denote ignoring either all three requirements or even just the latter two. Where bank supervision is limited, authorities might focus on building a core of profitable banks, effectively licensing only a small number, which will be easier to supervise.

25 An exception might be if the banking industry were to be turned over to well-known foreign banks (Uruguay has followed something like this approach; there is only one domestic commercial bank and one domestic housing bank, both public, although these banks are by far the largest in their respective markets). In this case these banks typically would guarantee the deposits themselves; the bad publicity to such a bank from bankruptcy in a small market would outweigh the costs of providing the necessary additional capital. Of course, the authorities have to ensure that the entrants are in fact such banks, and must be able to cope with a number of political negatives in turning over the country's banking industry to foreigners.

26 In the nineteenth century, many U.S. and German banks held capital equal to 25% to 35% of their assets, at times even higher. It is difficult to believe that these economies were any more risky than many small developing economies are today.

Bibliography

Ada, Z. 1991. Interest policy and its impact on Turkish banking system. Mimeo, State Planning Organization, Ankara. (In Turkish.)

Adhikary, Ganesh P. 1985. *Deregulation in the Financial System of the SEACEN Countries*. Kuala Lumpur, Malaysia: The SEACEN Centre.

Ahmed, Sadiq, and Basant K. Kapur. 1990. How Indonesia's monetary policy affects key variables. Policy, Research, and External Affairs Working Papers, WPS 349, World Bank.

Aigner, D., C. Lovell, and P. Schmidt. 1977. Formulation and estimation of stochastic frontier production function models. *Journal of Econometrics* 6:21–37.

Akkurt, A., D. Hakioglu, A. Karayalcin, N. Koc, C. Ozcet, A. Senel, N. Usta, and D. Varol. 1991. Developments in the Turkish banking sector: 1980–1990. Mimeo, Central Bank of the Republic of Turkey.

Akyuz, Y. 1984. *Financial Structure and the Relations in the Turkish Economy*. Istanbul: Industrial Development Bank of Turkey Publications.

——— 1990. Financial system and policies in the 1980s. In T. Aricanli and D. Rodrik, eds., *The Political Economy in the 1980s*. London: Macmillan.

Alkan, A. 1990. Auctions for Treasury's domestic borrowing. Mimeo, research report prepared for the Central Bank of the Republic of Turkey. (In Turkish.)

Amsden, Alice H., and Yoon-Dae Euh. 1990. South Korea's financial reform: What are the lessons? Paper prepared for the UNCTAD Secretariat, March.

Aoki, Masahiro. 1990. Toward an economic model of the Japanese firm. *Journal of Economic Literature* 28 (March): 1–27.

Atiyas, Izak. 1990. The private sector's response to financial liberalization in Turkey: 1980–82. In T. Aricanli and D. Rodrik, eds., *The Political Economy of Turkey: Debt, Adjustment, and Sustainability*. London: Macmillan.

——— 1992. Financial reform and investment behavior in Korea: Evidence from panel data. Mimeo, World Bank.

Atiyas, Izak, Mark Dutz, and Claudio Frischtak, with Bita Hadjimichael. 1992. Fundamental Issues and policy approaches in industrial restructuring. Industry and Energy Department Working Paper, Industries Series Paper No. 56. World Bank.

441

Atiyas, Izak, and H. Ersel. 1992. Customer patterns and credit rationing in Turkish banks. Research Department, Central Bank of the Republic of Turkey.

Atje, R., and B. Jovanovic. 1992. Stock markets and development. Mimeo.

Balino, Tomas J. T., and V. Sundararajan. 1986. Financial reform in Indonesia. In H. S. Cheng, ed., *Financial Policy and Reform in Pacific Basin Countries*. Lexington, Mass.: Lexington Books.

Banerjee, Abhijit, and Andrew Newman. 1991. Occupational choice and the process of development. Mimeo, Princeton University.

Bank Negara Malaysia. *Annual Reports, Quarterly Bulletins,* and *Monthly Statistical Bulletins,* various issues.

1989. *Money and Banking in Malaysia*, 3rd ed.

Survey of Private Investment in Malaysia, various issues.

Bardón, A., and F. Bacigalupo. 1980. Algunas Notas sobre el Proceso de Apertura en Chile. *Boletin Mensual Banco Central* 53 no. 631 (September):1703–31.

Barry, P. 1991. Role of domestic saving. New Zealand Treasury Paper.

Bayazitoglu, Y., H. Ersel, and E. Ozturk. 1991. Financial market reforms in Turkey between 1980–1990. Mimeo, Central Bank of the Republic of Turkey.

Behrman, J. 1976. *Foreign Trade Regimes and Economic Development: Chile.* National Bureau of Economic Research. New York: Columbia University Press.

Bencivenga, Valerie, and Bruce Smith. 1991. Financial intermediation and endogenous growth. *Review of Economic Studies.*

Bernanke, Ben. 1983. Nonmonetary effects of the financial crisis in the propagation of the Great Depression. *American Economic Review* 73, no. 3 (June):257–76.

Bernanke, Ben, and Mark Gertler. 1987. Banking and macroeconomic activity. In William Barnett and Kenneth Singleton, eds., *New Approaches to Monetary Economics*. Cambridge: Cambridge University Press.

1989. Agency costs, net worth, and business cycles. *American Economic Review* 79 (March):14–31.

1990. Financial fragility and economic performance. *Quarterly Journal of Economics.*

Blejer, Mario, and Silvia Sagari. 1987. The structure of the banking sector and the sequence of financial liberalization. In Michael Conolly and Claudio Gonzalez Vega, eds., *Economic Reform and Stabilization in Latin America*. New York: Praeger.

1988. Sequencing the liberalization of financial markets. *Finance and Development* 25:18–21.

Blundell-Wignall, A., F. Browne, and P. Manasse. 1990. Monetary policy in the wake of financial liberalization. Department of Economics and Statistics, OECD Working Papers No. 77.

Blyth, C. 1987. The economists' perspective of economic liberalization. In A. Bollard and R. Buckle, eds., *Economic Liberalization in New Zealand*. Wellington: Allen and Unwin.

Bollard, A., and R. Buckle. 1987. *Economic Liberalization in New Zealand*. Wellington: Allen and Unwin.

Borts, George, and Jerome Stein. 1964. *Economic Growth in a Free Market*. New York: Columbia University.

Brock, Philip L., ed. 1992. *If Texas Were Chile*. San Francisco: ICS Press.

Bryant, Ralph. 1987. *International Financial Intermediation*. Washington, D.C.: Brookings Institution.

Buckle R. 1987. Sequencing and the role of the foreign exchange market. In A. Bollard and R. Buckle, eds., *Economic Liberalization in New Zealand*. Wellington: Allen and Unwin.

Buffie, E. F. 1984. Financial repression, the new structuralist, and stabilization policy in semi-industrialized economics. *Journal of Development Economics* 14 (April):305–22.

Calomiris, Charles W. 1989. The purpose and optimal structure of deposit insurance: Lessons from the historical record. Mimeo, Department of Economics, Northwestern University, March.

1992. Regulation, industrial structure, and instability in U.S. banking: An historical perspective. In Michael Klausner and Lawrence J. White, eds., *Structural Change in Banking*. Homewood, Ill.: Irwin.

Calomiris, Charles W., and R. G. Hubbard. 1990. Firm heterogeneity, internal finance, and "Credit rationing." *Economic Journal* 100:90–104.

Calomiris, Charles W., and Charles Kahn. 1991. The role of demandable debt in structuring optimal banking arrangements. *American Economic Review* 81 (June):497–513.

Calvo, G. 1988. Servicing the public debt: The role of expectations. *American Economic Review,* **78:**647–61.

Campbell, J. Y., and N. G. Mankiw. 1991. The response of consumption to income: A cross-country investigation. *European Economic Review* 35:723–67.

Caplin, A., and J. Leahy. 1991. State-dependent pricing and the dynamics of money and output. *Quarterly Journal of Economics:*793–8.

Caprio, Gerard. 1992. Policy uncertainty, information asymmetries and financial intermediation. WPS 853, World Bank.

Caprio, Gerard, Izak Atiyas, and James A. Hanson. 1990. Research proposal: The impact of financial reform. Financial Policy and Systems Division, Country Economics Department, World Bank.

Caprio, Gerard, and Patrick Honohan. 1991/1993. Excess liquidity and monetary overhangs. Policy, Research, and External Affairs Working Paper, WPS 796, World Bank, 1991. Reprinted in *World Development* 21, no. 4 (1993):523–33.

Caprio, Jr., Gerard, and Ross Levine. 1994. *Reforming finance in transitional socialist economies. World Bank Research Observer,* 9, no. 1 (January):1–24.

Caprio, Gerard, and Lawrence H. Summers. 1993. Finance and its reform: Beyond laissez-faire. World Bank Working Paper. (Forthcoming in *Financing Prosperity into the 21st Century*. New York: Macmillan.)

Chant, John. 1987. *Regulation of financial institutions – a functional analysis*. Technical Report 45, Bank of Canada, 87 pp.

1992. The new theory of financial intermediation. In K. Dowd and M. K. Lewis. *Recent Developments in Monetary Economics*. New York: Macmillan.

Chant, John F., and Mari Pangestu. 1987. The analysis of efficiency of Indonesian banking. Mimeo, Department of Economics, Simon Fraser University.

Chari, V. V. 1989. Banking without deposit insurance or bank panics: Lessons from a model of the U.S. national banking system. *Federal Reserve Bank of Minneapolis Quarterly Review* (Summer):3–19.

Cheng, Hang-Sheng. 1986. *Financial Policy and Reform in Pacific Basin Countries.* Lexington, Mass.: Lexington Books.

Cho, Yoon-Je. 1986. Inefficiencies from financial liberalization in the absence of well-functioning equity markets. *Journal of Money, Credit, and Banking* 18 (May):191–9.

1988. The effect of financial liberalization on the efficiency of credit allocation. *Journal of Development Economics* 29:101–110.

Cho, Yoon-Je, and David C. Cole. 1992. The role of the financial sector in Korea's structural adjustment. In V. Corbo and S. Suh, eds., *Structural Adjustment in a Newly Industrialized Country: Lessons from Korea.* Baltimore: Johns Hopkins University Press.

Cho, Yoon-Je, and Deena Khatkhate. 1989. Lessons of financial liberalization in Asia: A comparative study. World Bank Discussion Papers, No. 50.

Christian, J., and Pagoulatos, E. 1973. Domestic financial markets in developing economics: An econometric analysis. *Kyklos* 26, no. 1:91–6.

Cole, David C., and Ross H. McLeod. 1991. *Cases on Financial Policy and Banking Deregulation in Indonesia.* Yogyakarta: Gadjah Mada University Press.

Cole, David C., and Betty F. Slade. 1990a. Development of money markets in Indonesia. Mimeo, Harvard Institute for International Development.

1990b. Financial development in Indonesia. Mimeo, Harvard Institute for International Development.

Cooley, T. F., and B. D. Smith. 1991. Financial markets, specialization and learning by doing. Mimeo.

Corbo, Vittorio, and Jaime de Melo, eds. 1985. Liberalization with stabilization in the Southern Cone of Latin America. *World Development* (August).

Corbo, Vittorio, Jaime de Melo, and James Tybout. 1986. What went wrong with recent reforms in the Southern Cone. *Economic Development and Cultural Change* (April):607–40.

Corbo, Vittorio, and Sang-Woo Nam. 1992. The recent macroeconomic evolution of the Republic of Korea: An overview. In V. Corbo and S. Suh, eds., *Structural Adjustment in a Newly Industrialized Country: Lessons from Korea.* Baltimore: Johns Hopkins University Press.

Corbo, Vittorio, and A. Solimano. 1991. Chile's experience with stabilization, revisited. Policy, Research, and External Affairs Working Papers, WPS 579, World Bank, January.

Cruse, P. F. J. 1990. Monetary aggregates on targets for monetary policy. Reserve Bank of New Zealand Working Paper W90/1.

Dammon R. M., and L. W. Senbet. 1988. The effect of taxes and depreciation on corporate investment and financial leverage. *Journal of Finance* (June):357–73.

De Gregorio, J. 1992. Liquidity constraints, human capital accumulation and growth. Mimeo, International Monetary Fund.

de Juan, Aristobulo. 1987. From good bankers to bad bankers: Ineffective supervision and management deterioration as major elements in banking crises. Financial Policy and Systems Division, World Bank.

1988. Does bank insolvency matter and what to do about it. Mimeo, World Bank, November.

de la Cuadra, S., and S. Valdés-Prieto. 1990. Myths and facts about financial liberalization in Chile: 1974–82. Working Paper no. 128, Instituto de Economia Universita Catolica.

Deane, R. S. 1986. Financial sector policy reform. In *Financial Policy Reform*. Reserve Bank of New Zealand. Wellington, N.Z.

Deardorff, Alan, and James Hanson. 1978. Accumulation and a long-run Hecksher–Ohlin theorem. *Economic Inquiry* 16 (April):288–92.

Denizer, C. 1991. Market concentration and bank profitability in Turkey. Mimeo, World Bank.

Diamond, Douglas. 1984. Financial intermediation and delegated monitoring. *Review of Economic Studies* 51 (July):393–414.

1989. Reputation acquisition in debt markets. *Journal of Political Economy* 97:928–62.

Diamond, Douglas, and Philip Dybvig. 1983. Bank runs, deposit insurance, and liquidity. *Journal of Political Economy* 91:401–19.

Diaz-Alejandro, Carlos. 1970. Direct foreign investment in Latin America. In C. Kindleberger, *The International Corporation*. Cambridge, Mass.: MIT Press, pp. 309–44.

1985. Goodbye financial repression, Hello financial crash. *Journal of Development Economics* 19:1–24.

Domar, Evsey. 1950. The effect of foreign investment on the balance of payments. *American Economic Review* 40:805–26.

Dooley, Michael. 1988. Capital flight: A response to differences in financial risks. *IMF Staff Papers:* 422–36.

Dooley, Michael, Jeffrey Frankel, and Donald Mathieson. 1987. International capital mobility: What do the saving investment correlations tell us? *IMF Staff Papers:*503–30.

Dooley, Michael, William Helke, Ralph Tryon, and John Underwood. 1986. An analysis of external debt positions of eight developing countries through 1990. *Journal of Development Economics* 20:283–318.

Dooley, Michael, and Peter Isard. 1980. Capital controls, political risk, and deviations from interest parity. *Journal of Political Economy* 88:370–84.

Dornbusch, Rudiger. 1976. Expectations and exchange rate dynamics. *Journal of Political Economy* 84:1161–76.

1983. Real interest rates, home goods and optimal external borrowing. *Journal of Political Economy* 91, no. 1 (February): 141–53.

1984. External debt, budget deficits, and disequilibrium exchange rates. NBER Working Paper 1336, National Bureau of Economic Research.

1986. Special exchange rates for capital account transactions. *World Bank Economic Review:* 3–32.

Dornbusch, R., and A. Reynoso. 1989. Financial factors in economic development. *AER Papers and Proceedings of the 101st Annual Meeting,* May.

Easton, B. 1987. The labor market and economic liberalization. In A. Bollard and R. Buckle, eds., *Economic Liberalization in New Zealand*. Wellington: Allen and Unwin.

Edwards, S. 1984. The order of liberalization of the external sector in developing countries. *Princeton Essays in International Finance,* No. 156.

1985. Stabilization with liberalization: An evaluation of ten years of Chile's experiment with free-market policies, 1973–83. *Economic Development and Cultural Change* 33 (January):223–54.

1985. Money, the rate of devaluation, and interest rates in a semi-open economy: Colombia 1968–1972. *Journal of Money, Credit and Banking* 17:59–68.

1987. Sequencing economic liberalization in developing countries. *Finance and Development* (March):3–9.

1988. El Monetarismo en Chile, 1973–83: Algunos Dilemas Econmicos. In F. Morande and K. Schmidt-Hebbel, eds., *Del Auge a la Crisis de 1982*, ILADES, Santiago, Chile.

1989. On the sequencing of structural reform. NBER Working Paper 3138, National Bureau of Economic Research, Cambridge, Mass.

Edwards, S., and Alejandra Cox-Edwards. 1987. *Monetarism and Liberalization: The Chilean Experiment*. Cambridge Mass.: Ballinger.

Edwards, Sebastian, and Mohsin S. Khan. 1985. Interest rate determination in developing countries: A conceptual framework. IMF Staff Papers 19.

Edwards, S., and Sweder van Wijnbergen. 1986. The welfare effects of trade and capital account liberalization. *International Economic Review:*141–8.

Errázuriz, Hernan Felipe. 1982. Evolucion de la Legislacion Bancaria y Financiera (1973–81). Chapter V in *Legislacion Economica Chilena y de Comercio Internacional*. Central Bank of Chile, February.

Ersel, H. 1992. The potential for secondary market for government domestic debt instruments in Turkey. Discussion Paper, No. 9201/A, Central Bank of the Republic of Turkey, Ankara.

Ersel, H. and E. Ozturk. 1990. The credit delivery system in Turkey. Research Department Discussion Paper 9003, Central Bank of the Republic of Turkey, Ankara.

1993. Liberalization attempts and the financial structure of Turkish corporations. In *Financial Liberalization in Turkey*, Central Bank of the Republic of Turkey, Ankara, pp. 219–251.

Fazzari, Steve, Glenn Hubbard, and Bruce Peterson. 1988. Financing constraints and economic activity. *Brookings Papers on Economic Activity.*

Fischer, Stanley, and Jacob Frenkel. 1974. Interest rate equalization, patterns of production, trade, and consumption. *Economic Record* 50 (December):555–80.

Fisher, Irving. 1933. The debt-deflation theory of great depressions. *Econometrica* (October).

Fleming, J. M. 1971. *Essays in International Economics*. London: Allen and Unwin, ch. 12.

Frank, J. 1990. Monopolistic competition, risk aversion, and equilibrium recessions. *Quarterly Journal of Economics:* 921–38.

Frenkel, J. A. 1983. Panel discussion on the Southern Cone. *IMF Staff Papers* 30, no. 1.

Frenkel, Jacob. 1976. A dynamic analysis of the balance of payments in a model of accumulation. In Jacob Frenkel and Harry Johnson, eds., *The Monetary Approach to the Balance of Payments*. Toronto: University of Toronto.

1982. The order of economic liberalization: A comment. In K. Brunner and A. Meltzer, eds., *Economic Policy in a World of Change*. Carnegie Rochester Conference Series. Amsterdam: North Holland, pp. 99–102.

Froot, Kenneth, and Jeremy Stein. 1991. Exchange rates and foreign direct investment: An imperfect capital markets approach. *Quarterly Journal of Economics* (November):1191–1218.

Fry, M. J. 1972. *Finance and Development Planning in Turkey*. Leiden: E. J. Brill.

——— 1978. Money and capital or financial deepening in economic development? *Journal of Money, Credit and Banking* 10 (November):464–75.

——— 1980. Saving, investment, growth and the cost of financial repression. *World Development* 8 (April):317–27.

——— 1988. *Money, Interest, and Banking in Economic Development*. Baltimore: John Hopkins University Press.

Gale, Douglas, and Martin Hellwig. 1985. Incentive-compatible debt contracts. *Review of Economic Studies* 152 (October).

Gelb, A. 1989. Financial policies, growth, and efficiency. Policy Planning and Research Working Paper, WPS 202, World Bank, June.

Gertler, M. 1988. Financial structure and aggregate economic activity: An overview. *Journal of Money, Credit, and Banking*, 20, no. 3, August.

——— 1992. Financial capacity and output fluctuations in an economy with multi-period financial relationships. *Review of Economic Studies*, July.

Gertler, M., and Glenn Hubbard. 1992. Corporate financial policy, taxation and macroeconomic risk. *Rand Journal* (Summer).

Gertler, M., and Kenneth Rogoff. 1990. North–south lending with endogenous domestic capital market inefficiencies. *Journal of Monetary Economics*.

Gertler, M., and A. Rose. 1991. Finance, growth and public policy. Policy Research Working Papers, WPS 814, World Bank.

Gilchrist, Simon. 1990. An empirical analysis of corporate investment financing hierarchies using firm-level data. Mimeo, Board of Governors.

Giavazzi, Francesco, and Alberto Giovannini. 1988. Can the European monetary system be copied outside Europe?: Lessons from ten years of monetary policy coordination in Europe. NBER Working Paper Series, no. 2786. National Bureau of Economic Research, Cambridge, Mass.

Giovannini, A. 1983. The interest elasticity of savings in developing countries: The existing evidence. *World Development* 11 (July):601–7.

——— 1985. Saving and the real interest rate in LDCs. *Journal of Development Economics*, 18 (August):197–217.

Goldsmith, Raymond. 1969. *Financial Structure and Development*. New Haven, Conn.: Yale University Press.

Green, Edward. 1987. Lending and the smoothing of uninsurable income. Mimeo.

Greenwald, Bruce, and Joseph Stiglitz. 1988. Information, financial constraints and economic activity. In M. Kohn and S. C. Tsiang, eds., *Finance Constraints, Expectations, and Macroeconomics*. Oxford: Oxford University Press.

——— 1990. Macroeconomic models with equity and credit rationing. In R. Glenn Hubbard, ed., *Asymmetric Information, Corporate Finance, and Investment*. Chicago: University of Chicago Press.

Greenwood, Jeremy, and Boyan Jovanovic. 1990. Financial intermediation and growth. *Journal of Political Economy*.

Gros, Daniel. 1988. Dual exchange rates in the presence of incomplete market separation, long run effectiveness and policy implications. *IMF Staff Papers*:437–60.

Gurley, John, and Edward Shaw. 1955. Financial aspects of development and growth. *American Economic Review* (September):515–38.

Hachette, D. 1989. The opening of the capital account: The case of Chile 1974–82. Mimeo, Instituto de Economia, Universita Catolica.

Hall, R. E. 1978. Intertemporal substitution in consumption. *Journal of Political Economy* 96:339–57.

Hanson, James A. 1974. Optimal international borrowing and lending. *American Economic Review* 63:616–30.

    1986. What went wrong in Chile. In A. Choksi and D. Papageorgiou, eds., *Economic Liberalization in Developing Countries*. London: Basil Blackwell, pp. 227–32.

    1992. An open capital account: A brief survey of the issues and the results. World Bank Policy Research Paper no. 901, June.

Hanson, James A., and J. de Melo. 1985. External shocks, financial reforms, and stabilization attempts in Uruguay during 1974–83. *World Development* 13, no. 8 (August):917–39.

Hanson, James A., and Craig Neal. 1986. The demand for liquid financial assets. Mimeo, World Bank.

    1986. *Interest Rate Policy in Selected Developing Countries 1970–82*. Industry & Finance Series no. 14. Washington, D.C.: World Bank.

Hanson, James A., and Philip Neher. 1967. The neoclassical theorem once again: Closed and open economies. *American Economic Review* 57 (September):869–78.

Hanson, James A., and Roberto Rocha. 1986. *High Interest Rates, Spreads, and the Costs of Intermediation*. Industry and Finance Series, no. 18. Washington, D.C.: World Bank.

Harberger, A. 1979. Vignettes on the world capital market. *American Economic Review* 69:331–7.

    1982. The Chilean economy in the 1970s: Crisis, stabilization, liberalization, reform. In K. Brunner and A. Meltzer, eds., *Economic Policy in a World of Change*. Carnegie Rochester Conference Series. Amsterdam: North Holland.

    1985. Observations on the Chilean economy, 1973–83. *Economic Development and Cultural Change* 33, no. 3 (April):451–62.

Harper, D. A., and G. Karacaoglu. 1987. Financial policy reform in New Zealand. In A. Bollard and R. Buckle, eds., *Economic Liberalization in New Zealand*. Wellington: Allen and Unwin.

Harris, J. R., F. Schiantarelli, and M. Siregar. 1992. The effect of financial liberalization on firm's capital structure and investment decisions: Evidence from a panel of Indonesian manufacturing establishments, 1981–1988. Working Paper 997, World Bank, October. (Published in *World Bank Economic Review* (January 1994).)

Hart, Oliver, and Bengt Holmstrom. 1987. The Theory of Contracts. In Truman Bewley, ed., *Advances in Economic Theory*. New York: Cambridge University Press.

Held, G. 1989. Regulacion y Supervision de la Banca en la experiencia de

Liberalizacion Financiera en Chile 1974–1988. IC/R 758, May 3, ECLAC, Santiago, Chile.

Helpman, E., and A. Razin. 1978. *A Theory of International Trade under Uncertainty*. New York: Academic Press.

Hernández, L. 1991. Credibilidad, problema "peso" y comportamiento de las tasas de interes: Chile 1979–82. *Cuadernos de Economia* 28 (December):385–410.

Hinds, Manuel. 1988. Economic effects of financial crises. Policy Planning and Research Working Paper No. 104, World Bank.

Honohan, Patrick, and Izak Atiyas. 1989. Intersectoral financial flows in developing countries. Policy Research Working Paper 164, World Bank, March.

Hoshi, Takeo, Anil Kashyap, and David Scharfstein. 1989. The role of banks in reducing the costs of financial distress in Japan. Mimeo, University of California, San Diego, November.

1990. Bank monitoring and investment: Evidence from the changing structure of Japanese corporate banking relationships. In R. Glenn Hubbard, ed., *Asymmetric Information, Corporate Finance, and Investment*. Chicago: University of Chicago Press.

1991. Corporate structure, liquidity, and investment: Evidence from Japanese industrial groups. *Quarterly Journal of Economics* (February):33–60.

Hubbard, Glenn, and Anil Kashyap. 1992. Internal net worth and the investment process. *Journal of Political Economy*.

Hunn, N., D. Mayes, N. Williams, and S. Vandersyp. 1989. Financial deregulation and disinflation in a small open economy. New Zealand Institute of Economic Research Monograph 44.

Inada, Ken-Ichi. 1964. On the stability of growth equilibria in two sector models. *Review of Economic Studies:*127–42.

Institute of International Finance. 1990. *Financial Sector Reform: Its Role in Growth and Development*. Washington, D.C.

Iskenderoglu, L. 1989. Money Demand and Currency Substitution in Turkey: A Dynamic Model Approach. Unpublished M.Sc. Thesis, Middle East Technical University, Ankara.

Iskenderoglu, L., E. Ozturk, and T. Temel. 1991. The Turkish banking system: Income statement (1983–1989) and balance sheets (1981–1989). Research Department Working Paper, February 18, Central Bank of the Republic of Turkey, Ankara.

James, Christopher. 1987. Some evidence on the uniqueness of bank loans. *Journal of Financial Economics* 19, no. 2 (December).

James, Christopher, and Peggy Weir. 1990. Borrowing relationships, intermediation, and the cost of issuing public securities. *Journal of Financial Economics* 28, no. 1–2 (November–December).

Japan Development Bank. 1993. Policy-based finance: The experience of postwar Japan, Final report for the World Bank. January. Japan Economic Research Institute. Kozo Kato, Tsutomu Shibata, Aiichiro Mogi, Yuichiro Miwa, Yoshikaz Niwa, Nobuhiko Ichikawa, Masahiro Furuta.

Jappelli, T., and M. Pagano. 1992. Saving, growth and liquidity constraints. *Quarterly Journal of Economics,* forthcoming.

Jaramillo, F., F. Schiantarelli, and A. Weiss. 1992a. The effect of financial liberalization on the allocation of credit: Evidence from a panel of Ecuadorian firms. World Bank Working Paper 1092, February.

1992b. Capital market imperfections, financial constraints, and investment: Econometric evidence from Panel Data for Ecuador. Mimeo, Boston University.

Joannon, Felipe. 1984. Paridad de Tasas de Interes: El caso chileno 1976–83. Instituto de Economia Universita Catolica, Santiago, Chile.

Johansen, S. 1988. Statistical analysis of cointegration vectors. *Journal of Economic Dynamics and Control* 12:231–54.

Johansen, S., and K. Juselius. 1990. Maximum likelihood estimation and inference on cointegration – with applications to the demand for money. *Oxford Bulletin of Economics and Statistics* 52:169–210.

Johnson, Harry. 1961. Equilibrium growth in an international economy. *Canadian Journal of Economics and Political Science*. Reprinted in H. Johnson, ed., *International Trade and Economic Growth*. Cambridge Mass.: Harvard University Press, pp. 120–49.

Johnston, R. Barry. 1991. The use of monetary policy instruments by developing countries. In Gerard Caprio, Jr. and Patrick Honohan, eds., *Monetary Policy Instruments for Developing Countries*. Washington, D.C.: World Bank.

Jung, Woo S. 1986. Financial development and economic growth. *Economic Development and Cultural Change*:333–46.

Kaufman, G. G. 1973. *Money, the Financial System and the Economy*. Chicago: Rand McNally.

Keeling, W. 1992. Shake-out may be imminent. *Financial Times,* June 6, p. VI.

Kehoe, Timothy, and David Levine. 1990. Debt-constrained asset markets. Mimeo, University of Minnesota.

Kemp, Murray. 1964. *The Pure Theory of International Trade*. Englewood Cliffs, N.J.: Prentice-Hall.

Keynes, J. M. 1920. *A Tract on Monetary Reform.*

Khan, Moshin, and Nadeem Haque. 1985. Foreign borrowing and capital flight. *IMF Staff Papers*:606–28.

Khan, Moshin, and Roberto Zahler. 1983. The macroeconomic effects of changes in barriers to trade and capital flows: A simulation analysis. *IMF Staff Papers* 30, no. 2:223–82.

Khosaka, A. 1984. The high interest rate policy under financial repression. *Developing Economics* 22 (December):419–52.

Kim, Pyung Joo. 1990. Financial institutions: Past, present, and futures. Presented at the Honolulu Workshop on Korea's Political Economy, August, East-West Center, Hawaii.

King, R., and R. Levine. 1993a. Finance, entrepreneurship, and growth: Theory and evidence. *Journal of Monetary Economics* 32:513–42.

1993b. Finance and growth: Schumpeter might be right. *Quarterly Journal of Economics* 108:717–37.

Kong, Myungjai. 1991. Tobin's Q, internal finance, and investment in a developing country: Evidence from a panel of Korean manufacturing firms. Ph.D. dissertation, New York University.

Kouri, P., and M. Porter. 1974. International capital flows and portfolio equilibrium. *Journal of Political Economy* 82:443–67.

Krueger, Anne. 1981. Interactions between inflation and trade-regime objectives in stabilization programs. In W. Cline and S. Weintraub, eds., *Economic Stabilization in Developing Countries*. Washington, D.C.: Brookings Institution.

———. 1984. Problems of liberalization. In Arnold Harberger, ed., *World Economic Growth*. San Francisco: ICS Press.

———. 1986. Problems of liberalization. In A. Choksi and D. Papageorgiou, eds., *Economic Liberalization in Developing Countries*. London: Basil Blackwell, pp. 15–31.

Kuala Lumpur Stock Exchange. 1990. *Investing in the Stock Market in Malaysia*.

Kumcu, E. 1989. Some evidence on currency substitution in Turkey, Unpublished manuscript, Central Bank of the Republic of Turkey, Ankara.

Kupiec, P. 1991. Financial liberalization and international trends in stock, corporate bond and foreign exchange market volatilities. OECD Department of Economics and Statistics Working Paper no. 94.

Kwack, Taewon. 1985. *Depreciation and Taxation of Income from Capital*. Korea Development Institute. (In Korean.)

Lacker, Jeffrey. 1990. Collateralized debt as the optimal contract. Mimeo, Federal Reserve Bank of Richmond.

Lagos, L. F., and F. Coloma. 1987. Expectativas de Devaluacion, Credibilidad y Sustitucion de Moneda en Chile. Working Paper no. 108, Instituto de Economia, Santiago, Chile.

Lagos, L. F., and A. Galetovich. 1990. Los efectos de la indizacion cambiaria y salarial en el control de la inflacion: el caso de Chile, 1975–81. *Cuadernos de Economia* 27, no. 82 (December):357–80.

Lal, Deepak. 1987. The political economy of economic liberalization. *World Bank Economic Review* 1, no. 2 (January):273–300.

Lane, Christopher E., David C. Cole, and Betty F. Slade. 1991. Monetary policy effectiveness in Indonesia, 1974–1990. Overseas Development Institute Working Paper no. 44.

Lanyi, Anthony. 1975. Separate exchange markets for capital and current transactions. *IMF Staff Papers*:714–59.

Larrain, F., and P. Meller. 1990. La experiencia socialista-populista chilena: la Unidad Popular, 1970–73. *Cuadernos de Economia* 27, no. 82 (December):317–56.

LeFort, G., and C. Ross. 1985. La Devaluacion Esperada. Una Aproximacion Bayesiana: Chile 1974–84. Documento Serie de Investigacion no. 72, Departamento de Economia U. de Chile, Agosto.

Lee, Chung H. Forthcoming. The government and financial system in the economic development of Korea. *World Development*.

Leipziger, Danny M. 1988. Industrial restructuring in Korea. *World Development* 167:121–135.

Levine, Ross. 1992. Financial intermediation and growth: Theory and evidence. *Journal of Japanese and International Economies* 6 (December):383–405.

Levine, Ross, and Sara J. Zervos. 1993. What have we learned about policy and growth from cross-country regressions? *American Economic Review* 83, no. 2 (May): 426–30.

Lim, J. 1987. The new structuralist critique of the Monetarist theory of inflation: The case of the Philippines. *Journal of Development Economics* 25 (February):45–61.

Little, Ian, Tibor Scitovsky, and Maurice Scott. 1970. *Industry and Trade in Some Developing Countries: A Comparative Study.* Oxford: Oxford University.

Lucas, Robert. 1988. On the mechanics of economic development, *Journal of Monetary Economics* 22:3–42.

Lummer, Scott L., and John J. McConnell. 1989. Further evidence on the bank lending process and the capital–market response to bank loan agreements. *Journal of Financial Economics* 25, no. 1 (November):99–122.

MacDougall, Ian. 1968. The benefits and costs of private investment from abroad: A theoretical approach. In R. Caves and H. Johnson, eds., *Readings in International Economics.* London: Allen and Unwin, pp. 172–94.

Mankiw, N. Gregory. 1986. The allocation of credit and financial collapse. *Quarterly Journal of Economics* (August):455–70.

Marcus, A. 1984. Deregulation and bank financial policy. *Journal of Banking and Finance,* 8 (December):557.

Matte, Ricardo. 1983. Politica Monetaria y Movilidad de Capitales en Chile entre 1975 y 1983. Thesis, Instituto de Economia Universita Catolica, Santiago, Chile.

Mayer, C. 1990. Financial systems, corporate finance, and economic development. *Asymmetric Information, Corporate Finance and Investment.* In R. G. Hubbard, ed., Chicago: University of Chicago Press.

McKinnon, Ronald. 1973. *Money and Capital in Economic Development.* Washington D.C.: Brookings Institution.

1982. The order of economic liberalization: Lessons from Chile and Argentina. In K. Brunner and A. Meltzer, eds., *Economic Policy in a World of Change,* Carnegie Rochester Conference Series. Amsterdam: North Holland, pp. 159–86.

1988. Financial liberalization and economic development: A reassessment of interest-rate policies in Asia and Latin America. Occasional Papers no. 6. International Center for Economic Growth.

1991. *The Order of Economic Liberalization: Financial Control in the Transition to a Market Economy.* Baltimore: Johns Hopkins University Press.

McKinnon, Ronald J., and Donald J. Mathieson. 1981. How to manage a repressed economy. Princeton Essays in International Finance, No. 145, December.

McNaughton, Diana. 1993. *Banking Institutions in Developing Markets.* 2 vols. Washington, D.C.: World Bank.

McNelis, P., and K. Schmidt-Hebbel. 1991. Volatility reversal from interest rates to the real exchange rate: Financial liberalization in Chile, 1975–82. World Bank Working Papers 697, June.

Meek, Paul. 1991. Central bank liquidity management and the money market. In Gerard Caprio and Patrick Honohan, eds., *Monetary Policy Instruments for Developing Countries.* Washington, D.C.: The World Bank.

Mehra, R., and Edward Prescott. 1985. The equity premium: A puzzle. *Journal of Monetary Economics* 15:145–62.

Michaely, Michael. 1986. The timing and sequencing of a trade liberalization policy. In A. Choksi and D. Papageorgiou, eds., *Economic Liberalization in Developing Countries*. London: Basil Blackwell, pp. 41–59.

Moran, Theodore. 1974. *Multinational Corporations and the Politics of Dependence: Cooper in Chile*. Princeton N.J.: Princeton University Press.

Morande, F. 1991. Flujos de Capitales hacia Chile, 1977–82. Chapter 5 in F. Morande, ed., *Movimientos de Capitales y Crisis Economica,* ILADES, Santiago, Chile.

Morisset, J. 1993. Does financial liberalization really improve private investment in developing countries? *Journal of Development Economics* 40:133–50.

Mundell, R. 1968a. *International Economics*. New York: Macmillan.

1968b. International trade and factor mobility. In R. Mundell, ed., *International Economics*. New York: Macmillan, pp. 85–99.

1968c. Capital mobility and stabilization policy under fixed and flexible exchange rates. In R. Mundell, ed., *International Economics*. New York: Macmillan, pp. 250–71.

1984. Capital mobility and the relation between saving and investment rates in OECD countries. *Journal of International Money and Finance:*327–42.

Myers, S. 1977. The determinants of corporate borrowing. *Journal of Financial Economics:* 147–75.

Nam, Sang-Woo. 1988. Readjustment of the business boundaries of financial intermediaries in Korea. KDI Working Paper no. 8822, December.

1989. Liberalization of the Korean financial and capital markets. Paper Presented at the Joint KDI/IIE Conference on Korean Financial Policy, Washington, D.C., December 12.

Ord Minnett Securities-NZ-Ltd. 1991. *Saving and Superannuation: The Reduction of Government Involvement,* Wellington, New Zealand.

Orden, D., and L. A. Fisher. 1990. Financial deregulation and the dynamics of money, prices and output: Evidence from New Zealand and Australia. The University of New South Wales Discussion Paper No. 90/9.

Ortiz, Guillermo. 1983. Dollarization in Mexico: Causes and consequences. In Pedro Aspe, Rudiger Dornbusch, and Maurice Obstfeld, eds., *Financial Problems of the World Capital Market: The Problem of Latin American Countries*. Chicago: University of Chicago Press, pp. 71–95.

Owen, P. D., and O. Solis-Fallas. 1989. Unorganized money markets and unproductive assets in the new structuralist critique of financial liberalization. *Journal of Development Economics* 31:341–55.

Papageorgiou, Demetris, Michael Michaely, and Armeane M. Choksi. 1991. *Liberalizing Foreign Trade, Vol. V: Indonesia, Pakistan and Sri Lanka*. Oxford: Basil Blackwell.

Park, Yung Chul. 1987. Financial repression, liberalization and development in developing countries. KDI Working Paper no. 8704, May.

Pehlivan, H. 1991. *An Analysis of Financial Liberalization and Financial Development in Turkey, 1980–1989*. Unpublished Ph.D. dissertation, University of Bradford, United Kingdom.

Pehlivan, H., and C. Kirkpatrick. 1991. The impact of transnational banks on developing countries' banking sector: An analysis of the Turkish experience, 1980–1989. Paper presented at the British Society for Middle Eastern Studies Annual Conference, School of Oriental and African Studies, University of London, July 10–12.

Persson, T., and Lars Svensson. 1985. Current account dynamics and the terms of trade: Harberger-Laursen-Meltzer two generations later. *Journal of Political Economy* 93:43–65.

Pfeffermann, Guy P., and Andrea Madarassy. 1991. Trends in private investment in developing countries, 1990–91 edition. International Finance Corporation Discussion Paper No. 11.

Pitt, Mark M. 1991. Indonesia. Part I in Papageorgiou et al. *Liberalizing Foreign Trade, Vol. V: Indonesia, Pakistan and Sri Lanka.* Oxford: Basil Blackwell.

Reserve Bank of New Zealand. 1986. *Financial Policy Reform.* Wellington.

Reynolds, Clark. 1965. Development problems of an export economy: The case of Chile and copper. In Clark Reynolds and Markos Mamalakis, eds., *Essays on the Chilean Economy.* Homewood, Ill.: Irwin, pp. 203–357.

Reynoso, A. 1989. Financial repression, financial liberalization and the interest rate elasticity of savings in developing countries. Unpublished Ph.D. dissertation, Massachusetts Institute of Technology.

Rieffel, A. 1987. Exchange controls: A dead-end for advanced developing countries? Special Paper No. 12, *AMEX Bank Review,* July.

Rodrik, Dani. 1987. Trade and capital account liberalization in a Keynesian economy. *Journal of International Economics:*113–29.

Romer, Paul. 1986. Increasing returns and long run economic growth. *Journal of Political Economy* 94:1102–37.

Rossi, N. 1988. Government spending, the real interest rate, and the behavior of liquidity-constrained consumers in developing countries. *IMF Staff Papers* 35, No. 1 (March).

Roubini, N., and X. Sala-i-Martin. 1992. The relation between trade regime, financial development and economic growth. Mimeo.

Sachs, Jeffrey D., and Susan M. Collins. 1989. *Developing Country Debt, Vol. 3: Country Studies – Indonesia, Philippines, Turkey.* Chicago: University of Chicago Press.

Saint-Paul, G. 1992. Technological choice, financial markets, and economic development. *European Economic Review* 36:763–81.

Samuelson, Paul. 1965. Equalization by trade of the interest rate along with the real wage. In *Trade, Growth and the Balance of Payments, Essays in Honor of Gottfried Haberler.* Chicago: Rand McNally; Amsterdam: North-Holland, pp. 35–52.

1948. International trade and the equalization of factor prices. *Economic Journal:*163–84.

Sargent, T. 1983. Comment on G. Ortiz, "Dollarization in Mexico: Causes and consequences." In Pedro Aspe, Rudiger Dornbusch, and Maurice Obstfeld, eds., *Financial Problems of the World Capital Market: The Problem of Latin American Countries.* Chicago: University of Chicago, pp. 95–106.

Schmidt, P., and R. Sickles. 1984. Production frontiers and panel data. *Journal of Business and Economic Statistics* 2.

Schmidt-Hebbel, K. 1988. Consumo e Inversion en Chile (1874–82): Una Interpretacion real del Boom. Chapter 6 in F. Morande and K. Schmidt-Hebbel, eds., *Del Auge a la Crisis de 1982*. Santiago, Chile: ILADES.

Schwarz, A. 1992. Growing pains. *Far Eastern Economic Review* (April):45–6.

Schwert, G. W. 1989. Why does stock market volatility change over time? *Journal of Finance* 44:1115–53.

Shaw, E. S. 1973. *Financial Deepening in Economic Development*. New York: Oxford University Press.

Sheng, A. 1993. *Bank Restructuring: The International Experience*. World Bank.

Sinai, A., and Stokes, H. H., 1972, Real money balances: An omitted variable from the production function. *Review of Economics and Statistics* 14, no. 3 (August):290–96.

Siregar, M. 1992. Financial Liberalization, Investment and Debt Allocation. Unpublished Ph.D. dissertation, Boston University.

Sjaastad, L. 1982. The role of external shocks in the Chilean recession 1981–82. Working Paper no. 5, Centro de Estudios Publicos, September, Santiago, Chile.

Spencer, G. 1990. Monetary policy: The New Zealand experience 1985–1990. *Reserve Bank Bulletin* 53.

Spencer, G., and D. Carey. 1988. Financial policy reform – The New Zealand experience 1984–1987. Reserve Bank of New Zealand Discussion Paper G88/1.

Stein, Jerome. 1962. *The Nature and Efficiency of the Foreign Exchange Market*. Princeton Essays in International Finance No. 40.

Stiglitz, Joseph E., and Andrew Weiss. 1981. Credit rationing in markets with imperfect information. *American Economic Review* 71, no. 3 (June):393–410.

1983. Incentive effects of terminations: Applications to credit and labor markets. *American Economic Review* 73:912–27.

1988. Banks as social accountants and screening devices for the allocation of credit. NBER Working Paper No. 2710, October, National Bureau of Economic Research.

Stockman, Alan. 1988. On the roles of international financial markets and their relevance for economic policy. *Journal of Money, Credit, and Banking* 20:531–49.

Svensson, Lars. 1988. Trade in risky assets. *American Economic Review:* 375–94.

Sundararajan, V., R. Vaez-Zadeh, and In-Su Kim. 1985. A study of interest rates in Malaysia: Deregulation, its consequences, and policy options. International Monetary Fund, February.

Sundararajan, V., and Tomas J. T. Balino. 1990. Issues in recent banking crises in developing countries. Mimeo, International Monetary Fund.

Suwidjana, N. 1984. *Jakarta Dollar Market: A Case of Financial Development in ASEAN*. Institute of Southeast Asian Studies, Singapore.

Tanzi, Vito, and Mario Blejer. 1982. Inflation, interest rate policy, and currency substitution in developing economies: A discussion of some major issues. *World Development* 10:781–89.

Taylor, L. 1983. *Structuralist Macroeconomics: Applicable Models for the Third World*. New York: Basic Books.

The Treasury. 1984. *Economic Management.* Wellington: Government Printer.

Titman, S., and R. Wessels. 1988. The determinants of capital structure choice. *Journal of Finance* 43:1–19.

Tobin, James. 1983. Comment on domestic saving and international capital movements in the long run and the short run by M. Feldstein, *European Economic Review:*153–56.

Townsend, Robert. 1979. Optimal contracts and competitive markets with costly state verification. *Journal of Economic Theory:*265–93.

1988. Private information and limited insurance: The revelation principle extended. *Journal of Monetary Economics* 21:411–50.

Tybout, James. 1986. A firm-level chronicle of financial crises in the southern cone. *Journal of Development Economics:*371–400.

Valdés-Prieto, S. 1987. Depression, disinflation and recovery in Chile, 1930–34. Essay Three of Ph. D. thesis, Massachusetts Institute of Technology.

1988. Ajuste Estructural en el Mercado de Capitales: La Evidencia Chilena. Report to the Central Bank of Chile. Instituto de Economia Universita Catolica.

1989. Control de Cambios en Paises en Desarrollo: Implicancias para una Ley de Banco Central. *Cuadernos de Economia* 77 (April):115–44.

1989. Origenes de la Crisis de la Deuda. *Estudios Publicos* 33 (Summer):135–74.

1990. Regulacion Bancaria: ¿Exclusiva del estado o de todos los acreedores? Working Paper No. 129, Instituto de Economia Universita Catolica.

1992. Financial Liberalization and the Capital Account: Chile 1974–84. Mimeo, Instituto de Economis Universidad Catolica, Santiago, Chile.

Van Wijnbergen, S. 1982. Stagflationary effects of monetary stabilization policies: A quantitative analysis of South Korea. *Journal of Development Economics* 10 (April):133–69.

1983a. Credit policy inflation and growth in a financially repressed economy. *Journal of Development Economics* 13 (August):45–65.

1983b. Interest rate management in LDC's. *Journal of Monetary Economics* 12 (September):433–52.

1985. Macro-economic effects of changes in bank interest rates: Simulation results for South Korea. *Journal of Development Economics* 18 (August):541–54.

Veneroso, Frank. 1986. New patterns of financial instability. Mimeo, Financial Policy and Systems Division, World Bank.

Villanueva, Delano, and Abbas Mirakhor. 1990. Interest rate policies, stabilization, and bank supervision in developing countries: Strategies for financial reform. IMF Working Paper WP/90/8.

Vittas, D. 1991. Measuring commercial bank efficiency: Use and misuse of bank operating ratios. World Bank Working Paper, WPS 806.

Wallace, Neil. 1988. Another attempt to explain an illiquid banking system: The Diamond and Dybvig model with sequential service taken seriously. *Federal Reserve Bank of Minneapolis Quarterly Review* (Fall):3–16.

White, B. 1991. Banking supervision policy in New Zealand. *Reserve Bank Bulletin* 54.

Wilcox, J. A. 1989. Liquidity constraints on consumption: The real effects of real lending policies. *Federal Reserve Bank of San Francisco Review.*

Williamson, Stephen. 1986. Costly monitoring, financial intermediation and equilibrium credit rationing. *Journal of Monetary Economics* 18 (September):159–79.

1987. Costly monitoring, optimal contracts and equilibrium credit rationing. *Quarterly Journal of Economics:*159–79.

Wirjanto, T. S. 1991. Testing the permanent income hypothesis: The evidence from Canadian data. *Canadian Journal of Economics* 24:565–77.

Woo, Wing Thye. 1991. Strengthening economic management in Indonesia. Mimeo.

Woo, Wing Thye, and Anwar Nasution. 1989. Indonesian economic policies and their relation to external debt management. In Jeffrey D. Sachs and Susan M. Collins, eds. *Developing Country Debt, Vol. 3: Country Studies – Indonesia, Philippines, Turkey.* Chicago: University of Chicago Press.

World Bank. 1991. *World Tables 1991.* Baltimore: Johns Hopkins University Press.

1989. *World Development Report.* Oxford: Oxford University Press.

Yoo, Jung-Ho. 1989. The Korean experience with an industrial targeting policy. Mimeo, Korea Development Institute, May.

1990. The industrial policy of the 1970s and the evolution of the manufacturing sector in Korea. KDI Working Paper No. 9017, October.

Zeldes, Stephen. 1988. Consumption and liquidity constraints. *Journal of Political Economy* 95:1196–1216.

Index